THE
SELECTION
EFFECT

How Consciousness Shapes Reality

HERB MERTZ

Penn Wolcott Press
Princeton, New Jersey

Copyright © 2020 by Herbert Ian Mertz
Published by Penn Wolcott Press

All rights reserved. Printed in the United States of America. No part of this book may be reproduced in any manner whatsoever without written permission except in the case of brief quotations embodied in critical articles and reviews.

ISBN 978-1-7335080-0-1 (paperback)
ISBN 978-1-7335080-1-8 (eBook)
Library of Congress Control Number: 2019918430

Illustrations: Herb Mertz
Photographs appear courtesy of ICRL/Brenda Dunne

Publisher's Cataloging-In-Publication Data

(Prepared by The Donohue Group, Inc.)

Names: Mertz, Herb, 1953- author.
Title: The selection effect : how consciousness shapes reality / Herb Mertz.
Description: Princeton, New Jersey : Penn Wolcott Press, [2020] | Includes index.
Identifiers: ISBN 9781733508001 (paperback) | ISBN 9781733508018 (ebook)
Subjects: LCSH: Mertz, Herb, 1953---Philosophy. | Mind and reality--Research. | Consciousness--Research. | Reality--Effect of mind on--Research.
Classification: LCC BD418.3 .M47 2020 (print) | LCC BD418.3 (ebook) | DDC 128.2--dc23

TABLE OF CONTENTS

Acknowledgments i
Prologue 1
Introduction 3

Part I: Unexpected Moments 19
    Chapter 1: The PEAR Lab 21
    Chapter 2: REGs for Everyone 31
    Chapter 3: Clueless 39
    Chapter 4: The Crash House 49
    Chapter 5: The Challenge 59

Part II: Stepping Back 65
    Chapter 6: Out of My Control 67
    Chapter 7: What Should Happen 79
    Chapter 8: Moments, Models, and Webs 89
    Chapter 9: Into the Subconscious 99

Part III: Mirror Maze of Mind 113
    Chapter 10: Digging Deep 115
    Chapter 11: Who Am I, Anyway? 129
    Chapter 12: From the Outside In 141
    Chapter 13: Alternative Reality 159
    Chapter 14: The Home Stretch 167
    Chapter 15: The Finish Line 175
    Chapter 16: Some Life Lessons from the REG 181

Part IV: When Worlds Collide 191
    Chapter 17: Stories 193
    Chapter 18: Science and the Selection Effect 209
    Chapter 19: Interlude—REG at a Distance 221
    Chapter 20: Psychofeedback 233
    Chapter 21: Fast, Slow, Self-Aware 245
    Chapter 22: The Age of Meaning 257

Supplemental Material 269
    Units of Meaning 271
    Running Your Own REG Project 291
    Mind Lamp Games 305

Appendices 309
    Appendix A: Random Output and the XOR Mask 311
    Appendix B: Z_{max} Score Monte Carlo Simulation 313
    Appendix C: Terminal Z Score Table 314

Glossary of Terms 315
Notes 323
Index 347

ACKNOWLEDGMENTS

I owe a debt of gratitude to many: John Valentino as my business partner and for the many hours of discussion we have had on these topics in years past, as well as his valuable reader comments that led to a much better book. Robert Jahn and Brenda Dunne for encouragement, for advancing the field of anomalies, and for creating a context and foundation for my project. Some of the members of the Psyleron team: Adam Curry, Justin Wilson, Ian Cook, and Nicolas Haw, as well as our wonderful assistant, Lynn Ann Cornell. Roger Nelson of the PEAR Lab and Global Consciousness Project. My editor, Paula Planter, of EditAmerica, and my publishing consultant, David Wogahn. My early influences on relevant concepts—Frank Sudia and Nancy Beth Orr—as well as the influences of Rev. Michael Gardy, Rev. William Kirby, and my business mentor Martin Tuchman. And of course, I thank my wife, Fran McManus, and our son, Ian, both of whom gently stepped around me as I spent hours pressing the computer space bar over and over and over.

PROLOGUE

Green fills your mind, raining down with rich hues and a warm glow. You bask in the images of deep green grass, shimmering green leaves, and an azure ocean. Ready now, you open your eyes and gently press the space bar on the computer keyboard. A green square appears on the screen and a target line edges upward and across it. Success! You press the space bar again and again and receive a green square as the line continues upward. Yes! One more press and another green—and then more success.

Staying in this groove feels right and effortless now as greenness suffuses and bathes you. You glance sideways at the gently blinking light on the device that is the source of the green squares. There is an equal chance that each new square will be red rather than green. But you are successfully using your mind and only your mind to get many more greens than reds. No physical brain waves are involved; you are fully untethered from the device. You are selecting what happens just by thinking about it—in tune with the world in some undefinable way.

With so many greens, your game score is now much higher than chance would dictate. You press the key again and a RED occurs—the opposite of the desired green—and the line edges slightly downward. You tell yourself, "Well, a few REDs will always occur of course, so never mind." Another GREEN and another GREEN and yet another. Ah, this must be the definition of a flow state. Amazing, so strong it is—as if it is its own reason to exist. You feel cut loose from the normal world with this elixirlike state of mind, your own brilliant reality. How can you explain it to people—this sense of pure meaning that now paints the screen as if an extension of your own being? More GREEN. You can do no wrong.

But, you think to yourself, this whole thing is a little unnerving. Do I even have a right to affect stuff in this way? Maybe I'm going crazy. I'll just press again now, a bit timidly—RED. OK, no big deal. I'll just put the feeling out of my mind, and yes, there it is again. Got it. GREEN! But you can't shake that slight feeling of anxiety that is creeping in. Maybe there's something a little freaky or even wrong about too much success. You wince slightly and gingerly tap the space bar. RED, RED again.

Tension begins to well inside you, and you're tightening up but try to remain calm. A GREEN, good, thank God. RED. RED. RED. The anxiety is palpable now as your mind goes slightly blank. RED. RED. Now panic is setting in. You can't seem to access the part of your mind that you could just moments ago. RED again. It all seems to be laughing at you as the string of reds pounds inside your head relentlessly each time you press the key. Now your world is full of red. What is this state of alarm that is pushing out all other feelings? But you are defiant. You will turn it around. You have to! You can't stop now, you're in too deep, and you won't let the score end back at zero, with all of your brilliant work gone, as if it never existed.

You hold down the space bar and rapid-fire: RED. RED. GREEN. RED. RED. RED. RED. Dammit! The line and the score will soon go below zero. How can this be happening? Your heart sinks as you manage to pull your hand from the keyboard just as the line dips below zero. You shudder and squeeze your eyes shut. What the hell just happened?

INTRODUCTION

On the evening of February 13, 2011, Prof. Garret Moddel of the University of Colorado Boulder and one of his graduate students, Zixu (James) Zhu, huddled over a small table in a university laboratory. Way across the country, in Princeton, New Jersey, coresearcher Adam Curry of Psyleron Company paced the floor expectantly. On the table in Boulder, splayed out and connected to a set of wires, was an electronic circuit board. The board had a heartbeat of sorts—in the form of an ongoing stream of random ones and zeros emitted by the circuit. The numbers flowed past the screen like the trace of a hospital monitor showing a patient's vital signs. In this trace, the ones were high, and the zeros were low. What the researchers planned to do was to disturb the circuit to see how it would react. The reaction they were looking for was more than physical. They wanted to know how the circuit would *feel* about being disrupted. Could the circuit give some evidence of a conscious self?

Attempting to affect that target circuit board, which we will call the *prisoner*, was another circuit, which we will call the *warden*. The warden's job was to periodically and abruptly cut the power to the prisoner. It would do so using its own random circuit by spinning an internal roulette wheel, and when it came up double zeros, it would cut power to the prisoner and shut it down. The process would occur over and over—analogous to, say, a sleep deprivation process. The question was, How would the prisoner react?

Of course, once it got shut down, the prisoner would fail to respond at all. That would provide no evidence for anything. Furthermore, one could not alert the prisoner ahead of time to tell it what was about to happen, because any physical signal sent to it prior to the event could affect its functioning. A change in behavior at that point could be attributable to the signal itself, in no way indicating the presence of consciousness. A better measure was needed—a more creative concept of how the prisoner might display a burst of consciousness or awareness of its situation.

In fact, a number of studies in the past decade with human subjects have seemed to show a unique signature of consciousness. In one type of study, a subject sits in front of a blank computer screen on which a picture suddenly appears. The image is either a disturbing one, such as a gory auto accident, or a neutral one, such as a common landscape. Before a picture appears, the subject presses one of two buttons to "guess" whether the next picture will be disturbing or not. For added intrigue, the computer does not select which type of picture will be shown until the instant it is displayed—and well after the subject has pressed the button. Nevertheless, the subjects in these studies have been able to pick out or intuit future disturbing pictures at rates significantly better than chance. From a conventional scientific standpoint, of course, that makes no sense. How can a signal travel from the future back to the present and affect a subject? But as reported by one of the world's foremost social psychologists and replicated a number of times in other studies, somehow it does happen.[1]

A related study design is even more striking. In experiments involving the modified design, human subjects are wired up to track their vital signs. And instead of pressing buttons, subjects sit passively in front of their blank screens, waiting for the next disturbing or neutral picture. It has been statistically confirmed that their bodies react ahead of time to disturbing pictures and not to neutral pictures. The data show small, added spikes in the subjects' heart rates and skin conductivity in the seconds leading up to the event. So, without being told when the next event would take place or what it would be, their bodies nevertheless react as if they know. Their bodies brace for the image with an intuition.[2]

The research team in the Colorado study postulated that perhaps their prisoner would react in the same way as the human subjects. That is, if the prisoner does have some sense of self, then why shouldn't it display a similar anticipatory response? Maybe its response would be even stronger given the simplicity and straightforward nature of this isolated, single circuit. The heartbeat might show a response—a recognizable shift in its otherwise random stream of ones and zeros—in anticipation of the target event. For example, the circuit might produce more ones or more zeros than would be expected by chance just before the power is cut. Such a response would indicate some active inner experience of electronic intuition.

Garret, James, and Adam built the devices to eliminate all other possible sources that might affect the random variation of the output. And by means of extensive control runs and testing, they assured themselves that that was the case. So, all the team had to do was to run the program many times and then analyze the few seconds of data just prior to each cutting of the power.

On that February evening, the equipment was ready to go. James pressed a button to start the apparatus, and it would run all night. They turned off the lights and left the building.

In the morning, they returned and shut down the system to give the prisoner a rest. Their analysis of the data—to their amazement—revealed a recognizable dip in the number of ones that were produced just prior to each time the power was cut. The output contained far more zeros than ones starting at about one second before each event. It appeared that the prisoner anticipated what was about to happen to it.

The researchers' first thought was that the system might be malfunctioning in spite of their thorough testing and control efforts. They ran through the system tests again, and everything checked out fine. The prisoner's heartbeat appeared to be giving random ones and zeros at all other times. The researchers then ran the experiment a second night to see what would happen.

In the morning, they found results that were equally robust. And so, yet again, and without becoming overly excited, they ran the system a third night. In the morning they found more strong results— again of exactly the same type and at the same points in time. When they compiled the data from all three nights, the overall result was staggering from a statistical standpoint. The chance that the result could have occurred by chance was almost nonexistent. The odds were greater than a billion to one that the system showed the proposed effect.[3]

At that point, Garret, James, and Adam could relax a little after their years of planning and anticipation. They shared looks of incredulity back and forth—perhaps in the form of images of the Nobel Prize ceremony running through their heads. This was big, really big. It appeared as if the computer circuit was alive and had a self that was at least barely aware of its relation to the world and outside events. But the results were also scary: Why was this effect so robust? And once looked for, why was it so easy to see? How could they as researchers present these findings to the scientific community before they had a better handle on them?

They stepped back and put on new analytical hats—in effect challenging the circuit to show them just how robust the results could be. To that end, they adjusted some of the instrument settings to see what effect the changes would have. They lowered the rate at which the prisoner produced its ones and zeros. Then they started the experiment and left for the night.

In the morning, the data were analyzed but showed nothing at all. There was no effect. Apparently, the lowered output rate lost the effect. So, they increased the output rate to be faster than the original, so they could check again how much that condition might enhance the effect. But upon reviewing the results, they saw no effect there, either. This was confounding, because it meant they had originally stumbled onto the exact right settings to maximize the signal. There must be a narrow band of settings that hit the sweet spot. So, they returned to the original settings and ran the experiment again. This time, they got no effect. The original settings gave nothing at all. So they tried again. Nothing. And yet again, nothing. The apparatus never gave another positive result. Today the prisoner and the warden sit on a dusty shelf in a storage room at the University of Colorado.

※ ※ ※

In a normal world, that sequence of events would not happen. Odds of a billion to one against chance don't suddenly appear in a data stream at exactly the right point, only to disappear without a trace. For one thing, this type of circuit would not malfunction in this way. Similar circuits are used routinely in most computer encryption security systems throughout the world. And though they *can* produce wild swings in their ratios of ones and zeros because their output is based on uncertainty, the likelihood of any given swing at any given time is fully calculable. The precise spike found in the

Colorado data on multiple occasions is about as likely to occur as is drawing a needle out of a stadium-size haystack.

Laboratories have variously adapted these devices, called *random-event generators*, or REGs, for studying the mind. So-called mind-over-matter research has been carried out for decades using them. In most studies, a person sits in front of a REG, connected to a computer giving feedback, to see whether the person can shift the output simply by thinking about it. The devices can also be placed at a remote site rather than near the person, so as to make sure—beyond the already extensive shielding—that no brain waves or other conventional force is involved. Hundreds of studies—including work in high-profile laboratories at Princeton University and Stanford Research Institute (now SRI International)—have produced a pattern of overall positive results. In 1992 and again in 2000, a compilation of all reported studies showed an apparent, highly significant impact of the mind on the devices.[4]

There are certain major drawbacks to the results, however: Even though highly significant, the physical effects are small overall and often inconsistent—even backward at times. And perhaps most perplexing, a recurring pattern is seen—one similar to the Colorado results—wherein early positive findings are followed by declines or disappearances.[5] As data go, none of those properties reflect the solid, stable patterns that scientists like to see.

Nevertheless, one would think that *any* measurable positive results would spark high interest among the wider scientific community. How fascinating that the mind might be able to directly affect physical reality—even if just a little. But the scientific community has remained unimpressed by that argument, because most damningly, no theory would explain how it could work. The capability of a mind to directly affect matter and events does not fit with our largely mechanical understanding of the physical world. To punctuate that rejection, in a 1994 interview about the positive mind-over-matter results found at the Princeton laboratory, Nobel laureate physicist Steven Weinberg stated:

> If there were anything to [these findings,] that would really be the discovery of the century. In fact, it would be more than that. It would overturn all the centuries of work since the birth of

> modern science at the end of the sixteenth century. Those centuries of scientific work have given us a picture of nature. We understand why things are the way they are. We understand them in a way that doesn't put human consciousness in any special position. Parapsychology, if there were anything to it, would undo those centuries of effort, and we would be back at the beginning—without any real idea of what kind of world this is that we live in.[6]

Because of that chilly response and others like it, most scientists have avoided this subject area—that is, except a few intrepid souls who are either tenured or retired.[7] Another clue as to why these studies have struggled to be noticed has to do with where they are run, which is largely in engineering environments. The studies are conducted there because their focus is almost always on the devices themselves: how they can be configured, refined, and otherwise tweaked to increase the signal if indeed there is a signal at all. But over time, the lack of success in that approach has taken a toll, and interest has waned.

A more natural place for such studies is in the field of psychology. After all, we're talking about a possible mind effect. The real action in these studies may be not with the devices but with the people involved and what's going on in their minds as they try to affect the REG output. To date, most reports that we do have on subjects' states of mind are anecdotal. People "working" the REG device report moments of feeling a deep connection followed by the output's turning positive. Or they imagine the device as a pet or otherwise being alive such that they feel momentarily bonded with it. On the flip side, they might be doing well and suddenly feel they're going to lose the connection—and so they do. They freeze up and then start to do poorly. The foregoing prologue tries to convey how rapidly one's feelings can shift while trying to influence the REG output.

In spite of the more natural fit with the field of psychology, this field is not inclined to take up mind-over-matter studies. Psychology has always struggled for respectability next to the hard sciences of physics and chemistry, and it does not want to risk falling out of step with those fields. And so, given that rejection by both the hard and soft sciences, the Colorado experiment sits abandoned as one more random blip of data with no meaning or use. It is wrapped up and filed away—trucked to the back of a mile-long warehouse like in the final scene of the movie *Raiders of the Lost Ark*.

But there may be more to the Colorado experiment than meets the eye. A close look at the study suggests an entirely new possibility: that it may validate something many have long suspected about the power of their feelings. This may be one of those accidental discoveries that changes everything.

To explain such a prospect, we'll look at the study through different eyes. First, it's probably not the case that the circuit showed evidence of consciousness. If the circuit *had* shown evidence of consciousness, the results wouldn't have disappeared so abruptly. The circuit would have continued showing some response—even if low-level and fluctuating, which didn't happen. Instead, we turn to the other reasonable alternative: that the researchers themselves somehow produced the results. Perhaps it was their changing emotions and attitudes that were reflected in the ones and zeros of the output. So, we'll take a closer look at the setting in which the study took place.

Before the study began, Garret, James, and Adam were of course excited and wanted a positive result. Research scientists feel that way about their studies, or they wouldn't spend the time and commit the resources required to set up and run them.[8] In mind-related studies, however, attitude is known to play a central role. When researchers are enthusiastic, or are "believers," as they are called, they often get good results.[9] In contrast, if they're "debunkers" of the subject matter or even if they're highly critical, they usually get nothing. Detractors have used that pattern of results to say that believers must somehow be biasing their studies and that once the bias is eliminated, the effect goes away. But looked at from a different perspective, experimenters are coaches for the participants in a study. If a coach sits morosely with the players and tells them they have little or no chance of winning, then the players probably won't win. So, other things being equal, an upbeat, positive coach gets positive results, and a dour, negative coach fails to deliver. The presence of a positive emotional bias, then, is not a scientific problem but is the whole point. Subjects have to believe they can produce an effect in order to produce one.

The Colorado experiment was run by "believers" and therefore had positive experimenter attitude going for it. But if that were all, then one would expect the results to be only *mildly* positive, as has usually been the case in other mind-over-matter studies. But in fact, the Colorado experiment's results were extremely powerful—far beyond any expectations for a single short-term study. That's why there must have been something more involved in it. In that regard, we can look to the uniqueness of the study design itself—specifically, that it involved no human subjects present and trying to influence the REG. Instead, the researchers proposed that the prisoner REG might be conscious enough to affect its own actions. But if that wasn't what happened, then the only way to make sense of the result is if the researchers *had projected the idea of a self onto the circuit*. That is, they envisioned the state of mind the device would take on if it truly cared what happened to it. Even further, to grasp the idea that the prisoner was going to feel pain, the researchers had to *actively imagine* that pain, the pain the prisoner was going to feel. Thus, they were inflicting pain on the device while also caring deeply about its well-being—not unlike being forced to run a cruel experiment on your own pet.

In summary, then, the idea of the circuit's feelings became part of a powerful story that the researchers lived into. And by emotionally or empathetically reaching beyond themselves, they changed the course of real events. If true, it is here that we find empirical evidence for a belief we often suspect but have no real way of knowing: that powerful human emotions literally bond us to one another in love, caring, and empathy. When we care about others' well-being, many of our normal self-regulation processes are momentarily set aside. We give over to an outside need and are all in. The researchers may have inadvertently shown how powerful their own feelings could be when they weren't looking.

Finally, we turn to the moment when the results disappeared, which further makes the point. Once the researchers fully accepted their own positive results, they changed their attitude. They stepped out of the story and began to evaluate "more objectively" what might have happened and why. Now they had become detached scientists, putting on their white lab coats and adopting a steely-eyed, more analytical demeanor that made them ready to see how high they could push the results.[10] Using this new hands-off—or emotions-off—attitude, they ran further tests. But without their personal engagement, there was nothing to drive the results.[11]

❉ ❉ ❉

That explanation is plausible.[12] And although the conclusion isn't what the Colorado team had intended, this experiment raises important questions and challenges about certain long-held beliefs in science. One of those beliefs is that all activity in the universe stems from a defined set of known physical forces. For instance, such forces as gravity and electromagnetism are understood and well quantified. But here something different appears to be at work. That is, given that the brain is purely physical, the brain could not be the source of the effect; the mind is doing something outside the scope of our current understanding. Further, if the mind can do something the brain cannot do, that suggests that the brain and the mind are not identical things. There is at least *some* difference between them.

A clearly defined break between brain and mind—of any sort—is something that has been imagined for centuries but never empirically confirmed. Indeed, cracking that tight brain–mind symmetry has long been the holy grail of mind-over-matter research. It is also a defining difference between classic brain research in neuroscience and what may emerge as *consciousness research*. A convincing demonstration of that break, once accepted, would indeed send a shock wave through the field of neuroscience. And because it would so deeply shatter the field's current model, the bar for acceptance has been set almost impossibly high. As neuroscientist Sam Harris put it, "It remains a fact that any argument or experiment that put this philosophical assumption in doubt [that brain and mind are the one and the same] would be a landmark finding *for* neuroscience—likely the most important in its history."[13] Doubling down on the issue, another scientist quipped, "I wouldn't believe it if it were true."[14]

However, if it *is* true, then we humans are not fully controlled by the neurological activity of the brain. That would suggest some measure of freedom from the brain to exercise choice: a self with elements of free will. The prospect also hints at the possibility of consciousness after death—or even of immortality—a topic of course highly charged and that would have invalidated any further discussion even a decade ago. But since then, this topic has infiltrated the domain of science—or at least technology. Most of the immortality discussion revolves around the prospect of keeping the body alive forever or transferring consciousness to silicon-based entities. But more and more reports by people with various medical conditions experiencing altered states include encounters with larger realities of which we know very little. And as technology enables the mind to take on new abilities, we may increasingly encounter these new realities.

In any event, the relationship of brain and mind is heightened by the REG, which becomes a potential window into this mystery. And given the need to shift the research from engineering departments to psychology and neuroscience departments—and given the dim prospect that many departments might take this on—I decided I would try to solve this mystery myself. I was not in a position to set up and fund a lab to do formal multi-subject trials in the usual cross-sectional style of study, but I figured that that approach might not work anyway. Finding out what goes on in subjects' minds as it occurs is notoriously difficult. And that's doubly true when trying to link mental states with the weak and often fleeting signal we're seeing. So, I developed an entirely new research design for the study: In this project there would be no outside subjects. I would be the only subject and would produce results myself in an extended, longitudinal study. What was unique about this design was that in addition to being the subject, I would also be the experimenter. As the experimenter in my own study, I would have direct access—*from the inside*—to the mind (my own) trying to affect the device. I was going undercover, so to speak, to explore my own inner workings. The observing part of me would be watching as I explored my own states of mind to see how they might succeed at influencing REG output. I could note the feelings in relation to the output and record those experiences. And if I could learn to correlate states of mind with REG success, then maybe I could explain it to others and help them do the same.

The second goal of the project was the true driving force behind the entire effort. I wanted to develop a theoretical model that would describe how this REG mind effect might work. As I hacked deep into my own experience,

I could begin to detail the structure and functions involved and how it is that that structure and those functions might affect those outside physical events. I could test my insights by feeding suggestions back to myself as subject and would then implement them to see what happened. Over time, I hoped to find a solid model that reinforced itself through experience.

I was prepared for the long haul with this research project, expecting it could take as long as a year of intense personal work. But in hindsight, I obviously had no idea what I was getting into. That expected, single year turned into many, involving more than 11,000 hours on the REG device and more than 2,200 pages of notes about the experience. It was difficult and tedious work, but at each point along the way, I gained just enough strange, new insights to continue pushing me forward. The project took me into emotional waters more deeply than I expected and into conceptual paths I never could have predicted. I encountered parts of my psyche that operate below the surface of consciousness and that have mental subroutines with their own agendas. In the process, I mapped out areas of my brain and functions of my mind and gained an unexpected sense of an inner meaning space. I had to face my own inner contradictions in the form of a divided mind with such unruly parts that it resembled attempts to herd cats. Furthermore, it seems that the mind is purposefully constructed in that way—with checks and balances, sets of regulators, reflexive self-control, and more than a touch of inner chaos. It seems we are natively out of alignment with ourselves so that we can avoid becoming too fixated in our minds or too bold in our actions. Safety is often secured by being hypervigilant to our surroundings as well as by not standing out in a crowd. And so, I had yet another concern: how advisable is it that I root around and make changes to the structure of my own mind?

My associates, friends, and family have been taken aback by how much time and effort I put into this project. I admit it reached the realm of obsession. However, for me it has also been a privilege. To deeply explore the nature of the mind has been a lifelong dream of mine. Indeed, for most of my life, I have been utterly fascinated by the experience of my own conscious mind. And though that fascination followed a path of scientific interest and discovery, early on I was transfixed by simply being able to think at all. My first personal memories of wonder stretch back to the third grade, when I would lie in bed conscious at night for hours, fascinated by the experience of being awake. With my eyes closed, I could create a little voice in my head that would say anything I wanted, and I could visualize sweeping, colorful landscapes and meander through them. One night, my parents came into my darkened bedroom long after bedtime just to check on me, and I said, "Hello." They were startled that I was awake and sounded quite worried. I told them not to worry; I was just thinking.

In middle school, I sought to dig more deeply into my own consciousness. Growing up in Bethesda, Maryland, outside Washington D.C., I would ride my bicycle into the neighborhood of Georgetown to visit a metaphysical bookstore called Yes![15] Yes! opened up new worlds for me when I found the books *Cybernetics within Us*, *Psycho-Cybernetics*, and *Self-Hypnosis*. I began practicing self-hypnosis to see whether I could get to the depths of my mind. But whatever I learned, the mystery only deepened.

In high school, I wanted to test the limits of what we know about the mind, to see whether the mind could demonstrate strange abilities. I came across an early electronic test device called the Aquarius 1000. This gadget had four small buttons that were targets arranged in a square. There was also a larger, start button at the bottom. When you pressed the start button, it selected one of the four targets but didn't tell you which. You had to guess the right button by pressing it. If you were correct, the button would light up and you heard a pleasing ding-type sound. If you were wrong, it blew you a raspberry. The idea, of course, is that over repeated trials, you would try to do better than chance, which amounted to one correct target out of every four tries. To succeed on a consistent basis would favor the idea of extra powers of mind. I didn't do very well—no better than chance, as I recall it. Undaunted, however, I moved onto harder stuff. I tried to use my mind to make a candle flicker while it was shielded behind glass or to move a sewing needle around as it floated on a dish of water. No luck there, either.

I shelved that effort for quite some time because other aspects of growing up intervened. I resolved to study engineering in college. It wasn't that I wanted to be an engineer; I wanted to understand how the world works. In fact, what I *really* wanted to know is whether the mind and the self are just complex physical machines like computers. When I learned that Princeton University required its engineering students to be deeply schooled in the humanities, I was sold. My family and I visited the Princeton campus on a bright spring day with a crystal-clear blue sky, and we got lost in the vast expanse of Gothic Hogwarts-style buildings. That was it; I had always wanted to live in a castle. What I did not know as I began my studies there is that Princeton would become a pivotal location for the subject of mind over matter.

That was many years ago, and since then, mind-over-matter research has of course continued—but always and only on the outskirts of science and in a world largely unaware of its presence. Today, however, there's an additional impetus for resolution of the subject: Humanity is on a collision course with the development of artificially intelligent computers and robots. And that course is posing difficult questions about humanity's own place in the world. Through these silicon entities and steel bipeds, we come face-to-face with—well, we don't yet really know what; and if, as many suggest, mind and consciousness are simply physical aspects of the brain, then perhaps artificial intelligence (AI) will emerge with a consciousness of its own. And if that's the case, then it is perhaps inevitable that AI will surpass humanity in most ways—or all ways—and robots will replace us as the dominant species on Earth.

However, if mind and brain show separation from each other, then it is less certain that consciousness and intelligence are linked inextricably. There may be one without the other: intelligence without consciousness, suggesting that humans have different roles to play in the world than do our AI creations. Complex consciousness may be more evolutionarily significant than science currently thinks it is, and the development of empathy, caring, and other higher impulses may be clues to where we're headed. And they may form a hopeful narrative for our human place in the future.

There's even more at stake than a better understanding of ourselves and where we might be headed as a species. We can use the new awareness to change our own present experience. That is, we learn to step back from our own brains, and we alter our brains' activity to better suit our needs. We have many neurological circuits left inside us from a more-primitive time—circuits involving urges that no longer support us in today's highly complex society. And achieving the highest quality of life both personally and institutionally may depend on a new way of managing and channeling our deeper urges.

※ ※ ※

This book is organized into four parts. Part I describes the early phases of the REG project. The narrative involves much more than background information, however, because unless one grasps the utter cluelessness with which this work began, it's hard to follow the path of its evolution. In part II, I step back to analyze my experience and findings and compare them with current concepts in psychology—in particular, the brain's responses to winning and losing. In the process, I synthesize a model of the mind's structure and begin to tackle such concepts as self-integration and self-alignment. I suggest that the mind may affect the brain in the same way a mind affects a REG. A breakthrough leads me back into the project after a long but productive hiatus. In part III, I apply this new knowledge to the project and bring it to completion, including some key lessons learned. Finally, part IV examines ways that the direct impact of mind in and on society appears to be happening even today. Seen through a different lens, it becomes clear that a new narrative of mind and matter fits the data much better than the narrative more generally held today.

I would like to believe that through this project, I boldly went where no one had gone before. In the process, I became convinced that our future understanding of ourselves sits directly across the table in the form of this REG device, which promises to become a tool that will break the logjam of centuries of philosophical debate conducted in the absence of data. The REG enables us to reject the idle speculations of the endless circular reasoning that results when the mind muses on itself. Instead, the REG puts a stake in the ground to narrow the discussion and takes us on a journey of discovery and understanding that seems waiting to unfold.

But all journeys begin somewhere, and this one begins in the basement of the massive engineering building at Princeton University. Here the mind's ability to do things it shouldn't be able to do was coaxed out of a background of noise. We began to develop a more sophisticated concept of mind over matter, using the term *selection effect* to more accurately describe the process. With the selection effect, the mind chooses, or selects, a preferred outcome from a set of possible outcomes and then helps bring the outcome into being. Under this concept, we don't move matter with our minds as much as we use our minds to guide the course of events toward a desired outcome—a process that may include an effect on our own brain states.

This is the story of the selection effect as a critical element of consciousness research: its past, its present, and—most important—its future as *our* future.

PART I: UNEXPECTED MOMENTS

CHAPTER 1:
THE PEAR LAB

In the spring of 1976, a Princeton University student approached the dean of engineering with an unusual question. Would she be permitted to conduct an independent research project on the subject of mind over matter? The student proposed to study whether the mind could have a direct influence on physical matter.

In the mid 1970s, Princeton University did not do mind over matter. To even suggest it inside the institution's hallowed halls would be like swearing up a blue streak in St. Peter's Basilica. Princeton's School of Engineering and Applied Science was known for its theoretical approach to complex engineering problems, which put this student's research interest way out of bounds. But in prior discussions with the dean, she became aware of his wide-ranging interests in both the humanities and sciences. So, she had taken the chance to broach the subject.

Dean Robert G. Jahn, a research professor in the mechanical and aerospace engineering department, was duly taken aback. But he knew this young sophomore to be an exceptional student, so she could not be dismissed out of hand. He responded as professionally as possible, asking her to describe exactly what she wanted to do. She explained that a former Boeing scientist named Helmut Schmidt had developed an ingenious device to see whether people could mentally affect its output.[1] His random-event generator* output an endless series of random ones and zeros—like 101101001110100—and the task was for someone to shift the pattern of digits coming out of the

---

* Also called a *random-number generator (RNG)*. However, I will use the term *random-event generator (REG)* based on the concept that the output of different numbers represents different physical events in nature.

device in such a way that the computer could recognize that it is no longer random. Unusual results would indicate that the person somehow shifted the output through intention or will.

Jahn's own research was in the field of rocket propulsion, making him, literally, the proverbial rocket scientist.** But in spite of Jahn's focused area of expertise and impressive mainstream credentials at the time, he was intrigued by the student's unusual request. The likelihood of any effect was of course slim, but if there were even the hint of an effect, the implications might be huge. And in truth, as far as Professor Jahn was concerned, almost any question could generate a learning experience if formulated well and approached rigorously. So, he agreed to oversee the study himself on one condition: the guiding philosophy would be that the results would have to speak for themselves. There would be no wishful thinking—only hard data making the case for or against the proposition.[2]

Indeed, against all reasonable expectations, the results of the study turned out to be highly positive. The data supported the hypothesis that people could mentally direct changes in the behavior of this physical device. Professor Jahn was once again taken aback but forced to accept his own position—namely, that research results trump our preconceived notions. Without necessarily believing that human minds had created the effect, he concluded that the subject warranted further study.

While the rest of the school quickly forgot the research, including the student who had initiated it, Jahn didn't. He pondered the scientifically unthinkable. What if direct mental interaction with sensitive machines were possible? If so, then parts of our technological society might be at risk of disruption—or even sabotage. And even more striking were the implications of this direct mind–matter interaction for the nature of reality and, indeed, the very foundations of the universe.

So, after much soul-searching, Jahn decided he would establish a laboratory to study the phenomenon. It was a big gamble, given general academic hostility to the subject matter. He would be putting his career at risk. But his

---

** Jahn passed away in November 2017, with more than 200 research publications to his credit and having received an industry lifetime achievement award for his pioneering work on electric propulsion systems for deep-space travel.

research side had the strong suspicion that there was something there. As dean of engineering, Jahn had the authority to open a laboratory of his own personal interest as long as he could obtain outside funding. He had close ties to major foundations and wealthy individuals, and James McDonnell, founder of McDonnell Aircraft Corporation, was interested and agreed to initial funding. So, while Jahn remained focused on his mainstream rocket studies, he resolved to create a laboratory to study the subject.

The lab would be called the Princeton Engineering Anomalies Research laboratory, or the PEAR lab. It would focus on anomalies wherein mind may directly interact with matter in unexplainable ways.[3] The lab program's main goals were to determine (1) whether such anomalies exist and if so, (2) how active—or even disruptive—they might be in our lives and society both now and in the future. Further, based on Princeton's tradition of theoretical studies, another goal was to gain an understanding of the basis of such phenomena and their impact on our current model of the world. It all depended on how reliably such anomalies could or could not be produced in a laboratory setting.

Professor Jahn—or Bob, which he didn't mind being called—decided he needed a psychologist to counterbalance the lab's engineering-heavy backdrop. When he met Brenda Dunne, a developmental psychologist from the University of Chicago who had already done work in the field of anomalies,[4] he knew he'd found the lab's other half. Brenda knit the lab together synergistically, rendering the whole more than the sum of its gadgetry parts. Bob offered Brenda the position of lab manager, she accepted, and the two remained collaborators and friends for the whole of the lab's existence (figure 1.1).

In July 1979, the lab was set to open—against the strong sentiment of the administration and most of Jahn's peers. And as the university had feared, some people—upon hearing of the new lab—wanted their "psychic abilities" tested. For that reason, the university developed strict rules for the lab such that it would not be used for feeding people's self-delusions. Participants were to be told explicitly that the lab was not validating such abilities. The truth is that the lab didn't have the slightest interest in such people or such claims. Rather, it wanted to know whether such abilities

FIGURE 1.1. Brenda Dunne and Robert Jahn shortly after the PEAR lab opened.

are latent or hidden in all of us. To that end, it planned to welcome any and all participants. Volunteers would be encouraged from all walks of life: students, faculty, townspeople, passing visitors, and people of any age or gender. The engine of science had taken a strange new twist, ready to tackle one of the most profound questions that could be posed about reality and human existence.

※ ※ ※

Personally, I was a terrible student at Princeton. At least that's what it felt like to me. I thought everyone was smarter than I was. In the engineering school, I was surrounded by young wizards of the highest caliber, and I was really not engineering material. In fact, as noted earlier, I wasn't there to become an engineer. I was there to understand from a technical perspective how the world works and whether the mind is just one more physical thing in nature. At one point, I wrote a paper for an upper-level psychology course whose 15-page assignment ballooned to 65 pages. The paper discussed how engineering terms such as *energy, momentum, power, force,* and *acceleration* are also used to describe psychological states. One might say, "I have real *momentum* in this project; it's going to be a *force* in the industry, with real *power*." Such dual usage of those terms seems quite natural and not surprising. What *is* surprising is the fact that those terms have the same complex relationship to one another in both the physical and mental domains. In other words, the world of mind and the world of matter seem to have parallel internal structures.

I loved research, and after graduation, I moved into the town of Princeton to work as a consultant to Educational Testing Service, the famed producers of the SAT and the GRE. I worked in the company's perception research labs, doing engineering design work and fabrication for many studies. It was a way for me to begin blending my engineering interests with my psychology interests.

I didn't know it at the time, but a few blocks from my house on the university campus, a laboratory was about to open—one that promised to fulfill my dream of studying unusual powers of the human mind. I don't remember how I found out about the PEAR lab, but I instantly knew it presaged a long and fruitful association. I went looking for the lab on campus but had trouble finding it. It clearly wanted to keep a low profile by being buried in the C-wing basement of the school's massive engineering building. I introduced myself to Brenda, and Bob came down from his office. I had met Bob before because he was a professor in my own department of mechanical and aerospace engineering. And of course, he was also dean of engineering. I offered my services as a volunteer in the form of a part-time intern at the lab. He told me immediately that one of the devices was not working right and needed some fresh eyes. The device was called "Murphy" because everything that could go wrong with it during construction had gone wrong. I set to work and called in a friend of mine to help rebuild the electronics of the counting module.

Murphy was an imposing structure in the entrance room of the lab. It was a large, 10-foot-high, floor-to-ceiling pinball machine that dropped 9,000 marble-size polystyrene balls through a series of pegs on its way to the bottom. At the bottom, the balls fell into a series of bins spreading from the center outward to the left and right. Under normal circumstances, the balls would fall pretty much symmetrically—from the center outward to either side. The goal was to see whether, in the chaos of the bouncing, a person could use only the mind to shift the overall distribution to the left or to the right. A Murphy run would take about 15 minutes and make an awful clatter, with all the balls dropping and careening off the pegs and one another. It was quite hilarious to see people standing in front of it trying to get the distribution to shift left or right. They looked like skiers leaning into a run as they bent their whole bodies one way or the other to add a bit of body English to the bounces. Murphy can be seen behind Bob and Brenda in figure 1.1.

A wide array of other devices built in the lab were more refined and precise than Murphy—more of what you might expect from hard-core engineers. One of them was a carefully calibrated swinging pendulum placed inside a Plexiglas housing. The period of the arm swing was very precisely measured by sensors, and the question was whether someone could affect the period of the swing just by staring at the device. Perhaps one could slow it down or speed it up via a sense of merging with it in some way. In a similar fashion, there was a music drum with a regular beat, and the subjects were tasked with subtly influencing the frequency or amplitude of the beat. There were also interferometers, an undulating fountain, a random-walk table, and a host of other gadgetry.

Finally, the lab also built its own version of the REG device that had birthed the lab in the first place. Figure 1.2 is a picture of that early REG. As can be seen, it was quite large—about the size of a microwave oven. The output of each trial showed up on the screen as feedback, was stored on computer, and was printed out, as shown at the right.

The REG turned out to be an exceptionally good device for this research. It churns out large amounts of data, and, most important, it does so without causing many of the engineering headaches the other gadgets caused. Its output is digital and can be designed as rock-solid, without the kind of signal drift that had to be dealt with in virtually all of the other instruments. Appendix A describes how software is also used with the REG to ensure

The PEAR Lab   27

FIGURE 1.2. The original PEAR REG device, with digital feedback and strip printer.

complete randomness and lack of influence by any outside physical force such as heat or brain waves or magnetic fluctuations.

With many of these initial devices in place, the lab set about collecting data to see exactly what study participants could do.

❊ ❊ ❊

Seven years into the life of the lab, Bob and Brenda had amassed a large body of highly provocative data. They published their first book, *Margins of Reality: The Role of Consciousness in the Physical World*, in which they laid out a picture of positive effects far too numerous to be accidental or coincidental. The book sparked much discussion, selling well both nationally and internationally. However, it was met with great skepticism from the mainstream scientific community because no one knew what to make of it. It's not that the scientific community could fault Jahn's research credentials or even his methods. Even ardent skeptic magician the Amazing Randi, having visited the lab and seen the methods and data, said in an unguarded moment that he was impressed with the research going on there.[5] Later, Randi tried to walk back his earlier positive response, ostensibly because of pressure from his colleagues. And being soft on this research did not mesh with his skeptic stage routine.

Many of the scientists who responded to the findings appeared not even to have reviewed the work. They seemed to have decided a priori that the mind could not possibly do what was being suggested. Any positive results, therefore, must be silly or absurd. But other laboratories around the world were showing positive results as well.[6] That's not to say that all such studies were significant. Some were not—a fact critics jumped on. The elusiveness of the phenomenon did indeed perplex even the researchers. This effect did not play by the normal rules of an engineering study, wherein results should be solid and consistent once found. Still, as noted in the introduction, the combined significance of the studies reached probabilities that were hard to deny.[7]

Following are a few of PEAR's findings as reported in *Margins of Reality*[8] and summarized in Brenda and Bob's paper "Science of the Subjective."[9]

- People tend to experience the strongest effect when they first start. As time goes by, their effectiveness declines, with no learning or experience benefits being observed. It looks very much like beginner's luck that seems to decline over time.
- Both males and females show significant results, but males show more-directional results, and females show stronger results overall, with greater variability.[10]
- Pairs of casual friends working together do about as well as individuals alone, but bonded pairs of individuals in deeper relationships show the most-volatile profile, with significantly greater overall results. The whole appears to be more than the sum of the parts.
- The overall effects measured are small even though at times they appear dramatic. The results are not visible but, rather, show up as strong deviations from what would be expected by chance.

- The distance between the participants and the REG device does not seem to matter. The process can be completed from different rooms or even from different locales.
- Some evidence suggests that time itself is not a factor, because participants show an effect on data that were generated previously in time—or an effect even on data that will be generated at a later time.

※ ※ ※

Well into the 1990s, the lab was abuzz with activity as well as high hopes of cracking the mystery of the anomalies. There was ongoing construction of new devices driven by new ideas, and the lab had progressed the field in many ways, not the least of which was to give credibility to researchers beleaguered with otherwise endless assaults on both their characters and their methods. The goal was to zoom in on the effect itself and isolate it from the surrounding variables, as any good research process would do.

What was not evident at the time, however, was that the lab had in some ways already peaked. And even though it continued to exist for many more years, it produced relatively little to match the excitement of the early years. Many more papers were produced, some of them dealing with theory or variables such as gender or the decline of results over time. And, perhaps tellingly, the entire lab's results seemed to be showing a decline. In retrospect, the lab was locked into a no-win situation. On one hand, in order to hone in on the effect, one had to apply more constraints to the study designs. On the other hand, the anomalies seemed to thrive only under conditions of uncertainty. In other words, the tightening constraints seemed to allow less room for the effect to take place. So, although tighter controls gave the critics less to complain about, the effect itself was evaporating.

In the end, it seemed as if things were following the old adage, "You can't get there from here"—or at least beyond a certain level of effect. Something was wrong with the whole approach. Or, rather, the current approach had nothing more to offer. For whatever reason, this phenomenon was not complying with our image of what it should do, and so it remained strangely elusive. As Brenda noted, it was "spritelike." And how indeed does one go about studying sprites?

※ ※ ※

In February 2007, after 28 years, the PEAR lab finally closed its doors. On closing day, a large group of us sat around the lab's overstuffed orange couch reminiscing. For hours, we talked about the experiments, the interesting people who'd found their way into the lab, and the famous visitors who had included royalty, astronauts, movie stars, musicians, and TV networks from around the world. There had been a constant stream of military higher-ups, including a US secretary of the navy who had told Princeton's administration to "keep its hands off the lab" and let it do its work.[11] There had even been a Russian scientist suspected to be a KGB agent working in the lab as a technician for more than a year.[12] So there had always been a bit of intrigue and larger-than-life quality at the lab. Indeed, not long after the lab's closure, best-selling author Dan Brown included references to the PEAR lab by name in his book *The Lost Symbol*.[13] The book even had a character named Trish Dunne, clearly modeled after PEAR manager Brenda Dunne.[14] During a television interview, Brown said that he believed that "the human mind really does have the ability to affect matter."[15]

The New York Times ran a feature story on the lab's closing. It quoted Professor Jahn as saying, "It's time for a new era, for someone to figure out what the implications of our results are for human culture, for future study, and—if the findings are correct—what they say about our basic scientific attitude."[16] At the time, Jahn was voicing his frustration, but one of my colleagues and I were already on the job: we had come to the same conclusion and were plotting a new course of action.

CHAPTER 2:
REGS FOR EVERYONE

Several years before the PEAR lab closed, I met a new student intern there named John Valentino. John had just finished high school, so I noted wryly that he was younger than the lab itself. John had read about PEAR on the Internet, and after visiting it to observe some of the ongoing experiments, he decided to take a gap year after high school to work there. Even at that young age, John made himself invaluable to PEAR research. He had a knack for study design and possessed technical expertise in both hardware and software, electronic circuitry, and computer programming. It was also interesting that he had had virtually no exposure to the scientific paradigm before coming into the lab. So, as far as he was concerned, the lab's experiments and its largely positive results were simply to be accepted at face value. He had no idea that the subject area held a black-sheep reputation within the scientific community. However, over time, he came to experience—like the rest of us—the vehement reactions, anger, and fear that the subject engendered.

John and I got our first chance to sit down and talk later that year, when PEAR hosted one of its academies, which it held every few years. The academies brought together former and current interns, scientists, philosophers, donors, and friends of the lab to discuss topics ranging from philosophy and physics to art, music, and, of course, the latest PEAR lab findings and other lab findings. At the 2003 academy, John and I discussed the utter failure of the whole field of anomalies (parapsychology) to make significant inroads into either science or society. We knew that something had to change, or the field would continue to stagnate. As I noted earlier, it appears that few come to believe in unusual powers of mind unless and until they have a personal experience with them. John was largely convinced of the existence of such powers from his own personal experience even before he arrived at the lab.

John and I were so absorbed with the thought of bringing personal experience to the masses that I remember little else about that academy. The discussion continued after the academy, back at the lab, and then at my house. We couldn't stop talking—as if trying to wear down the universe until it gave up a solution. Finally an idea began to emerge. The workhorse device used at PEAR was the random-event generator. But PEAR's version of the device was huge and clunky, and it used archaic DOS-based software. We needed a sleek and inexpensive USB-based REG with engaging, graphical software. Such a REG might just democratize the experience, enabling the formation of a wide community that could talk about REG experiences and begin to advance the science. What we needed, then, was a company that could produce such a device—and it seemed like something we could do. We had the required hardware and software expertise. Unfortunately, neither John nor I was in a position to start a business at the time. John was just about to enter Lehigh University as an undergraduate, and I had just been promoted to run a sizable public company. So, we simply reconciled ourselves that one day we would do it.

* * *

Two years later, both of our lives had settled a bit, so we decided it was time. We called our new company Psyleron—a mixture of *psy* for *psychology*, and *leron* just because it sounded cool. We set up shop initially alongside the Lehigh campus, where John was still in school. Psyleron's first goal was to build the compact, commercial REG we had dreamed about. John set to work on the new design. He used the PEAR circuit template and updated it to contain more-modern chips. The original PEAR microwave-size REG had been of mostly discrete components, but the new, Psyleron REG-1 would use more-integrated circuitry and would be the size of a small cell phone. It took almost a year to develop a fully debugged circuit and basic software applications to use it—and it turns out that randomness is not easy to produce. So, though it seems to be ever present in the chaos that is life, in fact *pure* randomness is rarely seen in nature. Rather, correlations of some measure are almost always found between an event and its prior conditions. With randomness, however, an event cannot have even the slightest relation to past events.

When we finally hit the market with our first commercial product, we had a backlog of interest and orders. We were encouraged enough to move our office to Princeton, with the goal of developing more products. By far, the most exciting thing for me was that I finally had a REG in my personal possession and could begin my own exploratory study with it. I was ready to train, to see how much I could influence the device's output.

In proposing my own training, the first issue I faced was that training presumably doesn't work. As noted earlier, the PEAR lab and others have found that people tend to get their best results at the outset, and the longer people keep trying to produce results, the weaker their impact seems to become.[1] At some point, that decline does seem to level off or even slightly reverse itself, but given that the effect isn't strong in the data to begin with, at this point the effect can be so small that it might not be seen at all.

The training problem is even worse in my case because I've shown neither prior talent nor a gift for such an unusual ability. I tend to be balanced and analytical—traits that might in fact work against good results. In general, I'm much more comfortable analyzing what others can do. In other words, I'm better as an experimenter than as a subject. In fact, as much as I've been drawn to it, the whole subject area scared me at a deep level. For example, a colleague and I were at a remote-viewing conference in Las Vegas selling our products. We participated in a so-called spoon-bending party—an event that had become a kind of yearly spectacle at this annual conference—to see whether attendees could go beyond papers and seminars to a moment of personal experience. About 70 attendees each picked up a spoon or fork from a large pile in the middle of the room. They began lightly rubbing the neck of the spoon and focusing on it mentally, with the idea that the neck would suddenly become soft and pliable. At some point, a first person in the group gets it going and naturally exclaims aloud, at which point the room goes electric. The energy, excitement, and sudden confidence in the room causes or enables others' spoons to bend. And that indeed happened—to lots of people but not to me at that event. My spoon remained hard as a rock, and I was so freaked out by the whole thing that I just wanted to hide under a table.

The story had another strange twist for me, even more telling. At the conference were a husband and wife who had earlier in the day purchased some of our products. And even at the time they did, I made a note to myself that the man had a strange lightness of presence. Not flashy or dynamic, but kind of fluid or luminous. Sure enough, his spoon bent. In fact, once he got it going, he kept picking up spoons and with a surreal cadence, just kept bending them one after the other. Furthermore, he did the most-difficult kind of bending, which is to twist the neck a full turn or more on the utensil's axis—like the swirl of a scoop of soft ice cream in a cone. As he was doing it, I started asking him questions about his state of mind and the inner experience of what he felt he was doing. But after a few more spoon bendings, he said: "I'm done. Your questions made me lose it." I felt like an idiot. Even so, he did give me several of his bent spoons to take home, and they are utterly remarkable. I also took home one of the unbent spoons and tried to bend it by clamping it onto a table vise and twisting it with a pair of vise grips. The spoons in the batch were not thin metal but quite thick at the neck. Even bracing myself against the workbench and with a great deal of torque, the spoon did not twist as cleanly and tightly as the man had been able to do with seemingly no effort at all.

So, I realized that I'm not the best subject to be trying this personal training project myself. Nevertheless, I decided it would be my tenacity and my persistence that would have to make up for my shortcomings.

※ ※ ※

Psyleron developed two software applications for the REG. We called one of them the *Reflector*. The idea was that it reflects one's mental state onto the output. Its basic computer-game screen displays feedback to the user in what's called a *random-walk chart*, or, sometimes, a *drunken-walk chart*. The chart is imagined as a walk across a blacktop, as shown in figure 2.1. When pressing a key on the computer, one gets a result either *in* the stated direction (a hit) or *against* the stated direction (a miss). Each result is called an *individual trial*. And with each new hit or miss, a solid line begins to build on

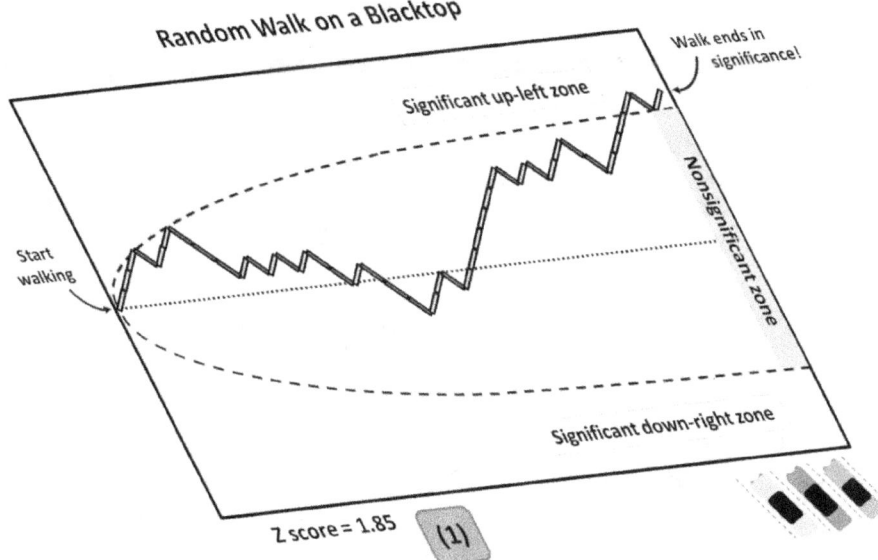

FIGURE 2.1. The random-walk chart as a blacktop. The REG results walk forward left with each hit and forward right with each miss.

the chart, starting from the point indicated at the left. A hit takes the line up as shown, and a miss brings the line down. Through many trials, the line builds itself randomly across the blacktop from left to right.

With a random-walk, one expects to stay reasonably close to the center dotted line. That is, overall there should be about the same number of hits as misses—or greens as reds or ones as zeros—such that the ending point is still somewhere near the midline. But it can at times wander quite a lot to the sides. The goal in playing the REG game is to skew the results as much as possible to the side—a side that one has selected ahead of time and then "intends." In figure 2.1, for example, perhaps the player is trying to have the results go up/left. Thus, if the result ends *above* the dotted parabolic line, as it does in the figure, then the result is considered statistically significant.[2] If the result ends *anywhere inside* the parabola, it is considered normal. And if the result ends *below* the parabola—in a case in which the player is trying to go in the other direction, it is considered *significant*—but in the wrong direction. That is, rather than psi hitting, it is psi missing.

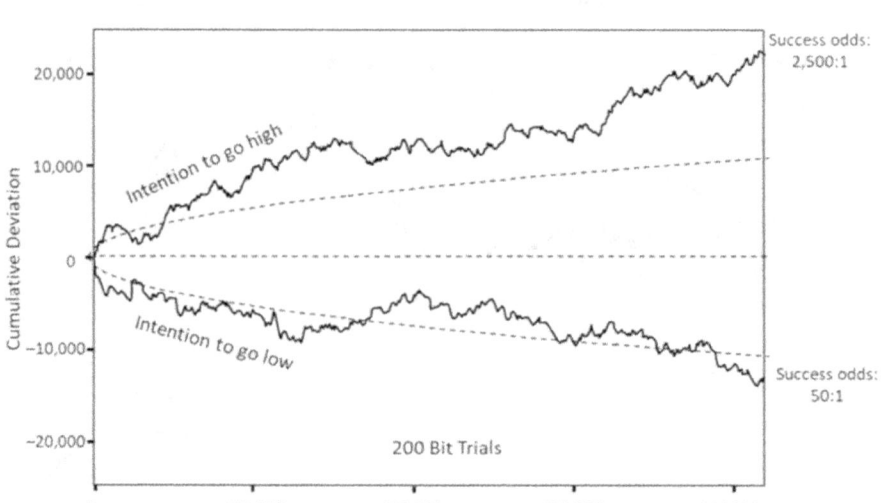

FIGURE 2.2. The PEAR REG data set showing high-intention and low-intention conditions, including odds against chance associated with the results.

Most of PEAR's original REG research was reported in this random-walk chart form, though the software did not display the data on the screen until it was later analyzed. Figure 2.2 combines a decade of data collection from PEAR research involving 91 participants in 522 session series. The two data lines represent two different conditions. In the upper line, the subjects were tasked with trying to make more ones than zeros (called *go high*). Indeed, they succeeded overall in a big way, with odds against chance of 2,500:1, as shown. Similarly, in the lower line, subjects were tasked with trying to make more zeros than ones, (called *go low*). Here again, the results were significant, but at odds of 50:1 against chance, they were not as significant as in the go-high condition. The combined odds against chance of both of these data lines together is more than 14,000:1, and it's hard to overstate how visually striking the results are when displayed in this manner.[3]

✳ ✳ ✳

In addition to the random-walk chart, the Reflector gives an ongoing score that lets you know during a session how well you're doing relative to chance. That score is a statistical measure called the Z score. I'll keep the discussion of Z scores to a minimum, preferring whenever possible to report results in terms of odds. However, I'll sometimes refer to them in a specific context. And because there are different meanings for the Z score depending on how it's applied during a session, I describe them here for the statistically inclined.

Z score: The basic measure of significance during the session. The Z score ending value can be translated into statistical odds against having occurred by chance.

Z_{max} score: The maximum score reached at any point during a session, as calculated from the start of the session.

Finally, the screen also includes another simple feedback visual with each new trial. A red or green square appears (figure 2.3) based on the latest output. (The square can also be seen in figure 2.1.) Within the square, a number appears in parentheses to indicate how many of the same result have occurred in a row. In figure 2.3, the number (2) means this is the second green result in a row.

FIGURE 2.3. A square appearing green on the computer screen with current run-length indicator.

If the next trial result is red, then a red square appears with the "run" indicator reset to (1). The way I played the game, I was always trying to get greens. I didn't want to confuse my brain any more than necessary by shifting my intention back and forth.

※ ※ ※

That's pretty much all there is to the Reflector game and the logistics of my would-be project. Once the hardware and software had been completed, I was to be the first user—or the power user I hoped to be.

So, with everything in place, one sunny spring afternoon more than 12 years ago I sat down to play the game. I was to become an expert at this unlikely process in nature that we called the selection effect. That is, I would use my mind to influence a physical device, guiding its output in a prespecified direction. I had a new laptop computer, a new REG device, a cup of tea, and high hopes of solving this mystery of mind and maybe even changing the world. And the only thing I had to do was to create more greens than reds on a computer screen.

Really, how hard could that be?

CHAPTER 3:
CLUELESS

For the first six months of my project, I stared at the computer screen and had no idea of what I should be doing. I tried to "think" the line on the screen to go up. I tried to think green. I tried to imagine a high score. I tried all of those strategies again and again, but nothing worked. And if, as the saying goes, insanity is doing the same thing over and over and expecting a different result, well, I was clearly certifiable.

Even though I could not see my thoughts reflected in the output in any way, in retrospect something *was* going on. I experienced a few moments that seemed to connect—if only subtly. But I was primed to deny anything that might be merely subtle, not wanting to fool myself into creating meaning where there wasn't any. I would admonish myself every time my attention was drawn to a moment that seemed to hold promise. I was looking for big results and ignored as unacceptable anything that might be less so.

What became clear, however, is that the real action of the game was not on the screen. It was in the way I began to feel. New states of mind began to emerge, and I had moments of thinking, "I don't ever remember feeling this way." I couldn't place the experiences. Over time, as those new feelings and thoughts continued without reference, some of the lyrics of an old Jackson Browne song became my slogan: "It's like a song that is playing right in my ear / That I can't sing / I can't help listening." I was riveted, trying to grasp something that seemed right in front of me yet remained elusive.

In the seventh month of the project, I had my first profound experience. I was playing the game, when unexpectedly and without warning, I knew with certainty that the line on the REG chart was suddenly going to shoot upward. I could feel it and almost see it, and the hair on the back of my neck stood up. That glimpse of the future, however brief, had been laid out in front of me. And sure enough, immediately thereafter, I began hitting a multitude of greens, and the line on the chart shot upward dramatically.

The feeling was so intense and so strikingly clear that there was no way I could deny it. I had just then encountered a certain inner awareness and a certainty of the future that I should not have. That future was playing out right there on the computer screen. I wondered: did I cause the result, or did I just sense what was about to happen? I couldn't tell, but either way, something was real here. In that moment, I knew there was more to reality than what our current worldview would admit. After a lifetime of wondering, I had personal proof of a direct connection between mind and matter. I was astonished, happy, and a bit shaken up.

※ ※ ※

My brief instant of certainty did not return for quite some time. I continued with the REG but had become so unnerved by the experience that I seemed to be blocking it from happening again. In some very real way, I *didn't want* to experience it again. It had been eerie, spooky. It wasn't so much that I did anything strange so much as I had encountered myself in a new way. The experience had created fear, almost a fear of my own beingness that was too raw, too vital. Nevertheless, I redoubled my efforts to overcome the fear, because nothing in my environment suggested there was any cause for such fear. I was sitting in a chair in a quiet room, about as comfortable and safe a situation as could be imagined. But still, a feeling of fear remained, suggesting to me that this game was more than just a game because it was beginning to uncover profound aspects of my inner life.

Over time and after many data trials and experimental sessions, other notable patterns began to emerge. As before, they occurred at unexpected times, seemingly without my consciously causing them. Surges of feeling would well up inside me that felt like waves pushing me forward. At those times, the REG output invariably responded in a positive direction. That period would be followed by a sense of cresting and running out of steam, in the expectation that the REG output would slide back down. And the results complied, heading back downward just as I predicted. Oddly enough, it felt good and right when the chart would peak and then head down. It was what *should* happen, even though presumably, I was still trying to keep the line going up. The complex feeling of wanting the REG results to go up but secretly sure they were going to go down added to the inexhaustible number of perplexing and confounding inner states that were beginning to emerge.

Figure 3.1 shows three examples of my random-walk data (with approximate trend line overlays) in which periods of misses (reds-down) and hits

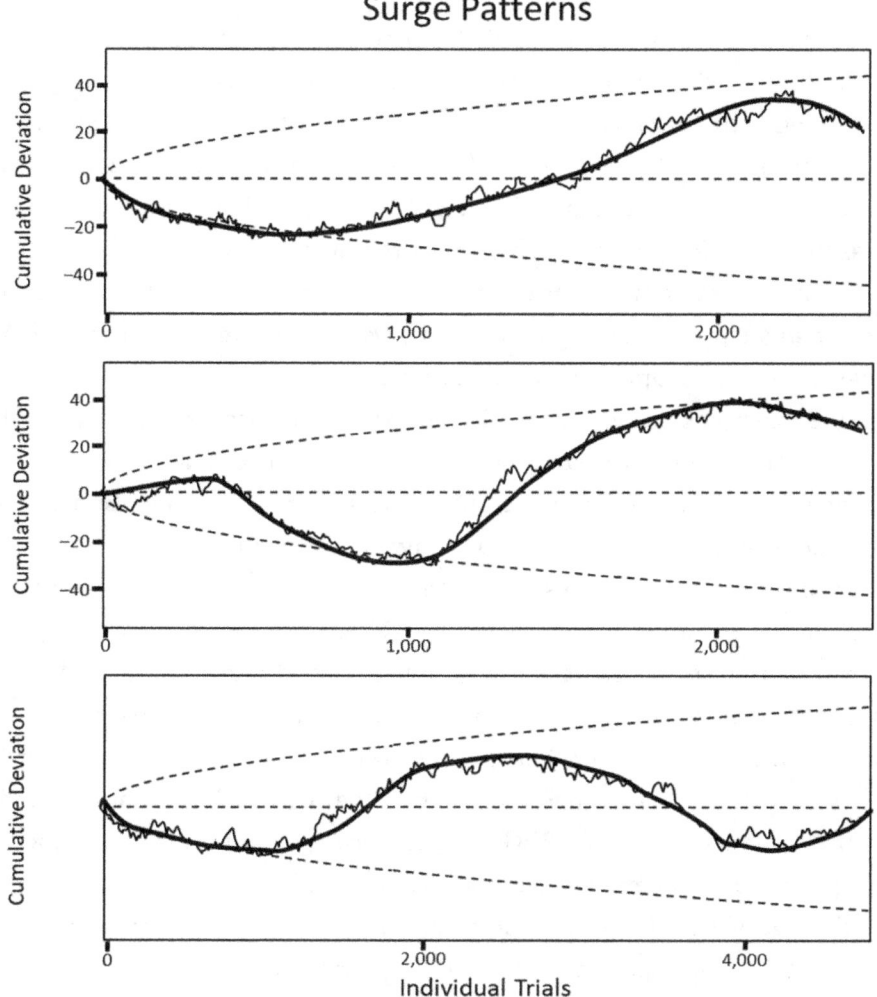

FIGURE 3.1. The wave experience with overlaid trend lines to highlight the pattern. Three examples wherein the inner feeling of emotional surges and declines (chart line rising and falling, respectively) precedes the actual output.

(greens-up) alternate, creating a wavelike pattern. The waves as shown roughly alternate between the upper and lower parabolas. As soon as they reach or get close to the boundaries, they reverse in a relatively smooth motion. And the real key to the experience is not just how the charts look but how feelings *precede* the results that occur. By paying attention to those feelings as they occur, I became able to predict the curves ahead of time.

※ ※ ※

The experience of being in a short-term positive zone with the chart going up and then losing momentum and having the chart go back down became a recurring pattern. In fact, it began to happen so often that I gave it a name: *a rubber band*. A rubber band usually occurs in the game when I'm achieving an unusually high score and then suddenly notice that fact. For whatever reason, my noticing it causes the results to immediately reverse themselves, to be pulled back down. It was like a stretched rubber band that tightened and then snapped back. Figure 3.2 displays three examples of rubber-band charts, again with approximate trend lines.

The experience described in the prologue is a classic rubber band. And the experience tends to leave one a bit shaken because an anxiety and a fear accompany a rubber-band event. The feelings seem to have no rational basis, but there they are anyway. And once again, although such events can also occur by chance, the key lies in how the feelings precede the action seen on the screen. In conversations with other REG study subjects over the years, everyone reports the same thing. In our circles, the term rubber band has become a staple. The specter of having a rubber band hovers over the game as if built in. In fact, there was a time I was giving a talk to a group of 12 neuroscience graduate students at Laurentian University in Canada. Some of the students were using REGs in their research, and I was describing the surges, the phenomenon of pulling back, rubber bands, and more.

Several of the students came to see me afterward and said they'd had exactly the same experiences but had never put them into words.

The rubber-band experience also has a counterpart in day-to-day life. It's when things are going too well, and one suddenly steps out to notice the fact. One begins to get a little nervous about it, with the sense that something will *have* to go wrong. The thought produces a kind of background anxiety that is hard to shake. And it's strangely self-fulfilling, because the sudden feeling bounces one right out of that frame of mind that had just before been working so well.

The knock-on-wood ritual is one way of reversing a foreboding feeling, to try to shake off its effect. So, though the idea of jinxing oneself is usually

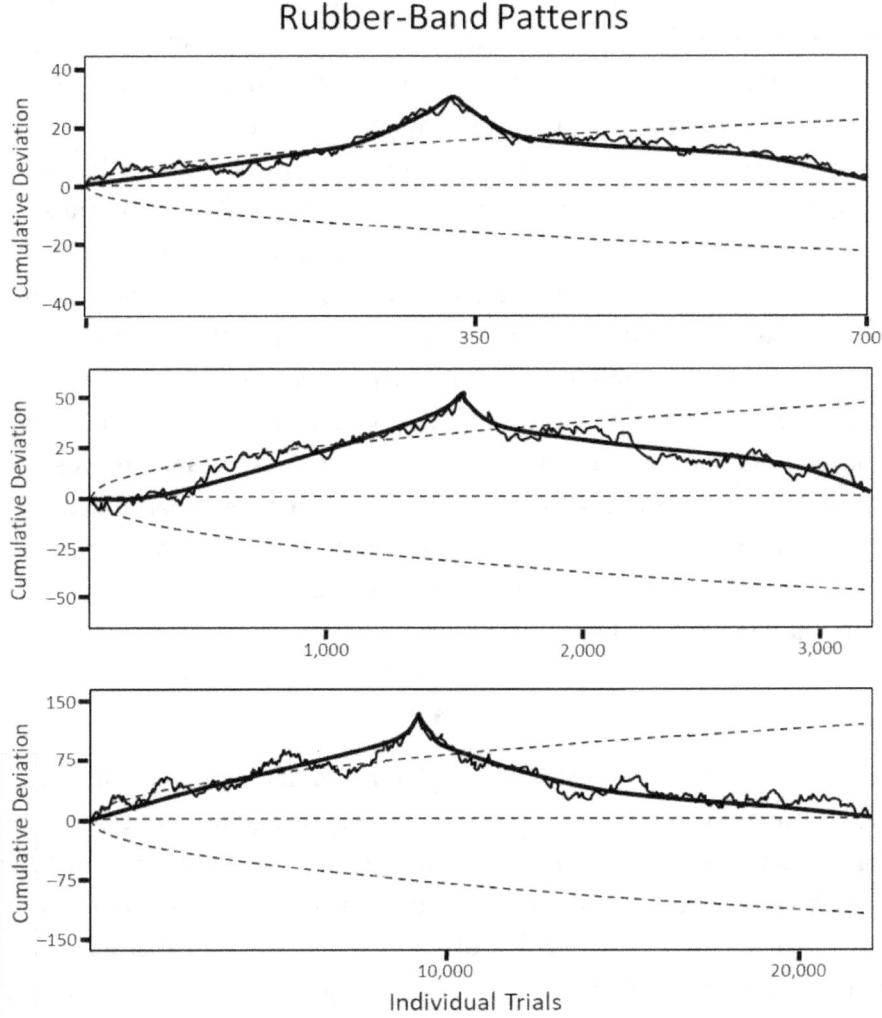

FIGURE 3.2. The rubber-band experience—with approximate trend lines—to highlight the pattern. Three examples where initial feelings of confidence and positivity give way to a fear of loss, which in turn appears to reverse the direction of the output.

considered just a superstition, as far as my REG experience is concerned, it's very real. It's more than imagination—even though it originates in our imagination. My colleagues and I use the term *micropsychology* to describe how quickly the mind changes from one state to another as reflected in both feelings and the REG output that tracks the feelings.

Rubber bands can wipe out good scores as quickly as the scores get produced. To the outside world, therefore, it appears as if nothing unusual happened. The score ends up back near zero, where chance dictates that it belongs. For the player, however, the experience of the climbing score and then the rubber band is full of feeling and meaning from start to finish. In that regard, I would argue that the full mind-over-matter, or selection effect includes *both the up period and the down period*. That is, rather than there being no effect at all, there are very clearly *two* effects. So, the overall effect is double the value of the peak, and the question becomes whether they can be teased apart. If so, we might be able to harness both actions for some useful purpose. The situation can be compared to devices that tap the ocean's tidal energy: The tide powers the device as it comes in as well as when it goes out. Energy can be extracted and available for use during both periods, even though the ending position of the tides is the same as the starting position. If the ebbs and flows of the REG process could somehow be harnessed, maybe we could similarly use them to perform work. This up and down cycle was my first clue that the direct impact of the mind on the environment both in the lab and in life might be extremely understated.

※ ※ ※

A year into my project, I asked the Psyleron programmers for some help. I had become so tired of ending up back at zero after going through an emotional roller coaster that I asked them to slightly bias the output in my favor. Even though I knew the system would be rigged, I just wanted to feel what it would be like to see a big effect on the screen: "Let me experience being really good at this REG thing even though I know I'm terrible," I requested of them.

They wrote a clever program for me by changing the way each trial was scored before being presented to me as red or green. Each time I pressed the space bar, instead of generating a single REG data bit that was either a red or a green, the program internally grabbed a larger fixed number of bits. If more than half of the bits grabbed were green, then the result would be green. If more than half of the bits grabbed were red, then the result would be red. And if there were a tie—in the form of an equal number of reds and greens—they called it in my favor. Over time, that small bias of green over red continued to build. And the more I played, the more I couldn't help but succeed.

Sure enough, as I played, my chart fluctuated somewhat but began to climb overall. I became exhilarated as the chart inexorably headed upward. After some minutes, my current score went past a Z score of 2, then 3, then 4, then 5. I was so engrossed with this elixir of success that I felt I was in an altered state of consciousness. I could not fail, which gave me complete confidence. I didn't even have to worry about rubber bands because any momentary backsliding got quickly washed away; the results simply ran right over them. I was unstoppable. When it was over, I had a Z score of 9 (essentially, an infinite probability), and I was literally giddy with euphoria. Everyone who came into the room got a good chuckle over my head-spinning ridiculous grin.

After I returned to Earth, however, my colleagues found something remarkable. What had *actually* come out of the REG was a result I had never seen before. I ended with a real Z score of more than 4. The odds of such a score's happening by chance (one-tailed, fixed end) is about one in 30,000. Now: one might want to say I was overdue for such a score anyway, but that's not how randomness works. One can never predict what will happen next. Furthermore, it overlooks the quality of that particular moment: this event was the *first and only time* we created a dramatic program alteration, and my artificially induced mental state was the most dramatic positive emotional experience I had experienced with the REG. Apparently, the emotional exhilaration of that moment and the sheer personal confidence I felt were reflected in the REG results.

We never repeated that experiment. Had we done so, it would have been a vastly different experience. The meaningfulness of the previous experiment would no longer have been there. Instead, it would have been replaced with a self-conscious state of mind with an awareness that I was trying to trick myself. Such a state would have been very unlike the original one.

※ ※ ※

Early in my REG work, shortly after my first striking experience, I realized it's important to record my impressions on paper. So, I began keeping an experience journal, which helped me sort through the strange new states of mind and reflect on their meaning for me. What I didn't realize at the time was how important such a journal is to those engaged in a REG learning process, because it turns out that one hardly remembers anything that happens during the sessions.

It took me a while to determine why that seeming amnesia occurs. Simply stated, once a state of mind is no longer the current state of mind, it is gone. With the REG, every moment is basically like every other moment (a nondescript red or green), so there are no distinct cues for access to previous moments. And specific feelings, as unique as they might have been in the moment, also fade. Dreams perhaps make the best comparison. When one awakens, dreams fade unless one writes them down. At least then, one can reread what was written and have a glimmer of remembrance.

The journal also disciplined me in putting mental states into words. It's often difficult to make this translation because of our lack of vocabulary about an expanded variety of mental states. REG-facilitated states can be additionally nuanced and quite unusual, which only adds to the challenge. The states are not like those of feeling happy or sad or perplexed. They have more to do with relationships being formed in various parts of my own mind. Here's a short entry from my journal.

> Okay: I am dealing with my thoughts as if I am outside them and watching them. I started the session very relaxed, and indeed it went backward [down] as per my mind's thinking that I am goofing around and not really intending with any focus. I watched it happen, kind of amused at how predictable it was. It was so easy to watch myself going negative. No effort. Then I decided to battle back to a positive score. I became very focused

on shifting my inner state, and it was very intense. Suddenly I wasn't watching anymore, but had "become" my thoughts, pulling on them in a certain direction.[1]

Reading such an entry at a later time helped me develop an awareness of how my mind can be switched from *being* a thought to *watching* that thought as if from the outside. And oddly, after a while, I developed the ability to do both at the same time.

*   *   *

The early years of the project convinced me that it was something real and important but one I had little or no control over. In that regard, the effect was not at all what I had originally expected. It certainly was not suitable to make me a hit at parties by performing mind tricks. Rather, the more the project progressed, the more it became focused inside myself. People would ask me: "What could you possibly be doing with this game for so many hours? Isn't it incredibly boring?" In fact, it's just the opposite: it's endlessly fascinating to explore new and different states of mind. Even if I couldn't control them, certain feelings and thoughts clearly engaged the REG output. It was right there on the screen.

Unfortunately, the meaningfulness of all of those ups and downs depended on people's believing that any of it mattered. All my self-reporting in the absence of hard facts wasn't going to fly within the scientific community or really anywhere else. I needed a way to demonstrate an effect in some dramatic way, or my project was going to be a failure. I could engage in a formal study of results, but my lack of confidence made that unappealing. I didn't feel nearly good enough to put my abilities on the line, because my current results seemed terrible relative to the big effect I had been hoping for. And frankly, given all the time I had put into the project, my performance was embarrassing. It was clear that I needed a push.

CHAPTER 4:
THE CRASH HOUSE

Bill Higgins, our third Psyleron partner and board member—after John and me—has (admittedly) a bit of attention deficit disorder. It's hard to keep him on one subject—that is, except when you can get him talking about his past. Bill was an FBI agent for many years. He was involved in a controversy in a regional office where he exposed some highly-out-of-spec bureau activity—actually, corruption. For that he was fired because the supervisor to whom he blew the whistle was in on the scheme. He spent the next 10 years clearing his name, which he finally did successfully—and with a commendation. Bill has that archetypal FBI agent look, with a very upright and solid posture stemming from a navy background. And he has bright eyes, an engaging smile, and lips that are almost always slightly parted as if he's about to say something important. Bill went on to a highly successful career in New York real estate. During that time, he met and married Barbara Corcoran, another budding real estate tycoon who went on to become a star on the TV show *Shark Tank*.

Bill begins virtually every Psyleron meeting with the same question: "What are we measuring?" In other words, this selection effect thing is real enough, but what is it? Bill's burning interest has always been to understand the basis of the effect. Bill is deeply involved in the process called *remote viewing*—a clairvoyance process whereby someone tries to envision the scene of a remote sight. Obviously, to do such a thing reliably would be a boon for gathering intelligence behind enemy lines, and Bill worked with the main figures who conducted in the 1980s the US military's previously classified Stargate project on remote viewing. (The program was profiled in the movie *The Men Who Stare at Goats*.) Bill himself is very good at remote viewing, having often achieved remarkable results. Once again, personal experience is the key to both interest and belief.

Bill often donated money to PEAR and was a major financier of a previous PEAR business venture in the 1990s called Mindsong that ended in failure for a number of reasons. One might say that it was just ahead of its time. Bill also rescued another high-profile anomalies research laboratory from financial demise: the Rhine Research Center in Durham, North Carolina. The center was started by J. B. Rhine in the 1930s, and Rhine popularized the use of playing cards and Zener cards for card guessing via ESP.

Bill was instrumental in our deciding to move Psyleron's headquarters to Princeton from its first location next to the Lehigh campus. It was just after the PEAR lab closed, and Brenda and Bob were also looking for a place in which to operate their nonprofit International Consciousness Research Laboratories (ICRL). Brenda found a building in town that seemed suited for both groups. We prevailed upon Bill to buy yet another building for yet another science project and give manageable rent to both Psyleron and ICRL. After some deliberation, Bill decided he couldn't support the building from New York. In the end, I stepped in and bought it—thereby deepening even more my wife's suspicion that I had been taken over by aliens.

The Golden Year of Development

By the time we moved Psyleron to Princeton, we had sights set on other devices and products, which began our golden year of development. John put together a group of young whiz kids mostly from Lehigh who worked on new products. And when a house came up for rent across the street from our building, we grabbed it. It became the crash house for this motley crew of young engineers, including Adam Curry, who had been part of the Colorado experiment, and Justin Wilson, Ian Cook, and Nick Haw. John lived in an upstairs apartment in the office building. Bob, Brenda, and Roger Nelson, the former PEAR lab statistician who ran the Global Consciousness Project, all lived within a few blocks of the building. I lived just across town. If ever there was the image of a Silicon Valley seedpod blown over to the East Coast, this was it. Over the course of the year, the team brought to life a bunch of new products based on the REG circuit.

The Psyleron Mind Lamp™

The Psyleron Mind Lamp is a frosted-glass table lamp with a REG built into its base. The REG drives the LEDs in the lamp to make its whole body change color. The idea is that people might somehow change the color of the lamp through the mind. In one of its two modes, the lamp stays white most of the time and periodically changes color to one of eight colors. In the other mode, its color meanders randomly around a color wheel in one direction or the other. Sometimes it just perches on one color for an extended period before moving again.

When the Mind Lamp was first developed, we had no idea of how it would be used. It was just very cool to look at. Our first prototypes kicked around the office, and periodically, a few people would stare at it and try to change its color. Others just noticed that at certain times of the day, it seemed to act differently—perhaps linked with the staff's various attitudes, like sluggish after a big meal. One day not long after our first prototype was built, we received a visitor who'd been to a couple of the formal PEAR academies. The lamp caught her eye, and she asked what it did. In response, a couple of us said she should pick a color, and we'll make it turn that color. She said red. Within seconds, the lamp abruptly turned to bright red. We all high-fived ourselves, and the woman was amazed. It had clearly been beginner's luck. And being beginners, we were excited and so had not yet put mental constraints on it. I guess we just kind of expected it to work, and so it did.

SyncTXT

John and the team had an idea for a text-messaging system that would send messages of advice to a user just when such advice might be needed. The user would create a list of messages ahead of time, and then, maybe four or five times a day, SyncTXT would send one of them. Both the timing of the message and exactly which message was sent would be chosen by a REG driving the system. The theory was that the user's subconscious would choose the message and its timing, thereby giving the advice the user needed—just when the advice was needed.

When John was testing the system before it was released, one of the messages he could receive was, "I know you are thinking about me." He was giving SyncTXT a life of its own, such that it would pipe up and speak when it knew John was thinking about it. Of course, with that message being only one of a number of possible messages, and because a user received only a few messages per day, this message should not occur often.[1] But John got this message frequently—and exactly at times that he had turned his attention to SyncTXT. One time, he was giving a talk about SyncTXT at a conference, describing the very fact that he receives this "I know you are thinking about me" message far more than would be expected. Just then, his phone buzzed in his pocket, and as he confirmed later, it was that message again.

We released SyncTXT in 2008. We later got a patent on it and enhanced it in various ways. We added some fixed message sets that users can select from rather than creating their own. The messages comprise 15 sets of aphorisms, from the Bible, the law of attraction, Western philosophy, Beatle lyrics, and so on. And now, years later, there are endless stories of humorous and poignant synchronicities with SyncTXT. The website posts ongoing user-contributed events, and I have had more than my share that I could catalog. One day, when my wife and I were headed out the door for the evening, we implored our teenage son to "Be good—no parties at home." He smiled. At that very moment, I got a SyncTXT alert, from a message set of more than 200 African proverbs. I read it aloud: "When the master is away, the frogs hop into the house." We all got a good laugh—and the point was made. Another time, several Psyleron staff were visiting a house to see whether we might rent it for them to live in. The owner was going to move into the garage out back and would need to come into the house daily to shower. The whole arrangement was strange and creepy. As we left the house, Adam got a SyncTXT message: "Be afraid, be very afraid." We fled, laughing and didn't look back.

SyncTXT can be both profound and hilarious. Sometimes a message may be merely background noise, and you don't give it a second thought. But because messages happen infrequently, they do make you stop and think. As I was writing here—and feeling that I would never finish my REG project—I got a message from seventeenth-century playwright Molière that said, "The trees that are slow to grow bear the best fruit."

FieldREG

FieldREG was developed at PEAR and can be characterized roughly as the idea of measuring the meaningfulness of an event. The REG is run unattended in the background of an event to record an impression of how the event was experienced. For example, a hotel chain explored having FieldREG running while concierges interacted with customers. FieldREG would record the quality of the encounter. During the PEAR era, FieldREG was run at seminars, movies, and even focus groups to see what points touched the audiences. It's even been reported used on first dates to see whether the parties feel chemistry.[2] FieldREG is the second major application running on the Psyleron REG, after the Reflector. The software is very similar to the Reflector's, except that it can be set on a timer to record a period of time. Later, the output chart can be reviewed for inflection points and other patterns of interest.

Justin, one of our developers named earlier, is a FieldREG power user. At one point, he injured a leg playing pick-up soccer and was sidelined for half a year. When he returned to action, he described his first game and the excitement and exhilaration of being back on the field. However, he also knew he was rusty and not feeling like a great asset to the team. But about half an hour into the game was when things began to click for him. From that point on, he really felt in the groove or in a flow state and had a great game.

Justin had set up FieldREG to run for the two-hour duration of the game, and a chart of the event is shown in figure 4.1, with an approximate trend line. For the first half hour or so, when Justin reported being excited but rusty, the curve arced upward. The rise can be thought of as a heightened emotional state of excitement, expectation, and some nervousness. Once Justin got into a flow state there appears to have been a dramatic shift. The chart reverses direction in a kind of easing of tension, and that mode plays out for the rest of the game. In this case, the chart's going down represents a good thing.

Interpretation of the results, then, is a highly personal and subjective process. One is free to interpret the data however one wants to. Naturally, that will cause critics to cry foul—that this is an example of humans' creating meaning where there is none. But Justin's story and that chart do

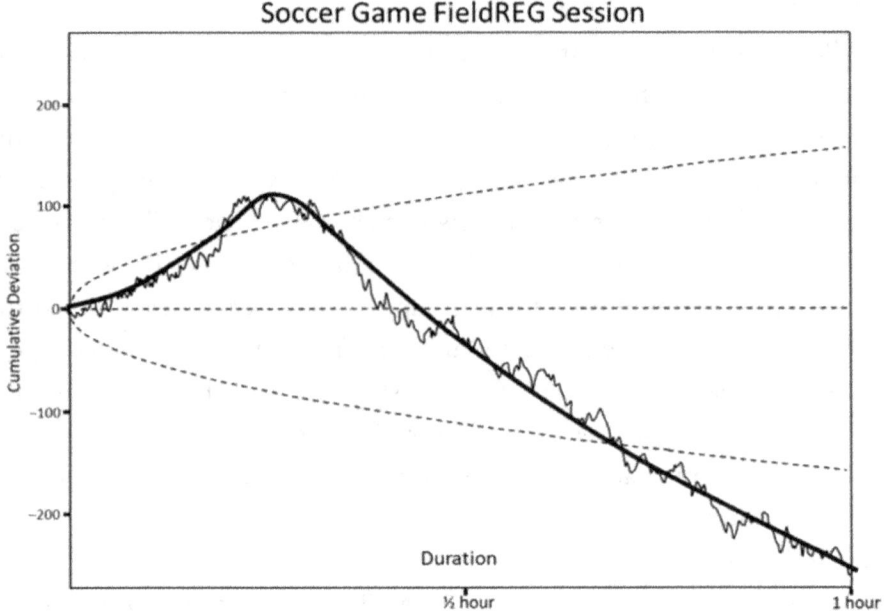

FIGURE 4.1. A FieldREG session with approximate trend lines. The session narrative involved initial anxiety (the rising line) followed by a sense of flow state (the falling line).

clearly go together, even if we cannot explain exactly why. And in any event, the experience is intended to be fun and intriguing. We don't have all the answers. But I imagine that someday there might be professional consultants who have trained themselves to be sensitive conduits for this kind of feedback. Event organizers would contract with those "sensitives" to run FieldREG sessions and then interpret the results. Who knows.

I'll tell one more FieldREG story: It was an event that occurred a couple of years later that involved an internationally known street magician who visited Psyleron and the ICRL offices. He came to buy some REGs and discuss their use. Because he is a true television celebrity and routinely parodied on high-traffic YouTube videos, we were all pretty excited. We set up a FieldREG session to begin at the time of his arrival and ran it for the almost three hours of the visit. The chart of the full event is shown in figure 4.2. The chart seems to show a high level of excitement and engagement from the very start, and it stayed that way throughout the entire length of the visit, which included, as expected, some very entertaining magic tricks.

As the magician was leaving the office, Professor Jahn asked him if he ever used "the stuff we do here" in his performances. In other words, has he used mind over matter or other such abilities during his magic routines. To our surprise, he said, "All the time." Not that he builds such effects into his routines or expects or requires them on cue, but that they surface at odd times. And when they do, he can feel them and use the knowledge to advantage. He recounted to us a time when he performed some card tricks at the Pentagon. The attendees included the US secretary of defense as well as a four-star army general. The magician started a trick by asking everyone to think of a single playing card—any of the 52 cards—but not to say it aloud. At that moment, he just *knew* that the general and the defense secretary had somehow settled on the exact same playing card—whatever card that might be. So, he said, matter-of-factly, "As part of this trick, General, you and Mr. Secretary have selected the same card. What card did you think of?" The general stated his card—at which point, as the magician recounted—"The secretary of defense turned white and ran out of the room."

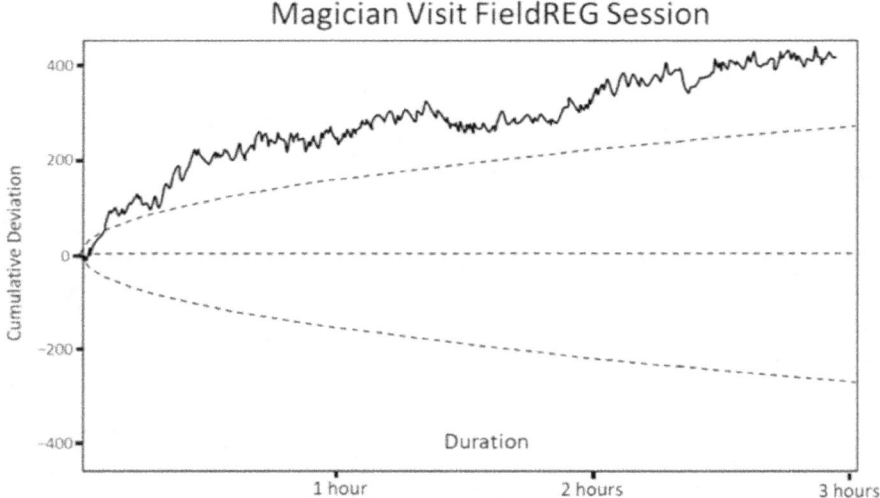

FIGURE 4.2. A FieldREG session started one-hour before a magician arrived at the Psyleron/ICRL offices and ending shortly after he left.

I would go into the Psyleron crash house periodically, and one of the guys might ask me how it was going with my own REG training. I would mumble something evasive—say, that I was still working on it. One day, Ian was especially insistent. So, I said that although I wasn't sure I was succeeding overall, a particular pattern seemed to be recurring but I couldn't be sure because it was too anecdotal. So, Ian said he would look into it by examining my data. But he ran into a problem. As the REG software was being developed, it went through a number of revisions. Often, the revisions made prior data formats incompatible, which made the data chunks all different. Fortunately, he found a large section of data in the central server that was in the same format, so he extracted it.[3]

Ian's analysis showed that probably nothing was related to the pattern I thought might be there. However, it did show that I had created a pretty strong effect relative to my basic goal of getting more greens than reds. The random-walk chart in figure 4.3 displays that data set. As can be seen, there's an early dip in the data, which is followed by a long-term trend upward, ending well above the significance parabola. That data set represents more

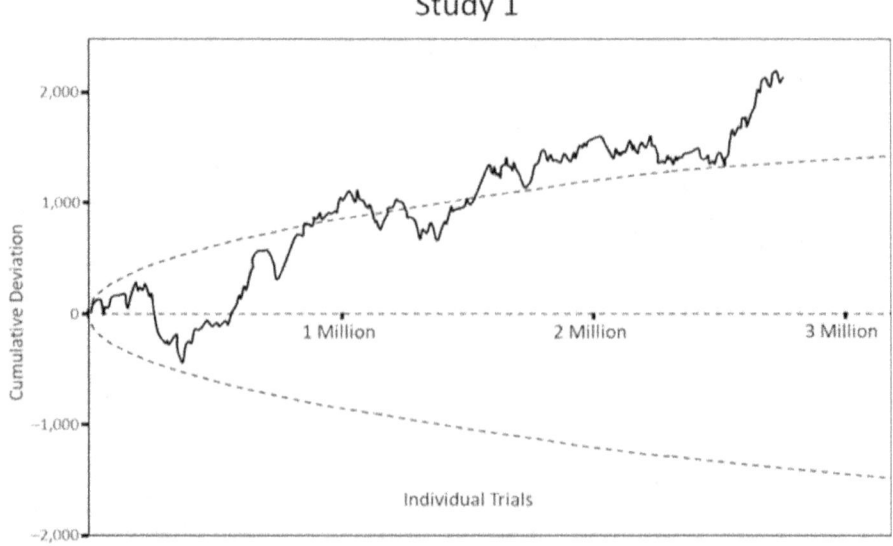

FIGURE 4.3. A large set of data in a consistent format randomly extracted from my REG data. This data set became known as Study 1.

than 2.5 million individual trials, each being a red or green result. (Note that trials can be fired in rapid succession by holding down the space bar.) The probability against the occurrence of that result by chance with an arbitrarily selected data set is about 200 to one. Those odds are better than the usual 20 to one required to indicate the possibility of an effect. So, in my mind, that was pretty good. On the other hand, with respect to my training goals, it still didn't feel like that much of a success. I had produced only a small deviation from chance. Compounded over so many trials, that rate had become quite significant. But it was certainly of no practical use.

In spite of my own lack of enthusiasm over the results, I got some attaboy pats on the back from the group—and some jovial ribbing about being lucky. The encouragement, however, was just what I needed to push myself forward. It emboldened me to undertake a new, formal study to see if I could replicate my good results, and because the effect size overall was quite small, it seemed doable. I would do a set of a million more trials with the goal of scoring at least as well as the first data set—and maybe better.

CHAPTER 5:
THE CHALLENGE

Over the course of some months, I was able to produce a second study set, or Study 2, to compare with my first set. The random-walk chart of the results appears in figure 5.1 with the solid dark line. The final score for this experiment was not quite as good as the first set, but pretty close. The odds were about 170 to one of their being more than chance.

The dotted line on the chart is the control data set. That line was produced by running another million trials on automatic, with no one present trying to affect the output. The control process is for helping confirm that the REG is working properly by producing random results when not being focused on. As can be seen, the control data set meandered around zero and was not significant.

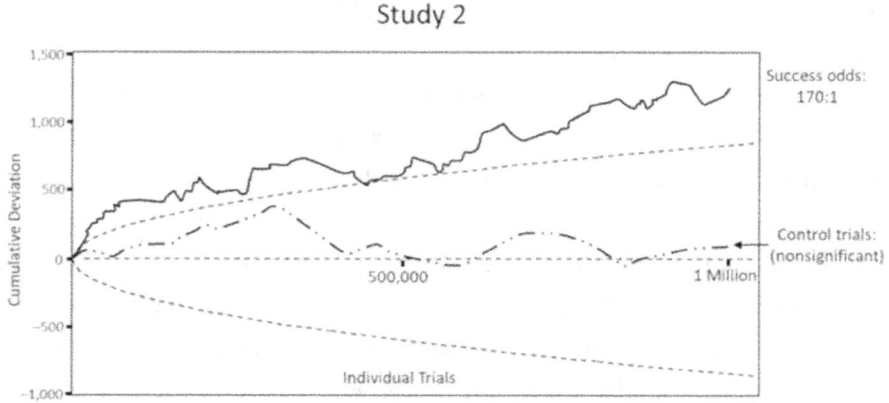

FIGURE 5.1. Study 2 data set of 1 million trials showing significant odds against chance of 170:1. The dotted line represents the control conducted with no one present.

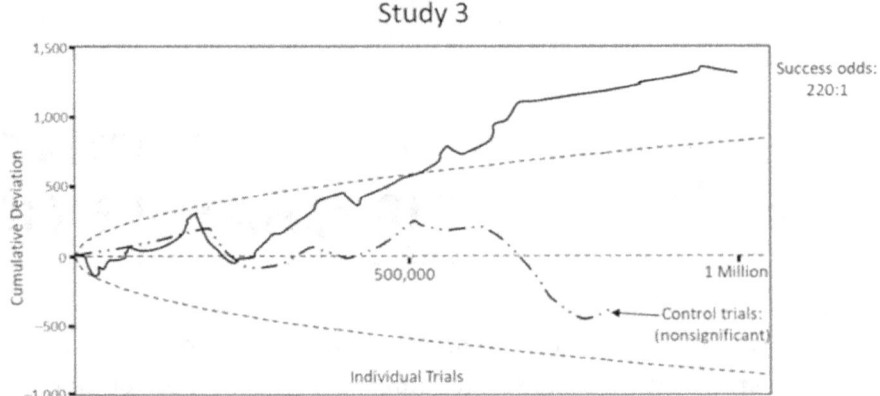

FIGURE 5.2. Study 3 data set of 1 million trials, showing significant odds against chance of 220:1. The dotted line represents the control conducted with no one present.

At that point, I was pleased but did not immediately announce my results to anyone. I was becoming aware that announcing things like this shifted one's mind-set. It's like bragging and then having the universe hit you in the face—or, in my lingo, a rubber band. So, I decided to do yet another set and to see whether I could do just as well or better again. So, some months later I felt ready to see if my so-called training during that interim period would make a difference. I undertook another 1-million trial study. Figure 5.2 shows the results of that study: Study 3. The overall score was slightly better than the first two, but again remarkably similar, with odds in favor of an effect being about 220 to one. The control line again meandered around zero through most of the automated trials, though I stopped at 800,000.

In reviewing all three data sets—the original and the two replications—I found it uncanny how they ended with such similar scores. There's no statistical logic for the similarity, and in fact, it would be totally unexpected. In retrospect, I feel certain that this is not a coincidence. I believe the result was driven by how well I expected I would do in general, given the outcome of the first data set. The first set showed how I roll, so to speak, so the next results should be similar. With each study, I confirmed this same basic relationship—not much better or not much worse. I developed a sense of normalcy about that level of results.

* * *

It did not occur to me during either of the two new studies that all the data could be considered as one large data set. Combining all of the data together is fully allowed by the statistics here, because the whole would represent *all* of the formalized data. There was no picking and choosing, selectively excluding for any reason any of the data trials of any of the three studies. Combining all three data sets into a single, larger data set creates a level of significance much greater than the individual sets alone. The random-walk chart of all data is produced by appending the second set to the end point of the first one—which is already north of the parabola. And the third is of course added onto the end of the second. The random-walk just keeps going higher and higher. The three studies together form a single set with odds of an effect being 116,000 to one. Figure 5.3 displays the combined random-walk chart.[1]

I have no doubt that if I had thought about combining the studies *while I was producing the results,* I would not have ended up with such a high score. Being aware of the rising significance would have spooked me into a rubber band. So, because of that fortuitous disconnect wherein I did not keep track of this overall score, I was now staring at a pretty amazing combined result.

It's sometimes said that when statistical results reach a level of odds of one in a million, the hypothesis about the target variable is pretty much confirmed. My overall results were close enough to that one-in-a-million mark that I became captivated by the idea of actually getting there, and that became my new personal challenge. If I could add one more good data set to the previous three—say, another million trials—I might reach that target. Figure 5.3 also indicates that target point at the upper right—the point I would hope to reach with a final data set.

The problem, of course, is that now I would have to operate under the full weight of the knowledge and the significance of my prior results. To fail would be to risk ruining the entire set of data. If I went only slightly positive or drifted negative or, God forbid, rubber-banded, with a massively negative result—which could easily happen—the overall score would quickly plummet. And once a study is slated for inclusion, the protocol says one can't take it back. Just thinking about it gave me cold chills. On the other hand, the

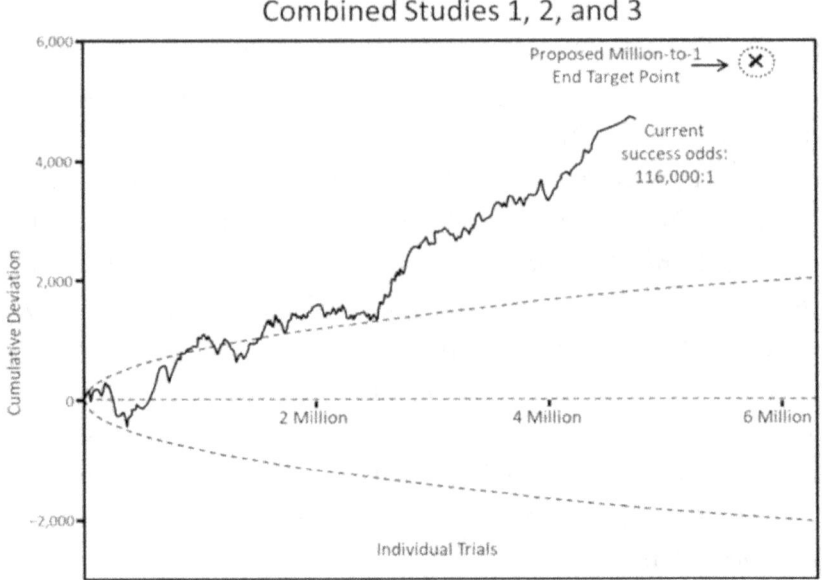

FIGURE 5.3. Combined results of Studies 1, 2, and 3, showing highly significant odds against chance of 116,000:1. The proposed final Study 4 target of a million-to-1 odds against chance is shown.

goal presented an enormous challenge to understand the rubber bands that inevitably threaten when results get too good. All in all, I had created for myself a personal high-stakes laboratory for research.

※ ※ ※

By that point, it was clear to me that running the REG game is more than just pressing keys and hoping for the best. I now saw the game as a window into my own mind—whatever that might hold. It seemed that an unusual state of mind was needed—one that included less self-doubt and less self-sabotage. I later called that quality *self-alignment*, and I used the sense of that self-alignment as a sort of metric to evaluate my progress.

Given the REG goal I had just embraced, I knew I was setting myself up for failure if I started right away. I would not succeed, in part because I had no real handle on or even an idea of what I had to do. I did have a vague notion of aligning conscious and subconscious elements of mind, but I wasn't sure what that actually meant. Furthermore, or perhaps because of that, I knew

I could not maintain the even-keeled frame of mind that would seem to be required. I was emotionally all over the map once I started a session. So, even though I continued to practice with the REG, I stepped back to search for guidance from the body of psychology literature.

It would be two more years before I would start producing data for the final study. In the interim, I practiced. I had many REG experiences and began to form a theory about how and why the selection effect works the way it does—and why I react so emotionally in the process.

PART II: STEPPING BACK

CHAPTER 6:
OUT OF MY CONTROL

One day, while in an otherwise unremarkable REG session, I suddenly thought of my grandmother wearing a funny green hat. The image was completely made up. I gave her a green hat because green is the REG hit color, so it put green into my mental imagery. I had a special fondness for that grandmother, who passed away many years ago, so the whole image filled me with profound feelings of love and nostalgia. I suddenly got a surge of REG hits, and the chart line went up dramatically. I stopped and thought about it in puzzlement. A minute later, I tried it again—just letting myself embrace the feeling and the image. It worked again. I was excited. A few minutes later, I tried it yet again, and it worked yet again. I felt I had finally found a lasting strategy. Who would have thought my grandmother was to become so historically important?[1]

Like a moth drawn to a flame, I decided to try the image one more time. This time, oddly enough, I had *less* confidence than before. I even asked myself at the time why I should suddenly be tentative with this approach given my success. But I became introspective—against my own better judgment. I knew this could be a rubber band in the making, that I might start reversing direction if I thought about it too much. So, I sheepishly tried the image, and sure enough, it didn't work. I tried again, and it didn't work. In fact, it went backward—way into the negative. Along with the plummeting score, I was cascading downward mentally, as if I had lost my footing. My grandmother in a funny green hat never worked again.

That is not how training is supposed to work. One is supposed to get *better* over time. But it does mirror the findings of PEAR and other laboratories where REG training seems to work in reverse. As noted, people tend to do their best work when the experience is fresh and novel—the proverbial beginner's luck. The results get worse over time, and rubber bands seem to be part of that decline effect. Strangely enough, the rubber-band moments seem more emotionally potent than the positive-going periods. Furthermore, that negative-going effect is so highly predictable. Many times, I've felt like an emotional Ping-Pong ball buffeted by those two opposing forces.

The strength of the negative-going feeling and its apparent impact on the REG led me to reframe my approach to one of understanding the selection effect process. Rather than focus on the seemingly capricious moments of success, like suddenly thinking of my grandmother in a funny green hat, I was facing a much more-consistent negative-going effect. The rubber band *always* kicks in for me when I feel that the results are getting too good. So, although each positive-going experience needs something new and different each time to bring it on, the rubber-band frame of mind is always the same: it is reactive and against anything positive. It occurred to me that perhaps the study of anomalies was forever locked in a hit-or-miss proposition because it was looking in the wrong direction. That is, instead of learning how to succeed, I'm locked into the fear of losing what I have. I pull inward as if protecting my ego from what might happen if the score drops. In such moments, I'm aware that I don't want to feel this way, because clearly negative thoughts are self-fulfilling. But at such times, I have no choice about how to feel.

In looking for research studies that involve winning and losing, I found a number with similarities to the REG game. Such studies often involve gambling tasks that give participants choices and immediate experiences of gain and loss. Recent experiments include the monitoring of participants' brain activity so as to examine brain states while participants make their gambling decisions. As it turns out, these experiments have a lot to say about what we do to ourselves without any conscious control. Indeed, I needed to understand the experience and find a way through it. If I couldn't shake fears of loss that simply overtook me, I would never succeed. And for some reason, while playing the game the sense of impending loss felt more powerful than impending gain. Why?

Winning and Losing in Nature

During the course of evolution, losing can be far more dramatic than winning. For our prehistory ancestors, winning against, say, the mastodon meant a full belly for a week. But losing to the mastodon meant game over—forever. So, not surprisingly, at a very deep emotional level, we've developed an aversion to loss that is stronger than the taste for gain. And so it is that loss aversion, brought by the sense of danger, can be a more potent emotion than its more general, positive-going counterparts of happiness and contentment.[2]

Loss aversion manifests itself in the brain primarily through two almond-shaped organs of the brain called the amygdalae. One of them is tucked underneath and inside each hemisphere of the brain, and even though the two can have slightly different functions, they are typically spoken of in the singular. One's amygdala becomes activated when a present-day version of a mastodon appears unexpectedly in one's environment. The amygdala can go so far as to help shut down all nonessential analysis of the brain as it generates the sensation of fear necessary to act decisively in the primal survival mode. Of course, not all situations are life threatening, but whenever a situation of potential loss is determined and there is something to protect, the amygdala activates emotional concern and readiness to act.

Brain scan research has shown how the amygdala becomes excited during games of winning and losing. In psychology studies, when a gambling task was framed in terms of winning, the subjects' amygdalae did not become active. For example, the statement "You have a 60% chance of winning" did not activate the amygdala. Even when the chances of winning were not good, like "You have a 20% chance of winning," there was no response from the amygdala. But when the game was described to the subjects in terms of losing—no matter what the odds—the amygdala became excited, as in "You have a 20% chance of losing." The mere suggestion of loss set it off. In this state, subjects tended to bet far more cautiously than was warranted. However, sometimes subjects could see through the way the game is framed and managed to still bet rationally. But interestingly, even *their* amygdala showed the same level of excitement. Those participants simply had the ability to contain their emotions, overriding the signals to make decisions more rationally.[3]

In life, during periods of sudden doubt, we may reframe an experience in terms of loss. With the REG, that doubt seems to be self-fulfilling; it may be that the amygdala takes over the REG game and begins to drive the results backward. The process snowballs, such that pretty soon a full-fledged rubber band ensues. During those periods, it becomes impossible to shake the fear of loss by trying not to think this way. Cognitive linguist George Lakoff titled one of his books: *Don't Think of an Elephant!* Clearly, it's tough *not* to think of something once it's suggested. Then there's the famous scene in the movie *Ghostbusters* when Harold Ramis's character, Dr. Egon Spengler, tells his fellows, "Clear your minds, boys, because the first thing you think about will manifest." And almost immediately, the 10-story Stay-Puft Marshmallow Man comes lumbering down the street.

I've often wondered in such moments why I don't just stop playing the game and allow myself to calm down. That is, when there's a sense that things will get only worse—and then they always do—why don't I pull my hands from the keyboard, take a few breaths, read the paper, and chill out? However, another factor is present in gambling tasks that makes stopping emotionally difficult. That factor is perhaps one reason so many people have gambling problems. It again has to do with the wiring of our brains. Neurologist Richard Restak, in *The New Brain: How the Modern Age Is Rewiring Your Mind,* reports on studies at the University of Michigan in which students were given the gambling task of betting on the red and black squares (like my red and green squares!) of a roulette wheel. As the students bet, the researchers were able to correlate the students' decision-making process with an imaged area of the brain called the *medial frontal cortex*. The reaction of this part of the brain showed that every time there was a loss (picking the wrong color), the brain predicted a change of fortune on the next try. The more losses in a row, the more this part of the brain predicted a turnaround.[4] Thus the students seemed compelled to continue, compulsively and frenetically betting more and more, even as their losses mounted.

That behavioral response is called the *gambler's fallacy:* that excessive loss must be followed by a turn in fortune. In a random system like a roulette wheel or the REG, however, each trial is independent of the next, and no prior string of losses has an impact on the probabilities associated with the next result. Nevertheless, the participants gained a sense of urgency as this fallacy fueled escalations in the amounts of money they were willing to bet; they desperately wanted to make back their lost ground. That's exactly what happens with the REG game. As I am losing ground, I become almost maniacally fixated with gaining back the lost ground. To stop or quit is to accept the fact that the great score of a moment ago is permanently gone. Rather, I continue playing, fixated on trying to turn the tide of my fortune. How often I have said to myself, "Let me just get back to where I was before, and then I'll stop." And even though I know from experience that there's a slim chance of recovering due to my own deep sense of being out of control, there is something paralyzing about the situation. And the more I push to succeed, the more my fears seem to be used against me. One part of me is literally driving the results down while I seem neurologically compelled to continue. And a third part of me is watching the score plummet in horror and disbelief.

I seem, then, to have found some neurological bases for why the REG game creates such a powerful negative-going experience: my brain is doing something I cannot control. That was my first clue to how my brain circuitry is deeply involved in the REG process. And even though REG results cannot be caused by the brain alone—based on the definition of what physical things can and cannot do—the brain is clearly playing a central role. Such a conclusion is perhaps unpopular in the ranks of anomalies research, in which the brain is generally ignored. But the brain clearly controls parts of my mind, even if I might somehow learn how to manage its impact.

As I became aware of that brain influence on REG output, there arose something even more striking: it's the way these negative-going periods first come on. They appear abruptly, kind of out of the blue. They're like a switch being suddenly flipped or the instant interrupt of a flash news bulletin. "We interrupt this game to let you know that you could lose." And it all goes downhill from there. The question is, exactly when do conditions become right to fire this trigger? There must be some reason why at any given moment, my current state gets interrupted.

Logically speaking, for one to suddenly fear loss there must be an associated feeling that there's something to lose. Without some prior gain, there would be *nothing* to lose. So, at some moment, deep in my mind, I must decide I have something worth protecting. This occurs in life, of course. Whether it's a new relationship, a good job, or any number of other things, we can quickly shift from bold outward fearlessness to a fearful pulling inward so as to protect a position. We don't necessarily notice ourselves doing it, but with the REG, the moment of switching is evident. It's a feedback loop between state of mind and REG response that builds on itself. The REG game becomes a window on the activities of the deeper psyche.

The Prediction Process

In the early 1960s, Harvard experimental psychologist Richard Herrnstein was studying learning processes in pigeons. He used classic stimulus–response methods that were common at the time (behaviorist B. F. Skinner was then at Harvard). Herrnstein built an apparatus that would dispense a small piece of bird food to a pigeon when one of two buttons, left or right, was pecked.[5] The researchers could change the probability associated with each of the buttons. For example, both buttons might dispense food 75% of the time they were pecked. If that were the case, there would be no reason for the pigeon to favor one button over the other.

When the probabilities attached to each button were different, however, the most effective strategy was to favor the button with the higher probability. Herrnstein found that the pigeons quickly picked up on patterns of such probabilities and matched them with their pecking patterns. That is, if the right button dispensed food more often than the left, the pigeons began pecking more on the right. Although that might not be surprising, what *was* surprising was how precisely the pecking strategies mirrored the dispensing percentages at that time. The exactness defied the imagination, as if the pigeons were using a hand calculator to exactly determine what to do (except that handheld calculators hadn't been invented yet). Clearly, the pigeons' mental calculations were not performed at the analytical conscious level. It was a strong indication that neural networks in the brain train themselves to make the best-possible predictions.

Researchers at Stanford ran a similar experiment with monkeys. Instead of pecking one of two buttons to receive a reward, the monkeys registered their selections by looking at either a red circle on the left of a computer screen, or a green circle on the right. A sensor trained on their eyes picked up the direction of their gaze. The monkeys received a squirt of juice in their mouths if their selection was correct. The research showed that the monkeys exhibited the same matching process as the pigeons. In fact, research to date gives strong evidence that most if not all animals have their own built-in circuitries for this prediction function. With the monkeys, a regression analysis was done to see exactly how their mental neural networks were "thinking" in order to make their choices. The analysis showed that a monkey's choice involved a complex algorithm spanning the previous 20 choices and results. The most-recent trials carried the most weight in this algorithm, but even the 20th trailing event was factored in as part of their decision process.[6] These results speak to just how evolved such calculating and modeling processes are.

Humans, too, show matching capabilities, sometimes on display in dramatic real-life situations. There's the legendary story of a British radar operator in the 1991 Desert Storm war who became fixated on a blip appearing on his radar screen. To the radar operator's eye, the blip on the screen moved exactly like an allied fighter jet returning to the aircraft carrier, and it had the right altitude and speed. But something about the blip deeply disturbed him. Some intuitive feeling told him the blip was in fact a missile headed for the allied ship. His alarm rose to such a level that he made the extraordinary decision to authorize a missile strike on the moving object. He knew that if he were right, he would save a ship and hundreds of lives. But if he were wrong, he would kill an allied force pilot and certainly end his career. Fortunately, he was right. In the debriefing, however, the radar operator could not say what triggered his intense emotional response to the blip on the screen. The screen tapes were reviewed for hours until finally the clue was determined. When the radar blip first came into view on the screen, it appeared close to but not exactly at the edge of the screen. That is, it wasn't caught by the first few sweeps of the radar sensor. That type of appearance indicated that the target had risen into radar view from a lower altitude the way a ground-to-air missile in the area would do. This radar operator's years of experience in front of a radar screen had ingrained a deep neural expectation of normalcy, and his subconscious patterns had become violated.[7]

The story pinpoints how our predictive neural networks give us uneasy feelings, or even alarm, when events deviate from their norm. Those feelings, often outside our conscious awareness, alert us to unusual patterns and situations. We stop and try to reflect on what is disturbing us, so that we can take action. Figuring out what's causing the feeling may take some time, as with the experience of the radar operator. Or it can happen in the blink of an eye, as when a sinister figure steps out in front of us from around a corner.

The presence of such a predictive system suggests why the fear of loss kicks in when it does during the REG game: it occurs when certain neurological circuits decide that a pattern in the environment is worthy of attention. When one achieves a REG result that's too good relative to the individual's inner sense of normalcy, an alert can fire. It is certainly an odd concept that these circuits raise alarms when the score is perceived to be *too good*. The player may actually be very pleased with the current scoring, but the alarm is designed to always make one feel uneasy. That uneasiness is first and foremost the concern that one is heading from familiar ground into the unknown. That fear of loss—this time a loss of normalcy—no doubt kicks in a response from the amygdala. Once engaged, the response feeds on itself, particularly as it affects the REG results.

The Mental Regulator

In real life, the regulating process described previously involves a three-step sequence. First is an expectation of how things should be, which becomes a norm. Second is a violation of that expectation or norm, which comes with an alert that something is amiss. Finally, there's the attempt to correct the deviation through some action and thereby return to the norm. A thermostat is an example of such a regulator. It has a set point, such as 70 degrees Fahrenheit. It gathers information from around it about the current temperature of the room and fires an internal alert when conditions stray too far from the set point. The alert triggers a mechanism that causes hot or cold air to flow until conditions are restored to the set point. This is also called a *negative feedback cycle* because it counters events that are moving positively away from a norm. The goal of negative feedback is to make sure a system stays as close as possible to its set points or equilibrium conditions.

It appears to me that our minds have such circuits designed to regulate such inner set points. For example, the radar operator had inner set points with regard to the ways friendly radar blips act. The blip he saw was not friendly, and he took steps to restore normalcy. Such experiences occur all the time in our daily lives, as mentioned earlier. For example, think of all the set points you have in place when it comes to, say, the common act of driving your car: set points for how the engine will sound, for the precise way the gas pedal will give power, for the constant adjustments you make to the steering wheel, and for the ways other drivers will act. Most of these expectations sit below the surface of awareness.[8]

Oddly, with the REG game, no specific pattern or sequence of greens and reds is expected at any given time. There are no rules for the sequence, no norms or set points for the neural circuits to learn and act upon. The inability to find lasting patterns in the output must be confusing to our matching circuits, because such pure randomness is rarely encountered. But there's one basic and overriding pattern in the output of the REG. Over the long term, the results should trend toward 50/50 greens and reds. So if the matching circuits have any general rule in the experience, it is that the basic set point of the REG output is 50/50. Therefore, when results stray too far from that set point—even in the short term—it would seem to set off an inner alert cycle.

This concept of an internal regulator became very useful to me. For shorthand, I've given it the simple name *mental regulator*.[9] The action of the mental regulator seems to be buried in our neural circuitry and explains why rubber bands suddenly appear. Like the radar operator's blip rising into view on the radar screen, my score rises to a level that no longer fits with a sense of normalcy. From simply being engrossed in the game, I suddenly bounce out of the experience with an uneasy feeling. Again, it is quixotic that an uneasy feeling occurs when the results are unusually better than expected. It seems that the mental regulator's circuits make no value judgments about any one set point. Like a thermostat, the mental regulator is not concerned about right and wrong or good and bad except insofar as being closer to the set point is good and being farther from the set point is bad. Furthermore, the mental-regulator set points are established at such a deep level that thinking about them or consciously urging them to be different does not change them.

Here's a simple example of the way a mental regulator operates in day-to-day life and how it lacks value judgment regarding a set point. Imagine that a neighborhood cat arrives at the back door every afternoon, scratching the door for food—at precisely the same time every afternoon. The time of day forms a set point. If one day the cat does not appear at this time, a deep-seated expectation has been violated. You don't have to be looking at a clock. At some point, your mental regulator lets you know something is amiss. The mental regulator doesn't care what time the cat usually arrives—just that the normal pattern has been violated.[10] And as noted earlier, an alert can fire even when the deviation from the norm is *beneficial*. To emphasize that point, imagine that a man—rather than a cat—comes to your house every day at dinnertime and demands $50 from you. Begrudgingly, you always give it to him. Now, one day, you're involved in some activity and forget about the time. Suddenly, your mental regulator alerts you to the fact that something is wrong: the man hasn't shown up. The key is the language "something is wrong." The mental regulator is simply tasked with alerting you to the difference between expectation and reality.

Indeed, that alert mechanism would seem problematic in cases where one is excelling and moving away from a norm. There are some life situations in which this process can ruin otherwise good moments, such as when one has a string of good fortune or, say, when an athlete is "on a tear." Too great a success may even force a reevaluation of one's very identity: "I can't be doing this well; it isn't me," or "Who do I think I am? And who would I be?" and so on. In fact, psychologists note that highly positive moments can produce anxiety precisely because they can seem so unfamiliar. That anxiety involves the fear that something unusually good sets you up for a big fall, and so instead of feeling the moment you brace yourself for a loss.[11]

In this regard, our image of ourselves may be highly constrained by a personal "upper bound." This is a theme that will recur throughout my project and is addressed later at length. Before this project I never would have believed that we shy away from success. But this phenomenon is not about the accomplishment daily tasks as much as about the deep sense of social position in relation to others. The subconscious mind maintains a self-image within a narrow band and appears to want to stay there. It is not rational by any means, but finding it active in oneself may be a key to new levels of personal freedom and well-being.

The mental regulator would appear to have evolved within us in an earlier, simpler time, when success issues were almost completely physical in nature. In that era, to excel meant to stand out; and standing out often made one a target. It was perhaps safer in general to live within the normal expectations of both the physical and social environments. As noted, gain seeking was not nearly as important as loss aversion, and so the mental regulator learned to chart a conservative path. It's only recently that our lives have reached a level of social complexity such that high levels of uncertainty in one's future can lead to gain without the downside risk of debilitating physical loss. The mental regulator does not seem wired for this changing environment. The REG experience is a case for this, because there's nothing to get excited about in some basic survival sense. An estimated 18% of Americans, or more than 40 million people, are considered to have mental disorders related to anxiety of one sort or another.[12] And as life gets ever more complex, it would seem beneficial for us to at least partially rewire this mental regulator so we can relieve the anxiety alerts it creates.[13]

❊ ❊ ❊

On the whole, I find it extraordinary to think that there is a complex set of predictive calculations running below the surface of consciousness. The mental regulator constantly evaluates normalcy and significance and serves up alerts about aspects of the environment that stray from their set points. The mind is split, with the conscious mind often pulling away from a norm, while the subconscious mind pulls toward it. As I worked the REG process, I could take on the experimenter role and watch that drama play out in my own mind. The fact is that for whatever reason, the subconscious mental regulator, once invoked, always seems to win the REG battle—at least in me. It doesn't seem to matter that such experiences wreak havoc on my peace of mind. I guess inner peace is not something evolution worried about during our development. Physical safety seems to be its evolutionary origin and raison d'être to this day. In any event, that knowledge forms a starting point for understanding the REG process—and for me, the deeper workings of my own psyche.

CHAPTER 7:
WHAT SHOULD HAPPEN

Following is a log entry from my journal. Figure 7.1 displays the random-walk chart from the session.

My score jumped up initially and managed to get above the parabola. I wanted to keep climbing but began to stall. I had the image of pushing up against a ceiling and continued to try to press higher. All the while, I was feeling a sense of heavy effort and trying to keep my mind on the positive—as if I were trying to rally troops to keep pushing. But I seemed to be moving through molasses. And even though I wasn't falling back, no matter what I tried I couldn't break out and go higher. Finally, it was just too much effort, and I let go. It was a big relief to stop trying, and I wanted to see what would happen next. I fully expected it would go straight back to zero because only my extreme effort had been holding it up. From that instant, it did immediately start dropping, with a powerful local Z score of minus 4.4, which actually felt great. When I got back to zero, I leveled out and was done. I knew there was no point in continuing, so I stopped.[1]

My certainty about the score's dropping back to zero was deep and natural. No other course of events would have seemed logical. In my mind, it was *what should happen*. The word *should* in that phrase connotes a strong expectation. One might say, for example, "The package *should* come tomorrow," meaning that this is normal and expected based on experience. The

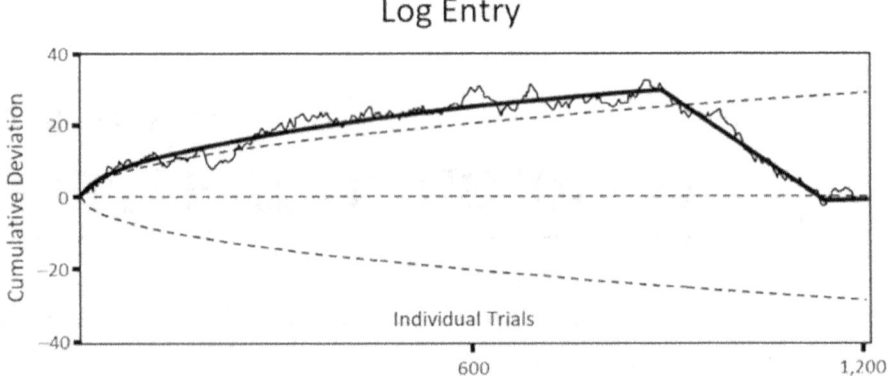

FIGURE 7.1. Chart of a personal log entry—with approximate trend line—showing an emotional shift from holding up the results to letting go, at which point the results dropped sharply.

statement itself could be expanded to read, "I got a notice on my door, so the package should come tomorrow." Many such expectations are deeply embedded in our daily lives, and we pay no conscious attention to most of them. When you turn the knob on a door, you expect the door to swing open rather than fall on top of you. We all internalize many deep models of how the world works.

It is only through training with the REG that I have learned to catch myself having momentary expectations with regard to the next results. Such awareness can be tricky, because it can bounce one out of the current frame of mind and thus shift the experience itself. Nevertheless, I've come to see how those deep expectations literally play out on the screen. At first, it was shocking, and now it's so commonplace for me that I don't react to it: what should happen *is what I think should happen*.

It also makes me wonder how often in life we make unlikely events occur because at the time we didn't realize they were unlikely. In seeing them as normal, they just happen and pass unnoticed. In fact, if we had noticed them, it was probably because we realized logically that they *were* unlikely. A colleague of mine tells a story about his childhood, when he often used a vending machine that dispensed one of four possible card packs. The machine had no buttons for selecting which card pack would come out; the card packs were dispensed randomly. But my colleague was too young to reason that out, and when he dropped a coin into the machine, he simply expected to receive the pack he wanted. And he always did. And because he didn't understand the way it worked, he had no reason to believe a different pack would come out. His internal model expected the right pack. It was only years later that he realized that by logic, that should not have happened.[2]

If certainty can have that effect on the environment, then of course we would all love to create expectations about future events we want to happen. The popularized concept of the law of attraction says you attract to yourself what you expect to have. The problem, however, is that given how our matching circuits lock onto previous experience, we cannot easily convince the subconscious of something new. In fact, if you try to convince yourself that something unusual is normal, the very effort tells your subconscious it is *not* normal and therefore is unlikely to happen. All of the huffing and puffing put up by the conscious mind just confirms to the subconscious that what you're proposing is out of bounds.

Nevertheless, one can adopt a generally positive attitude about life that can feed on itself and over time become more of a habit. A generally positive attitude tends to envision positive outcomes in situations. Studies have shown that generally positive people are more successful in life.[3] And though that may be due primarily to putting extra effort into tasks—and perhaps life in general—the selection effect would also seem to be at work. When the selection effect does bend reality in your favor, the people around you of a less cheery demeanor may shake their heads and say, "Why are you always so lucky?" But in fact, you're making your own luck.

How the Mind Overlays Itself on Reality

If the mind's beliefs about what should happen are driven in part by the selection effect, then there must be a process or mechanism that drives it. One place to turn involves new thinking on the nature of perception. The old image of perception is that we receive information through the senses and store it in our brains much the same as a recording device does. But now we see that the mind operates in a more active, multistep feedback process.

First, and as noted earlier, current events invoke prior experience through models. The simplest such model is the unconscious matching circuitry we've already discussed. But complex models may also involve a great deal of internal processing. The way one relates to one's father, for example, involves far more than a simple matching circuit. It encompasses years of rich and nuanced reflection. Such models appear to be formed in the higher regions of the brain.[4] The purpose of a model is very straightforward: it is to help you predict what will happen next. Science is now finding that the way we face new situations is to *actively overlay* our prior models onto current reality.[5] Projecting such a model most thoroughly prepares one to respond to such new events. And if new events do deviate from expectation, then one adjusts one's behavior and updates the model so as to become even better prepared for the next time.[6] Think of a baseball batter who's facing a pitcher he has seen before. The batter has a model of how this pitcher will pitch, and he overlays the model onto the pitcher. Then, with each new pitch, he modifies the model. But the action is not wholly conscious; rather, the nervous system becomes the update process, and the whole body absorbs the new information.

Now we can return to the REG selection effect. As noted earlier, by design and definition REG output displays no pattern in each next output. Nevertheless, the mind forms opinions about next results anyway. In a moment, it may overlay a trend regarding what should happen next. That overlay would seem to be more than just "in the head" but also involves an attempt to impose itself onto reality and make reality conform to the image of the model.

Think about a parent dealing with unruly kids. The kids are operating out of spec relative to being models of behavior. So, as the parent admonishes the aberrant behavior, there is an additional sense of urgency. The parent is literally trying to impose the model on the kids. I think that almost any parent can remember doing this. It's more than communicating about bad behavior but, rather, is thrusting out a model onto the kids as if to directly control their behavior.

With the REG, the controlling aspect of this overlay can be seen. It bends reality to conform such that events come to mirror the overlaid model. What the mind decides *should* happen *does* happen, which in turn reinforces the very process of asserting such *shoulds*. (I will continue to italicize the word *should* when it is used as a noun in this way.) The deeper the conviction, the more potent the effect. And because these should-based models come from the subconscious, they can become so sure of themselves that they may leave little room for alternatives.

Broadly speaking, the propensity to overlay often complex models on everything around us (unruly children notwithstanding) makes us a highly successful species. In effect, we are *meaning machines* because we project all manner of supposition onto situations in which supposition may or may not exist. At least sometimes, the expectations may paint themselves onto the canvas of reality. Meaning structures overlaid on reality become self-fulfilling. That's one of the first powerful lessons of the REG. Further, and as noted earlier, it suggests that the selection effect may operate in our lives in ways we never suspect or pick up on. We affect reality by bending events toward an unlikely outcome, but no mental-regulator alert gets fired, because at the time, the outcome seems natural. In contrast, because the REG has such a defined theoretical structure (binomial distribution), it becomes clear when it deviates from expectation. One can stand back and catch the process in action, perhaps saying to oneself, "Even though this high score seemed perfectly natural at the time, in retrospect it should not have happened."

The Other *Should*

Even though deeply held expectations result in what we can term *shoulds of prediction*, or *predictive shoulds*, there's another, equally important, type of *should*. This one is based on values. In this case, the *should* comes from what is considered right to happen. For example, one might assert, "You should brush your teeth twice a day." That statement has nothing to do with a prediction or expectation. Value-based *shoulds*, like their prediction counterparts, span the gamut from relatively mundane subjects like brushing teeth to highly significant ones like, "You should love your neighbor as you love yourself," or, "You should honor your parents," or "You should join the jihad and become a martyr." Such values may be learned, or they may be self-generated. A self-generated *should* might be, "Whether or not they actually win, my candidates should win because they have the best positions."

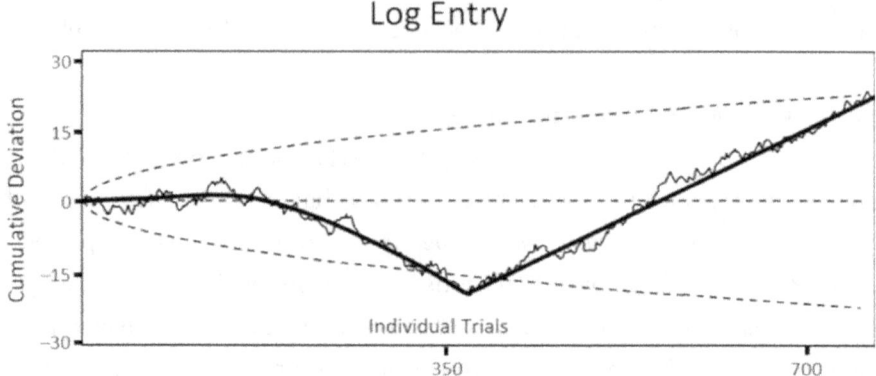

FIGURE 7.2. Chart of a personal log entry—with approximate trend line—involving an initial period of increasing frustration over the results, followed by a sudden emotional shift to righteous indignation and leading to an abrupt turnaround.

A careful look at those value-based *shoulds* shows that they also appear to be based on models—but of slightly different sorts. They represent moral or ethical frameworks for looking at the world—whether big or small. Following is an example of a self-generated value-based *should* or *should of rightness*, as chronicled in my REG log. Figure 7.2 shows the random-walk chart of the experience.

> I started the session feeling positive, and the chart responded by trending ever so slightly upward. I got a bit spooked and immediately started losing my grip. I kept trying to reassume earlier thoughts but couldn't, and so the trend line just kept heading downward; I simply couldn't stop it. Once I dropped into negative significance—in the lower parabola—I stopped and stepped away and became really ticked off. I sat there glaring at the screen, feeling strangely indignant, and said to myself: "This is not what I want for myself." I then suddenly felt a surge of emotion—as if someone had done me wrong—rather than the lower bound I should be at in the upper bound because I can do it and because I have earned it. I felt at that moment that I truly deserved to be at the point of positive significance: in the upper parabola. When I restarted a couple of minutes later, I used that

deep sense of entitlement to head straight for the upper bound.
I stopped when I got over the line.

That sequence was not driven by a matching circuit predicting a change in direction after a long drop. The issue was that my efforts at trying to succeed were being ignored in some larger-universe sense. I should be going up, not down, because it was my right to succeed; I had worked hard and earned it. I became very angry during the session. Nature needed to step up and do the right thing, rebalancing the ledger of fairness. Of course, that sense of justice is itself a model. But it comes from a different place—one that expects that nature has some higher structure built into it.

The relative potencies of the first type of *should*—the one of expectation or prediction—and the second type—the value-based *should of rightness* themselves make for an interesting subject that certainly merits future research. For example, the predictive *should* of figure 7.1 produced a Z-score value of minus 4.4 during the period of decline. The value-based *should* in figure 7.2 created an even more significant Z score of just over 5.0—this time in the plus direction. Both are very strong local effects, with the value-based *should* being the stronger of the two. And though this comparison is anecdotal, I do experience differences in the strength of the two effects. For me, prediction-based *shoulds* tend to dissipate quickly once events trend in accordance with the *should* that drives them. The movement toward resolution almost immediately lightens them up, because it seems that this is mostly what they want to see anyway. But the emotionally charged, value-laden *shoulds* can stand their ground much longer. The sense of rightness can cause anger and even the desire for revenge. There is no forgiveness in them until they are satisfied, and that may go beyond anything rational. I suspect we will find that this experience activates—or is activated by—some primal neural circuitry.

Shoulds and the Mental Regulator

The concept of *shoulds* seems tightly linked to the action of the mental regulator. Both types of *should* involve norms that are largely outside the control of the conscious mind. Figure 7.3 depicts a way to think about the mental

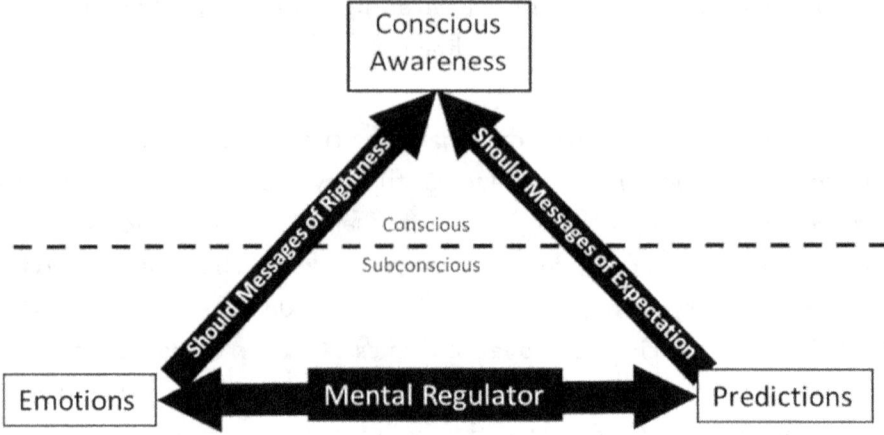

FIGURE 7.3. Two subsystems—emotions and predictions—sitting below the surface of consciousness that are connected to form the mental regulator. The subsystems each send their respective *should* messages upward to conscious awareness.

regulator and its relation to conscious and subconscious influences. It depicts how *should* messages rise to the level of consciousness from the two subsystems of emotions and predictions. Predictions lead to *should* messages that arise from *expectation-based shoulds,* and emotions lead to *should* messages arising from *value-based shoulds.* The mental regulator itself is formed by the interaction of the two subsystems that sit below consciousness. Note that in this schema, the mental regulator has no direct connection to the conscious mind; it does its work with relative freedom from interference.

In this diagram, I show only messages passing upward. Later, we'll discuss how the conscious mind can send messages back down the line as well. But I do want to say here that higher-level cognitive functions play roles in the formation of the norms that become the basis of models that sit below the surface of awareness. It is conscious thought, for example, that establishes the significance of Z scores. This is an abstract concept—not initially a matching circuit. So, when one sees a high Z score, such as 3 or 4 or 5, one knows consciously that it is significant. It is that conscious calculation that can trigger a mental-regulator alert. The point is that you have no choice regarding this message of significance that gets sent to the subconscious. The *score* is significant, and until you achieve it on a regular basis, you can't make it *not* significant. Further, a norm is self-reinforcing and mitigates against that set point's ever changing.

There is one more experience to look at—one I consider humorous. Figure 7.4 shows an example of a REG session with a chart I call *brain-dead*. It has the look of a trace on a hospital monitor that is flatlining. This type of output typically results when I've been playing the game too long at one sitting and have lost all sense of energy. I continue to play out of sheer stubbornness. It also reminds me of the Black Knight scene in the movie *Monty Python and the Holy Grail*. The Black Knight keeps wanting to fight his opponent even as his limbs are being cut off one by one. In my case, I've even dozed off pressing the space bar while in effect mumbling: "C'mon, gimme that next bit. I'll show you." My subconscious knows I cannot win, and so every momentary surge or change for the better dies an immediate death and falls back to the ground state. There is a foregone conclusion that I don't have what it takes to sustain anything of interest.

One might initially surmise that such a dull state of mind is disconnected from the REG output. Because I'm not going anywhere, so to speak, maybe I'm having little or no effect. Indeed, the very idea of no energy sounds like a recipe for no impact. But that clearly is not the case. The chart displays a very distinct pattern showing I'm still tightly connected. It's not a random-looking chart, but, rather, it stays too close to the baseline. PEAR discovered that phenomenon via subjects in certain frames of mind and called it *baseline bind*. That is, there appears to be a binding of the output to the zero line that

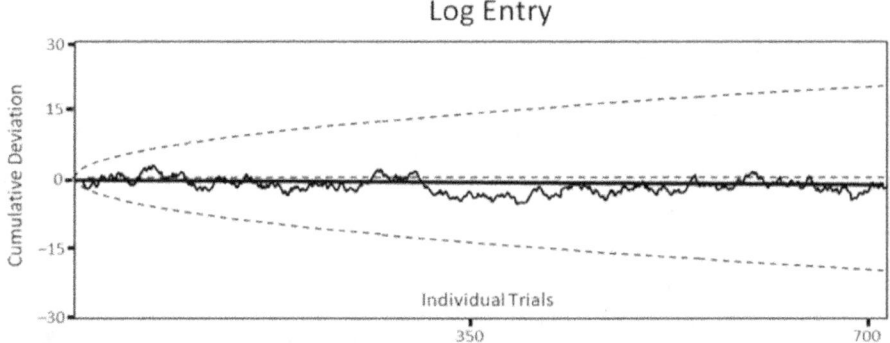

FIGURE 7.4. Chart of a personal log entry showing a brain-dead session—with approximate trend line—when I was too tired to continue but too stubborn to stop.

is far stronger than randomness would dictate.[7] Baseline bind is another way the selection effect shows itself.

※ ※ ※

As I continued to process *what should happen*—based on expectations, values, and awareness of my own state of mind—my arsenal of concepts about the selection effect was growing. I was getting a handle on why they so often regulated back *toward* the zero line—and occasionally away from the zero line. The emotion and prediction systems became very real to me: underpinnings of a new awareness. It was exciting to have a window into my own mental functioning and why and how I relate to the world the ways I do. But clearly a lot more remained to be discovered. The varied pieces of this puzzle of the mind were starting to knit themselves into a more comprehensive picture.

CHAPTER 8:
MOMENTS, MODELS, AND WEBS

When I was 20 years old, a friend once held a tulip to my face and asked me what I saw. "A tulip, of course," I replied. "Look again," she said. I looked more intently, and suddenly, I was right there with that *particular* tulip, its colors, and its contours. This tulip was more than the notion of *any* tulip. It was there with me in that moment, and I could almost imagine it staring back at me.

The English language does not make a clear distinction between those two types of experiences. The usual experience of a tulip is to recall previous times of having seen one. We all know what a tulip is and how it acts, so any present tulip should look and act like any other one we've seen. We just notice that it is in fact a tulip, recognized as such through its color and shape. But this *heightened experience* of the tulip is very different, conferring a sense of being in a unique moment and locked in the here and now.

When my friend put me into that very-present-time state of mind, it showed me how little I'm tuned in to my surroundings most of the time. It's easy to take things for granted as we walk through the routines of daily life. The memory of that tulip event always stuck with me, even as the heightened feeling accompanying it faded. But now, with the REG, I was having glimpses of that feeling again. I would have occasional lucid and heightened such moments, and with them, the REG output abruptly changed.

The experience of *those moments,* as I came to call them, is one of newness and excitement. Moments suggest an unbounded future, when they occur, because they're not about the past. They're new and real-time relationships that can lead to any number of outcomes. And there's no prior agenda—only the feeling of being in truly uncharted territory. Further, one puts aside the fears that can come with newness in favor of the compelling lucidity offered. Chapter 6 opened with an example of a moment wherein I suddenly thought of my grandmother with a funny green hat. The experience gave me a heightened sense of meaning and engagement. In that case, the moment had not been brought on by a dramatic event in my physical environment but by my own shift in thinking. It's an example of how we create our reality.

This concept of moments is set against the lessons of the previous chapter about models and the feeling of *what should happen*. The *model* state of mind appears common and humdrum when compared with *moments* as being rarer and more exciting. From this point forward, and to this day, I think about REG experience in terms of *models* and *moments*. Indeed, once alerted to that differentiation—fresh moments on one hand and recalled models on the other—I now see much of daily life in those terms as well. The promise of moments is that they can result in REG scores or life events that move away from prior norms. Moments want to go wherever they go—and that's usually away from the current norm—whereas models do the opposite. This chapter looks at those two states of mind and leads to a more comprehensive framework of the mind. Ultimately, that framework can make one more self-aware and more effective in many aspects of life.

Moments

Almost everything we encounter as young children is such a moment: most things are new and fresh and exciting and unknown. The intensity of such experience is evident as a parent points out new objects to a toddler, naming each one as the child takes it all in, staring wide-eyed, watching, and listening. Perhaps because of that more heightened state, subjective time passes more slowly for children than it does for adults. Over time, though, as daily life becomes more routine and there are fewer noticeable or memorable points on a constant basis, fewer points of reference are provided for memory. The few high points seem to be closer together—something American psychologist William James first articulated more than a century ago and which has been studied since then.[1]

Of course, at any age we can and do have moments. A moment might be thrust on us, such as in the instant of a near automobile collision on the highway or suddenly encountering a long-lost friend, or placing first in a competition. Sometimes a moment might involve a creative insight or a shift in awareness: "Aha! I've got it!"

Moments are cut loose from models and their set points—really by definition. And interestingly, because they operate without prior set points, moments seem to shut down the mental regulator. The mental regulator must have set points; otherwise, it doesn't know what to regulate to. So, during moments, the mental regulator gets literally sidelined, waiting for more-solid reference points to be established. I believe that's why moments feel so different.

Figure 8.1 gives an example of a REG chart in which I had the experience of what I consider a moment. It was abrupt and emotional and seemed to have creative insight to it. The accompanying journal entry that follows records my impressions during the experience.

> I was going nowhere and facing down a sense of being stuck. But each time I thought I might make headway, it still went nowhere. I was hugging the zero line and just able to keep from giving up and stopping as I edged downward. But then, suddenly, I shifted to the top of my head, and it felt as though a window had opened upward—like a channel or a tunnel through a

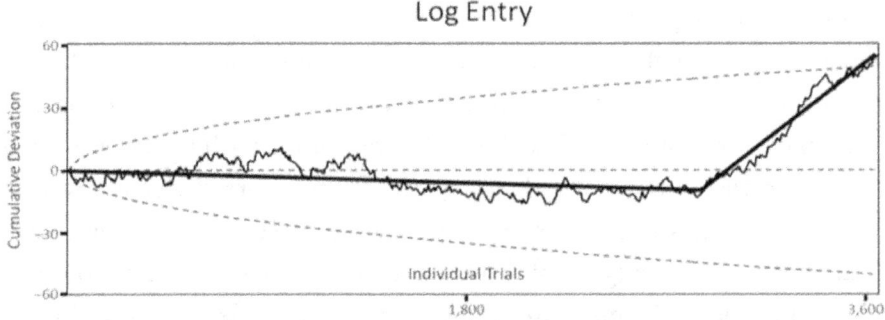

FIGURE 8.1. Chart of a personal log entry—with approximate trend line—showing a frustrating initial period followed by an abrupt mental shift out the top of my head, wherein I felt suddenly free, with good results coming easily.

> barrier. I opened to it and felt a sense of a freedom and wonder as my inner conflicts dropped away. From that instant, I soared upward with an exhilarating sense of joy. The output tracked the experience, and when I got to positive significance, I stopped to marvel at the whole thing. I later analyzed that moment to find that the Z score of the period was over 5.

When such a moment is over, it will never return in exactly the same way. There is no going back to a pre-moment state and experiencing the moment again—whether with the REG or in life. For example, a group of friends might have a terrific time spending a weekend together and resolve to "do it again." However, when they do return and try to recapture the moment, they're disappointed because the experience falls flat. A new and meaningful experience can be had, but it must be on its own terms rather than a replay of the past. If you try to make a model out of a moment by having it again, it becomes just that.

Moments may help explain the oft-cited decline effect in REG studies—for example, as described in the Colorado experiment in the introduction. Such periods begin with an unbounded sense of reaching out to unusual possibilities when the sky's the limit. But the mental regulator recovers from watching-and-waiting mode relatively quickly as it begins to form a new experience into a new model with its own set points. Further, as one reflects on the experience, one may step out of the experience itself—and the moment is past.

In the field of psychology, a close term for that sequence of events is *habituation*. Habituation tracks how we learn and how we integrate new experiences, and it's been studied extensively—especially with young children.[2] In one area of research, children are presented with images projected on a screen to see how long they pay attention before their eyes wander away. Researchers study that wandering of attention in relation to measures of intelligence. One might think that the smarter children pay attention longer, but exactly the opposite is the case: smarter kids tend to assimilate images more quickly and become bored, looking around for something new. The content and experience of moments then get processed into models.[3]

I was once in an intense dinner discussion with a chef and a psychologist about this idea of moments and models. I was making the case for moments as a specific, distinct state of mind. The psychologist was arguing against such a uniqueness. The chef was tentatively on my side, nodding some agreement but not quite grasping it. Then I said that a cookbook tells how long a steak should be grilled based on a model—a general set of rules. But the actual experience of grilling a steak provides the opportunity and in fact requires one to form a relationship *with the very piece of meat there on the grill*. The steak will be great if the cook relates to that individual steak, listening to its sizzle, so to speak, and acting accordingly. With that, the chef lit up saying, "That's it! That's it!"

More on Models

The opposite of a moment is a model, as described previously and in the prior chapter. So, we'll simply emphasize how widespread models are in the mind—from simple to complex. A chair, say, is a simple model. So is a car—or any object that is familiar. They're models largely shared with others in the backdrop of society. But we can move on to more-complex models, such as how a particular friend behaves or what it means to be an American. There can be many different such models, and we may each develop our own. Even models of the universe, origins, purpose, and destiny can be different based on culture or religion. People even sometimes fight to the death to affirm the rightness of their models.

When events do not meet a prior model's expectations and the breach is minor, the model simply gets updated. However, if the breach is significant, then the mental regulator may fire an alert. The purpose is to alert you to possible danger from the unexpected. And more than that, as discussed earlier, the mind may try to literally force the model onto reality, trying to make reality conform to it. This is an attempt to press the world back to normal—or at least challenge the deviation to show itself strong enough to override your attempt. If the force driving the change is stronger than your subconscious' ability to press it back into line, it becomes even more clear that your model needs updating.

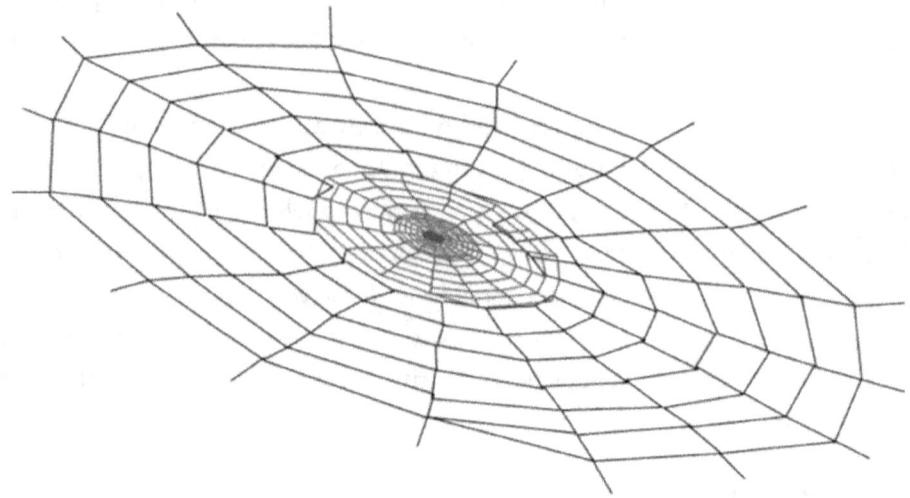

FIGURE 8.2. A simple spider web model of the mind's associative links.

Putting It All Together

The concepts of models, moments, and the mental regulator can be fitted into a relatively simple image such as a web of thought or, more specifically, a web of associations like the hyperlinks in the Internet. So, in consideration of the World Wide Web, we can call your mind a *personal-wide web*. In your web, concepts link to each other such as trees to branches, to leaves, to insects, to flies, and so on. Figure 8.2 depicts the basic idea of a web of mind stylized as a spider web.

Web concepts are already part of our lexicon. One might say, "She was caught in my web," or "I have a vast web of contacts." Webs involve *threads* that connect thoughts and represent associations. We use such language as in, "I will include you in that e-mail thread," and "I'm losing the thread of this argument." As one gets older, one's personal-wide web expands to become denser with threads of association. So, just like a cloth formed from tightly knit threads, the web becomes the fabric of one's mind. Figure 8.2 depicts the center area, which has become a tighter fabric of associations over time. Furthermore, the web shown in the figure might be just a subweb or a layer within a larger web. In other words, like the Internet, one might deal with just one small section of the whole at any given time.[4]

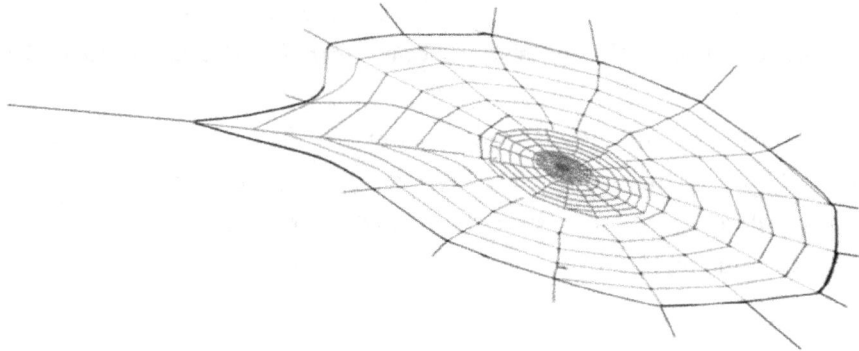

FIGURE 8.3. The web model showing how threads of association can be stretched by outside connections, as embodied in the phrase "the idea stretched my mind."

This image captures the notion of *models* and *moments*. A web holds itself in place or holds its shape by virtue of the threads making it up. The fabric defines a set of norms around which the web is designed. And like any other fabric that has been knitted together, it is durable. It resists outside influence, with belief systems held in place. It can be poked and prodded, and like most fabrics, it will spring back to its prior form. However, people with more-rigid webs may not bend or roll with the punches very well. Such people may also be prone to snapping if too much pressure is put on their webs.

Figure 8.3 depicts a web of mind or a subportion of it being stretched—perhaps by a new idea or a relationship in crisis. That puts tension on other threads, which would seem to evoke emotion. After the new idea gets assimilated or the situation abates, the tension subsides, and things return to normal. However, some of the threads might be stretched permanently so that they do not return to the old norms.[5] New norms get established in this way.

The idea of moments connotes the stretching process itself. A moment can be brought on by a pull from the outside, as shown in the figure. Or it may come from one's own thrusting of a new thread outward, like Spider-Man's sending a thread to a distant wall and pulling himself forward. In either case, the web can be altered in the process such that it settles out with connections and new norms.

Finally, it becomes apparent that the mental regulator is a natural part of this web model. When the web is poked, pulled, prodded, or otherwise put under tension by something new and nonconforming, the experience initiates mental-regulator activity. The mental regulator feels tension that causes alerts as calls to action. The conscious mind feels the breach of normalcy through the uneasiness of the web structure. Over time, a more elaborate mental-regulator-and-alert system seems to have formed that involves both predictions and emotions.[6]

❖ ❖ ❖

The concepts of the mental regulator, webs, moments and models, and *shoulds* turned into a growing body of theory and explanation with respect to the REG process. Furthermore, the concepts seemed in line with current scientific thinking about the mind. With those tools, I began correlating defined states of mind with how the REG output responded. Time after time, the concepts showed themselves to be relevant in linking results with experience, and I was sure I was onto something.

On the other hand, my growing knowledge was *not* leading to any sense of mastering the process. I was less frustrated now than when I was clueless—but not much less. I was perplexed by the fact that this knowledge should result in an advantage with the REG, but it didn't. Quite the contrary. There were times when the very act of framing my thinking seemed to make a model out of what was going on, and that caused me to drop out of whatever moment was being successful. Furthermore, the instant I thought I knew what I was doing, my deeper mind would find a way around that thought and stick it to me from behind.

The experience reminded me of the movie *The Matrix*, when computer hacker Neo finds fleeting references to the Matrix on the Internet. Every time he tries to follow the trail of such references, they disappear. Even when he returns to pages just viewed, the references have vanished. Finally, Neo meets Morpheus, who presents him with a choice: he can take the red pill and learn to know the Matrix for what it is (a computer simulation that everyone is trapped inside) and in doing so join the resistance movement against it. Or he can take the blue pill and go back to sleep and remain part of the Matrix. He chose the red pill.

I wanted the red pill. I just couldn't find it. There was neither a Morpheus to give me the pill nor any instructions to follow; I was on my own. So, even though I saw fleeting references to how the direct interaction of mind and matter might work to create the selection effect, I couldn't do anything about it. I was getting more positive results with the REG game, but I was also getting more negative results. I was like an infant flailing arms and legs, trying to learn how such limbs feel. Furthermore, the negative periods seemed to feed on themselves emotionally, always breaking in and sabotaging my good results. I knew when that would happen, and it did. I began to think that maybe I'm the most fearful person on the planet, constantly experiencing rubber bands and undermining myself when maybe others would not. It seemed that being able to know and describe what was going on would give me a leg up on success. That had always been my experience with any psychotherapeutic or self-reflective program, wherein bringing awareness to a problem causes it to loosen up. Indeed, that was happening to some extent, but the mental regulator always seemed to have the last word—and the last laugh. I didn't have the slightest idea how to get around it.

I could only conclude that my intention to succeed was not strong enough and that I would have to redouble my efforts. As Admiral Farragut said, "Damn the torpedoes, full speed ahead." But maybe it was more like Pickett's Charge: running straight ahead into a merciless barrage of gunfire of my own making. Either way, I didn't know. I just needed that red pill.

CHAPTER 9:
INTO THE SUBCONSCIOUS

In the spring of 2009, representatives of Psyleron were invited to meet with a group of 60 high school freshmen in central New Jersey and talk to them about mind–matter interaction. We decided it would be best to give the students some firsthand experiences to see how their youthful dynamics would play out in the results. We wondered whether they'd allow themselves to become engaged or be too "cool" to apply themselves.

As a warm-up exercise—and to help the kids understand how the process works—we ran the original PEAR REG game, which has three conditions: go high, go low, and keep to the baseline. The ongoing results were projected onto a huge screen in front of the room during each try.

In both the high and low conditions, the kids succeeded, achieving significant results, which was quite impressive. For the baseline condition (keeping to the midline), the group produced a flat line that was so closely tracking the center of the chart that one of my colleagues is heard on the videotape of the event saying, "That is the best baseline I have ever seen." The verbal reinforcement of their good results clearly got the kids' attention. They were both engaged and proud of their results.

We had another game for them, this time using the Psyleron Mind Lamp, which had recently been developed (and is described in chapter 4). Because it was a new product, we were intrigued to see how they might take to it. Would its rich visuals create even more meaningfulness than the rather clinical-looking REG chart?

The lamp has two modes, and in the one we planned to use, it remains white most of the time; but every few minutes on average, it will briefly change to one of eight colors. The colors have equal probabilities of

99

occurring, with the timing and the color chosen controlled by the random stream of data from the REG built into the lamp's base.

The students were divided into groups of six kids each, and each group was given a Mind Lamp. The group task was to select a color in advance and then try to have the lamp change to that color as its very next color. If the group succeeded, it scored a hit. If not, it scored a miss. A new color would then be selected, and the process repeated. The kids had exactly 30 minutes to do their best to see what percentage of time the lamp turned to the color they chose.

To help the participants, the lamp is designed to give a peek to a color without necessarily fully turning that color. Peeking creates a preview of the color direction the lamp is taking. So, if the preview color is the *right* color, the idea is that the group mentally pull on the color and take it over the threshold into the full color. If the lamp peeks any other color, then the idea is to throw it back, so to speak, and redouble efforts toward the right one.

When the starting bell sounded, all hell broke loose. It was as if ten different stories had been let loose in the room. Some kids began standing up and shouting orders to their lamp, yelling, "Blue, blue, blue!" Some started waving at it. Others began holding hands around their lamp, slowly chanting "Green, green, green." Still others were singing to get their lamp to turn yellow. The scene was that of a high-energy circus, and the teachers were laughing and shaking their heads at seeing many otherwise cool freshmen losing their cool over these lamps—and maybe even succeeding.

Indeed, when the half hour was up and scores tallied, the results were impressive for the groups. The probability of occurring by chance was about one in 750. (However, the groups were self-scoring, so the actual score cannot be confirmed.) The students were proud of their results and high-fived one another.

What was not mentioned was that during the excitement and chaos of the game, another story unfolded. It is the story of group seven. Group seven was the serious group—the totally intent group. Group seven kids didn't jump up and down or chant or wave or sing. They only focused all of their attention and concentration directly on their lamp.

This group chose red as the first color, and red was indeed the first color that their lamp peeked to, which was no doubt both exciting and perhaps a little unnerving. And maybe because of the startling response of the lamp, the group couldn't put the color over the threshold to the full color. That is, after peeking, the lamp went back to white. No score. The kids bemoaned the failure and resolved to redouble their mental efforts. The lamp peeked red a second time but once again returned to white. There was more upset. Then it happened again. And again. And again. It happened—by the kids' account—more times than they could keep track of. Not once did the lamp actually become fully red but returned to white each time. Further, they reported that the lamp *never fully turned any color at all* during the entire half hour.[1]

There was nothing wrong with group seven's lamp, as confirmed afterward, though certainly that's what the group members wanted to claim. What was striking in this incident was the impact of group seven's intent. By all standards of how we normally think of the power of intention, group seven should have yielded the most positive results. But if anything, they did worse. The lamp acted more like a stuck record than like something obeying the group's intention. That wasn't the first time we'd seen this. In my own personal experience and as reported by others, staring intently at the lamp makes it become sluggish and fixed rather than energetic and active.

The dilemma of intention can be looked at in terms of language already developed here. The groups with good results created *moments* for themselves. The groups were free-flowing and having fun while emotionally engaged. In contrast, group seven seems to have framed the exercise in terms of a *model*. This group was very clear: it wanted to move the lamp from what it was doing now (idling or peeking just to red) to a future state that would represent success. In doing so, they set up a model that turned success into an unusual condition. That is, success would occur if they "forced" the lamp into a new and unlikely state. This is a surefire way to tell the subconscious that it is indeed unlikely. So, while the conscious minds were saying, "I want this new thing to happen," the subconscious minds were saying, "Such an event *should not* happen." The subconscious says in effect, "The current state is normal, and I expect that it will continue to be normal." All the grunting and effort just make it more certain of its conclusion.

That finding, which is so clear in the experience, is a powerful statement about concepts such as the law of attraction that do and do not work. As indicated earlier, the law of attraction says events will trend toward what one deeply expects to happen. But by definition, new goals are not the norm. If they were the norm, then they would already have happened and wouldn't exist as goals. Therefore, to use the selection effect for such a goal, one must truly believe that it *should* be the norm. I cannot overstate how much this has been driven home to me for years with the REG. For years, I strained to press the REG to do something different, unique, and special. But all the while, I was building greater internal resistance and alienating my subconscious mind from the very thing I wanted.

※ ※ ※

The revelation that intention can be used against oneself forced me to revise my entire REG approach. Rather than focusing directly on REG output as I had been doing, I needed to turn my intention inward. I had to try to affect my own state of mind and let the REG results indicate how I was doing. As with a patient monitor, the doctor acts not on the screen itself but on the patient and lets the patient's change in condition affect the monitor. Maybe that was the piece of that red pill of knowledge I needed.

Of course, learning to tune in to my inner states is a daunting task and does not itself mean I can change those states. Presumably, that would involve an alignment of the conscious and subconscious aspects of mind. I use the term *subconscious* rather than *unconscious* because *unconscious* sounds too remote and inaccessible. The subconscious mind seems like something one can delve into and then use to at least try to bring consciousness.

That theory seemed logical and worth pursuing, so I framed a three-step process that became my mantra and guide. The three steps can be remembered by the maxim *reflect, connect, direct*.

> The first act of conscious intention is to *reflect* on the workings of the conscious and subconscious minds.

The second act of conscious intention is to *connect* with and engage the subconscious mind in a dialogue.

The third act of conscious intention is to *direct* the subconscious mind into alignment with the goals of the conscious mind.

This program sounded exciting to me. It might lead to more self-integration and allow me more-consistent influence on REG output. I did realize, however, that to truly make progress here would require many iterations. I would go through the three steps again and again, perhaps shaving off layers of resistance as I went. I was also intrigued by how it might affect other areas of my life. I seemed to be embarking on a reengineering of my personality. Let me explain each of the steps, as they relate not just to success with the REG game but also with the game of life.

Step 1: Reflect

The subconscious mind is described in many ways in a large body of literature. My interest was highly specific and thus drove my description. I wanted to flesh out the *structure* of the subconscious (how it is built and what it does) rather than its specific content (repressed memories, father complexes, etc.). Psychoanalytic theory does speak about some structure—for example, the separation into the id, ego, and superego. But my own foray into self-reflection was yielding new concepts such as models, moments, *shoulds*, webs of meaning, threads of association, and the mental regulator. Those concepts had become very real to me, but something was still missing from this structure. The structure did not convey the vibrant chaos that seems to rule the subconscious. The subconscious is constantly shifting and not at all consistent. It is, as Brenda Dunne notes, "spritelike." Indeed, whenever I thought I knew what was going on, something unexpected would happen. What, I wondered, causes my own mind to be so squirrelly?

I turned to the field of artificial intelligence, which incorporates a structure and a framework that seemed to match the complex inner dynamics I'd experienced. The late Marvin Minsky of MIT, often called the father of artificial intelligence, basically gave robots a subconscious mind. He found that for a robot to act intelligently, it needed hundreds if not thousands of subroutines at work below the surface of actual decision making. Some of those subroutines do things such as parse language, estimate distances, link names to faces, and unpack complex visual shapes. Minsky concluded that the vast array of neural nets in physical brains must do the same. He called that concept of subroutines *agents*.[2]

Both humans and robots, therefore, need large amounts of internal cognitive support in the form of such agents. Minsky constructed his agents to in effect argue and compete with each other for relevancy in whatever problem solving was taking place. So, what looks from the outside like a calm set of decisions made and actions taken is not that way at all below the surface. The agents live in a chaotic cacophony of cross-chatter, at times working together and at times competing for control and relevancy. Minsky calls that complex and flexible hierarchy of subroutines the Society of Mind theory.[3]

Minsky's concept of a society of mind seemed to explain why I experienced my subconscious mind as a process like herding cats. There are many subroutines in my own mind, each of them doing its own thing. They make a variety of calculations and provide numerous checks and balances. And there seemed to be something even more shocking about my own inner society of mind. I suspected that the feelings that emanate from my depths have, in effect, a life of their own. They are separate minds, each one of them with its own volition. And most surprising of all, it appeared that these agents were sources of impact on the REG output. They are the ones having the direct impact, and what I think of as "me" is a sideshow, just along for the ride.[4]

Interestingly, in the second release of his book *Society of Mind*, Minsky replaced the term *agents* with the term *resources*.[5] He may have taken flak from colleagues for the idea that the subroutines were sounding too anthropomorphized. In shifting from *agents* to *resources*, he removed the sense of their own inner drives or volitions. The change was also consistent with Minsky's view of the mind itself as simply a complex (robotlike) mechanism. In my experience, however, the subroutines within my own mind are *both* agents and resources. First, they are agents to themselves, seemingly with opinions and intent. Second, they are resources to my conscious mind, able to help me manage my top-level activities. But the key is that in their agency, they aren't neatly controlled. They have to be engaged before they can be coaxed into alignment.

That new image of my subconscious shifted my thinking when it came to how to progress the relationship. Through reflection, I had to isolate the agents that are relevant to the selection effect. I had already identified the prediction and emotion resources/agents, so I needed to examine them more closely. To do so, I had to find the context or framework in which they are embedded. My goal was to wrap my arms around what they were doing (so to speak) so that I could more reliably connect with them.

Step 2: Connect

Eastern and Western cultures take different approaches to engaging the deeper elements of mind. Freud pioneered talk therapy, which became the West's preferred method of raising subconscious activity to conscious awareness. However, in my project, I had no one to talk to except myself; and talk therapy is notoriously ineffective when done solo. I could ask myself such questions as, "What *should*-based feeling is causing these results?" and, "Why do I suddenly feel like I'm going to do well in the next few minutes?" There was some promise there, but the real issue was how to connect the conscious and subconscious aspects of mind to get them in dialogue.

The East takes a different approach—through its rich tradition of meditations with the goals of greater inner awareness and self-integration. Because I had to integrate those agents with my conscious mind, the Eastern approach also seemed to hold some promise. In mindfulness meditation, for example, one sits quietly, clearing the mind, and watches as thoughts bubble up from below. In that process, layers of blocked or locked-in emotions and bound energies can be released to help connect the conscious and subconscious minds.

A number of studies have shown that meditators perform better than nonmeditators as psi subjects.[6] However, studies to date have relied on self-identification of the meditator.[7] No one to my knowledge has controlled metrics related to who might be a more-effective meditator and how that measure correlates with REG results. In any event, one might expect that meditators are subject to the same mental-regulator effects as nonmeditators are—even if perhaps less so. For example, one day we had a visitor at the Psyleron/ICRL offices who was one of our consultants and a meditator himself. He wanted to show us a frustrating experience he was having with the REG. We set up the game, and he closed his eyes and went into a meditative state. When he gave the signal, we started the session. Sure enough, the random-walk chart headed solidly up and into the significant zone. Then he opened his eyes and began watching the screen. Immediately, the chart reversed course and went directly back to zero. "What the hell?" he complained. "This always happens." It was a classic rubber-band response. So, although the fellow's meditation training may have helped with the positive results, once his conscious mind saw what was happening, the dynamic changed.

Given the constant specter of that rubber-band experience, the mental regulator seemed like the best entry point for a connection with the subconscious. At least I knew it was there, or something like it, because I could feel it operate and could see it in the REG results. To really delve into it, however, it seemed I would need to work through the prediction and emotion agents. As the earlier figure 7.3 shows, I seem to receive messages from the two systems through *should* feelings as well as other impressions and alerts that are sent upward to consciousness. Figure 9.1 modifies the earlier diagram by

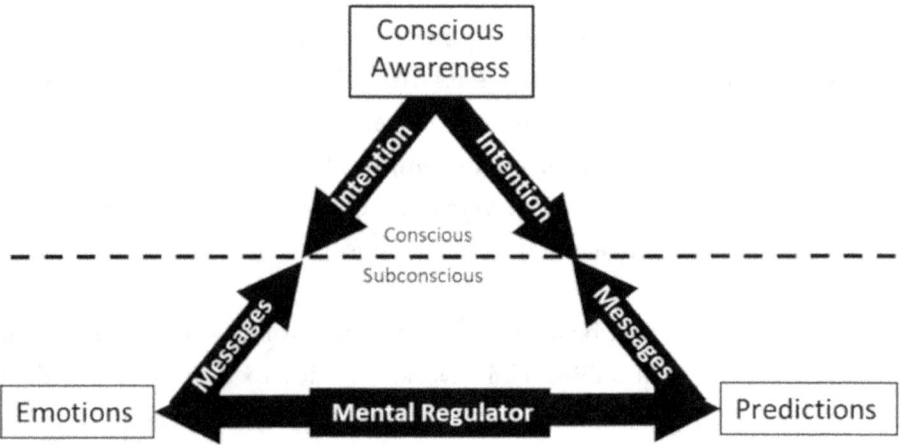

FIGURE 9.1. Two subsystems—emotions and predictions—sitting below the surface of consciousness and sending messages of significance to the conscious mind. The conscious mind can also use its own attention and intention to influence the two subsystems.

making the arrows bidirectional, thereby indicating that through intention and awareness, the conscious mind can establish two-way communications with these agents. As I began to recognize patterns in their actions, I became able to empathize with the reasoning that drove them. And that growing empathy seemed to itself forge the connection.

Step 3: Direct

Through more than a year of inner reflection and connection, I began probing and poking the two agents. I also became able to see how the emotion and prediction agents engage each other. For example, I might be doing very well with the REG—being very much in a flow—when the prediction agent decides the results have become too significant. The mental regulator shunts that message to the emotion system, which then responds by generating conscious-level, somewhat uneasy feelings about it. If the REG results continue to rise, then at some point the mental regulator may authorize an alert. I can feel the alert as it disrupts my current state. It instantly frames next events in terms of loss, which causes me to pull back, with changed expectations. And that new attitude can quickly drive the score downward. However, if I do keep pressing forward in opposition to what the mental regulator wants to happen, then at some point it freaks out (technically speaking) and begins (amazingly) to systematically shut down my ability to continue. My conscious mind gets cloudy and slightly disoriented and feels a weird tingling sensation—until I agree to stop trying. It reminded me of the scene in *2001: A Space Odyssey,* when Dave starts pulling circuits from the computer HAL, and HAL begins shutting down as he loses higher functions. Watching as if from the outside, I could see this all very clearly happening to me—in real time.

Conceptually, I saw a solution to the problem, though a difficult one. If I could hold an alternative mental model wherein high scores are normal, then the prediction system would allow it and would not excite the emotion system to fire an alert. I have had brief periods of certainty regarding such a model and have seen this work. That is, if I am truly confident that I can alter the REG patterns, then normal becomes my ability to succeed rather than any prior fixed result.

Such a shifted model, however, does not usually last long because my very success becomes too significant to me; something inside me can't abide it. So, even if the mental regulator doesn't fire an alert over the score, it fires an alert about my changing who I am. A shift in my self-identity becomes the cause for alarm.

Overall, then, the appeal to a changed model with changed norms did not seem as if it would work—at least not now. I therefore turned to the other class of experience. As will be recalled, moments are full of fresh meaning, excitement, and insight, and they trend natively away from current norms. They shut down existing models for the brief time as they explore unfamiliar connections. The problem with moments, of course, is that they tend to be spontaneous and not easy to produce on demand.

A way forward did present itself, however. I discovered that there is an aha instant that is often part of the reflect–connect process. That is, as I watch for messages coming from the subconscious, when I see a new one it provides a moment of recognition: "Aha! I see what is happening!" And so, for that brief moment—and it is a *moment*—the mental regulator is disarmed. The conscious mind has the upper hand, and it becomes possible to insert a purposeful message into the subconscious. That message can be that the REG output will rise.

The window of time for the message is small, however. It may be only seconds. Still, a few seconds is long enough to fire off a burst of trials that skew the output in my favor. Then the mental regulator regains control by stepping back behind my conscious state of mind. That's just how the mind works: as you sit reading here, your subconscious activity watches vigilantly from behind—scanning for irregularities—and is ready to give you feelings about your environment.

The game isn't over at this point, however. Seeing the mental regulator step back to gain control can itself create a new moment. "Aha! The mental regulator is reframing the moment!" That can create a new moment that can shift back behind the mental regulator and drive another round of good results. The process becomes a cat-and-mouse game with elements of mind.

The process sounds like it might go in circles, but it does lead somewhere. The moments of self-revelation lead to a longer-term process of self-integration. Each time I'm able to see the action of the subconscious, I bring more of it to conscious awareness. And because the process involves both the prediction and emotion systems, I believe it builds both emotional intelligence and cognitive intelligence (whatever that might mean in this context). It does feel like a path is forged to the deeper self. It may even help create a deeper self.

Unfortunately, the process does terminate. The cat-and-mouse game ends when the mental regulator finds a wider framework than I am currently able to handle. So, even though I may see the subconscious shift back, it shifts to a level that disappears from my mental sight. And though one's depth of awareness in this regard should grow over time, progress appears to be slow. Perhaps because this action is not required for survival, evolution did not include natural support for it. To excavate our minds, we have to build our own apparatus.

Layers of Mind and Their Alignment

The process of stepping backward in the mind makes the mind feel organized into discrete layers. With the REG game, such a layering becomes apparent. The first and simplest layer of the REG experience is attention to the very next trial: red or green. Each next REG result is the most immediate issue as it arrives and then passes. It feels simple and immediate, not concerned with anything else that might be wider in scope. We can call each such experience a *unit of meaning,* albeit a small one.

From that simple experience, next layers form. Within a session, one senses a trend developing. That is, one might feel "on" or "hot" for some period and know that the trend will continue as long as the feeling remains. Such trends are themselves layered. A broader one involves the way one feels about the results of the most-recent session or one's sense of how the next session will go. The same can be true of recent days or weeks. And it reaches even wider—into one's personality in general. It reflects one's basic senses of optimism and pessimism—that is, how positive or how negative one's overall outlook tends to be. Finally, the layers seem to extend even beyond individual personality to the web of society. There's a way we know ourselves by reflecting off that social web—while also influencing it. All layers can be active *and* interactive at any given time, which is one reason the results themselves are so complex. It's as if multiple waves combine to reach the next result.

I like the term *wider* for those layers because they seem to wrap around each other like a series of blankets, but in this case, the blankets mean fields of some sort. I tend to think of them as *meaning fields* rather than energy or information fields.[5] Our physical body seems to have nested layers of these meaning fields moving outward from the body. Wider layers, like the layer of personality, influence and shape the activities of the narrower ones. Over time, I've begun to define those layers, even if the boundaries I put on them are arbitrary. Following is a rough pass at seven layers of the REG experience. Included with each description is an example of how the layer can be seen as part of daily life. That is, life, too, is wrapped in similar layers of these meaning fields—from short-term, simple experiences outward to more-complex ones.

Layer 1: *The firing of the next REG trial with an expectation of a specific outcome.* In other aspects of life, this can be any momentary action, like eating a spoonful of soup. It is immediate, simple, and important in its own right. But it comes and goes quickly.

Layer 2: *The set of next trials that are the same color in a row—what's called a* run—*like getting four greens before a red occurs.* In life, this can be thought of as short-term tasks taken one after another or multiplexed, like household chores. One sees how far one can get before completion or before other factors intervene.

Layer 3: *The trending of the REG output over a short duration—in particular, what one feels about what is likely to happen in the near future.* In life, this can be thought of as what one feels about next events' falling into place—or perhaps falling apart.

Layer 4: *A longer-term trend involving REG results over the course of the last number of sittings or sessions.* In life, this might be compared to organizing a small project, like a family gathering.

Layer 5: *The wider sense over the past days or even weeks of how REG results have been trending, with an ongoing expectation of what will happen next.* In life, it can relate to whether one feels that things are headed in the right direction over the course of days or weeks. This is the first level that may trend out of one's sight because one may or may not imagine that there are such trends. Indeed, many outside forces can intervene to derail trends. But a lesson of the REG is to pay attention to those wider frameworks because one's expectations can help shape otherwise flexible and uncertain outcomes.

Layer 6: *The way one's very personality becomes reflected in the wider results.* Is one optimistic or pessimistic? This is the level at which the REG game and life become blended such that there is no separate comparison. One's outlook and how one feels about oneself are similar in all instances—REG and otherwise. The REG merely provides an indicator of these deeper self-structures.

Layer 7: *The social and cultural reality in which the REG experience exists and finds meaning, complete with sets of norms and expectations as well as the reaction to their violation.* This level blurs into life experience insofar as how one accepts or challenges social norms as they currently impinge on the self.

The seven levels can be compared to the structure of a book. A book is layered in units of thought. It begins with individual letters that make up words, which roll up into sentences, which become paragraphs, which become sections, which become chapters. Each of us is a book of life.

※ ※ ※

The lengthy period of stepping back from the project and finding out about my mind gave me a very rich experience. I gained appreciation for the complexity of my own mind and learned that real progress can be made in coming to understand consciousness and what it entails. I had developed a schema that by all rights had some firepower to it. It involved tools and methods I could apply. I had no idea how extensive this self-auditing process might be or how well it might translate into REG success under pressure. Nevertheless, I felt sufficiently armed to go forward.

PART III:
MIRROR MAZE OF MIND

CHAPTER 10:
DIGGING DEEP

By early 2010, I was applying my program of *reflect, connect, and direct* in a structured way. I had targeted the two subconscious agents: the value-based emotion system and the expectation-based prediction system. My REG results were more consistent, and I was feeling a sense of mastery over myself. I was playing a chess game with my subconscious mind and winning. Further, new mental states were affecting my daily life and activities. I felt much calmer, cleaner, and clearer inside, as if I had removed a clutter of kinks and twists. And in other areas of life, I was handling certain long-standing resistances. Finally, after an almost-two-year hiatus, I was ready to begin the million trials of the last REG study.

The focus on my own REG work, however, did not help Psyleron move forward as a company. By this time, all of the original investment money had been spent. And though we had money coming in, it wasn't enough to match our expenses. Almost everyone had to find another job. Justin, Nick, and Ian were snapped up by engineering-based firms in Virginia, North Carolina, and Texas. That left only John, Adam, and me. The need to downsize was in fact no surprise to John, who had said from the beginning that we look more like a nonprofit company that might do better with grants and donations.

John was unhappy also because he felt I'd mucked up the company in various ways. For one thing, I had a habit of asking our staff to do things that derailed them from their other work. It also messed up lines of authority. The staff didn't come here to work for me; they came to work for John. But because John and I were partners, the staff could hardly blow me off. All in all, John was pretty disgusted, and a cloud hung over the operation. Further, it seemed as if I didn't care whether we succeeded or not. My personal obsession with the REG was an opiate that shielded me from the reality we faced.

While John and I weren't seeing eye to eye, the business nevertheless muddled on. Adam was getting us bits of publicity here and there. We were selling just enough REG-1 units, Mind Lamps, and SyncTXT subscriptions to stay solvent while we tried to figure out a next move. And in spite of our differences, John and I continued our endless discussions about the nature of consciousness and the REG effect—an activity that also took a lot of time away from other activities. We were like a couple who couldn't get along except doing this one thing. Both of our significant others, however, didn't see the point of our long conversations. They voiced their concerns that this had to stop.

※ ※ ※

When I began my fourth and final REG study, I started with great success. In the first few days I jumped to an impressive ongoing Z score of 3.35 (with odds against chance of more than 100:1 as estimated from the Z_{max} table in appendix B) and stayed there. I felt like I'd finally mastered the process. All I had to do was ride out the study by using this method to prove it could be done. My target was to end this fourth data set with a Z score of at least 2.0, which would give me the one-in-a-million score when combined with the three earlier ones. I was on track to blow far past the target.

Two days later, John called with more concerns about the business. Our bank balance had dipped below zero for the first time. He needed some positive news. Normally, I would not have said anything about my current REG strategies and scores so as not to jinx or rubber-band myself. However, I decided to chance it and explained to him my new concepts in my training program and how I felt I was now able to consistently get high scores. I reminded him that I am not given to hyperbole, so that when I step out to say I'm really onto something big, I'm *really* stepping out. However, I added that this mental strategy was still relatively new to me, and the newness effect could be what was driving a lot of the results. In any event, both of us knew it's dangerous ground to announce such a breakthrough. In fact, even as we spoke, I felt something shift in me, and I knew I was in trouble.

Upon returning to the REG game, I had the most massive rubber band I ever remembered. It was all just too absurdly predictable. My score plummeted. It rallied slightly and then plummeted even further. I was riveted in a compulsion to continue, locked in my gambler's fallacy and amygdala-mediated deer-in-the-headlights frozen mode. By the time the rubber band subsided, in one long disastrous sitting I had undone weeks of meticulous good work. In fact, I was now below zero. The random-walk chart created a devastating symmetry: way up and way down. I was angry—and incredulous that this should be happening. I walked away and tried not to think about it for days.

Unlike some earlier strategies, however, this approach has some built-in corrective elements. I replayed the events in my mind, noting how I had shut down as part of a reactive fear process. All was not lost, though; just a good score was lost. I was only a tenth of the way through the million trials and had plenty of time to recover. When I restarted with a calmer frame of mind, I was able to begin moving more cautiously in a positive direction by using the same strategy. It took me another 200,000 trials just to get back above the zero line. Then, over the next month and with another half a million trials, my current Z score continued to pull higher toward my target. I was vigilant about monitoring my attitude, trying to keep from incurring additional large setbacks from similar mental meltdowns. I did have two relatively small ones but managed to stop and regroup each time.

As I approached the targeted end Z score of 2, however, I began to falter. My results began trending slightly downward, and I had a sense that the score would continue downward. At this point, I found the unaccustomed wherewithal to stop—thankfully, because examining my data at that point revealed a distinct pattern in the making: one that would have doomed results had I continued.

Figure 10.1 displays the data for the fourth study, with approximate trend line up to the point of stopping. This graph is a little different from previous ones in that the vertical axis displays the current Z score as the study progressed. That measure enables one to see the early fluctuations more easily, including the strong start and the rubber band. Also evident

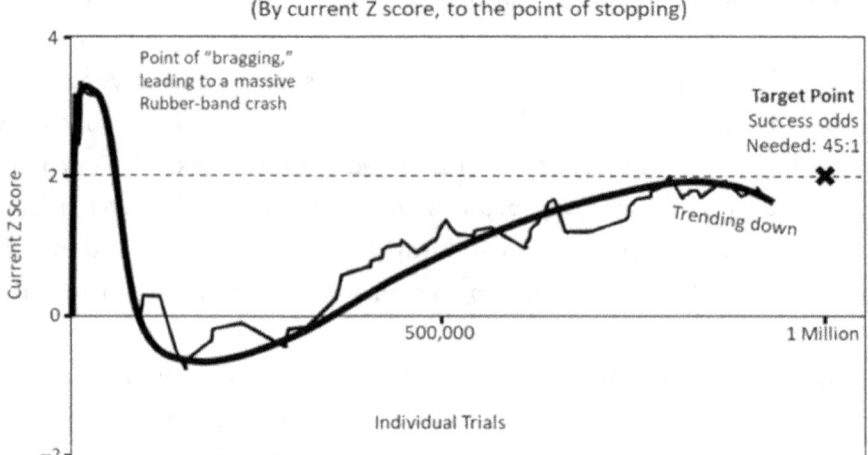

FIGURE 10.1. A Z-score-based chart—with approximate trend line—showing initial success, followed by a strong rubber band, followed by a long slow rise, and finally, followed by an apparent repulsion from the ending target Z score of 2.0.

is the subsequent slow climb heading for the required ending Z score of 2. I briefly crested at a score of just over 2 before edging downward.

The psychology surrounding the approach to a target is complex. On one hand is the desire to reach the goal. On the other hand, fears start to rise up. With each later trial, one is closer to the end, which means that any misstep has less time to recover. So, one begins to feel one is sitting on a knife edge, trying to maintain a mental calm. But there is a second fear as well. It is the fear of success. If I succeed, it will force me to change my understanding of myself. My web of identity is thus threatened, and in many ways, I would feel more comfortable failing.*

In spite of the faltering toward the end, the overall result for all four studies combined to this point is strong. Figure 10.2 shows the random-walk chart, where the small "x" marks the targeted end point yet to be reached. At the point of stopping, I had achieved a probability against chance of 856,000:1—that is, had the study been slated to end at this point. Visually, it looks ever so close to that million-to-one mark.

---

* The issue of target-based psychology is examined in the supplemental material chapter entitled "Units of Meaning."

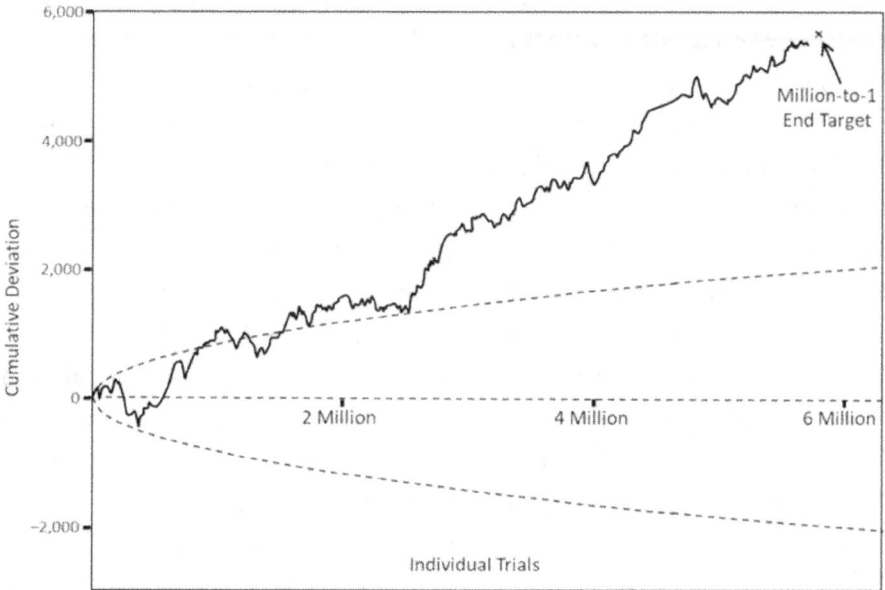

FIGURE 10.2. The random-walk chart combining Studies 1, 2, 3, and 4 to the point of stopping. The odds against chance (if this were the final Z score) are 856,000 to 1.

The Mental Pen and the Occlusion Process

In each of the previous three studies, I had run the trials of the study from start to finish without any REG "training time" in between. This fourth study marks the first time I stopped in the middle of a study to regroup. Taking such a break is permitted *as long as it is decided ahead of time*. And note that any attempt to "time" a restart based on how many reds or greens have recently occurred makes no difference, because according to the principles of physics and randomness, any next trials are fully independent of previous trials.

As I continued to practice, it became clear that most of my previous training had been shallower than I thought. The new training allowed me to survey my past work—like an explorer who reaches the farthest point of a previous expedition. I really had not progressed past layer three in my schema, which is the layer of short-term trends on the order of minutes. So, I tried to address wider layers that are involved in personal acceptance of success, as well as more-specific, long-term personal goals. I could see how blind I am most of the time to those more-entrenched layers, with their deeply rooted *shoulds* and expectations. They had always been active—but outside my conscious awareness.

A method for working with the wider layers suggested itself, so I went with it. It's somewhat counterintuitive, however, because I first had to forget about them. That is, I needed to narrow my focus and allow myself short bursts of unconflicted greenness. The clarity of that narrow sense came from my training and excluded everything except the next trial. In effect, it is lowest-level layer-one strategy. I called this strategy the *mental pen* because I seem to literally write *green* on the screen—almost like pushing green out of my eyes. It is a kind of perception in reverse. That is, instead of using the eyes to perceive green, I use them to paint green outside me. Those short bursts with the mental pen would tend to drive the process forward with three or four greens in a row. Using it became quite reliable.

There's a catch, however. When I apply the mental pen successfully a number of times during a short span, my wider self becomes alarmed by the very reliability of it. That alarm reaches out to block continued success. Thus, the use of the mental pen flushes out a mental regulator associated with a wider layer of the self. As I use the mental pen, I can watch for this to occur, as it inevitably does. I have found that a mental regulator works by putting up a mental wall that keeps me from using the mental pen. Parts of my mind become blocked from use through an occlusion process. I can literally feel how I am shut out from assuming a state of mind I had moments before. And it seems that the more successful I am, the more the occlusion wants to kick in. The mental regulator goes into protection mode—this time protection from too much self-awareness.

I was fascinated by this occlusion process and realized how it plays out in other areas of life. For example, it often kicks in during public-speaking engagements. When I get nervous about what I'm going to say—even if I'm prepared—a critical part of my mind shuts down. As if the doorway to the resources I need is walled off. I blank out.

Seeing this process at work with the REG game gave me some sense that I might counter these automatic responses. I began to gain some mastery over the occlusion process, which runs on various levels or layers, so it isn't a matter of just getting through it once. The marginal success I was having against it seemed to alarm my mind even more. So, as I continued, subconscious agents of my mind found other ways to block me. I became aware of another evolutionary trait built into our psyches—presumably to help keep us safe. But it wreaks havoc with the REG game. I call it the *exploratory response*.

The Exploratory Response

Think about a time you approached a traffic light with, say, three lanes of stopped traffic. You scanned the lanes to decide which one looks best to line up in. To make your decision, you looked at the number of cars in each lane, the presence of big trucks, and so forth. You made your best guess and committed to a lane. But almost immediately, your mind played devil's advocate. Maybe the right lane would have been better—

The REG game has its own version of commitment to a path. It's a mental path in this case. For example, I might adopt a certain frame of mind and find that it is working. A good frame of mind continues to work. That success can set off alarms internally, but let's say for the moment that I'm in a flow and loving it. Suddenly, I find my mind thinking about jumping to another mental strategy. For some reason, I hedge my bets against the state of mind I'm currently using. Something won't allow me to just stay the course. I find it crazy that I do this to myself, because it is clearly counterproductive. At first, I thought it was only an issue of mental discipline. Maybe my mind is just too noisy and needs some Zen training or something. Over time, however, it became clear that there's something systematic—almost diabolical—going on within me. It is structural, a self-interrupt that seems built into the mind. The REG process just seems to highlight what occurs unnoticed—and perhaps even exaggerates it.

To search for what possible evolutionary value this mental second-guessing might hold, I went back to the books. A further review of Richard Herrnstein's research on matching circuits described in chapter 6 found an answer. Herrnstein (and others) showed that animals' matching circuits have a second crucial aspect to them: they always engage in what he called *exploratory responses*. So, even as matching circuits provide you a best course of action, they immediately begin to test alternatives. For example, when one of Herrnstein's pigeons learned that the left button dispensed food 70% of the time it is pecked and the right one 10% of the time it is pecked, one would expect the pigeon to forget about wasting time on the right one. Always pecking the left button would be maximally effective on a per-peck basis. But how did the pigeon learn that left-side bias in the first place? It was by exploring the action of both buttons until it figured out the current pattern. So, if it does not continually explore alternatives, then it would not know when environmental conditions change to a new pattern—one that might suddenly begin favoring the right side. Failure to keep pace with new and changing conditions could be wasteful or even deadly.[1] Ants, for example, form a single tight column when headed to and from a source of food. But occasionally, one ant will randomly break from the column and literally wander off. That ant is in the random exploratory process. Even though the ant column knows the value of what it is headed for, the column might be walking right past an even better and closer source of food. And inevitably, sooner or later, the current source will run out. The time to explore is before resources become depleted or conditions turn bad.

Today our current method of foraging for food tends to be in the form of walking the aisles at the grocery store. That would seem to obviate the need for the exploratory response. But there are other times that it could be critical. We can look at the dangers that arise when the self-interrupt process fails to occur, such as texting while driving. Most of us know how it becomes possible to stare at the screen and instantly and completely forget where one is. One need be absent for only five seconds to land in a ditch—or worse.

On the other hand, in many instances today one is completely physically safe and needs to simply focus on something and stick with it. In such cases, that jumpy-mind syndrome can keep one from putting the power behind a goal that it requires. The grass may be greener on the other side, so the exploratory response proposes. Thus, whereas we often go around beating ourselves up for our attentional shortcomings, our brains appear simply wired that way. Sure, we can overcome it to some degree (tell that to someone with ADHD), but rather than being solely an individual character trait, it's in part how our brain is designed. And though constant self-interrupts can mess with a sense of inner peace, as noted before it appears that our bodies were not designed for inner peace but for survival.

When I first recognized exploratory actions at work with the REG trials, I called the output resulting from it *disrupter bits*. The REG activity seemed to reflect a shift in the mind that is exactly the opposite of what was currently working and racking up greens. The exploratory response becomes an alternative hypothesis that overlays the exact opposite image on the REG output. And immediately, disrupter bits flow forth. I know this because I literally feel the occlusion from my previous state of mind—and the imposition of my mind now overlaying red on the output. Both the occlusion and exploratory responses form a deal killer.

The exploratory response calls to mind the Necker cube phenomenon. See figure 10.3. The image appears to you with the front square either down and to the left or up and to the right. Whichever way the image appears first, it will shift to the other orientation within a few seconds in spite of conscious efforts to the contrary. The inability to hold one image for any length of time again speaks to the idea that our subconscious is constantly looking for alternatives. Perception remains limber, so to speak, to make sure we fully explore all the possibilities in the environment. And because perception becomes an overlay on reality, as the image shifts so do expectations of reality. The situation becomes very similar to a shifting expectation of "seeing" a next REG result as red or green in order to test reality—and in doing so, literally causing the expected result. Studies show that for normal Necker cube subjects, the image changes back and forth on average about every six seconds. Meditators do somewhat better: about every eight seconds.[2] So, even with mind training, this exploratory response is tamed only minimally.

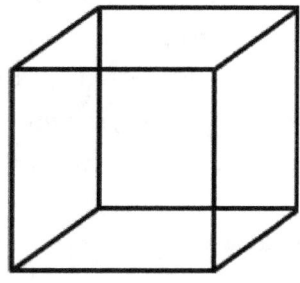

FIGURE 10.3. Necker cube.

The exploratory response is very bad for REG results. The conscious mind wants green, while the subconscious tests reality and presses for red. But it gets worse. There's another function of mind that also causes yet another reversal of results. I call it *posing*.

Posing

The REG game is a mental feedback process. One tries to be fully engaged while having at least a toe outside watching what's going on. When I find or see a state of mind that is giving good results, I try to mentally grab it so that it can be maintained. That causes me to instantly "pose" that frame of mind. I make it into a thing so that I can reapply it.

The problem with posing is that it is no longer the original experience. To pose is to create a *model* out of the original frame of mind, and then use the *model*. Now somewhere in my mind I know this is happening, and I know I am no longer being genuine or real about it. In fact, that lack of authenticity or present-time meaningfulness tells the mind it should produce the opposite results in the REG output. Thus, this attempt to use feedback to watch the mind, grab a working state, and re-present it can reverse the output. So, given this process, how is one supposed to train?**

As a kind of experiment, and frankly out of frustration, I decided to see what would happen if I combined the effects of exploratory disrupter bits with this mental posing. I would watch for a disrupter process at work and would then pose it. Or, said another way, I would create a mental pose of the disrupter process. So, in a session, I began this test. I watched myself posing a process of interrupting myself—which is two levels deep of self-reflection. I was going to feed the signal back on itself in a recursive disrupter-pose loop. I had no idea what it would do, though: like having created gunpowder for the first time and deciding to light it. When I tried this process, I was completely immersed in trying to get behind each disrupter bit with a new pose regarding the previous output. I was not paying close attention to the overall results. However, when I reviewed it, the output chart, shown in figure 10.4, is remarkable. This session easily became the most-significant

---

** Note that the mental pen described above is itself a pose, which is a reason it can be used only briefly. Overusing it leads to reverse results.

negative Z score (and larger than any positive score) of my entire REG career. At one point, it reached a current Z score of negative 5, with odds of at least 10,000 to 1 as drawn from the chart in appendix B.

The dramatic score was no doubt enhanced by the newness effect of my strategy—as is often the case—even though it was in the negative direction. Several immediate retries gave wild swings—but not this wild. I became far too self-conscious of the significance produced. However, a week later, I decided to try the process again in a formal way. This time I produced what I recall as a negative score almost as strong, about minus 4.6. But in an ironic and perhaps not coincidental twist, the computer crashed, and the final portion of the data session was lost. I find it interesting that the results always went negative—the embodiment of the sense of backing up.

※ ※ ※

The presence of the exploratory response and the problem of posing seemed like a brick wall against any classic notion of mental discipline and training. If disciplined mental states are continually undermined by their very own neural circuitry's testing of alternatives and then producing reversed results, how could one ever really master the process? And the more precise my state of mind, the more my posing bounced me out and the disrupter bits pressed the opposite. I was doing better and worse at the same time and

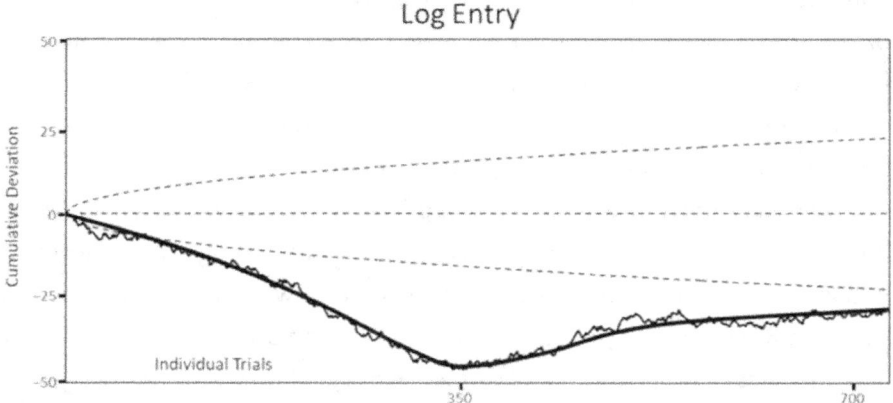

FIGURE 10.4. Chart of a personal log entry—with approximate trend line—involving an experience wherein the concepts of posing and disrupter bits feed back on each other.

was powerless to tell these deeper circuits to stop. I could anticipate the process and see it happen—and yet not control it. Even with awareness placed squarely on it, it would shift and still get behind me. So, my growing sense of personal mastery ironically seemed to increase the exploratory response's need to guard me against my very success.

Faced with that kind of self-inflicted checkmate—and in spite of my earlier revelations and successes—the only rational thing to do was to give up. Any other alternative would result in continuing to have my own efforts used against me in a variety of ways and with no escape. I became convinced that having tried for so many years, I had an answer to my original question. The selection effect exists, but it is not trainable in any normal sense. It felt like the ultimate defeat, finally breaking my unwavering determination. And persistence was futile.

For me, giving up was a moment of true despair. There was literally nothing left to try. And oddly enough, it felt natural and comforting. Letting go of my six-year-long unshakable sense that I would succeed left me with a sense of peace. All of my blustery ideas about how I was going to change so many minds and chart a new future for humanity dissolved before my eyes. I was serenely alone.

※ ※ ※

Once I adopted that attitude, however, my world began to transform. The moment caused me to open outward or upward and appeal to the universe for comfort. In a phrase that echoed beyond my downcast eyes, I said wistfully, "Hey, I tried to do something good here." It wasn't about my success anymore but was about facing a future without the aspirations of making a difference in the world. I wasn't special anymore.

It was then that my REG scoring suddenly shifted. I entered a flow state that didn't abate. I was getting great scores again and again. Ironically, or perhaps tellingly, I no longer cared. I was done. It was game over. I was just using the REG to display my feelings of serenity that did not care about the outcome.[3] All that mattered was the sense of freedom from the struggle.

As I continued in this more open frame of mind, I just let myself be part of the highest or most open level of mind I could grasp. I threw myself on the mercy of the collective-level aspiration we have for evolving beyond our current limitations. I clearly could not do this alone. For whatever reason, I wasn't up to it. In some small way, I had to die by myself. The experience was not something I ever could have imagined. The researcher in me had allowed the subject to be killed during the study.

CHAPTER 11:
WHO AM I, ANYWAY?

Ruth Rosenbaum is one of those straight-A overachiever types. An Ivy Leaguer from Brown, she studied literature on her way to a variety of career interests. After her master's degree, she worked in Paris as head of research for a new movie production and served as liaison between the French producer and the American director. One morning, in the middle of a meeting, she experienced an overwhelming sense of fear and horror. Because she had had many unusual experiences in her childhood, she knew to inventory her inner feelings to find out whether the experience was originating inside her or whether it was coming from the outside. In this case, she sensed it was coming from the outside. After dealing with her responsibilities, she excused herself from work and went home to process the growing sense of horror. Letting the experience unfold, she saw, in her mind's eye, debris falling from the sky; she heard agonizing sounds of people screaming; and then, out of nowhere, she saw what looked like an odometer starting at 000 and running up quickly to 346, where it stopped still. After a solitary walk, she returned home and fell asleep. It was not until the next morning that she learned that a plane had crashed just outside Paris, killing 346 people. Even more striking, the takeoff and crash had occurred about two hours *after* her intense emotional experience.[1]

After returning to America from Paris, Ruth became a journalist and wrote science articles for a national magazine. She has a good journalist's presence: petite and unassuming in a way that lets her blend into the background. Her gentle demeanor, however, belies a tenacious sense of responsibility that tends to make her a standout wherever she goes. Her intensely curious mind gets to the bottom of things, and in the process, she can become part of the story itself. Ruth cannot help but affect the world around her.

Ruth ultimately became a psychotherapist, and through the years she has had a full-time practice, which proved to be a rich outlet for her varied talents and abilities, including her intuition. She teaches courses at Columbia University's Teachers College as well as at a New York–based psychoanalytic institute.

I met Ruth at a weeklong PEAR academy in the April 2010. I presented on my project at the time, and we took a long walk around the pastoral Henry Chauncey Conference Center on the vast campus of Educational Testing Service in Princeton. I never forgot that walk because there's something about Ruth's ardent manner that is, well, unforgettable. About a year later, Ruth produced an influential article about the parallels between psi phenomena and the psychotherapeutic process. The premise was that some forms of communication between therapist and patient defy conventional explanation and can be understood in the context of psi. Ruth entitled the article "Exploring the Other Dark Continent," wherein the first dark continent (so named by Sigmund Freud) is the realm of female sexuality. Both domains involve so much mystery and depth that therapists often avoid the subjects.[2]

As Ruth described, "The psychotherapeutic process illuminates the existence of what is referred to as the 'intersubjective field' or some might call 'intersubjective space.' This field emerges from communications between patient and therapist, both conscious and unconscious, but which are greater than the sum of the two individuals' words and psyches. It is, in effect, a 'third entity,' with its own attributes and influences." In relating that phenomenon to the Princeton engineering anomalies research (PEAR) studies, she noted in a personal communication, "some of the more-successful PEAR subjects spoke of their experience as entering a space with the machine that felt like a blurring of boundaries between themselves and the machine, a co-created field similar to descriptions of the intersubjective field in the therapeutic situation."[3] In her article, Ruth further described some PEAR studies that involved two individuals with a close emotional bond working together giving positive results greater than either individual's separate efforts to alter the machine's output. The effects are more readily attributed to a new whole that emerges in the shared space that people co-create.[4]

Early in the development of psychoanalysis, Freud was intrigued with the notion of direct mental sharing, or telepathy. His deep interest led him to broach the subject in psychoanalytic circles. He went so far as to write a letter to a friend—which he denied but was later discovered to be true—stating, "If I had my life to live over again, I should devote it to psychical research rather than to psychoanalysis."[5] It was not until the field developed into a more rigorous academic profession that discussion of this subject became largely off limits. Overall, Freud had an approach–avoidance relationship with this research. Concerned about his legacy and his standing, he tended to confine the interest to private communications while repudiating them publicly.[6] One cannot help but think of Galileo, forced to recant many of his findings under the strong arm of the Roman Catholic Church.

Whatever one considers the intersubjective field or space to be, the effect itself can be important to the therapeutic process. People in distress are notoriously bad at working through the deeper elements of themselves on their own, needing someone else on the outside who can see into them and identify their issues. And when maximally effective, the patient–therapist relationship can bring moments of cocreation that avoid years of more-surface discussion.

As noted earlier, I did not have a therapist to dialogue with during the REG experience. I was trapped in the mirror maze of my own mind and had no reference points. The stark impossibility of finding my way through that labyrinth forced me to give up. The serenity and openness that ensued became the keys to unlocking a protective layer of self. I no longer had anything to protect.

I don't believe the presence of a therapist would have helped my situation. What I was facing was not the result of repressed memories, physical trauma, existential rage, or even spiritual crisis. Rather, my problem seemed to be the very structure of the mind itself. It seemed to me that human minds (and/or others) are designed through some basic, universal principles to explicitly avoid what I was trying to do. Minds have a myriad of checks and balances against the vulnerability that comes from opening up to the outside. As a mind reaches toward the outer boundaries of its own domain, it inevitably turns back to its safety zone. There can be moments of deviation, to be sure, but over time—and if it continues—there always comes a point at which the mind simply must turn back—or risk its sense of self. This suggests that the mind has a kind of mental membrane that surrounds its outer boundary and keeps us together. The REG experience can generate exceptional moments of poking at that boundary, but as a general principle, it is followed by a return to stasis—often driven by a rubber band. That common pattern seems to form an inviolable truth with the REG as well as with other aspects of life.

By this point, my training had become less about the score and more about exploring my own mental space. It was a convoluted mirror maze of a space, to be sure, bounded by a mental membrane that seemed purposeful in shielding me from the outside. Further, the selection effect seems to support the idea of the existence of a vast intersubjective realm outside each person's own mental membrane. The domain outside is a shared space—a kind of DMZ between self and other. One can cross the zone to the other side, but it is difficult, mostly because of our native protective mechanisms and the fact that our own network of internal associations is so loud.

Having nothing left to lose (as I perceived it) softened my defenses and brought the outer boundary into view. It may be foolish to play with these boundaries and their stability. Perhaps doing so would bring on a point of crisis—maybe even edging toward schizophrenia or other psychically porous states. But the effect was compelling to me, and I expected that under purely self-directed activity such as mine, it isn't likely that an otherwise balanced person could go too far with this. In any event, these feelings connected me with a domain that was bigger than simply me.

Pragmatic Spirituality

The experience of such complete resignation brought to mind one of the most-successful self-help programs of all time, which begins with the very point of hitting bottom. The first three steps of the Alcoholics Anonymous Twelve-Step Program are to (1) admit powerlessness over the present condition and that life has become unmanageable, (2) come to the belief that a power greater than oneself could restore sanity, and (3) turn one's will and life over to the care of that greater power. Regardless of what one considers that higher power to be, the point is that the sequence is a well-established one, and it works. Restated for the purposes here, one is forced to leap into the unknown toward higher ground rather than stay put with the prospect of slowly dying.

There is a spiritual connotation to this process, in which spirituality is defined as active engagement with a reality larger than oneself. Based on my REG experience, it now seems pragmatic to adopt a form of spirituality wherein the ego breaks down its rigid boundaries, and one opens upward and outward to some larger expression of reality. Innovation and creativity are possible only when one rises above the limitations of one's current viewpoint, model, or unit of meaning and looks from another, wider perspective. We do not realize how much we are constrained by the bounds of normalcy—and thus mediocrity rather than creativity—until we pry ourselves free from our own limitations to reflect on where we are stuck.

This notion of there being a higher or larger reality is of course a subject of much debate. And though some may regard that idea as a return to folklore or creation myths, science cannot presume to deny that which is currently beyond its scope. Nevertheless, there are certain such appeals that are clearly wrong and that give the whole concept a bad name. For example, in the middle of the 2011 professional football season, a young quarterback—a strongly religious person who wore "John 3:16" (a Bible verse) written into the black smudge below his eyes—was made the team starter. The team won eight straight games, and the sports world was mesmerized. It was a real phenomenon. When the public was polled, 43% of those surveyed said he was winning because God was on his side.[7] In the first playoff game, however, his team got thoroughly crushed. That was the end of the season—with nothing ever said again about God's role in his winning streak.

This is not to say that during that remarkable period there wasn't something unseen going on. And people simply use the best language they have. Without a better vocabulary for such phenomena, we resort to older ways of thinking about them. That is, by always attributing unusual outcomes to the God level, we have short-circuited any critical thinking about other possibilities. There may be larger realities that can momentarily coalesce and connect us but that are not as large as a catchall concept of God. Short-term zones or grooves may come and go based on real interactions with others. For example, it seems reasonable that members of the sports team described referred to were galvanized to become highly in sync with each other. They created an intersubjective space that had real power beyond our narrow concepts of the senses. That power includes the selection effect factor at a group level—the ability to help envision a shared future and then channel reality toward it. Said in more-familiar terms, the team got in a flow state and went on a hot streak. But that language should not be used for selling the experience short as simply an excited state. Rather, or in addition, the team's state enabled the players to connect into a greater whole. Such an intersubjective linkage may work for some time and then dissipate for any number of reasons. Perhaps disrupter bits or other inner alerts form at both individual and collective levels. The group may tell itself, "This is just *too* unusual and *has got to stop soon.*"

While notions of higher powers or higher layers of organization are largely dismissed in our society, my inner death experience made me look at things in a different way. That is, being in a moment of intense stress as I had put myself under, I looked for a way out; it is both logical and natural to look beyond the self for a greater context. It is perhaps only because we have rooted out all sense of the miraculous that we have mostly abandoned this mental exit hatch of opening to a larger unit of meaning. But maybe we should reconsider. It wouldn't mean a return to a prescientific age but, rather, would be the application of a native resource that connects our minds to create solutions we never would have thought of on our own.

In their book, *Why God Won't Go Away,* a neuroscientist and a physicist, both of whom are also medical doctors, discuss certain mental states associated with religious or spiritual experiences. The authors note that sometimes—during medical emergencies, meditation exercises, and other peak experiences—people report unusual moments of heightened and more-expansive connections to reality. At first, the authors said, they believed such experiences to be distorted, aberrant neurological states. But later they concluded that such states may represent real experiences rather than just tricks our minds play to help us cope with helplessness. These states may be wider perspectives that involve more than our usual and immediate sensory inputs. In the end, the authors suggest that a possible reason we have a mental faculty for such experiences is that such states may be adaptive, and the ability to directly connect self and other may be a useful aspect of reality.[8]

Multiple Selves

Through this experience of giving up, I inadvertently felt connected to a larger whole. And almost in spite of myself, that new feeling and its results resurrected my project. The REG game became light, free, and effortless. Unfortunately, after a period of time, that heightened sense of connection dropped back into a more normative state of mind, and the REG results began to moderate. I was my old dusty-ego self, again bringing on the REG decline effect as I tightened up. There was, however, a residual sense of how different I'd been during that period. So, even though that newly enhanced state of mind was gone, with some effort it could be brought back. It wasn't so much remembering the state of mind as the fact that there was *another me* who had experienced it. In other words, I could regain some level of access to the feeling by being the person I had been at the time. I was able to maintain both my normal self and this projected other self simultaneously. The contrasting selves became so vivid that I began to call this second viewpoint *the other*.

The presence of the other caused me to seriously ask myself questions: Who am I, anyway? Am I more than this current trapped ego, all day long second-guessing my own actions and making myself stressed and unhappy in so many ways—Minsky's competitive society of mind inside my head? Or am I this other, more connected self that taps into a larger reality beyond my self-imposed boundaries and that feels more serene and alive? Do I have to be either/or? And why is it that I can feel them both at the same time?

The concept of multiple minds seems a bit strange, but of course exists in clinical studies. Multiple personality disorder (MPD—more recently termed dissociative identity disorder, DID) shows how a person can have more than one top-level mind. Such a condition can surface as a coping method among children who have been seriously abused. It is an effective strategy because if one personality experiences abuse, another personality can exist who was "not present" at that time. The second personality has a different life with a different history and memories. The personalities can be so independent from each other that the characteristics of each appear to come from different individuals. For instance, one personality might love orange juice, and another breaks out in hives from it. One might have a lazy eye or need glasses, and another has sharp eyesight. Facial muscles may change so radically between personalities that it seems that the person had donned a new face.[9] Although MPD personalities are usually formed under extreme circumstances, they do point out what minds are capable of.[10]

MPD is treated in adulthood by helping the personalities get along with each other and even integrate to some degree. The new whole becomes an emergent figure from the various personalities, even if mediated by a central figure. In my case, I seemed to be having a mild version of multiple personalities. Further, the idea fit very well with the concept of mind as web or multiple webs. There is no inherent reason that the mind cannot have two high-level webs that cluster around different centers such that one can shift from one center to the other. Conceivably, the experience is a more functional and useful version of what appears in a pathological context. Nor is it that esoteric when looked at in terms of our daily lives. That is, psychologists have noted that people can display different clusters of personality traits in different work and home settings and even appear to be different selves in conjunction with different groups of people.[11]

Alan Hugenot, mechanical engineer and popular lecturer, describes his own clinical death following a terrible motorcycle accident that shattered much of his body. During his coma, he had a heightened emotional experience wherein he was a new person relative to his past. It was a brief period but had a profound and lasting effect on him. After resuscitation, he was able to revisit the second personality and again see the world through its eyes. He protects that personality from being brought together with his normal personality and becoming assimilated into his normal self.[12] The shift into that alternative personality gives him something of a vacation from his day-to-day self with its more normative way of looking at and relating to the world.

For me, the other took on an almost mythical quality. When I could assume its viewpoint, I felt in tune, or connected, with a larger reality. I adopted the name *connected self* for that viewpoint because it feels more connected in intersubjective space. Of course, this new self might be construed as so much more brain activity, but as with all things related to the REG, the question is how it succeeds in influencing REG output. Indeed, when I took on this viewpoint, my REG results showed continual traces of a heightened state. So, whereas the connected self might be my imagination, the correlation with REG output says something about just how real the imagination can be. Ultimately, I couldn't deny the correlations, so I just embraced them. And similar to conclusions put forth in *Why God Won't Go Away,* I've come to suspect that the experience of this connected self may develop precisely because it is an adaptive response to real conditions. Its presence is its own validation.

In contrast to the connected self, I continued to call my past self the *ego self*. It is a well-worn term of course, but one that's pretty easy to identify with. It's the normal, day-to-day way of facing the world, which includes much inner dialogue and chatter as well as strong identification with the body. The ego self's focus on personal needs overpowers the subtler senses of one's own web of wider connections. In contrast, the connected self has an abstract, ethereal quality and lives into this more expanded reality. The connected self feels more like the hub of a network than something with the solidity and inertia of the ego self. The comparison of the two selves sounds judgmental, but clearly both selves are needed: the ego self to run the body and its baser needs, and the connected self to help one explore and evolve into new realms.

As I observed the two selves in relation to each other, there was yet another perplexing aspect. Where does the conscious *me* who is writing about all of this fit in? Perhaps that me is my ego self or connected self at any given time. But it doesn't feel that way in the moments I reflect on them. When talking about these selves, I feel more like a moving awareness from the outside in. I'm trying to figure out what to do, how to manage these two selves in relation to each other. It reminds me of the classic cartoon of the guy with a little devil on one shoulder and a little angel on the other. Both are trying to tell him what to do, and of course they never agree. I'm the guy in the middle.

I called this third viewpoint the *analytic director*. It is the awareness of both the ego self and the connected self but from an outside position. It is somewhat like the awareness of someone else's self, like that of a friend. You are not the friend, but you can grasp the friend's self—just like you can view your own self or selves as if watching from the outside-in. This is still self-awareness but just a step removed. It may sound like splitting hairs, but the process of finding a place to stand outside a viewpoint creates a more stable point from which to observe it.

The growth of the connected self—largely through guidance by the analytic director—occurs by letting REG results show the way. While playing the game, I can become the connected self and try to maintain its viewpoint in part by looking back at the ego self. If I can see the ego self and can have compassion for it, I know I am not it. In fact, I can shape it and to some degree realign it. Equally important, in the REG process, *I ascribe only positive REG results to the connected self.* That is, if a session is not going well, it can be attributed to the ego self. That may sound like a cheap shot, but the strange thing about this kind of meaning structure is that it makes itself true. I find that the more I fashion the two selves this way, the more the connected self is free from inner contradiction—and thus self-aligned and effective from the start. So, while the two selves tussle for control over the REG, I find that the connected self grows larger in relation to the ego self. The goal is that over time it will replace much of the ego self's control. There is an important role for ego self—and its powerful subconscious agents—in affecting the REG output, but only if aligned and managed by the connected self. In any event, it is all quite fascinating.

※ ※ ※

One question arising from this dance of selves involves the relation between these selves and the brain. Indeed, the ego self appears to consist of firmly encoded layers of brain circuitry. It is our evolutionary past brought to the present. But as noted previously, the connected self seems to be different—at least to some degree. Affecting the REG output is a process that sits outside the bounds of what the brain can do. Because of that, it seems that the mind can construct a self that is not quite as brain based as the ego self is.

The relationship between mind and brain has been debated for centuries. And because it's pivotal here—in some ways the central question—we have to face it head-on (no pun intended). That is, until we build a theoretical model with more granularity than, "They're probably the same thing," we cannot truly explain the selection effect. And so, linking REG findings with some of the theoretical tools in our twenty-first-century scientific arsenal, we take up this critical subject.

CHAPTER 12:
FROM THE OUTSIDE IN

Phineas Gage was a railroad worker in 1848 when a detonating cap misfired and sent an iron rod through the left side of his face in an upward direction, through the neocortex, behind the left eye, and out the top of his head. He survived the accident, but the damage to his brain changed his personality. Where before he had been a polite and exemplary worker, he became rude, sullen, and forgetful, given to fits of anger. Over time he lost his job, wife, and family and became a drifter. He had acquired in many respects a different brain and become a correspondingly different person. Gage's new personality and changed self were clearly products of his damaged brain.[1]

Another case, also in the annals of clinical neuroscience, is that of a patient known as H.M. (not me). In the 1950s, H.M. had both hippocampi—the seat of general memory in the brain—removed to treat his epilepsy. It was not known at the time that removal of both hippocampi would mean no new memories could be formed. After the operation, when H.M. met someone, he could hold a conversation, but if he turned away and then back, he had no memory of the person or conversation. H.M. spent the next 55 years being studied for that brain condition. Clearly, his brain was no longer working correctly, and so he could no longer function as a normal human being.[2]

Gage, H.M., and other of brain-damage case studies show just how central our brains are to our personalities, our memories, and our senses of self. And if those examples are not enough to make the case, there's another smoking gun. More than half a century ago, the field of neuroscience gained the ability to selectively stimulate areas of the brain with small electrical probes. Such probing often elicits strong memories in subjects and, sometimes, a distinct smell or taste or other sensations. Scientists have become able to map the function of many brain areas and even individual neurons in this way, and they have found the areas for language, sounds, smells, different muscle groups, memories, and even higher-level reasoning. They've even found individual neurons that recognize a particular face and only that face. In one now famous study, a patient had a specific neuron that would fire rapidly each time he saw pictures of actress Jennifer Aniston.[3] The upshot of all of those findings is an ever-increasing conviction that the subjective experience of mind appears to arise solely from the brain's neuronal activity.[4]

In spite of such a large body of evidence to support the idea that the brain fully makes the mind, a number of celebrated neuroscientists have disagreed with the proposition. Among the Nobel laureates who have been the most vocal about an alternative are Sir Charles Sherrington, Sir John Sperry, Wilder Penfield, and Sir John Eccles. Dr. Wilder Penfield was one of the first architects of brain mapping through the use of electrical stimulation. He was also one of two neurosurgeons that patient H.M. was referred to in an effort to understand what had happened to H.M.[5] During a 40-year career of probing into open brains to treat epilepsy, Penfield concluded that the mind seemed to have aspects not present in the brain. He knew that such a position would be unpopular with his peers but felt compelled to say what he thought. He voiced concern that science was missing some evidence on the issue, and late in his career, he laid out his argument in his book *Mystery of the Mind: A Critical Study of Consciousness and the Human Brain*. Each of the other neuroscientists—Sherrington, Sperry, and Eccles—wrote highly unpopular treatises on why they believed the mind and brain are not one and the same.[6]

In open-brain clinical work, a neurosurgeon stimulates the brain—with part of the cranium removed—while listening to the subject's statements of experience. What ends up on paper as a record of events may lose much of the richness of the surgeon's close encounter with the patient. Penfield seemed to find that nowhere in the subject's subjective experience under electrical stimulation was there the act of decision making. That is, among all of the memories, muscle twitches, smells, tastes, and all other experiences that probing elicited in patients was a lack of the volitional quality of experience. Patients reported being affected by the probe and having experiences that were being given to them that they themselves did not produce. Something was being *done to them,* like reaching into a box and pulling various items out. Both doctor and patient were watching the brain from the outside in.[7]

Since Penfield's era, it has been found that there are prefrontal areas of the brain that operate in conjunction with the emotional regions that highly influence decisional processes. Thus, even decision making that might seem independent of the brain can be linked to the brain. Patients who are brain damaged in these regions can lose the ability to think through the making of decisions. Penfield himself worked with long-term brain-damaged patients who were decision impaired and did not develop cognitively or socially as independent individuals. So, he was clearly aware of this issue. It may be, then, that Penfield did not have the exact words to describe why he believed the brain is not the whole story of consciousness. In general, we have little developed language for discussing the relationship of mind to itself or another mind (in contrast to the brain). But in the case in which the doctor is literally peering at the seat of another's consciousness while engaged in a dialogue with that other, there could be some sharing that extends beyond our scientific expectations.

We may not fully understand what transpires between people even during normal social discourse. There is so much mental noise in the situation that we just process whatever presents itself. So, although Ruth Rosenbaum's intersubjective space, or what I have called *shared-meaning space,* may not be apparent or admissible as data in science, it doesn't mean it isn't there. I propose that Penfield and others were perhaps exceptionally good observers of patient experience in this regard, as well as their own, and experienced shared feelings beyond standard sensory cues.[8]

Brain Awareness

We become acutely aware of our brains when they fail to perform as we want them to or expect them to. One might say, "My brain just won't do math," or "My brain is tired, so I can't remember." One tries to access mental circuits that otherwise feel blocked or simply not there. One might then try a different route to some information, only to find once again that the brain sits like an impenetrable lump and will not comply. And that somewhat provocative outside-in awareness of brain is mild compared with the experiences of people who have suffered physical damage to their brains. For them, life is *all about* the experience of their brains.

Beth Jameson was in the hospital for routine surgery when her monitoring systems malfunctioned, and her brain was left without oxygen for more than five minutes. That condition, called *anoxia,* quickly kills cells in the affected areas of the brain. Beth lost much brain function, and when she awoke from unconsciousness, she had in effect a different brain. It is hard to imagine what that would be like: being the same person but having former parts of your usable brain simply gone.

Beth was still aware enough that she could work toward her own recovery and try to return to her old self as much as possible. Together with her husband, she chronicled that personal journey to recovery in a book entitled *Brain Injury Survivor's Guide.* One of the most striking aspects of the story is the intense scrutiny under which Beth put her damaged brain. She writes of her rehabilitation: "[It]… helped me begin to deal with the various areas of my brain that were damaged or lost entirely. The most noticeable to outsiders was the damage to my cognitive abilities." She continues, "Memory loss, which seems to be common among most brain injuries, was another area of my brain affected by my anoxic brain injury. In my case, it is the loss of my short-term memory. That has also been an area of my brain that was permanently and irreversibly damaged." And finally, "My frontal lobe was also affected as a result of the lack of oxygen to my brain. Most people can filter their thoughts before they speak. They still might choose to use rude, hurtful, or crude words. But, when a person's filter is damaged, what that person is thinking at the time just comes out. I have to admit I still struggle with my frontal lobe injury."[9]

That outside-in view of the brain is increasingly becoming part of our culture. Clinical psychology, for example, has developed an approach called *cognitive behavioral therapy,* or CBT. It is a method of metacognition similar to Beth's experience, only it is clinically structured. Patients undergo CBT when struggling with depression or other conditions, like addiction.

If a patient is thinking depressive thoughts, the situation can sometimes spiral into a full-fledged bout of depression. With CBT, a patient comes to understand that the brain is starting to connect to unwanted pathways. The patient then tries to interrupt the cascading sequence by forcing alternative thoughts and images. Such a totally artificial thinking process works only if the patient can step outside the current mental pathway and simply make the brain do something different—anything different. The key is to distract oneself in order to ride out the depressive neural groove until it passes, as at some point it will. With the spiral into depression averted, normal life can resume.[10]

The BioREG

CBT requires fairly high levels of self-awareness. During CBT-like moments, the brain becomes as an object outside the self. In my REG work, I began to develop a distance from my ego-self brain circuitry as described in the previous chapter. From an outside vantage point looking in on my own brain, I learned a version of brain probing. I could mentally poke parts of the ego self (presumably encoded in the brain) to see how they would respond—in some ways not unlike neuroscience's electrical probes. The process is not as precise, of course, but it has benefits. I found I could mentally "press a direction" onto the brain to try to influence the REG output. In other words, I used focused awareness to alter brain states, and then the brain states would affect the REG results. The striking conclusion was that both steps involve the same selection effect process: affecting one's own brain states though this probing is no different from affecting REG output. The brain can be guided or even forced into states as if it were a REG. *The brain is, in effect, a bioREG.*

The idea that brain states can be shaped by the mind is not that strange a notion.[11] It is how most of us might imagine we control our own actions. That is, when one makes the mental decision to raise an arm, the mental state is somehow impressed onto the brain, which then uses the nervous system to get the muscles moving. The scientific interpretation of that sequence is, of course, that the brain is simply affecting itself. However, science cannot rule out the possibility of causality's moving from a somewhat independent mind to brain, because we do not know the *complete* relationship. The bioREG concept is a description that fits into a reasonable schema for part of that relationship.

The bioREG concept sits alongside other theories being developed that give brain and mind some independence from each other. Most of the theories center on the concept of free will, because free will is fundamentally what is at issue. That is, if the mind is fully defined by particles bouncing around in the brain, then there can be no free will. Volition would be subsumed under the heading of physical forces that push and pull with precise and regular motions. Yet it certainly feels like we have free will when we decide to raise an arm and do so.

A favored line of thought that defends free will involves quantum uncertainty. Since quantum uncertainty is fundamental, if the brain exhibits such uncertainty, then there is room for free will. The present and future are not fully determined by the past. And to shape the next brain states, consciousness might use the opening that quantum uncertainty provides. There are tiny structures in the brain called microtubules that appear to display inherent quantum uncertainty.[12] Some theorists have made those microtubules the focal point for free will—that somehow consciousness alters their states. But others assert that any quantum effects found in microtubules are orders of magnitude too small to be of significance to actual brain states.[13] Further, no mechanism—or no reasonable one—has been proposed whereby trillions of isolated microtubules spread throughout the brain would become coordinated upward into something that functions as a whole.[14]

One of the advantages of the bioREG concept is that it does not have to coordinate all of those disparate events spread throughout the brain. Instead, the bioREG concept acts from the top down by guiding the brain toward desired future states. The selection effect is not a force mechanism, but a guiding process. Further, the bioREG concept does not depend on quantum uncertainty. Recent findings indicate that thermodynamic uncertainty can be just as fundamental as quantum uncertainty.[15] The brain—with upwards of 86 billion neurons, 100 trillion synapses, and a quadrillion or more synapse firings per second—in some ways simulates the molecular interactions of a thermodynamic system.[16] With so many events occurring, a slight variation in the timing of one firing to the other can lead to very different cascading physical states. This leaves room for the bioREG approach to the shaping of next events. Quantum uncertainty itself may play a role in this same timing process—because almost infinitesimally small selection effects on the chemical interactions within the synaptic cleft[17] may also shift the order in which neurons fire. Even the smallest of neuron-firing reorderings can be quickly amplified through complex subsequent events. And to cap it off, there appears to be an inherent random component to the exact moment of a neuron's firing, which itself might be subject to the selection effect.[18] On the whole, the bioREG concept is supported by the fact that predictions of future brain states become hopeless within a very short time frame.[19] All that is required for the bioREG model is that there be inherent uncertainty of virtually any sort, which there clearly is.[20]

Reconciliation of Mind and Matter

Most scientists today object to any separation of mind from brain (as in the earlier discussion) on fundamental grounds—grounds that trump any further discussion. The objection is called *dualism,* which states that if the mind is independent from the brain and is not of the same substance, then there is no common basis through which the two sides can interact. Oil and water do not mix. Yet clearly, mind and brain do interact, so there must be a common basis. This dualism issue forms a powerful argument for the assertion that the mind must be derived from the brain. What alternative could there be? In fact, there is one other alternative: that the brain is derived from the mind. The mind may be all there is. And although that position is radical, it may be forced on us by the REG results.

The full argument for such a proposition would be out of place here, but we will briefly explore its merits. I hope you will bear with it, as it helps explain the REG breakthrough that follows.

To begin, we note that the scientific community has changed its understanding of physical matter over the years. In the nineteenth century, matter was thought to consist of atoms as tiny, solid particles that were the smallest units in nature. In the early twentieth century, atoms were found to be constructed of yet smaller particles bound together and whirring around each other in specific ways. Thus, matter at the atomic level became a structure itself, consisting of interacting particles and mostly of empty space. Still later in the past century, Princeton physicist John Wheeler helped redefine the whole concept of structure in matter with the slogan, "it from bit." That is, all "its" of matter arise from bits of information. At the smallest, quantum level of reality, the stuff of nature is a churning soup of waves and particles perpetually coming in and out of definition. Things become fixed or solid only when particles interact with each other. So, just before two electrons bump into each other, they each exist in a cloudlike or wave state of their own separate realities. Bumping together gives them defined properties with respect to each other. They acknowledge each other's existence and properties as "things" outside themselves. The information contained in these interactions is all there is—nothing more.

We characterize electrons as having the power to "acknowledge" each other, because according to quantum mechanics, any statement made about an event must be made from a specific viewpoint. We are forced to look through the eyes of an electron to understand their interaction. Einstein, for example, took on the viewpoint of a traveling particle of light, and that exercise led to a new understanding of how light, space, and time are interconnected.

In physics, the requirement to adopt or assume a viewpoint in any interaction is called *observer-dependent reality*. No general statements about reality can be made that are not tied to a specific orientation, and it is through the interaction of the observer and the observed that the characteristics of nature are realized. To see how it works, suppose you, as observer, ask a friend, as the observed, what his favorite ice cream is. After a moment of thought, he responds, "Chocolate almond." Now, just because he answers in that way does not mean he was in a specific ice-cream state before you asked the question. He may never even have thought of the question before you posed it. So, through this interaction, you "collapsed" him into a fixed state whatever his prior thinking had been—if only in respect to you and if only for the moment. Later in the day, if someone else asks him the same question, the different context might result in a different answer. So it is with the nature of electrons, wherein their orbits and spins come in and out of definition through interactions with outside observers.

In observer-dependent reality, the observer is uncertain of what will be found in an interaction until it occurs. You didn't know how your friend would respond until you asked. That uncertainty is final; you don't know what you don't know until you do know. Of course, this sounds suspect as a general rule about reality—in the sense that just because you don't know about something, like the existence of a new planet, doesn't mean the something isn't already there. In our mind's eye, we imagine a view of the universe as a large space filled with planets and stars—including this proposed new planet—whether or not anyone knows about it. Indeed, it seems like the height of hubris and solipsism to say something comes into being "because of the way I see it." But, in fact, your creation of the image of an independent fixed universe projected from your mind's eye is itself another part of your viewpoint. You just can't get around it.

Of course, it still doesn't seem right, so we'll try to soften the blow even more. What we think of as fixed and real is so because our society includes others like us who are part of a larger agreement about what's out there. We have framed an image of the world that we collectively assert, so that even if I am unaware of parts of it, you or others might be aware. And when we find a new planet, we put that planet into a collective framework that includes the fact of its preexistence in a fixed universe with fixed properties. We lean on science as our arbiter of that truth.

But science is itself just a group viewpoint wherein we all agree about a set of common understandings. Even our vaunted mathematical theories of nature change over time. Newton saw gravity as a force. But Einstein realized that gravity is better described as a warping of spacetime under the influence of masses. And new insights today and tomorrow could change *that description*. Even more provocative, it's possible that the universe evolves based on its own interactions with itself. If that occurs, then hard-won and cherished constants of nature like the speed of light may someday be found to have changed.[21]

The final blow to our image of a universe as having fixed forms and characteristics whether or not we are aware of them comes from some of the most-advanced thinking in psychology. Cognitive scientist Donald Hoffman of the University of California, Irvine, shows that human perceptual apparatus has been fashioned solely by our evolutionary need to predict how things outside ourselves relate to us. That is, what we perceive and know of the world is defined by its relationship to our needs.[22] There are no generalized characteristics to anything in our known universe—only qualities that are relationships between our own mental apparatuses and models of what we need. As a simple example, think of how you perceive a lightly built wooden chair you intend to sit on. Now think about how a 350-pound person might perceive the same chair. That person may not see a chair at all. And if you retort that the person still sees the same physical object, the object is defined as much by what it means as how it looks. A bat (with no sight) or a cat (with a different visual color palette) will also experience the chair differently. And with regard to our earlier, hidden unknown planet, if no one is around to see it, do we think other planets that might be nearby "see" the planet the way we do?[23]

We continue along this line of reasoning: If the universe is known only through observers with different perspectives, it is fair to say that there are as many defined "universes" as there are observers to engage them. Each observer lives in its own reality of what it comes to know. Matter, then, is nothing more than the information obtained by an observer in an interaction. One might say, for example, "This is a critical *matter*." Here the term matter reduces all physical and psychological considerations to a common base of information. I myself am often heard responding to a new piece of data by saying, "Solid." Is that solidity physical or psychological—or both?

In quantum physics, the process through which observers gain knowledge about a quantum event has always been a sticking point. Raw physical information, when it is experienced by an observer, causes the observer to become *informed*. That moment highlights the yawning chasm between mind and matter as the two come face to face and miraculously manage to interact, in some sense defying dualism. Many quantum physicists have pondered and wrestled with that moment and that chasm in an attempt to understand this juncture.[24] What does it mean for one part of nature to become informed by another part of nature? One of the most penetrating thinkers (again) in this regard was John Wheeler, who developed the model of the quantum measurement process as a loop between two polar elements. One element is physics—or the matter side of the interaction, and the other element is the observer—who becomes informed in what Wheeler called the *meaning* side.[25] This framing of the issue asks how this loop of engagement is possible at all. Wheeler never succeeded in understanding the role and nature of meaning to his own satisfaction, writing: "That forward step has yet to be taken in the realm of meaning. Until it is, we will not have grasped the why of the quantum." He continued, "No model for such an [observer/observed] loop is available for us today except of information-theoretic character, the model of existence as a meaning circuit."[26]

Theoretical Physicist David Bohm, who worked closely with Einstein in the 1940s, also pondered the role of meaning in this quantum loop. He came to believe in an even deeper role for meaning. He stated, "Mind and matter are inseparable, in the sense that everything is permeated with meaning."[27]

In fact, we have laid the groundwork for the centrality of meaning in the mind/matter issue here, because we are not starting with matter and requiring it to miraculously transform into mind. Rather, we will use the tools we have already developed to *dissolve* the chasm. An observer is envisioned here as a web of associations, as discussed in chapter 8 and stylized in figure 8.2. Each electron, then, is *not* physical matter as we historically think of it, but is another small web of associations or meaning. When the electron encounters another electron, the two webs engage and interact in some fashion. In other words, these tiny observers have some level of sentience or subjective experience, however small. Therefore, it can be argued (as I do here) that some level of sentience and meaning exists at all levels of nature's observers. Furthermore, all the observed quantities in nature are themselves observers looking back at other observers. Reality consists fully and completely in the experience of meaning. Wheeler pictured nature as the image of a giant eyeball emerging from the physical universe and looking back on itself.[28]

The idea that everything in nature has a subjective experiencing component to it is called *panpsychism*. While explored in the early part of the Enlightenment, theories of panpsychism were gradually discredited by a growing conviction that all of nature (even humanity) is mechanical.

Subsequently, many aspects of this mechanical model were refuted by the implications of quantum mechanics, but these implications have been largely ignored. The concept here, however, supports the strongest form of panpsychism. That is, rather than matter's having a subjective component along with other properties such as mass and charge, in this concept there is no matter at all. Webs of association are all that is—and they are meaning itself. As Bohm put it, "If the electron were determined by a meaning, that would be its being." And in his stating, "while the degree of consciousness in the atomic world is very low, at least of self-consciousness," he implies that some level of consciousness is in fact there.[29]

The basic philosophical objection to this notion of sentience at all levels of nature is often raised through the example of a rock. How can we possibly construe a rock to be sentient—let alone to consist of nothing but meaning? The answer, at least here, is that a rock is not a sentient observer. The rock is not a web of associations that forms a singular integrated observer. Rather, it is a collection of trillions of molecular or quantum observers that are loosely linked by encountering one another. By way of comparison, when you are in a large crowd of people, there is no expectation that the group thinks as one. So, the many interactions that comprise the rock display average behaviors to the outside that are the characteristics we see, including its solidity and stability.

The idea of webs of meaning works for simple, electron-size observers and for complex, human-size ones as well. But there is a vast expanse between the two that has not been addressed. Humans had to somehow climb the ladder from the quantum level to our own level. That ladder is, of course, described by biology. Through biological evolution, reality layered itself all the way from quantum-level interactions to our own social world. The gap is filled by applying a new and central concept of the meaning-action pair.

Meaning-Action Pairs

When a web of association or meaning (like you or me), observes something outside itself, all it knows about this outside something is how the outside something behaves or acts. And though an observer might make additional inferences about the observed something, such as, say, the meaning of a strong handshake, the inferences are themselves part of the observer's own internal web. On the whole, then, what the observer observes outside itself is simply action. And any given occasion of such action can be called a unit of action. What observers observe are *units of action*.

Having given this "technical" definition to the observed, we need a similar definition for the observer. For the observer, we've been using the terms *web of associations* and *web of meaning*. In previous chapters, when the focus was on a relevant or active part of a web, the actor or agent was called a unit of meaning. So, here we will adopt that term as the more formal designation for an observer. Observers are *units of meaning*.

We can now reframe the old dualism of mind and matter with a new phrase: units of meaning experiencing units of action. In any given instance of an observation, the observer and the observed form a meaning-action pair, or MAP. Figure 12.1 shows two meaning-action pairs, in this case with two electrons. In the figure, we must take the observer perspective of each of electron A or electron B.[30] For each of them, the other electron forms a unit of action. Mind-matter dualism is eliminated because everything explicitly starts and ends with the observer side or meaning side of the MAP. A unit of action is not inert matter but is another observer that may or may not be looking back.[31]

In the interaction, each electron says to itself (these are very self-aware electrons), "I am meaning to myself, and I see action outside me." Rather than being matter, the electrons are each webs of meaning whose qualities include the properties of three physical dimensions, mass, and charge. And the properties can be shared among similar webs. In effect, those properties are known—and indeed exist—only through web-based interactions. Further, this framework changes the very idea of space. Physical space becomes just another quality—one that all observer units (in this case, electrons) happen to share and by which they interact. But what's

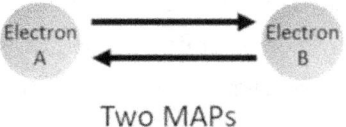

Two MAPs

FIGURE 12.1. Two electrons interacting to create two MAPs—one from each perspective.

more foundational to all qualities is a new concept of space inherent in a web concept called *associative space*. Associative space is a simple concept. It is created when you close your eyes and think of, say, a dog and a cat. Associations must have some way to spread out, to be differentiated one from another. A dog and a cat are concepts linked in associative space by differences in key qualities, such as size and behavior. Ever-more-complex associations build up into a highly complex associative space that becomes (effectively) an almost infinite dimensional space of qualities. This is not fanciful; the fields of mathematics and physics are thoroughly comfortable with and regularly use such higher-dimensional spaces.[32]

With reality defined as the interaction of observers through common qualities, we can now have a basis for intersubjective space. Intersubjective space is another term for associative space—during an encounter between an observer and an observed. When two independent associative webs come into contact with each other, they can share some associations. The sharing enables independent webs to merge or overlap—at least in some small way—into a single web. And the process ends up with larger webs that build reality toward more-complex states. Evolution into ever-more-complex units of meaning chronicles that process. Figure 12.2 reimagines the two electrons as mutually interacting in the intersubjective space based on their common qualities. Through interaction they can function as a single larger meaning unit—a new entity capable of forming meaning-action pairs with other outside entities.

In quantum physics, such interaction can result in what is called *quantum entanglement*. Through entanglement, two electrons can become inextricably connected—at least in some measure and for some period of time. Atoms can have entangled electrons, and molecules can have entangled atoms. Over time, larger units of meaning can build from complex organic molecules that sit at the base of biological evolution. And whereas quantum entanglement is generally considered to dissipate at layers larger than the molecular level, this may not be correct based on some more-recent theoretical research.[33] And in any event, whatever forces bind matter together at larger biological layers, the interactions are nevertheless considered here to be built as meaning-action pairs.

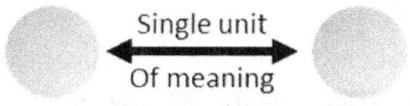

Intersubjective Space

FIGURE 12.2. Two electrons losing individual identities and forming a single entangled unit of meaning in intersubjective space.

At some stage in the development of nature's complexity, consciousness emerges as identifiable. That is, a consciousness must reach a certain level of sophistication before another, higher consciousness can recognize it as such. We can't grasp or imagine the consciousness of an ant. Further, the rise of such complex webs involves more than just a greater number of associations. As MAPs of biology build upward into larger units, they also remain as their original layers of smaller MAP units. For example, the MAPs that bind atoms together (the proton, neutron, and electron interactions) remain intact as they form the larger MAPs of molecules. The cells of the body function on their own to keep themselves intact, but they also act in concert with other cells, with which they cluster to form organs. And organs work together to build whole body systems like the nervous or limbic system. We can look at brain structure as well. The brain is built from neurons that form clusters that form subregions that form regions that form hemispheres that form the whole brain. The body is built from layers of meaning-action pairs at many levels.

To analogize the way in which layers interconnect as MAPs, we can think of an organism as a corporation. The CEO is the top-level agent. The CEO is to himself a unit of meaning, while the division heads are his units of action. Thus, the CEO forms a meaning-action pair with each division head. The division heads are to themselves units of meaning, with department heads as their units of action. Department heads are to themselves units of meaning, with managers as their units of action. And so forth. It isn't turtles all the way down—as the old expression goes—but MAPs all the way down!

One final analogy. A skyscraper under construction can be likened to the evolutionary process. Workers full of meaning cluster all over the skyscraper, building it upward story by story. Each new layer of meaning (design and construction) becomes a unit of action for the next layer to be built on top of it. Similarly, the brain is built layer by layer by the contributed change of untold generations through evolution. So, whereas science holds that the mutations of evolution are random and fully a process of trial and error, the process may not be as blind as we've thought. Generations of parents (the construction workers of the skyscraper) may have helped guide evolution by helping select into being desirable future DNA mutations to aid in adaptation. The bioREG concept suggests that units of meaning can bootstrap themselves to more-sophisticated states by altering the course of their own action sides. If true, then the selection effect becomes a natural part of self-directed evolution at both the individual and species levels.[34]

Higher-Order Meaning-Action Pairs

The development of the connected self was my way of adding another story onto the skyscraper of my mind. From this new position, I look down at the ego self as if it forms another person. Thus, the ego self becomes an outside unit of action. That unit of action, however, is not physical, but another part of me. I interact with the ego self from this position and even force changes in it. The process gives me firsthand experience that units of action need not be material or physical.

Extending the skyscraper analogy upward, society uses this same two-step process of building something and then separating from it in order to add a next layer on top. It is more than just physical stuff that gets layered; meaning is infused in those layers. Inventions are good examples of the process. An invention, such as a motor, already includes both meaning and action, and is itself a meaning-action pair. The meaning side involves the design and function bestowed by the inventors, as well as an action side in the form of the physical stuff that makes up the motor and how it behaves. But over time, new inventors revisit the motor and add new meaning. They might find better ways to build it by adding new, abstract thinking on top of what exists. They might also insert the motor into a different, larger device like a refrigerator. In that sense, the motor as a whole becomes the action side for the larger or new concept. And the process iterates over and over to build ever-more-complex and abstract layers of culture and society.

Austrian-British philosopher of science Sir Karl Popper went through that same analysis using his own terms. He called the progressive layering of abstractions in culture *World 3;* World 1 is the realm of physical things, and World 2 is the realm of neurological correlates to conscious experience. Popper was not a religious man but came to believe in effect that the world shimmers with layers of abstract form that culture builds over time. And he maintained that the World 3 layers of abstraction are in some way very real.[35] His confidence in that assertion came from the fact that our creations in World 3 become more than what we put into them. Once created, they feed back to us new and novel applications. They don't quite take on lives of their own, but they are nevertheless "out there"—similar to the reality of physical objects that populate World 1.[36]

British physicist Sir James Jeans captured the sense of that increasing complexity and abstraction in his famous statement, "The stream of knowledge is heading towards a non-mechanical reality; the Universe begins to look more like a great thought than like a great machine. Mind no longer appears to be an accidental intruder into the realm of matter... we ought rather hail it as the creator and governor of the realm of matter."[37]

※ ※ ※

My own REG experience continued into higher levels of abstraction and wider layers of self-reflectivity. And like culture, I seemed to be building new layers onto myself. The scope of who I was seemed to expand both outward and upward. That course of events was not planned and was never a focus or goal of my project. My goal was always to find better ways to influence and direct REG output. In the service of that goal, I remained focused, with my head down, so to speak, always looking back at my previous states of mind. Looking below me, I walked myself up a staircase, transfixed by what was happening with the REG output. And because of that single-mindedness, I was not paying attention to where I was going. I just assumed it would be the right direction, whatever that was. But whenever I did look around me, I found myself in new territory. The world around me was different; I was inadvertently walking my consciousness into a more rarefied and subtle sense of intersubjective space—a space that began to shimmer like

Popper's World 3. It was both ephemeral and palpably real, and the domain that emerged was filled with ghostly—or at least semitransparent—possible futures that I came to call *alternative reality*.

CHAPTER 13:
ALTERNATIVE REALITY

A lbert Einstein spent the last 20 years of his life working at the Institute for Advanced Study in Princeton. Each morning he walked up Mercer Street toward town and then down Alexander Street to get his morning paper at the local railroad station where the "Dinky" railroad line stopped. Both streets were lined with upright Charles Steadman–style white frame houses and manicured green hedges along their sidewalks and walkways. The children playing nearby would run up to him and say, "Good morning, Dr. Einstein."[1]

It was in a book in the library of my junior high school that I read that scene about Einstein's life. For some reason, it made an indelible impression on me. I imagined the kids in a bucolic 1950s setting looking up at the usually disheveled Einstein, beaming wide-eyed at him. It was pure Norman Rockwell. Years later, as a college freshman, I was walking outside the campus grounds when I had an eerie, déjà-vu experience. Looking around, it took me a moment, but I realized: this was the setting described in the book I'd read in seventh grade. It was not *like* the setting; it *was* the setting.

The experience was strange. I was clearly awake in real time but also transported back to the earlier time of reading the book. And further, I was living the imagined scene of Einstein in front of me, with a stooped Einstein and the kids running up to him. I felt tapped into all three realities at once.

That strange splitting of reality left as fleetingly as it had come and did not strike me again until one day when I was playing the REG game. The session had begun simply enough—by my using a strategy of imagining that the next result would be a green result. What I did was to fill myself with green, become green, and then hit the space bar to fire a trial. Sometimes, as in this case, I use this type of strategy after already having hit, say, four greens in a row. At that point, the screen will show a green square with the number 4 inside it, as shown in figure 13.1. At that point, I shift strategies and attempt to slowly and deliberately run the result up to ten in a row. Because ten in a row is unusual, if I get there I feel as if I've had a strong hand in the result.

FIGURE 13.1. Square showing a current run of four hits.

One day I had had four hits in a row when I decided to run it up to 10. I sat for a while as usual, filling myself with the idea of green. But as I stared at the screen, something totally unexpected happened. I began to experience a second reality superimposed on the first. The normal reality was clearly in front of me: solid and showing the green square. But there emerged in my mind's eye another reality that was less solid yet nonetheless very real. It seemed to sit below the surface, hovering in a transparency. In my mind's eye, I saw the number 5 in its own green square rising upward from the murky depths. It reminded me of the Magic 8 Ball when an answer rises into view from the blackness below.

I waited for a while before firing the next trial. I was enthralled by the dual reality, seeing both the current 4 and the future 5 at the same time. It seemed to be much more than imagination but without explanation. More than anything, however, it felt like a window into unstated questions I had about the nature of reality. I finally pressed the space bar to see what would happen. The 4 disappeared, and the ghostly 5 crystallized into the new, solid reality. I now had five in a row.

I focused on this unusual feeling to see whether it would remain with me. It did. This time I felt—or saw—or made—the number 6 rise up from the depths and superimpose itself on the number 5. Quizzically, I pressed the space bar, and the number 6 appeared, taking the place of the 5.

Although I was more than a little intrigued, on another level it seemed like part of reality that can be there if one wants it to be but not normally attended to. So, at that moment, I just stayed tuned in, letting it be what it was. The 7 rose up, and I pressed the space bar to solidify it into reality. At that point, subsequent numbers simply rose up without much attention or effort, though I knew I was somehow responsible for them. The 8 appeared, and the space bar made it real. Then 9. Then 10. Then 11. Then 12. As it continued, I had begun to step outside the experience and run an inner dialogue, saying, "This just keeps going. How does this process ever end? Can I live with what is happening? How can I live with knowing that this kind of reality exists?" As I talked my way out of the experience, I finally missed on (unlucky) 13.

※ ※ ※

Because of my work and interest in mind over matter, people often open up to me with stories of their encounters with alternative or nonordinary realities. A family friend once told me about an experience while cleaning up in her kitchen late one night. She suddenly had the sense of being visited by her uncle. She had been estranged from him, and they'd not spoken in years. But he came to her visually in an alternative-reality sense, and they had a conversation in which he apologized for certain past behavior, asking her whether she thought he had really acted that badly. When my friend replied that he had, he still beamed with radiant joy, shrugging his shoulders to indicate, "Well, whatever." Then he said he had to leave. She learned the next day that he had died that night.

Maybe, as the man neared death, he became able to reach into intersubjective space and connect with his niece. And although it is *not* the point here to validate everyone's strange paranormal moments, strange experiences can seem natural at some level when they happen. In the spoon-bending party described in chapter 2, it was the natural way with which the man in front of me engaged alternative reality that seemed to enable him to bend spoons so easily. Such events seem like openings to more-fluid spaces below the surfaces of normal events.

My family friend did not readily tell others about the incident with her uncle because talking about such things seems incongruous to events in the normal physical world. Such alternative-reality events seem more like dreams and don't fit reality as we know it. Further, the jarring and dismissive way others might react cautions one to remain quiet. But there seem to be a lot of us walking around with our own stories of various encounters with parts of alternate realities that we hold privately and close to our hearts.

My REG project was not undertaken in order to deal with such anecdotal, fleeting, and unusual incidents. I had planned to produce only laboratory-grade data that could be validated and repeated—and understood. However, the experience of alternative reality knocked me out of a certain sense of complacency. And though the events did fit squarely into my schema of life as mostly *models* punctuated with occasional striking *moments,* I never expected that any moments would be this strange.

※ ※ ※

My next attempt at encountering alternative reality bears some additional explanation. The experience just described occurred recently as I write here. And because of how vivid it was, it remains fresh in my mind. But also because of that vividness, I have not tried to bring it on again because it takes me to some edge of self that is unnerving. And in that way, the story intersects with the present. I do not know what will happen with this alternative reality or what I will be writing about next. In fact, with regard to the entire success or failure of the project as a whole, I am as much in the dark as you, the reader. (And if you read ahead, don't tell me how it ends.)

Reaching my goal of million-to-one odds is very different in this present moment from when it's looked at retrospectively. That is, at this moment, I have only one chance of success. I can't play the game or the project multiple times. This is very significant from a scientific perspective. That is, outside observers reading this after the fact might say that if I did in fact succeed, it was because a million other people also tried a similar project and planned to write about it. They all failed, and so their books were never finished or published. The one guy who happened to succeed writes about it and attributes all kinds of meaning to it—like lottery winners who after the fact tell how they "made it happen."

Realistically, of course, there are not a million people engaged in a similar project such that one of us is bound to succeed by chance. So, I do not feel like a number in a vast statistical sea. I am literally one person out of one. I have one chance at success—*and I don't want to be a failed attempt consigned to the dustbin*. But let's be fair: if I'm dealing with only a chance process, then by all rights I will not succeed, and the results will support the null hypothesis, which says there is no selection effect. However, I will already hedge my bets here. Although I may or may not completely succeed, my results so far do not resemble chance. I continue as a kind of one-man REG reality TV show or maybe a reality book being played out publicly. And just to note: while the present is now, I will continue writing in the past tense because writing is always about earlier events—even if they happened only moments ago.

※ ※ ※

After writing the above, I set up the game and challenged myself to find this alternative reality again. Writing about that strange experience got me reengaged with it. And describing it didn't seem quite as eerie.

I started a new session, and so no green or red square was already on the screen. I began to envision the underlying reality of the green square below the surface reality by imagining a green 1 rising to the surface. After some time, the image began to appear, though perhaps not as powerfully as the first time. I think part of me still wanted to run away. I pressed the space bar and got the 1. I got the 2, the 3, and the 4. I knew that I had it, but again, not quite as cleanly and effortlessly as the first time. I kept bouncing out of *being it* on one hand and *noting it* on the other.

I stopped after those four greens because at that point, I just *knew* I would miss the next one. After thousands of hours, I know when I'm losing my edge, or my *moment*. Getting five in a row, which is the prospect I now faced, crosses a boundary of significance. That is, to get five out of five—in the intended direction—has odds of one in 32, which is beyond the nominal significance level of one in 20. (Note that four out of four, where I was currently sitting, gives odds of one in 16.) To reengage with this process after months of self-instruction and achieve my first five out of five would be a personal victory. It would be another confirmation that I'm dealing with a real phenomenon—and personally making progress with it.

I returned to the game to continue. I wanted just one more green result, and I would stop. As I sat, each time I felt I had a fix on the alternative reality—like the viewfinder of my weapon system locking in on the target—I stopped myself just as I was about to press the space bar. Each time I was about to press it, my mind blanked out over the fear of seeing a miss.

I decided instead to go for a walk and cool out before continuing. In fact, a major value of such critical project moments is not the score but the state of mind it puts me into. I confront parts of myself that I never would have confronted otherwise. So, I stay with the feeling and explore it. I decided to keep with the feeling as I walked down to the coffee shop in the Princeton Shopping Center to get some coffee.

On my walk, I tried to maintain that sense of the alternative reality but kept getting caught up in the significance of what I was trying to do. The nagging importance of it wouldn't let go. In fact, I didn't see how I would ever lighten up, because it is a self-perpetuating feeling. Every time I got close to letting go of the fear, it shouted out to me: "But look what might happen!" I might fail, and that would be it; it would all be over.

As I sat sipping my coffee, I began to see how I was wrapped in my ego self, obsessed over my project and my success. But ultimately, it isn't about me; if this alternative reality is real, then it will speak for itself. That thought enabled me to shift my viewpoint to the connected self. As I let myself adopt that more elevated viewpoint, my energy level increased a bit (the coffee?), and I could feel myself separating from the fears of the ego self. The issue was no longer my grand plan for personal success but the meaningfulness of what I was trying to do for society.

In that heightened frame of mind, I looked around me at the people chatting and going about their day-to-day routines, and I marveled at the crazy world all of us are in. Things are not all they seem on the surface. I was again engaged in the two realities: the solid, physical one and this shimmering, alternate one. I noted that the connected self prefers to be in the alternative reality, with its waves of fluid futures. I felt alien and out of place sitting there, with normal life going on around me. It reminded me of Carlos Castaneda's accounts of how his mentor Don Juan would weave his way comfortably between normal and nonordinary facets of Mexican society.

My coffee break was ostensibly about preparing to fire the fifth REG trial. But it became more than that; it became a way forward. I had waited another 20 months since the previous trials of Study 4. And it was clear that my alliance with my connected self was the answer. The ego self would surely fail. So, I would force myself to stay as long as possible in the connected self and grow in it. The ego self would put up a fight, to be sure, but I knew what I had to do.

As I walked back to the office, I decided to end the current session as it stood—with the four hits. And instead, I would start a new session that would begin the final trials of the project. I felt ready. That fresh start would also help me diffuse the significance of the next trial I had been obsessing over for the past hour. In ending the current REG session, I would make the next trial part of a different unit of meaning. The next trial would be part of my final study more than it would be a continuation of my most-recent four trials. But of course, it would be both. I still needed to get that fifth trial, but now it was slightly cut loose from the significance I had attached to it.

I set up the directory for the final study trials and stared at the new session screen, ready to start. I kept envisioning the appearance of green, and I practiced pressing the key to fire the trial and make sure I didn't mentally pull back just as I pressed the key. I sat doing that for at least 15 minutes, during which I was inventorying my mental regulators, matching their action, having them get around me, and then matching them again. The longer I waited, the more significant it all became, but I could even see that occurring. I moved to get behind the state of mind—externalizing and encapsulating it—and successfully defused its hold.

And at this point, I should note that my chances of success on this one trial were not 50/50, as one might think. I have come to know that *I am fully responsible* for the next result. If my psyche is in the right place, I win. But if it is in *any other place,* I lose. There is a narrow path to success—like walking a hundred stories in the air along the I beam of a skyscraper under construction: one way to succeed—and many ways to fail.

Finally, I felt imbued with green and ready. I even felt ready to face failure should it occur. I was bigger than the event yet allowing myself to be part of it, to face its judgment of me at that moment. I envisioned the wider self and the world connected together and the purposes for which I was engaging in this process. I pressed the key. Got it!

CHAPTER 14:
THE HOME STRETCH

I shouted "Yes!" and raised my fists in triumph. And with that first new trial, I began my final push to the end. I sat back to take in the moment and declare a small victory. I had passed the test. I knew with certainty that the result was not chance. There were no proverbial file drawers with 31 other failed moments that went unreported. Now it was time to take the hill.[1]

To help me get in the groove, I set up an additional separate category of trials called *warm-up*. Warm-up would allow me to feel freer and loosen up without the pressure of real data. However, literally the moment I started with warm-up, it became clear that I could do much better in the warm-up category than in the one that counted—exactly because it didn't count. So, I decided to see if I could trick my subconscious by including that data in the real experiment. Sometimes the subconscious can be fooled that way, even though it knows better. Like taking a sugar pill you know has no power but makes you feel better anyway. It doesn't usually work for long, but nevertheless I decided to include any future warm-up results in the study (excluding the trials that had already been run). Unfortunately, given the high stakes, my subconscious was not fooled for a second. The next trials were negative, and I kicked myself for thinking this might work. Nevertheless, I had made the decision to include them, so what was done was done. I had to include the negative data—as well as any future results from either category of trials.

Over time, I used many strategies, but as it turned out, not so much the alternate-reality strategy, which was just too slow—and unreliable when used so deliberately. I couldn't keep the cats of my deeper mind herded and walking in the same direction. It may in fact be that trying to impose too much "actuality" onto the fluidity of alternative reality impedes its fluidity. But I did use it successfully for a few trials on numerous occasions, and whenever I did, I was once again amazed at the window into the world that it presents.

I continued using my tested strategy of self-awareness, which let me back up layer by layer each time I saw the mental regulator about to grab me. I tried as much as possible to avoid posing. And because I couldn't avoid disrupter bits, I had to give them space to play out. That felt like reeling in a fish, when sometimes one must let out some of the line in order to make headway. There were times when my score went negative, as when the mental regulator got behind my level of awareness. I would stop and inventory my mind to figure out what my subconscious was doing and get back on track.

The high-stakes aspect of the remaining trials left no room for large dropouts. That raised the internal significance level. And as I methodically gained on the target, the heightened state invoked what I've referred to as *layer 6,* or the *personality layer.* I could even feel elements of layer 7 social expectations, which are perhaps always pressing on us but rarely noticed. During that period, I could also see clearly how my surface-level intention has very little power to affect REG output. Rather, in order to succeed, I had to access my deep purposes for the whole project. The mental regulator was ratcheting up its resistance to my success, so I had to ratchet up my reasons for succeeding. I felt like the mother who lifts the car off her pinned child because she must: I had no choice in the matter; there were not enough trials left to risk letting my attention wander. Each time I found a wave of inner purpose, the REG results turned in my favor—and I felt changed.

After six weeks, I stopped to tally my results, thinking that I'd done enough trials. But a cursory tabulation showed I was still about 9,000 trials short of completion. The good news was that I seemed far ahead of the pace needed to win. At that moment, in fact, my score had me at odds well over a million to one for the entire study. But I wasn't at the end. I could still drop back. And knowing there were still 9,000 trials left to go rattled me terribly; I could easily rubber-band and blow it. And because it wouldn't be a good idea to continue while so out of kilter, I decided to take a break and do some research housekeeping.

Control Data

I planned to run a final control on my REG—standard protocol that would confirm it was working properly when no one was attending to it. However, the concept of a control becomes interesting in that it is impossible for me to not attend to it when I know it is running—kind of like, "Don't think of an elephant." I could have someone else run the control, but even so, I will see the results, and that could have an impact. In fact, giving the task to someone else would create the sense of my having lost control, and that alone might send the control itself into a rubber band.

I ran the control, setting the system on autopilot and focusing on other work. In that way, I generated 20 sets of 50,000 trials each. Upon review, half of the 20 sets ended with positive scores and half with negative scores. The overall result was not significant, though mildly in the positive direction (a Z score of about 1). And though that was well within spec, I would've been more comfortable had the overall result ended up closer to zero or even been negative. So, I decided to run a second control in which I'm specifically *trying* to keep the output at zero. From the standpoint of mainstream science there should be no problem with that, because according to the null hypothesis (there is no effect of the mind at all), it wouldn't matter what I did or didn't do. So, even though this is not a control run in the strict sense of my being absent, my attempt to keep the results at the baseline is just a more active version of *expecting* the result to wander around zero, as the device would normally behave. My active focus would simply help me control the fear that it might not be working right, which could become self-fulfilling. If that twisted logic is a bit hard to follow, just remember that the mind plays many internal games. The bottom line is that none of my complex thinking about what I was doing should affect the output if there is indeed no selection effect anyway!

I could not run a million trials while being engaged because it would take too long and require too much effort. But I could run 75,000 trials to match the number of trials I'd done since restarting the project. I could let them zip

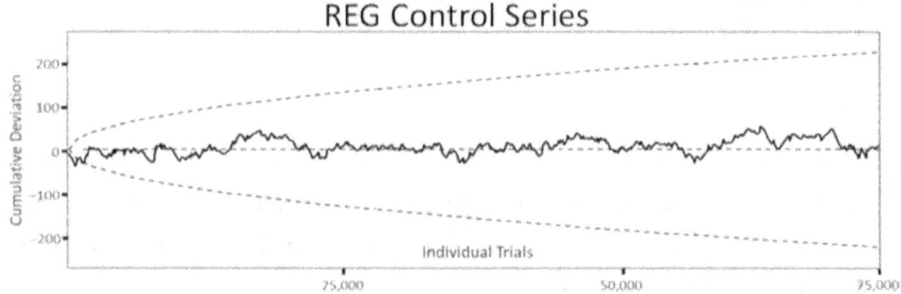

FIGURE 14.1. Random-walk chart of a REG control data set, but where I also attempted to mentally hold the results to the center line.

by at a fairly fast pace and just try to keep them as close to zero as possible. Figure 14.1 gives the result of that control session.

It looked good to me—supernormal, in fact. With that added sense of confidence, I stopped fearing the control runs and ran another set of 1 million unattended trials, with 20 more sets of 50,000 trials each. This time the Z score ended at close to −1 and brought the combined 2 million trials very close to zero.

❋ ❋ ❋

I had big plans to finish strong. I was almost finished writing this book, or so I thought at the time (there was no part IV), so I needed to wrap it up. But I was still feeling rattled about continuing, so I did not restart right away.

A couple of weeks later, before I was ready to begin again, I received an e-mail from John Valentino. By that time, John was married and living in Palo Alto, California, and working at a high-profile management consulting firm that kept him busy full-time. In the e-mail, John said he would be briefly on the East Coast at his parents' home in Philadelphia and might be able to meet me in Princeton before he flew out. I was happy to get together, but I knew we would talk about the book and the state of the project. I vividly recalled how I had bragged about my newfound mastery of the REG that had led to a massive rubber band. Therefore, I decided I had no choice but to try to preempt that possibility and finish the last trials before we met.

Later that day, I decided I would indeed begin again. In my first session, my score initially rose, but then the doubts came. And the score dipped well below zero. Typically, when I'm down, I feel that I want to climb back to a good score before stopping. But now I was burning up trials and didn't want to continue. But I didn't want to stop while I was still far in the negative—or, as they say, under water—during the session. Furthermore, I really hadn't planned on restarting at such short notice and so felt somewhat out of balance. That fueled the sense of not being "on." I did about 3,500 trials and was under water by about 50 misses over hits. I finally managed to pull my hands away from the keyboard.

After a few minutes of reflection, I knew I had to open myself to a more connected level, or a higher unit of meaning. Overall, things were not going the way I had envisioned—by achieving a triumphant finish. Instead of that lofty goal, I was struggling just to stay even. I thought it was humorous, though, that over the years I had kept stopping in the middle of this final study in order to regroup—like Zeno's paradox, wherein an arrow shot toward a target must always go half of the remaining distance in any unit of time before getting to the target. Thus, logic would say the arrow can never reach the target. With about 5,500 trials remaining, I was inching through ever-smaller increments to a finish line I might never allow myself to reach.

I woke up in the middle of the night before John was due to arrive in the morning. I was in a cold sweat and full of inner chatter: "What if my back-of-the-envelope calculation was wrong, and I was not up far enough to overcome the previous day's less-than-stellar results? What if I wasn't going to make it after all? What about the book? What was I going to say to John? I don't have the confidence I want to show. Maybe I should try to finish."

I should know better than to listen to my anxieties in the middle of the night. Nevertheless, I got up at 3:30 in the morning to write in my journal what was going on with me. I thought writing might help calm me. As I clacked away at the keyboard, the lure to continue and settle my concerns before meeting John was just too great. Even though I knew better—because I was hardly in the right mental frame of mind to continue—I began anyway. I started out doing well, but quickly went into a nosedive. My score plummeted to strongly negative. With my mind blanking out, I froze and couldn't pull out. How could I blow the whole thing so close to the end and after all my supposed training and all my profound blah-blah wisdoms and blah-blah insights? Finally, however, the fear of global failure at such a life level was greater than the blinding panic of the mental regulator, and I did manage to stop. I calmed down, regrouped, and started again. Once again, however, my score headed downward. Soon, a new disaster was forming, even worse than the last. Again in a panic, I managed to stop. I stepped away with less than 1,000 trials left. Why in the world had I started without really being mentally prepared? My reasoning about trying to bolster my confidence before the meeting had been horribly flawed. It was now five in the morning. I was exhausted and fell into a deep sleep.

When I awoke, the world didn't look quite so bleak. I didn't know how badly I had blown it, but I was fully prepared to face what had happened. This would not be a great Hollywood climax, for sure, but now I felt that *if I can simply make it successfully at all,* I'll be very happy. I analyzed the night's work. I was down about 80 additional misses over hits, which wasn't a complete disaster. By comparison (with something *really* bad), the rubber-band experience described at the beginning of this study 4 *after* my other meeting with John resulted in my being down 650 misses over hits. That rubber band had spanned many more trials.

Now I had only 675 trials left to complete, and the question loomed as to where I stood overall. This time, I did a full and complete data calculation of all of the existing data, adding each session end to end. The good news was that I had been so far ahead before my disastrous night that I was still on track to be well above one in a million. I checked and rechecked and concluded that statistically, I could not fail at this point. I would have to do more poorly than 34% hits on the remaining trials in order to drop below a million to one. Such a performance would require a Z score for those last trials that would be almost infinitely bad—well over 100 billion to one. So, I was faced with either succeeding at a level of million-to-one odds or failing at a level of 100-billion-to-one odds. The latter would be a rubber band even beyond my capability to shoot myself in the foot.

After all of that analysis, I sat somewhat stunned, knowing I had indeed made it. I would reach my goal. I felt ready to meet with John. I could say whatever I wanted and not worry about a rubber band. I let that sink in. It was exactly then that I received an e-mail with the subject line: "Unfortunately, I'm not going to be able to make it today."

CHAPTER 15:
THE FINISH LINE

My sixteen hours of failed judgment and poor sleep didn't matter anymore. The rest of the day, I floated above the ground. I was going to make it! After years of this mirage just hanging out in front of me, I was there. The sense of having conquered my inner demons, at least enough to succeed, was a warm glow emanating from deep inside me. I was Rocky Balboa, with arms outstretched in victory at the top of the museum steps. I was the REG Olympic Gold winner, the world champion. I had only 675 trials to go, and they sat out there like candy. I didn't have to worry about how I did; I could just savor them.

In spite of my elation, however, another part of me was let down. When the afterglow subsided, I had to face the fact that I hadn't mastered the process, as evident by this emotional roller coaster. I had produced only a small effect—not unlike so many other studies. However, in the process, I gained complete certainty that the selection effect does in fact exist. Now I was onto finding ever-more-sophisticated states of mind to enhance it. And those states would no doubt be valuable to me in their own right—that is, for applying to other aspects of life.

Having thought that, I still hadn't given up the original goal of creating a much stronger effect. I planned to finish the study as well as I could and also to keep practicing. To that end, rather than finishing the last 675 trials right away, I went back into training. I wanted to engage what I now knew of as the wider layers of mind and their deeper personal and social implications. As before, the pressure and the purpose provided the scaffolding for personal progress. I expected my last trials to show that I had clearly graduated from early training and was at least a REG Junior Jedi. So, I dug in once again—for literally, believe it or not, two more years.

* * *

In mid July 2014, after nine years of REG work and writing, I was done with this manuscript. Or again, so I thought. Either way, everyone around me was tired of hearing about it.

Still glaring at me were the 675 unfinished trials. I couldn't delay forever. Furthermore, one of my manuscript readers was so interested in the subject that he was planning his own magazine article about it. I didn't want to get scooped or be left behind. On the other hand, I had no intention of finishing until I felt ready. The problem was that such a moment might never come.

One day, I was doing some background reading the latest work by psychologist and neuroscientist Giulio Tononi on his integrated information theory. His book *Phi: A Voyage from the Brain to the Soul* is an extended fictional dialogue between Galileo and other historical and contemporary figures who teach him about the brain. Galileo starts out with objections to the implications of neuroscience—particularly neuroscience's rejection of free will. He gradually learns to see himself as a machine, that his consciousness consists simply of neurons firing in organized brain patterns. After becoming thoroughly convinced of that position, Galileo comes to grips with his own lack of a soul. There are two chapters in *Phi* in which the reader is led into a deep existential despair over the true nature of the self and reality, but the tone of the book is upbeat, noting that it really doesn't matter—because of course nothing really matters in some final sense—and one should celebrate living for its own sake and rejoice in more-limited aspects of meaning and the fact that we can experience beauty in nature.

That concept of mind as simply neurons firing is of course a prevalent theme in neuroscience. But given what I know about the REG and the selection effect, I naturally take strong exception. I skimmed the dialogue to grasp the author's arguments and point of view and watched myself become more and more upset over what I saw as a needless crushing of the human spirit. I went to my office and let loose with a sense of righteous indignation. The *should* of my own rightness looked like a good framing for finishing the last 675 trials—a kind of take-this-I'll-show-you! feeling. I would demonstrate how a meaningful state of mind defies what I was reading.

Normally, I require a little warm-up period with the REG, but I was so worked up that I told myself this is no time to be clinical about my method. So, I started off while muttering to myself in order to additionally fuel my mood. After an immediate upward surge and then backing off, I headed solidly upward. I went over significance—up to a Z score of 2. That success threw me for an moment, and I dropped back but stayed in the *should*-fueled *moment* and climbed back up. I felt my emotions cresting, so I pulled my hand from the keyboard. "Take that, Tononi," I said.

The moment was indeed satisfying, but now that driving feeling was gone. The indignation had dissipated by virtue of my success—which was premature relative to my goal of finishing the session above the significance line. When I stopped, I still had 201 trials to go. I felt a little silly, a little exposed; and my petulant mood was a little embarrassing—even to me. What do I do now? Even 201 trials done slowly, one by one, feels interminable, like watching the seconds tick on a clock.

Figure 15.1 shows the final 675 trials, with a marking of the point at which I stopped. It was Zeno's paradox again. I was another third of the way toward my target but never getting there because of the ever-smaller increments that lead forward. I should have just walked away and picked it up the next day or the next week, but as I've said many times before, even to

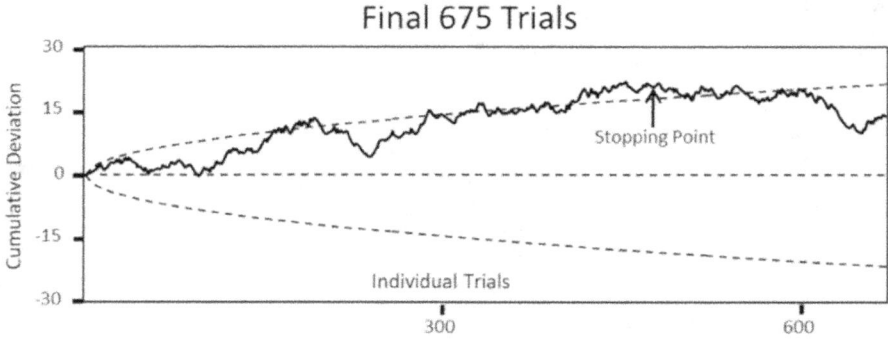

FIGURE 15.1. Random-walk chart of the final 675 trials of study 4, including the stopping point that led to an emotional shift.

the end of the project I just couldn't stop. Gambler's fallacy (neurologically speaking) strikes again.

I decided I would move slowly and deliberately to the end—as significant laden as that was. I ran a few more trials and was losing ground. I dipped below significance, and that rallied me to keep just above it. I hung at the significance line and couldn't push higher. Then I made the mistake of trying a go-for-broke strategy—a frame of mind that usually is either great (if it is pure) or disastrous (if it watches itself). I figured that if the universe wanted me to succeed with a deep enough purpose, it would keep me from watching myself too much. Bad move to play the self-importance card because it is too much oriented toward "me" rather than the value of the project. Furthermore, I had to watch myself to make sure I didn't watch myself too much.

I briefly fought with myself while trying to break out of the constraint but then doubted I could do it. Completely off-purpose at that point, I experienced a big drop. As it was happening, I pulled my hand from the keyboard. But I knew I wouldn't make it back over significance, because too few trials

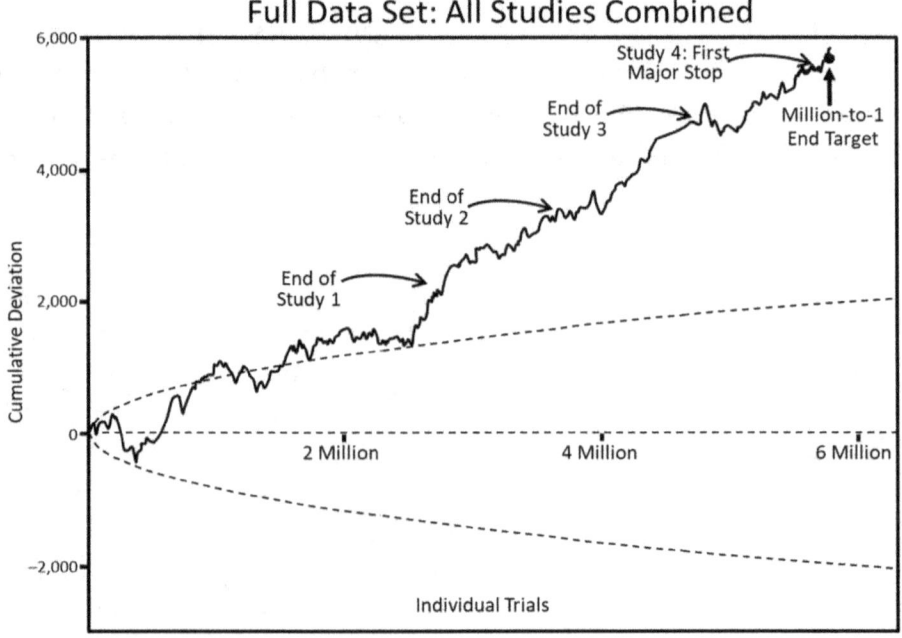

FIGURE 15.2. Random-walk chart of all four studies combined and completed, with final odds of 1.7 million to one against chance.

were left. With that, it all lightened up and I headed back up—just not fast enough to finish above the parabola.

The stats for this final group of 675 trials had a hit rate of 52.0%, so at least it was a number much better than my overall average, even if not significant by itself. The whole of study 4 ended with an overall probability of 84 to one against chance. And although that was somewhat less than each of the three previous studies, it wasn't bad, considering the extreme pressure I'd put myself under.

When I computed the whole study results, it showed odds against chance of 1.7 million to one. Figure 15.2 displays the set of the 5,755,888 trials, also noting the million-to-one target point. And so, once more with finality: *Take that, Tononi.*

CHAPTER 16:
SOME LIFE LESSONS FROM THE REG

My REG project was a solitary affair, but it holds lessons for everyone and speaks to the nature of the human condition. The following five lessons represent part of much more that can be learned by using this device and this method.

Intention and Purpose

The concept of intention often dominates discussions about the power of the mind. The general notion is that if your intention is strong enough, you can do anything—or at least a lot more than you think you can. Although I support that idea to some extent, I've found that intention plays only second position to the concepts of purpose and purposefulness. Purposefulness drives action and is the basis for mind's impact on the physical world.[1] *There is always a purpose behind intention.* For example, if you intend to go to the store, there's a reason or purpose for the trip: you need a specific item for some specific purpose. Purposes range from narrow frameworks such needing milk to incredibly wide ones such as planning for a meaningful life. Intention is the actor, but purpose forms the foundation and impetus to act. And as I found, direct intention has little effect on the REG. Intention is best focused on fostering brain states that guide and accentuate purpose and meaning. The latter is what drives the actual results.

Further, not all purposes are themselves equal, and the type of purpose matters. Recent studies have examined how people succeed in various aspects of life relative to purposes. A major distinction surrounds what are called *intrinsic motives* versus *instrumental motives*. The difference is made clear by a recent study. Newly entering West Point cadets (amounting to 11,320 cadets over the course of nine entering classes) were asked why they'd entered the academy—that is, what purpose or motive was driving them. One response, "the desire to get a good job later," was called an *instrumental motive* because it used the current relationship to the military and schooling as a tool for something unrelated. In contrast, the response "the desire to be trained as a leader in the US Army," was considered an *intrinsic* or *inner motive* because that purpose was intrinsic to the act of being at that institution. What the researchers found is that *the stronger the intrinsic motives, the more likely the cadets would graduate.*[2]

In summary, the selection effect does not work best as a detached or instrumental tool of intent. It works best when there is an intrinsic motive and reason for it. For me, that intrinsic motive has been to reframe my relationship to my mind, my self, and my understanding of the world. Intent still has an important role to play, but it becomes a specific tool. I use intent to look inward in order to explore myself—in part to unearth my deeper purposes. In general, one tries to align the deeper parts of the self with a greater sense of purpose and meaningfulness. With training, one can create that stronger inner alignment and use it to give more power to one's purposes in making changes in the outside world.[3]

Courage and Vulnerability

During the project, I had a REG session in which I set a difficult Z-score target for myself. I steadily climbed toward the score until I was one green hit away from reaching the target. I stopped for a moment. I know I have to stop, because the nervousness of getting that last hit or two will *always* kick off a rubber band. So, I took a moment to collect myself, rebalance, and prepare to continue. Once I stop in this way—if I can allow myself to—I can almost always succeed. But this present case was different. The target had been so significant from the outset and I was so "on" in getting right to the edge of it that *I could not accept what was happening.* I sat there staring at the screen and realized that I really *did not want to get to the target.* I just couldn't handle it emotionally, and so I sat there, with a kind of paralysis of mind. I felt a deep fear of success that seemed completely justified and rational at the time. The fear was that I wouldn't be able to pretend to struggle with my project anymore. That is, I was in the middle of a long research project, and to succeed in this way was too easy. It kind of begged the question of why I was making such a big deal out of all of this. I thought, if there is really nothing to success here except attitude, then what have I been doing for so long? I shuddered inside at such confusion. Giving in to the feelings, I let myself embrace the rubber-band sense of pulling back, and I held down the space bar. The score went right back to zero "as it *should*." I simply didn't have the courage to change my *model* of myself—who I thought I was and what I was doing.

A few minutes later, I followed with another session, wherein the exact same thing happened. I rocketed to within one hit of a difficult target and stopped. Again, I made the decision that it was just too much. And again, I let the sense of the rubber band take over and I plummeted back to zero.

I could have beaten myself up over my lack of inner strength or personal character, but at the time, I justified my decisions on the grounds that I was "doing research" and that monitoring my reactions and their impact on the data was more important than my success. That is true to some extent. The pronounced rubber-band failure was something I understood and could describe. In contrast, to succeed would render me speechless, with literally nothing to say about it. In any event, I know now that it takes courage to succeed beyond certain bounds. And in the sessions above, I didn't have that courage. I felt exposed and vulnerable, with a very real sense of impending loss of identity. There was a lightheaded, free-floating sense to it.

Once again, this situation is a contest of purposes. My conscious purpose was not strong enough to overcome my subconscious purpose of keeping my current boundaries of self. If I had let go to the vulnerability and allowed myself to feel my real passion to change, then I would have gained the last REG hits. Thus, this process can help train both vulnerability and unyielding purpose, and I have begun to use it in that way. Training can become profound as one begins to deal with the deeper aspects of self.

Empathy and Caring

This book's introduction began with the story about the Colorado study, wherein empathy and caring seemed to drive an extraordinary result. The nature of empathy can be misunderstood, however. I believe that a full understanding of it is necessary if humanity is to unlock the potential that resides in the selection effect.

In its purest form, empathy is neither sympathy nor compassion nor caring, as is often thought. It is, at least as I have come to know it, the ability to transfer one's consciousness to an outside viewpoint. It is the ability to look through someone else's eyes or to walk a mile in someone else's shoes, as the saying goes. It is to *actively* experience what someone else is experiencing. For example, empathy might enable a chess player to look at the game from the opponent's point of view and realize what the opponent is up to. Or there's a story about trappers who came across evidence that the wolf they were seeking had been in a location recently. By looking closely at the site, the trappers attempted to take on the mind of the wolf in order to divine where it had headed next. In both of those examples, empathy is not to the benefit of the objects involved. Empathy is an ability that can be used in a variety of ways.

The extended part of this message is that empathy is more than merely reproducing someone else's thought process in your own head. Rather, empathy would seem to involve the momentary sharing of a single reality among multiple parties—at least to some degree. One party locks onto the feelings of the other and shares some of the threads of the other party's web of meaning. The two parties' webs then partially overlap (as intersubjective space). As noted earlier, a good doctor, psychotherapist, or neurosurgeon is one who can empathize well enough to actually feel the deeper state of the patient or client.

That said, caring and compassion seem to be emotional states that most readily evoke empathy. One's heart goes out to another in love, caring, and consolation such that there is a level of active merging. The purposefulness behind such use of empathy makes it potent, as would seem to be the case with the Colorado experiment. The experimenters' minds formed a larger web with the REG and its output.

Oddly, I first began to experience empathy in the REG setting by turning it on myself. As I learned to see the world through my connected self, I could look "back" on my ego self. From that position, I could empathize with the ego self's sense of failure regarding the REG. The connected self grasped the ego self's fear, frustration, and despair. And because I could revert to the ego self (even simultaneously), I could check to see how well I seemed to empathize by virtue of the presence and support felt by the ego self. And as the experience of shifting between viewpoints occurred more often, it gradually loosened the grip of the moments of despair over my REG failures. In turn, this helped train my ability to empathize and become more mentally dexterous.

I see my REG experience as very much a laboratory for learning about empathy and how to apply it in life. Whenever one questions one's own motives, it means that two viewpoints are operating within oneself. It can be very helpful to stand outside both of the viewpoints in question. And from that analytic director viewpoint, it's possible to tune in to the other viewpoint and feel its feelings—without being as emotionally attached. I suspect that such an exercise builds overall emotional intelligence. Further, high levels of empathy help bind us together as a society in the service of long-term cooperation. Science is finding that such cooperation has been the main ingredient in the extraordinary success of our species.[4]

In summary here, it may be that one of the unique characteristics of human beings is our flexible skill at empathizing. Other animals, such as dogs and horses, are considered to have empathic connections with their owners, but only clever humans may be able to dial in to *any* other complex mind and momentarily become it. In that sense, it may not be hyperbolic to call humans *universal empathy machines*.[5]

Many Small Deaths

When engaging in the REG process for the first time, most people will have no personal norms or expectations about the results. For example, when you begin, you have only what you have been told about the game. And though the effort to affect reality in this way may seem strange or alien, you have little to lose because you haven't yet gained anything. However, with more experience, you gain moments of clear success. Then two opposite fears begin to surface: One is fear of failure as you pull back to protect what success you have achieved. That can lead to rubber bands, with the results clearly reversing themselves. The other is fear of success, which bears on your sense of identity, or how you define and think about yourself. That can cause your mind to go blank as it tries to protect you from yourself. The results of those multiple forces are internal confusion and a personal struggle that can cause you to tighten up and not know how to proceed. At some point, you may feel you have no choice but to give up—as I did—in abject despair.

These are moments I call *small deaths*. They are deep experiences that can rock one to the core. In fact, I've found that even if I'm aware that this process is taking place, I cannot stop it. That is, even if at the level of conscious awareness I may say, "Yes, this is predictable; I have seen it before," it doesn't help. I find that odd because knowing the sequence in advance would seem to obviate the strength of its impact. But it hits at a place much deeper than the conscious awareness can control or rationalize. Such deaths reverberate in a place that is deep and cathartic—as if latent and waiting to cry out.

As I noted earlier, when that happens, one experiences letting go at a primal level. In the aftermath, good REG results come effortlessly, though one no longer seems to care. But in fact, one does care—at a different level or layer, wherein a new relationship with self and reality begins to form. And that serenity and oneness constitute a highly desirable state—at least in my experience.

Unfortunately, over time, the ease and fluidity of that state once again begin to tighten up. Efforts gradually become bogged down, and one returns to feeling the same sense of rigidity and frustration. In my case, perhaps to the extreme, I gradually began to score backward far more than chance would dictate. It became so pronounced that it had a kind of parody quality to it. It was me being used against myself in ways I could not grasp. In my cluelessness and frustration, I had another moment of despair and giving up. And once again, the results shifted and it became easy again.

For me, that pattern repeated itself every few months. And it even increased in frequency as time went on. In fact, I was getting ready to give up because I was having to give up so often. But it occurred to me that this pattern is not treading water. With each small death, the more-primitive circuitry of the ego self becomes weakened relative to the growing, alternative viewpoint of the connected self. The balance begins to shift between those two selves, and over time, it becomes easier to slip into the connected self. And the key to the connected self is that it expands outward—the mental equivalent of taking in a deep breath of fresh country air and expelling it out across the land. In the end, it feels much better to have gone through it—in spite of the ego-crushing process it took to get there.

One morning in the midst of editing this section, the *New York Times* sports section included two human-interest stories (on the same page) about a major tennis tournament in progress. In one story, a top-ranked male player threw his racket in disgust, and the newscaster said later, "He basically gave up." The last set was 0-6, as he didn't win a single game and stalked off angrily.[6] In the second story, a top-ranked female player was so far down in the match (she'd lost the first set and was down 1-5 in the second) that, as she reported later, she just gave up. She said to herself wistfully, "It's over." But she then reeled off 12 of 13 games to win the match.

So, what was different in the two stories? It appears that the female player, in giving up, didn't turn inward in anger, frustration, or self-pity as it appeared the male player had. She reported that her "sense of resignation brought freedom."[7] In effect, she let go of having to win and relaxed into the game. And with that, everything lightened up and she entered a flow state.

Clearly, it doesn't take the REG to have such an experience of giving up and finding such a flow. But once again, the REG shows that the impact of mental shifts is not all in our heads. The world is changed, as are we in both our relation to ourselves and to the world.

No Limits

I have spoken extensively about the role of models and how our minds are organized around them. Based on the concept of significance, one's thoughts and actions tend to stay close to the set points of the models we have adopted. However, our models grow and expand—to the extent that the mind feels it can manage them and still stay in control. For some people, it's enough to manage a narrow set of personal affairs on a day-to-day basis. Others manage vast organizational empires. But the issue is that self-imposed limits can be fully reevaluated at any time because *the limits themselves are arbitrary and movable.* We just don't know it, because our models are transparent to ourselves. They are us, and so they are experienced as just the way things are.

A lesson of the REG is that one can learn to see the models from the outside in and in doing so, begin to adjust the models' set points over time. The thermostat doesn't care what its set point is; it will hold to whatever norm has been set. The issue is that any change will pull on the current threads of association in a way that can be disorienting. However, once such a pull is over, a new norm is set, and that new norm is functionally treated just like the old one. Many social norms change through such a process. For example, movie ratings drift through repeated stimuli, and what was once shocking becomes a new normal. The same is true of previously unacceptable language that through repeated use becomes part of everyday social discourse. And we all know that the first days of a faster Internet connection or a new smartphone are thrilling, but soon the added speed becomes expected, and one wants even more.

Given that description of the mind, it is reasonable to ask oneself, "Where am I less effective because I have bought into my own limits?" It's worth scanning your own mind in that regard, especially when events fall short of what you can imagine for yourself. Of course, just seeing your limiting set points doesn't mean it's easy to change them. You must also contend with society's models laid on you, which tend to define your place and position. How many times have I told myself that I will act differently in some recurring situation, but the moment I reengage with old relationships or threads of association, I am back to my old self.

What's important, however, is to become aware that who you are both to yourself and to society can change. Limits exist as natural parts of webs of self and society. If you think of your web as a harp and yourself as the harp player, you might imagine plucking strings to change the way the threads interact. As you crescendo, you might find yourself plucking new combinations that dramatically produce what I have called *moments*. Moments can shut down the mental regulator's drive to hold to current norms, because everything stops for a moment to the new music. At such moments, the only limits that exist are those we individually and collectively have agreed upon.[8] And they can change. Carpe diem.

I like to summarize these life lessons with the slogan "managing models and allowing moments." The two parts of the slogan relate to the two dynamics of our personal webs. The first term, *managing models,* speaks to how our minds create subwebs or units of meaning with their own norms. In practice, those units of meaning are the models by which we run our lives. The key becomes seeing the models and learning how to work with and manage them. You learn when a model is appropriate and when it is holding you back in a given situation. If it's holding you back, then you can run an inventory of other models and shift to one that might work better. For example, you might find that upon coming home from work, you're still at the office mentally and are interacting with family members as if they're coworkers. Stepping back and seeing this in action provides the opportunity to adjust. That flexibility is also the basis of emotional intelligence, which involves the ability to step back and examine your own reactions to determine whether a new orientation gives a more-adaptive and satisfying response.

The value of this process can be seen in the current social environment that is so highly polarized by political identity or so-called tribe. The tribal self is deeply invested in its own viewpoint and the larger polarized web in which it sits. And though most people shake their heads at how sad it is that we've crystalized into such incompatible identities, there's little discussion about the fact that it's all in our heads. Managing models involves the ability to almost literally step out of such a deep identity and look at it from the outside. From that vantage, one can see how incredibly limiting the ensconced viewpoint is and then move to supplement it with other, adaptive viewpoints as appropriate. It sounds hard or even undesirable—like giving up on deeply held positions—but it gives up nothing. It simply represents a shift from believing what is out there to first understanding that selves become deeply jealous and proprietary of their positions in the mind. Emotional intelligence accrues from being able to develop multiple selves and manage them effectively.

The second term, *allowing moments,* involves the freedom of spirit to embrace new ideas. One follows new paths to see where they lead and develops new and novel associations. The essence of creativity often involves giving in to the more-unconscious elements of mind that sometimes make wholly unexpected connections. In the process, you might develop new models that take you to new places and provide you with new personal tools and expanded awareness.

A recent study on creative and highly effective individuals characterized many of them as having so-called integrative complexity. Such people can shift between activities that involve big-picture models on one hand and detailed pieces on the other. They can see both the forest *and* the trees, grasp the whole ecosystem *and* get into the weeds. Luminaries such as Bill Gates, Elon Musk, Jeff Bezos, and the late Steve Jobs have been known to obsess over the smallest of technical details as well as the broadest of issues.[9] That shifting of attention between wide and narrow views or units of meaning is essentially a shift between models. And one expects that such mental dexterity leads to new moments of insight.

※ ※ ※

With the project successfully completed, I began to think about the selection effect in more-practical terms. If this phenomenon is as embedded in nature as it appears to be, where does it surface in society? As I reviewed both my own and others' experiences, as well as larger domains and activities of society, I began to see the phenomenon's subtle presence in many places. Therefore, I believe that the selection effect is a significant factor both in our individual lives and in society *even today.* The last part of this book attempts to show how this is true and proposes that the selection effect's influence will only increase in the future.

PART IV:
WHEN WORLDS COLLIDE

CHAPTER 17:
STORIES

The Psyleron Mind Lamp has a mode of operation whereby it naturally meanders from one color to the next around a color wheel, as shown in figure 17.1. The color transitions are smooth and gradual, sometimes happening at a slow pace and sometimes more quickly. And sometimes the lamp will simply just sit for a while on one color. All of that activity is determined by the random-event generator built into the base of the Mind Lamp. (And to reiterate an earlier discussion, the REG output is not moved by any physical force in part assured by inner data processing, as described in appendix A.)

The pattern of drift can go either way around the wheel. The clockwise direction, however, is dominant, as indicated in the figure by the darker,

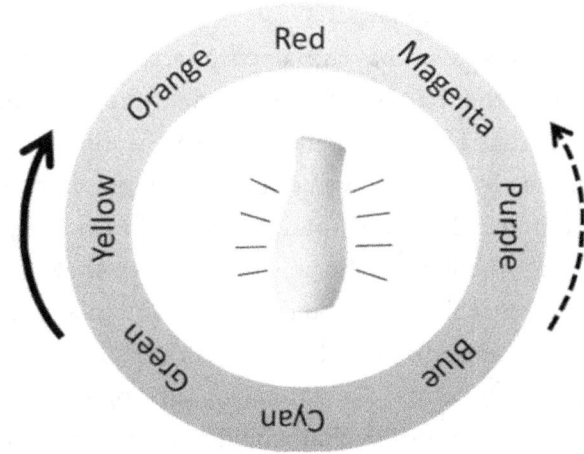

FIGURE 17.1. The color wheel of the Mind Lamp, showing how the color can drift in either direction around the wheel—but with one direction (solid line) favored over the other (dotted line).

solid arrow. Only occasionally will the color drift in the less-favored direction. Designing the lamp that way created a clear challenge of getting it to move in the less likely "backward" direction. To succeed gives a fair amount of certainty that the output of its REG has been shifted and is due to something other than chance.

I like the bold red color of the lamp. So, in a kind of meditation, I often try to keep the lamp situated directly on red for as long as possible. The task is to mentally fix red in place as it inevitably drifts toward magenta. If it does drift too far—past magenta into purple or blue—I usually give up and let it continue around the color wheel at its own pace until it returns to red again.

One day I was working with the Mind Lamp in one of the Psyleron/ICRL research rooms in our building, attempting to keep the color fixed on red for as long as possible. It began to drift into magenta. I tried to "pull" it back to red, but I didn't have the right frame of mind. I lost the sense of meaning or a reason that would keep it there. And so, it slowly drifted past magenta into purple and onward until it was almost blue. I found a faint, diffuse spot of purple remaining on the left side of the lamp (all of the colors are made from the mixing of three LEDs in the lamp's base, so the mixing isn't absolutely perfect if you look very closely), and I tried very hard to mentally pull on that spot to expand it. But it was to no avail, and instead, the spot blinked out and was gone. The lamp was fully blue, and I knew it would have to go around the color wheel before reaching red again.

But suddenly I had an idea. I imagined that the lamp was actually a living creature, and the trace of purple that had just disappeared on the left side of the lamp was an alien virus that had entered it and been absorbed into the lamp. In my mind's eye, the virus was now taking hold and growing. It was potent and beginning to infect the lamp. Totally engaged in my story, I could feel a shift taking place. The lamp color pulsed back with that lost spot of purple. Now I imagined that the virus could multiply and take over the whole lamp and might even spread to other lamps. With that, the lamp began to brighten, with subtle hints of purple and magenta reappearing. I imagined the virus creating a skin condition that would cover the surface of the lamp. Pretty soon, the lamp housing became fully purple and moved onto magenta. Now I imagined that the virus was invading inside the core of the lamp, growing in the lamp's insides, like in the movie *Alien*. In my mind's eye, a red glow began to emanate menacingly from deep inside the lamp, and the lamp, which was now fully magenta, complied—with a faint glow of red. The red brightened, and when it was almost fully red, I became totally unnerved, saying to myself, "My God, I really can't keep this up!" Immediately, I was out of my story of the virus, and the red began to fade—unnaturally fast—back to magenta and then purple.

Energized by my previous success, however, I decided to jump back into the story. I made the fading red a part of the plot line. It was fading because the lamp's immune system had fought back and was overcoming the virus. But now the virus had mutated into a supervirus—more potent than ever—and was assaulting the lamp again. Sure enough, as I engaged the lamp with this new plot line, the lamp reversed color direction once again and changed from purple to magenta. Indeed, within a short period, the lamp became fully and triumphantly red. I stared at it for a moment, trying to take it all in.

But I wasn't done yet. Not being content with clear success (which is not necessarily a good trait), I wanted to push the color further backward around the color wheel—into orange—just as icing on the cake. But now I'd lost my story altogether, as the plot was over and done. I was losing my mental grip, and once again, the color was heading unnaturally fast back to purple. Creating another story at this point seemed too artificial. Rather, I just sat back and noted to myself that I am clearly able to drive the lamp's output. I had just done it twice. So, I used that deep confidence and knowing to say to myself, *"I can indeed drive the color regardless of what happens now."* In my certainty and serenity of "having orange" no matter what might happen, within seconds the lamp reversed direction a third time, quickly turning magenta, then red, and finally, glowing bright orange. That was it. I was done.

I walked out of the research room and described the sequence in detail to colleague Adam Curry and then wrote it up in my research notes journal.

※ ※ ※

The behavior of the lamp was *extremely* unlikely to have occurred by chance—particularly that it would play out my story exactly as I had developed it. I have no reasonable choice but to believe—as I experienced at the time—that I had caused that sequence of events.

The experience involved a certain thrill as it was happening, but it was not until it was over that I felt its real weight. It caused me to reflect on the REG device that I had used in my long-term project, which seems highly abstract next to the physical presence and vibrancy of the Mind Lamp. Perhaps the more visceral relationship the lamp engendered is the reason it seemed so responsive. It is an everyday object, simply enhanced with some "advanced" technology. That ease of familiarity had enabled me to make a story out of it—one that seemed very natural at the time and flowed easily. And it was that experience that put me on the trail of stories as primary vehicles by which the mind influences its surroundings.

Many aspects of our lives, past ones and future ones, are organized into storylike narratives. A story involves a flow of events that is grouped together into a single unit of meaning. And whereas most of the units of meaning described earlier have been snapshot states of the mind, here they include the element of time or duration. Stories involve multiple decision points that lead to different sequences of events. In fact, the story *is* the story in part because of the unpredictability of how events unfold. The selection effect can be present when a story is good enough and compelling enough to impose itself on reality. And a powerful storyline may help bootstrap itself into being.

The Colorado experiment described in the introduction appears to be such a case. For the researchers, the study was imbued with rich theatrical emotion, and so the story played itself out in the course of real events. Similarly, my long-term project with the REG was a story that I lived on many layers. That is, I focused on each next trial of each session, but I also experienced the whole project as a larger unit of meaning. The REG program called FieldREG described in chapter 4 is in some sense a tool for stories. When one sets it up to monitor an event, the ensuing chart traces the ebb and flow of one's sense of meaningfulness during the event. In effect, the user retells the story of the event to herself through the lens of that meaning.

The explanation for our affinity to stories centers in part on the organization of the brain and how the brain holds information. We have what is known as *episodic memory*, wherein we encode and remember episodes of our lives involving both sensory and emotional detail.[1] Through stories, information becomes neurally associated or connected, allowing for easier retrieval. But here we reverse the causal order of brain to mind and put mind first. Meaning drives the development of biology through the presence of meaning-action pairs, with meaning as the architect and driver. Meaning continually builds scaffolding for itself in the brain–body and stands on what it builds.

Because of the binding of brain and mind, causal flows of influence back and forth are difficult to track. We can complicate that even more by looking at two people interacting, whose give-and-take very quickly leaves behind any predictability of what will happen next. The distinct states of the two brains and two minds involved in such an interaction are constantly changing in a somewhat entangled way. And so, it is in that maze of cross flows that we propose one unconventional link: the linking of one person's mind to another person's brain. That possibility is based on the idea of the brain as a bioREG, as discussed in chapter 12. A person's mind can affect the sequencing of neuron firing in the person's own brain similar to how a REG is influenced. So, here we imagine that one person's mind can affect another person's brain. But to bridge the intersubjective space between persons (after all, the REG influence is across space), there would have to be a powerful reason. I suggest that powerful stories told by master storytellers can bridge the gap.

Apple cofounder Steve Jobs was by all accounts such a master storyteller. It was said that when he described his product ideas and visions of the future, he created a "short-term reality distortion."[2] Everything he would say had a profound and compelling feeling of truth as experienced by all who were present. It was as if the listeners were *being given* an experience—in spite of any higher-level reasoning that might have objected. It was only later, once the moment had faded, that the spell of the story was broken. In my own personal experience, I had a business partner many years ago who had a similarly powerful effect on all those around him. When he talked, it was magnetic, and whatever story he wove became the way reality was at the time. It seemed as if he could paint the walls of the room a different color just by his presence. I once asked him about that power, and he said he was fully aware of it but didn't know why he had it.

The proposition here is that the storyteller influences another's brain in the same way that I, as storyteller, influenced the Mind Lamp. But if such cross-connections are possible, what about direct mind-to-mind influence? Such connections are reported occasionally in many contexts. If each of us is seen as a web of mind, then perhaps at times those webs can overlap. That is, although we do have mental membranes to keep us largely separate, it is all the same space. We just call it intersubjective space when it is between people. Indeed, these separate webs coming in contact with each other are like worlds colliding. And in brief moments, perhaps cross-connections can be made. It has certainly been reported in the psychotherapeutic process, as Ruth Rosenbaum wrote about and reported on Freud's own musing on telepathy. And so, we will continue to explore those direct connections in the context of how it is often, practically speaking, the power of stories that makes the link.

Shared Stories

Direct mind and brain connections, if possible, cause us to lose a portion of our personal distinctness and privacy. Just talking about it, I can feel myself pull back to guard myself. Of course, many positive aspects are possible as well, including how empathy and love may bind parts of our webs together. Groups of individuals might find themselves connected in ways they cannot explain but that lead to good outcomes. A common such example (used here before) involves members of a sports team gelling with each other. Suddenly, the team members are in sync such that they are playing "beyond themselves." The team begins to look like an integrated whole rather than a collection of individuals.[3] Figure 17.2 depicts a group mind forming into a shared web with multiple meaning-action units sharing information.

Science writer and journalist Lynne McTaggart conducted research on the power of groups to see how a group mind might affect a course of events. In one extensive set of studies, small groups tried to affect the growth rate of plant seedlings. The group members would focus on one set of seedlings in an attempt to help them grow faster. Another set of seedlings was the control group and not focused on. The studies produced significant results overall—that is, with greater growth evident in the experimental groups over the control groups.[4] The same result has been seen in other labs by using individuals rather than groups.[5] But McTaggart's particular interest was in learning how group bonding might affect overall impact. And after many experiments, she determined that bonded and cohesive groups are indeed more effective than single individuals.[6] Perhaps there's something about that size that enables the individual member webs of meaning to link and align—like the atoms of a molecule. If the molecule gets too big, it functions less well as a unit and tends to break apart.

The idea of a group web can also be examined in relation to social memes. Memes are concepts that get introduced into society for whatever reason and go viral. A meme can spread so quickly that within a short period, many

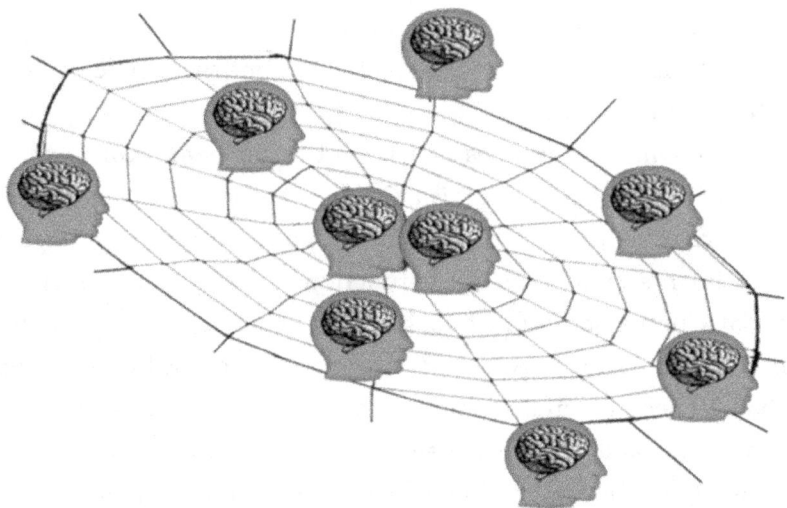

FIGURE 17.2. Representation of multiple brain-minds joined into a group web.

people within the grouping or society come to know and use it. With each new person who encounters it, it sticks further. One example of such a meme is the phrase "Call me maybe." It was introduced in a song in 2012 and for no apparent reason just spread. People would use it whether it made much logical sense in a context or not. It just became a thing. To help visualize the process, imagine the group web of figure 17.2 wherein the brain–minds are replaced by "Call me maybe," which spreads rapidly across the network.

The conventional explanation for memes or related phenomenon is that people share enough cultural concepts such that certain ones become easy for everyone to remember. They become relevant and simply catchy jingles. In fact, that explanation is identical to the web-based group mind indicated here. People are ready for the meme, and so it spreads. And because these two explanations are so similar, it might suggest that the model proposed here is superfluous and adds no value. But the group web as proposed here is *a real entity*—one that can create influences beyond normal expectations. The group web is a connection at a subconscious level, and so a meme is a singular entity spread within that larger web. When the meme is heard, it snaps a person into the awareness of what is already present in the person's subconscious in some indistinct or wavelike form. And as a result, the meme spreads more quickly than it would otherwise. For example, there are many historical instances when two or more people developed an invention or made a discovery almost simultaneously. The invention or discovery may have elements of a meme in the group mind but one that is relevant only to minds that are primed for it.[7]

The book *Connected* describes a variant of this phenomenon in the form of what is (clinically) called *contagion*. *Contagion* connotes the idea that people infect each other psychologically. For our purposes here, a contagion is a meme that is large enough in scope to function as a story—a meme story. For example, at a Tennessee high school in 1998, a teacher believed she smelled gasoline and became dizzy. A contagion regarding the smell spread to engulf more than 70 people, sending some to the hospital. The school was closed, reopened briefly, and then closed again with more casualties. However, in the interim, both the Occupational Safety and Health Administration and the Centers for Disease Control and Prevention were called in and concurred that there was no trace of any such substance. Two years later, a report in the *New England Journal of Medicine* concluded that it had been "psychogenic" factors or a "hive mind" that was to blame.[8]

Another case occurred in the town of Mattoon, Illinois, when many of the 15,000 residents were convinced that a madman was on the loose, opening windows at night and spraying people with a sweet-smelling anesthetic gas. The gas would leave some but not all persons in their bedrooms paralyzed for some period. Armed groups formed to roam the streets looking for the man in what later was deemed a construct of hysteria.[9] According to *Connected,* at least 70 cases of epidemic-hysteria incidents have been documented covering the period 1973 to 1993 and in which at least 30 people and sometimes hundreds of people were involved.[10]

Story-level memes may also be reflected in the mythological archetypes that Swiss psychologist Carl Jung proposed are buried deep within us. He suggested that as a species, we have "the wise old man," "the great mother," "the trickster," "the hero," and other figures lodged in our unconscious minds at a collective level. Those archetypes might appear to us in dreams or rise within us at times that we might need guidance or direction or need to see things in a new way. The idea of memes in a group mind or collective unconscious is a way of explaining their presence in each of us.

Historically, spiritual and religious rituals represent another type of group story designed to sync up the various parties involved. Rituals may involve storytelling through dance or other artistic forms. The engagement seems to create strong reality distortions among the participants and to shut down normal filters and barriers so as to allow more-direct connections between those involved. The shamanistic ceremonies move a group toward a single mind wherein a new reality takes hold. And people have reported healings, visions, and personal spiritual breakthroughs during such events.[11]

Even more broadly, a society's creation myth may sync up members into a group meaning and provide codes of moral conduct. Here again the story may entrain the members' brains (and minds) toward a common neurological structure that leads to increased harmony. If true, then creation myths become less about explanations of how the world came to be and more about a method for achieving social cohesiveness. So, although we tend to scoff at creation myths for their lack of scientific basis or rigor, the myths may work on a different principle with a different purpose. That principle involves what are called *received truths* rather than facts. A received truth is a story or statement that is readily adopted because it makes sense in the context of (the mind web of) all other available knowledge. The new received truth in turn reinforces the previous truths, and the story becomes deeper and richer. In fact, there is little evidence to suggest that before the scientific revolution, societies thought about facts as statements of verifiable data. Rather, everything was filtered for validity through *the listener's frame of reference*.[12]

Our current story of the big bang theory can be seen as simply our own creation myth. It is different from earlier creation myths only in that we call it scientifically confirmed. But again, in the wider sense, the very idea of being scientifically confirmed is just another part of our story.[13] In this story, we visualize the universe as a fiery ball exploding into existence, as if we were there and as if the event happened like any other event we might witness. That's not to say that the story is pure fantasy; we created it because it is part of a utilitarian body of data that is itself tied into our tools of analysis and our mastery of the physical world. But that story, too, will be superseded or at least modified by future scientific findings. We must realize that such theories are always bounded by the accounts of nature we are capable of grasping and that in the future, they will become stepping-stones to even-more-sophisticated stories. Their real value at any given time lies in how we share in their experience and how they help move society forward in constructive ways.

The Group Mind with a Life of Its Own

The group mind described previously involves individuals' syncing up together as shared webs or meaning spaces. But there is a level even beyond such sharing. It is a level at which a shared mind or a group mind begins to take on a life of its own. It is no longer just a repository of group thinking but begins to think on its own. This is a highly controversial concept, obviously, and requires a strong form of the web concept of mind.

We do, however, have instances when we briefly cross paths with that notion. A married couple, for example, may have interpersonal issues such that they seek help from a therapist. The couple's relationship may have been so long lasting and complex that it begins to weave a larger web in which both of the individuals become entangled. At some point, neither party really understands what is driving the relationship, which seems to create its own dynamics. In fact, relationship counselors often tell couples to think of the relationship as a third party. In that sense, the relationship counselor is aptly named—one who *counsels the relationship* rather than the individuals.

Again, in the book *Connected,* the authors discuss *emerging agency* in groups of animals. Some such groups display behaviors whereby a measure of individuality appears lost to the whole. The authors write, for example, that "mathematical models of flocks of birds and schools of fish and swarms of insects that move in unison demonstrate there is no central control of the movement of the group, but the group manifests a kind of collective intelligence that helps all within it to flee or deter predators. The behavior does not reside within individual creatures but, rather, is a property of groups." The authors go on to note that the group-level movements are not capricious in nature but that "even more important, the direction of movement is usually the best choice for the flock." Here the group mind looks to be more than a synthesis of individual minds but begins to show some level of its own intelligence.[14]

Focusing on such group dynamics is not intended to exclude the impact of normal sensory input. Sensory perception remains active and central at the individual level. The birds of the flock no doubt still attend to the visual movements of one another. But those cues may in fact follow rather than lead. The sensory feedback that confirms the graceful unity of action would reinforce to the group members that they can continue to sync up. One can give oneself over to the group when one can see that it is working and beneficial. That dynamic exemplifies the interplay of meaning and action on many levels.

The idea of ever-larger group minds reaches its zenith in what is called the Gaia hypothesis, which proposes that the entire Earth and its biosphere may function as a collective mind of some agency. The theory, put forth in the 1970s by James Lovelock and Lynn Margulis, holds that the Earth (as personified by Greek goddess Gaia) may have a consciousness of its own. And therefore, events play out on Earth not just as a clash of mechanical physical forces but in part as acts of Gaia as a meaning-action pair. In one of the more mythological versions of Gaia, she can become distressed by thoughtless acts of humans and can then spawn earthquakes and typhoons as allergic reactions to humans in an attempt to shake us off.[15] Such concepts are considered superstitions, but they may need to be revisited—not to the exclusion of other, "more-efficient" or "proximal" causal descriptions of such events but as higher-level organizing processes.

Fully grasping the Gaia mind, if there is one to be grasped, may be impossible for human minds. The Gaia web may involve configurations and associations that are so foreign to us that we cannot even imagine what they would be. However, given that humans are universal empathy machines as described in the previous chapter, we might use empathy to catch at least glimpses of the Gaia mind. Perhaps through meditation or other practices, it can be seen. Certainly, great sages and teachers have discussed achieving various forms of cosmic consciousness. Such awareness may become easier as society itself grows into an ever-larger group web. Maybe the gap between our individual selves and that hypothetical, largest group mind of Gaia will narrow, and we begin to share in it more naturally. On the other hand, as we ourselves get more sophisticated, so might Gaia and other larger webs of reality. They may continue to grow and evolve just as we do, and in that way, the greater whole may always remain steps beyond us.[16]

Stories Order Chaos

We have already discussed the idea of our lives' being experienced as stories and how those stories may invoke selection effects to influence the course of events. The very notions of the power of positive thinking and the law of attraction and similar concepts presuppose that whatever one's attitude, it begins to order nature around it. The problem is that our minds as webs of association engaged with society as webs of association can be firmly fixed. It isn't easy to suddenly change all of those threads. And the ripple effect tends to push things back the way they were. The idea of no limits still stands, but in practice, we are typically stuck where we are.

There's one condition that helps describe how webs work and how to use the selection effect to benefit. It has to do with situations in which conditions are exceptionally chaotic. In his book *Antifragile: Things That Gain from Disorder*, author Nassim Nicholas Taleb discusses how most people, systems, institutions, stock markets, and so on are highly risk averse and try to regulate out all uncertain fluctuations. As a result, naturally dynamic systems are constrained to tighter bands of regulation. This makes them *appear* to be controlled. But at some point, they will undergo unexpected shifts that are all the more violent. And when they do, there arise—as classically stated—both a crisis and an opportunity. Rather than be thrown by the chaos in such situations, I suggest that stories can play roles in the opportunity.

The opportunity comes by stepping back from the chaos and making a story out of what you would like to happen. That is, rather than getting lost and tangled in the chaos, you jump to a higher ground. From there you tell a story about what will happen next—a story that has a favored and beneficial outcome. As a simple example in my own life, when I lost tenants now and then in our commercial building, I used to get upset. It means more work, loss of income, an overall distraction. But I've learned that I can invoke a new story as seen from above. The jumbling has occurred because a better tenant is on the way, one who will be easy to work with. It sounds artificial, but I suspect that it helps the selection effect work and so tends to make itself true. From that higher vantage point, I can help guide the course of events through social fluctuations. It's just a simple situation, but the more chaotic it is, the more opportunity it offers as well.

Tennis is a game wherein attitude instantly translates into physical outcomes, so I like to use it in examples, as in the previous chapter. Here's another (and it won't be the last). In the 2018 US Open, a 20-year-old female player fended off 13 break points, gave up none, and won her semifinal match. These are very rare statistics. When asked how she did it, she said, "This is going to sound bad, but I wanted to play Serena."[17] *Serena* is Serena Williams, who would be her opponent in the final if she won this match. To play for a championship opposite this tennis legend would be an honor and a thrill for her. So, she created a larger unit of meaning wherein she was going to win to make the larger image come true. She was steeped in the story of an impending future that would be magnificent. In contrast, the losing player could be seen struggling with herself, trying to figure out what went wrong. What went wrong was that the young winner was playing a higher game—both on the court and in her mind.

I'll include one final example of adopting a higher unit of meaning—as controversial as it may be. We all remember that the ultimate outcome of the 2016 presidential election had been considered highly unlikely. One election site, based solely on state polls and historically highly accuracy, gave better than 98% odds in favor of the losing candidate.[18] So, we can look to the associative web concept and the selection effect for clues to how the outcome squeaked by on that 2% margin. Clearly, the election was very complicated, and there are perhaps as many theories about the outcome as there are people in the country. But in fact, the high level of complexity is *exactly the condition that allows for selection effects*. With so many possible scenarios and variables that could be critical, nobody will ever know what drove the end result.

During the campaign, the winning side, as we now know, gained intelligence about the inner workings, dynamics, and activities of the losing side. Certainly, the information could have been used in material ways to help the campaign. But the issue here is the way it elevated the campaign to a viewpoint above the battlefield, so to speak. To know what the enemy is doing creates the psychological perspective that one can win because one holds the high ground. One sees the opponent from a higher more-senior position or, in this case, web of thought. And that top-down sense of awareness and confidence held strongly enough, begins to order the course of events in one's favor. One ends up doing all the right things because the things necessary for bringing about an unlikely outcome simply surface to be acted upon. And as some of us have seen with the REG, if you're working for a highly unlikely outcome of a specific nature, the universe will rarely do more than is necessary to bring about the result (see my project results, figure 15.2). In that regard, the fact that the election was won on such a few votes in key places speaks to the structure of clarity and purposefulness imposed from the top.[19]

There's another lesson here as well. Because units of meaning are organized from the top down, attitudes that are more top down or authoritarian tend to be stronger and create more-targeted selection effects. They bend events in their favor more readily. The contrasting structure involves large numbers of smaller units of meaning linked together. This is the bottom-up structure of a grassroots-type organization. That structure, in order to be stronger than the top-down structure it faces, must itself function as a larger coherent whole. If it does, then it has power equivalent to the whole. If it doesn't, then we have what we saw in the election.

In conclusion, each of us has stories to live on many levels, and all of the stories in the world are what make it what it is. Stories have a habit of merging into larger ones, creating ecosystems of activity that often lose track of their own origins. We may even lose sight of where they're headed. That may be because larger webs of agency begin to shape events beyond our individual abilities to grasp or control. The world flows forward like a giant novel with an infinite number of nested subplots. Maybe the fabled Akashic records that compose the cosmic book of history not only hold the past but also include the ongoing story line that we create to help shape the future.

❋ ❋ ❋

Stories must be alive to keep their meaningfulness. Without aliveness, they lose power. If you see a movie too many times, it can lose its punch. What used to bring a laugh later brings just a smile and then later, perhaps a distracted and wandering mind. I earlier described the story of my grandmother in the funny green hat, wherein I "used" the meaningfulness of the story to drive the REG. But I used it so much that it began to lose its effect. There's a delicate quality to stories, and what starts out as new and fresh can fade.

The stories of the next chapter, which are accounts of mainstream scientific research, show how fresh new stories with powerful implications do indeed begin to fade. Like the Colorado study, when researchers step out of the living story they built around an experiment, initially positive effects can disappear. It is currently a great puzzle in science, but with the associative web model and the selection effect, we can provide science with new insights into this perplexing issue.

CHAPTER 18:
SCIENCE AND THE SELECTION EFFECT

In the late 1980s, two highly respected scientists, Martin Fleischman and Stanley Pons, discovered a formula they believed created a fusion reaction in a small container. The reaction occurred at room temperature, which led to the term *cold fusion*. Their repeated tests proved positive for the effect. They realized that if cold fusion were in fact occurring and if the heat it generated could be harnessed, then it would usher in a new era of almost unlimited energy. Fleischman and Pons were so excited by their own discovery that they hastily held a press conference to announce the news.

The announcement created a sensation and set in motion attempts by many other laboratories to replicate the effect. Unfortunately, most of the other labs produced no support for the proposed reaction. Occasionally, a new group would report initial success based on some modification of the process, but then the results would fade. Even today, this story continues, with a new breakthrough occasionally announced, only to fade again. Cold fusion has become a subject of both fascination and derision, as many contemplate why and how top scientists seem to have been led astray. Fleischman and Pons were too good in their field to be considered cranks. Something seems to have been at work other than a simply massive lack of judgment or blindness to real facts. Perhaps what they stumbled on wasn't fusion but was nevertheless something unusual and unexplainable—even if it faded over time.

* * *

In 2010, a provocative piece appeared in *The New Yorker* about other research studies that showed strong initial results but then declined over time. The article, written by Jonah Lehrer, was titled "The Truth Wears Off" and covered a variety of study areas, with a key one being clinical drug trials. Clinical trials with positive results can lead to approval by the US Food and Drug Administration (FDA). The problem is that once approved, a drug might show much weaker effect than the initial studies did. The FDA became so alarmed by how often that occurs that it formed a committee to figure out what to do about it.[1] The problem, which is still with us, doesn't seem to be fraud or even bad methodology in the studies; certainly, the last thing a pharmaceutical company wants to do is spend enormous sums of money on a drug that then gains a reputation for not working. The problem doesn't seem to be random. Nor does it seem to be accidentally significant results that come from testing so many drugs that one or two are bound to come up positive by the laws of chance. It seems to be something more systemic—but elusive as well.

The article also describes a related perplexing trend in another area of medicine. In the early 1990s, a second-generation class of drugs to treat psychosis was introduced that showed very strong therapeutic effects. For most of a decade, the drugs became widely prescribed and hugely effective—and profitable. But in the years that followed, the effectiveness of the drugs seemed to wane. In many cases, the drugs were no better—and were sometimes even worse—than the first-generation drugs of the 1950s.[2] At a convention in Brussels in 2007, scientists attempted to learn or at least describe what was happening. There had been no scientific reason for the declines. Antipsychotic drugs do not work like antibiotics, wherein over time, bacteria can develop immunities to them. And there was no reason that the psychophysical makeup of new patients should be different from that of patients in a previous decade. The decline simply made no sense from a normal scientific standpoint.

* * *

University of California social psychologist Jonathan Schooler became famous in late 1980s for an effect he identified and called *verbal overshadowing*. Verbal overshadowing occurs when a person is asked to describe an experience verbally, and the act of describing changes the way they remember the experience. The effect becomes critical with respect to, for example, crime scenes. If someone is forced to describe an encounter with an assailant, the act of describing the assailant might lessen the person's ability to later pick the person out of a police lineup. That is, something in the process of having verbalized the description of the encounter interferes with the person's sensory memories. However, after initial, strongly positive studies, the verbal-overshadowing effect in subsequent studies began to diminish. This was not a sudden disappearance of the effect, as if the original studies were flawed. Rather, it was a *gradual* decline, with each study tending to show an effect, but less than the previous ones. Schooler and his colleagues had no idea why.[3]

* * *

Perhaps inspired by Schooler's strange findings, in 2011 an associate professor at the University of Virginia began testing the replicability of studies within the entire field of psychology by asking whether many basic research findings hold up over time. He recruited more than 250 researchers to replicate 100 psychology studies that had given positive results several years earlier. The replication findings were announced in late 2015. Of the 100 studies, fully 62 of them did not hold up to replication. Only 35 did hold up, with the remaining 3 being inconclusive.[4] The findings generated a lot of finger pointing about what could have gone wrong. Some counterarguments indicated that things were not as bad as they might seem. But in any event, such a low level of replication called into question this entire area of life science.[5]

Since that time, the field has been attempting to find out whether or not the failure to replicate important studies itself holds up. In fact, it continues to be the case. Other long-standing landmark studies have fallen, including (1) the prison experiment in which normal subjects tasked with being prison guards quickly start to exhibit militant behavior; (2) the kids' marshmallow experiment, wherein kids who were able to defer getting one marshmallow immediately so they could get two marshmallows at a later time, became more successful in life; and (3) the concept of ego depletion, wherein repeated demands on our wills cause us to tire enough to make different choices. In each case, the original effects were seen as diminished or no longer significant at all.[6]

* * *

A growing list of scientific stories follows the similar pattern: an early, robust phenomenon followed by a subsequent decline. And that pattern is showing up—from psychology and neuroscience to ecology, medicine, artificial intelligence,[7] and, perhaps to some degree, in the natural sciences. Of course, the common initial response to the problem is that controls and methodology must be tightened up because study designs must have been sloppy to begin with. Another explanation is the file-drawer effect. That is, if one runs enough studies, some are bound to show significance by simple statistics—usually one in 20—and only the positive ones get reported in the literature. The insignificant ones are put in a file drawer and go unreported.

Some of those criticisms are no doubt valid. However, focusing on them alone obscures the REG-like selection effect that may also be present. The selection effect is not the result of bad ethics or bad design or bad anything.[*] It is the additional factor of how meaningfulness and significance directly bear on reality. Science was never designed to account for that factor. It may be the elephant in the room—one that will increasingly confound study results in the future. In fact, the tendency to create instabilities and to cause changes in outcomes is capricious and without an obvious cause, leading to wild-goose chases in search of answers.

---

[*] Note that the term *selection effect* is already in scientific use, referring to specific error processes in studies. One example is the file-drawer effect just noted, wherein one selects for publication only positive studies. Another example is the selection of a sample of subjects for a study that does not accurately represent the purported study population. These are "selection effects" of a different sort.

Historically speaking, the decline effect was identified in a scientific context during the very first ESP studies. These studies were conducted at Duke University by J. B. Rhine, founder of the modern field of parapsychology, who noticed that subjects' ESP results very often started strong and diminished over time. Originally, the pattern was an annoyance but later became institutionalized as a primary variable in itself. At the PEAR lab, that variable was called the *series position effect*, which examined the order in which subjects' results were produced. In such studies, each subject's early data was combined with other subjects' early data, and in general, all data were time-sliced into bins by order. The earlier bins showed stronger selection effects than the later bins did in what sometimes appeared as an almost linear decline in significance.[8]

It is not only study subjects who display such declines but also experimenters who conduct studies. For example, the PEAR lab had its most-highly-positive results early on in its existence, and they declined over time. A study late in the life of the lab failed to replicate the early findings altogether. The Colorado study seemed to show a strong, positive experimenter effect early on, with a subsequent abrupt decline. Quite recent research using REGs at the Ludwig Maximilians University of Munich resulted in a first study with highly significant results. But when a second study was conducted "to test the robustness of the effect," it produced results so opposite to the first study that it fully reversed their effects.[9] This attitude of testing robustness of earlier results, as noted in the introduction, is a clear sign that the experimenters shifted their emotional orientation in the study process. The thesis here is that REG research simply highlights experimenter effects that exist throughout all of science. Replication of studies in different labs can dampen that effect and the problem it poses—particularly in the natural sciences but perhaps not always. In the life sciences, however, it is perhaps more confounding. Life sciences studies more often involve what are called *threshold effects*. Threshold effects are subtle and do not hit you over the head—like the sighting of a bright pulsar in the heavens. Instead, they are results that statistically cross a threshold so to be considered positive or statistically significant. Threshold effects are often less stable and therefore may be more subject to fluctuations in experimenter attitudes and expectations. That said, even natural science experiments involving threshold effects may be at risk as well, such as with the cold-fusion controversy described earlier. In that instance, it may have been experimenter expectation—based in part on the strong theory the researchers had developed—that helped cause unlikely outcomes. *Unlikely* means an outcome that sits on one end of the probability curve of possible outcomes. By helping those outcomes occur more often than would be expected by chance, the effect reaches over a threshold and looks like a larger and more stable result than it is later shown to be.

Clinical drug trials may represent another example of the experimenter effect's changing of threshold values. In drug trials, the early environment is filled with excitement and expectation. The atmosphere is highly charged as the shareholders hope for big financial success, the scientists hope for enhanced reputations, and the staff hope for job security and perhaps generous bonuses. Under such conditions, selection effects might raise positive results over a threshold value, holding up for months or even years and perhaps all through the period of seeking FDA approval. But as the drug's success becomes integrated into the business, the drug becomes just one more business unit, and attitude mellows. The orientation may even shift to the defensive—in fear of the loss of what has been gained.

Selection effects in clinical trials no doubt involve patients as well. Patients stand to gain the most from the positive effects of a new drug. Whether they're in the treatment group or the control group—and typically will not know which they are in—the promise of getting better helps them select a better outcome for themselves than might otherwise be the case. That expectation is classically called the *placebo effect,* wherein people make themselves better just by expecting to get better. And that may be the strongest of all of the *positive* selection effects to appear on a consistent basis.

Mainstream science presumably attributes the placebo effect entirely to the impact of positive attitudes and expectations on metabolic and nervous system activity. But that's just a statement made in the absence of any real explanation of process. The selection effect proposes that there are meaning-action pairs at all layers of the body, and the meaning side works to select desirable outcomes by affecting the probability distribution of possible outcomes. That process includes the brain/mind as a whole—with its attitude and orientation—down to the level of intracellular structures. Meaning-based webs impose themselves on the action side to align the action side webs more with the meaning side. And remember that an action side of a MAP is also—from its own perspective—the a meaning side for another, usually less-complex, meaning-action pair. This next-level meaning side repeats the process on its associated action side, and the process cascades downward through the unconscious layers of the organism. This provides a top-down mechanism for self-healing.

That type of explanation, if on the right track, suggests how far we are today from grasping the *meaning side* of a fully human system. If meaning is infused at all levels of an organism, then it is ultimately as complex in scope as the physical processes are, and we need a whole new branch of medical research to begin identifying it.

Other examples of the decline effect in the foregoing stories can be seen in a similar light. Patients with psychosis are characterized in part by the mental noise and unpredictable moments that their brains produce. If we address the brains of patients with psychosis as wildly fluctuating bioREGs, then conditions are right for influence on these bioREGs. That can be from the patients themselves, but they usually get lost in the confusion from lack of self-stability. Rather, researchers, doctors, and other clinicians may *impose behaviors* on the patients based on strong expectations. Such models can apparently be sustained over long periods as the expected drug response becomes an institutionalized norm. Such a situation is not unlike the notion of a long-term contagion, fueled by a deep, web-level story and a highly suggestible patient base.

The story of verbal overshadowing broadens the discussion from the impact of the selection effect to include the basic nature of minds as self-aware and interacting webs. That is, when the human mind observes itself—and perhaps even when a social-level mind observes itself—it sets a feedback loop. Self-awareness changes the structure of the webs over time. Therefore, we can propose a new model of what happened to the verbal-overshadowing effect. Basically, becoming aware of their own responses, the webs changed their orientation to the verbal process involved in overshadowing.

That is, the group web changes its own associative threads, and the changes become reflected in the way we react to things. Our minds are different from what they were a hundred years ago—and according to that view—mostly because of web-based social-feedback processes that we ourselves create.

Jonathan Schooler himself speculated with the same line of reasoning. Having looked at all conventional explanations for the decline—including the idea that his first results were outliers—he rejected all normative explanations. The fact that the phenomenon declined gradually over time is incompatible with the idea of a momentary spurious result. Instead, as he stated in an interview, "I, I say this with some trepidation but I think we can't rule out the possibility that there could be some way in which the active observation is actually changing the nature of reality." And, "in this most radical conjecture, there could be some sort of collective consciousness that's habituating."[10]

* * *

Some years ago, the European Union announced a plan to spend €1 billion over a decade to map out the human brain and thereby duplicate the brain in software. The funding agency agreed to the approach based on what we think we now know about the brain's mechanisms. But more than 800 scientists signed a petition to stop the project and rethink the approach. They were saying that although they supported a mechanical worldview of nature, the brain is too complicated, too dynamic, and too organic for us to assume it can be modeled in the way we think it can. The objecting scientists feared that the wrong basic framework and chosen path could result in a huge waste of time, effort, and money. Indeed, within a couple of years, the project as originally conceived collapsed.[11]

Simultaneous to that project, the US government announced its own brain project with similar funding. Here again massive pushback arose in the scientific community. In that case, however, the criticisms caused the project design to be revised. The new approach focused on the need for better tools to study the brain in its various aspects. That is, rather than claiming we know enough to duplicate the brain in software, the US approach said we need new tools to probe the brain's complexity and dynamics more deeply.[12]

The selection effect is the kind of unknown factor that could derail any attempt at a purely mechanical or electrochemical modeling of brain function. And oddly, that selection effect factor may become more visible with the introduction of better tools. That is, in the past, unexplained brain behavior could be chalked up to levels of brain complexity beyond our ability to monitor or control. But as tools become more and more precise, those anomalies will become more and more glaring and apparent. They will only increase. And there will be less room to ignore or dismiss them.

Our current models will be left with loops of causality that disappear in one time–space moment and that pick up in another—as if coming out of thin air. The meaning side of the meaning-action pair is missing in the current model, and that causes gaps in causal continuity. For that reason, it may be that selection effects are poised to have an impact on neuroscience research. For example, one new area of research involves the goal of mind reading through brain monitoring. The idea is that as sensors and software become more sophisticated, we will become able to pick up thoughts in the brain to such a level that we can reproduce them—even visually—on a computer screen. With even further refinement, a computer might be able to display the ongoing imagery of a person's dream. Indeed, there's been some success in such mind reading, including picking out a correct thought from a target list of possible thoughts and determining whether a person is thinking yes or no or is lying or telling the truth. In another advanced-research program, subjects looked at simple shapes while their brains were being monitored. Later, the researchers analyzed the brain data to successfully guess the sequence of shapes as they had been presented to the subjects.[13]

The expectation based on those early successes is that higher mind-reading resolution will continue unabated. Such extrapolations are natural—based on a mechanical model of both the brain and the tools for examining the brain. Better tools and more experience should lead to better results. But the field of anomalies has been through this sequence many times before. The best success is usually achieved early on, and the more tightly one tries to constrain the variables in an effort to get the most-accurate results, the worse the results become.

New tools may continue to increase resolution, but only in the grossest of senses. Limits will be imposed as one moves from general observation to begin dealing with individual instances. That happens for at least two reasons: The first is the inherent uncertainty that is used in driving the probabilistic bioREG-like processes in the brain. The mind imposes selection effects on the brain, and it only *tends* to follow in response. And second, the mind tries to protect itself from outside exposure—from being too closely probed by outside minds. As a subject begins to feel that significance of being peered into, the subject's mind can find ways to change brain pathways—based on inherent redundancy[14] and thereby blur results. The sprites come out to renormalize the situation. It appears that this is just what minds do.

The field of physics is another area in which the selection effect may be active. This is not so much in the mechanical areas of physics, wherein ample quantities of matter stabilize results to give us the solid reality we know. Rather, there's a field of study called *foundational physics*, in which the research involves elementary quantum interactions. The REG, too, involves elementary quantum interactions to produce its output, and so it qualifies as a quantum research device. And like REG studies, mainstream quantum experiments often give surprising results.

Foundational physics recently developed a research method called *postselection*; and it's perhaps no coincidence that the selection effect shares part of its name. In the postselection methodology, researchers are interested in only one experimental outcome even when others are possible. In other words, the desired outcome sits in a probability distribution of all possible outcomes—just like the REG process. The specific outcome of interest, if and when it occurs, means that other, earlier events had to have occurred. And it's those earlier events that are what the experiment is really trying to get at—events that cannot be seen but can be only inferred by the final outcome. For example, in one experiment, the final outcome required that at an earlier time, two conditions had to have been met simultaneously: (1) that three photons were spread across two boxes but (2) that no two photons were in the same box at the same time.[15] That kind of paradox occurs in the quantum domain.

The relevance here is that the physics postselection process may contain elements of the REG experience. As noted, with the REG, one also selects a target outcome. In this case, however, one actively puts effort toward making that target state occur. So, although active effort and influence are not parts of postselection, there is an emotional bias toward its occurring. The suggestion here is that this bias may make the target outcome happen more often than it might otherwise. Of course, no one's checking for that factor in the postselection process. I feel certain that this is not the only potential sprite operating in physics today. These influences may become recognized only as our tools become more refined to the point that perplexing events begin to surface.

※ ※ ※

One of the differences between classical physics and quantum domain is the role played by physical distance. According to classical physics, the influence of forces drops off rapidly as one moves away from the source of a force. That's true of all fundamental forces: electromagnetism, gravity, and the nuclear forces.[16] But in the process earlier referred to as *quantum entanglement*, the role of physical space is called into question. Space often gets disobeyed through remote linkages—as if it weren't there. With REG research into the selection effect, such linkages have also been reported in the literature. Therefore, before finally leaving the experimental side of the REG discussion, I decided to take on the issue myself to see what would happen.

CHAPTER 19:
INTERLUDE—REG AT A DISTANCE

In January 2013, the *New York Times,* ABC News, and other media reported the strange case of Holly the cat. Holly had become lost during a family vacation, left behind in a city 200 miles from her hometown in Florida. But with no guidance and under her own power, she walked back to that Florida hometown, arriving after a two-month journey. She was spotted a few blocks from her home: scrawny, paws bleeding, and at half her weight. Of course, historically, so many dogs seem to find their ways home against all odds that we forget just how remarkable it is. When a cat performs that unlikely feat, it's a wake-up call once again to its sheer improbability. As one behavioral ecologist put it bluntly, "I have no data on this."[1]

A few animals—mostly birds—take navigational cues from subtle factors such as Earth's magnetic field or perhaps the angle at which the sun travels across the sky. We may conclude therefore that all such unusual actions are the results of purely physical mechanisms. But there is no known way to ascribe such a physical mechanism to Holly's journey. There is no remotely verified physical process by which we can say it occurred.

Rather than basing Holly's journey on external physical cues, we can speculate on something vastly different. We could propose that she undertook a search for the fulfillment and meaning she had known in her previous homelife. Being deeply attuned to the sense of love and safety she had at home with her owners, she let her inner feelings guide her. With empathy for her own past self, she tapped into the world of love she had experienced before. It was as if a beacon of warmth guided her toward a renewal of that feeling. If at times she was forced to move in a direction away from home, she might still feel that tether pulling her to navigate around the obstacles.

Those conditions may or may not have been operational in Holly's case, but the event needs some explanation—one that goes beyond our current scientific thinking. The suggestion here is that Holly shared intersubjective space with her owners and perhaps even her former self. Intersubjective space is based not on physical dimensions but on other, *psychological dimensions*. Distance is experienced in terms of similarities and emotional closeness. One can feel emotionally distant from another while in the same room or can feel close to someone on a phone call who is halfway around the world. As before, the concept of meaningfulness becomes key as we look at how the REG experience is related to distance.

Remote REGs

The REG work reported here always involved a REG device that was sitting next to me. That was a matter of convenience, as the REG was connected to the computer I was using. The PEAR lab, however, ran studies to test how distance from the REG affects performance. As noted in chapter 1, there were no reports of significant performance changes under remote conditions.[2] Nevertheless, I wanted to see for myself whether the inner experience of a remote REG might involve different feelings and might affect my scoring.

When Psyleron was first founded, John and I discussed that distance variable and tasked our team to stream REG bits across the Internet. In that way, the REG could be anywhere in the world relative to the person trying to affect it. But with our long list of programming tasks, the coding was never fully debugged. So, I had filed this issue away in favor of the more-immediate priority of trying to affect the output at all.

After completing my project, I felt ready to tackle the issue of distance. But I still faced the lack of necessary software. Then one day it struck me that I didn't need custom software at all. There was an obvious solution. Remote-command software is freely available such that one can run an application on a remote computer. All I had to do was set up a remote computer with a REG attached to it running our software and then access that computer from somewhere else.

I purchased a basic laptop computer, and it took all of 10 minutes to set up the remote operation. I placed the laptop in a closet in my house a mile and a half from the office. I accessed the remote computer from the office and initiated the Reflector software. The keyboard response was very quick, with literally no perceptible delay. And it soon became apparent to me that the experience with the REG output was the same. In fact, in some ways it was even better because I was more acutely aware of the need to reach out and connect in "mental space."

I decided to do a formal study that would confirm the feeling with hard data. But the idea of another long project like the one I'd just finished seemed like too much to undertake. Rather, there was another measure I often use informally. And it's more immediately gratifying than a long-term study. It is to see how high a score I could reach during a session—that is, before losing that new state of mind that drives results up. This is the REG equivalent of shooting a projectile up in the air and seeing how high it gets before falling back to Earth. The high point is called the maximum Z score, or Z_{max} score, as described in chapter 2 and noted elsewhere. The Z_{max} score does not have a simple theoretical probability distribution associated with it like the session-ending Z score does.[3] The primary way to determine the probability structure of Z_{max} values is by running what's called a *Monte Carlo simulation*. In such a simulation, one simply runs the program unattended many times over to see how often certain high scores get reached. Appendix B displays a table tabulated from the simulation of about 11,000 sessions.

Shortly after setting up the laptop at home, my wife and I hosted some good friends on their visit from California. During lunch, I described what I was doing, and they agreed to take the computer with the REG back to their home in San Francisco. They would set it up and leave it running so that I could access it whenever I wanted. We parted, and a week later, I was in business.

My first question involved how much keystroke delay there might be using a computer that was 2,500 miles away. Certainly, there would have to be some delay, and indeed, it was lengthy. It was less, however, when I pressed keys that must have a higher-priority interrupt, including Esc or Page Down. The letter keys and the space bar caused much longer hesitations. Anyway, when I started testing my experience, I found I simply couldn't adjust to keystroke delay no matter which key I pressed. Given the prior thousands of hours of experience with no delay at all, my mind rebelled at the slightest difference in feel. The hesitations had a kind of push–pull jerking effect, reminding me of learning to drive a manual-shift car.

After a few days of casual playing, I could feel that my subconscious was still not accepting the keystroke delay. The sense of being "off" was clearly driving results backward. Further, when I would let go and open myself to allow whatever would happen to happen, the backward results amplified to the point of being just plain ridiculous. If I could speak for my subconscious, it was basically saying, "Things are not right, and you are off; and so the results should reflect this and go backward." OK, I thought, if that's the way it is, then let me shoot for going down, or low, rather than high. As you may recall, PEAR had subjects go low as often as go high. So, during one session that was being notably bad, I decided to start a little study to see how far I could push the results down instead of up. I finished out the session and decided to keep adding to it until I could see how low I could get.

Of course, now that I was *trying* to go low, or backward, I expected that my subconscious would try to thwart me and go backward from going backward. However, in this case, the situation was more than my consciously deciding what I wanted to happen. The very real experience of the jerking action was independently disturbing. Neural circuits respond to patterns they see and experience and don't necessarily shift quickly based on higher cognitive reasoning. For example, just because you know a horror movie isn't real doesn't mean you can stop reacting to its horror. Anyway, I just wasn't sure how long I would keep going backward before my mind readjusted.

I reached a Z_{max} score of negative 4.2. At that point, it seemed my subconscious had somewhat readjusted to my intent to go downward. If I removed the initial session of this grouping (because I was in the middle of it when I first got this idea), the Z_{max} was still negative 4.0. Clearly, there was still a strong impact from the delay. After that score was reached, the results began to moderate. I ran two more starts in that way, achieving highs of negative 3.5 and a negative 3.1, respectively. It seemed as if each time I started a new session, my subconscious got back into its old, disturbed mode, and then each time it readjusted more quickly.

Based on the Monte Carlo simulation shown in appendix B (see the appendix for explanation), the following are the probabilities of reaching a specific Z_{max} score on any given start (one-tailed and reported as positive because the intended direction was established ahead of time).

> First try, Z_{max}: Odds of 835:1
> Second try, Z_{max}: Odds of 151:1
> Third try, Z_{max}: Odds of 44:1

Checking my results against the simulation set me—as usual—in a different mental mode. I had hoped that I was trained enough to shrug off feeling "the significance" in my results. But after this tabulation, I rather tentatively tried again. This time I reached a Z_{max} score of negative 2.75, just shy of statistical significance:

> Fourth try, Z_{max}: Odds of 18:1

As noted so many times before, the classic, decline effect is at work in the data. So, not only did each attempt itself decline after reaching a high point, but also the whole study showed a decline with each successive session. Figure 19.1 graphs the four tries in succession. The high-scoring first session and sharp decline are evident. The last try was in the same direction as the others but failed to reach significance. My mind clearly made multiple readjustments to lower the experienced significance. So, at that point, I abandoned the RED-going efforts and shifted back to GREEN.

A day later, I'd finally adjusted to the new conditions, having run this backward process into the ground, so to speak. I felt renewed and was doing quite well. I decided to do a quick formal study on GREEN to see how high I could reach. I reached a Z_{max} score of 5.1, with odds beyond the Monte Carlo simulation table, but presumed to be over 50,000:1. I engaged in six more starts, and while I never reached as high as the first one, I did have a start with a Z_{max} score of just over 4. So, while a decline set in, this result was also highly significant.

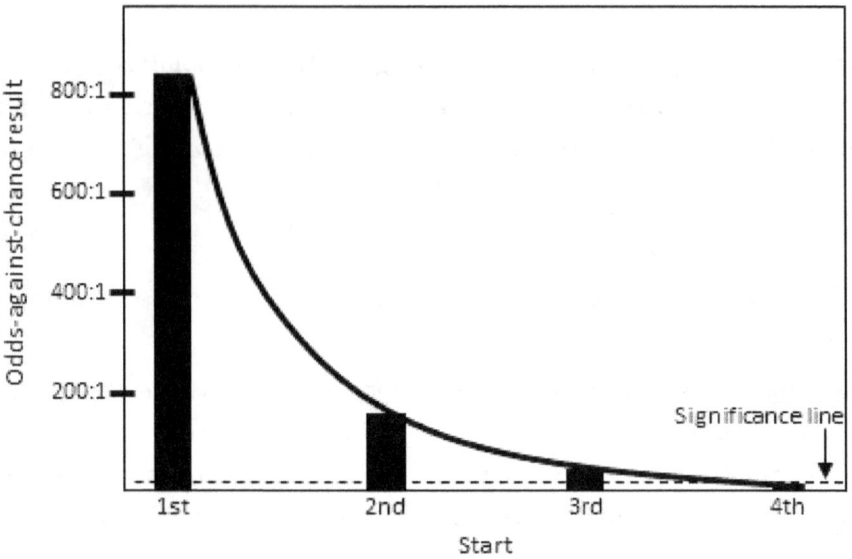

FIGURE 19.1. Four successive Zmax-score sessions—with approximate trend line—showing odds against chance based on a Monte Carlo simulation (see appendix B).

✳ ✳ ✳

The computer came back to Princeton after some months and was installed at my house, again one and a half miles from the office. With good (back-to-normal) keyboard response, I could sit at my office desk and continue my overall training. The distance issue faded into the background, and the REG may just as well have been beside me. I experienced emotional surges and anxiety-based rubber bands very much as in the past. Another common pattern, which occurred even at a distance, is one in which I am doing poorly for some period of time and then stop to regroup. I step outside the previous frame of mind, look back at where I'd gotten stuck, and in so doing can "turn around" my results. Figure 19.2 shows three such incidents of that experience, each one showing a before and after. The first incident is labeled *Locally Produced* because it occurred with the REG next to me. The second two cases are labeled *Remotely Produced,* because they occurred with the REG at remote locations. In each of the three cases, the left-side segment is the one I produced before stopping to regroup. The right-side segment shows where I restarted. The scaling on each before-and-after segment is the same on all axes, so the pair of data lines can be compared in an absolute sense.

This before-and-after experience is interesting in general, but what does not factor in is whether it was remote or local. That variable just seems to be

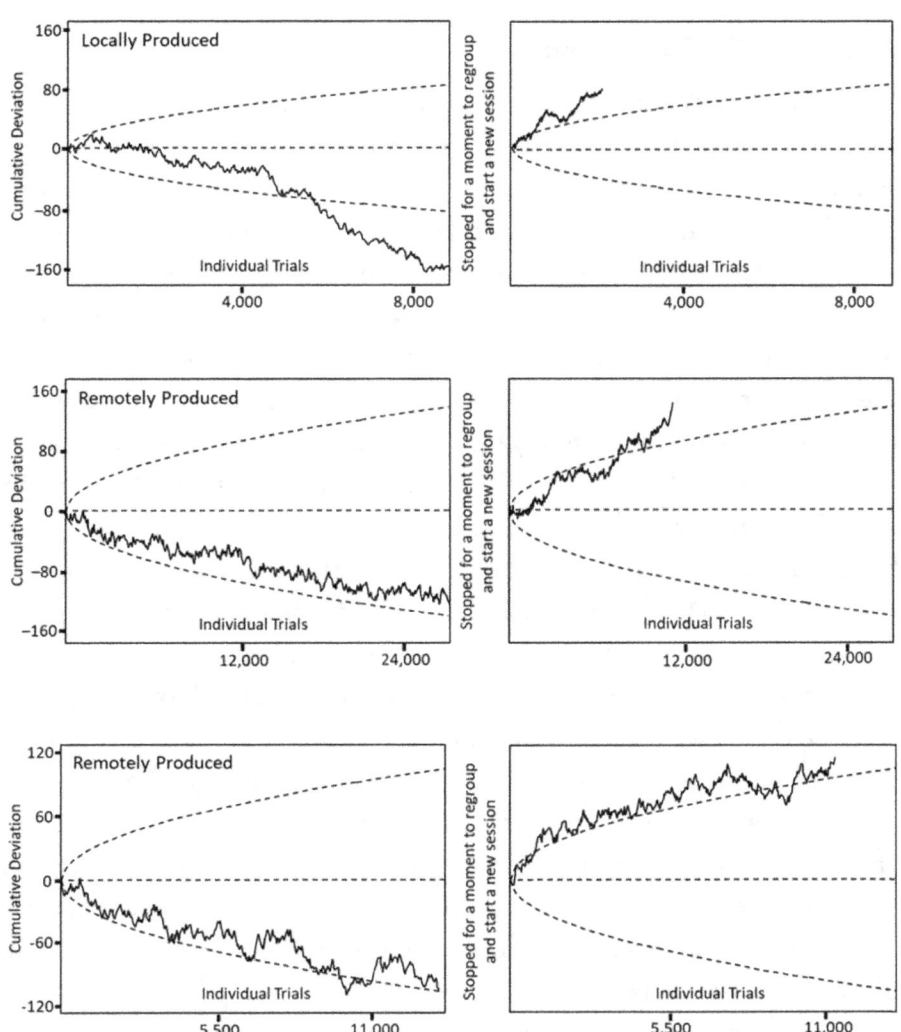

FIGURE 19.2. Three pairs of linked segments, in which the left-side segment of each pair was produced in one frame of mind, followed by a momentary stop to regroup, followed by a new start and new frame of mind giving the right-side results.

a nonissue. What's disturbing, however, is that the before-and-after parts cancel each other out, making it look like nothing happened overall. That is, when looking at the two segments as just one long data line, the casual eye might see only that they have reaffirmed the overall chance expectation. But this two-part experience is definitely not the same as if it had never occurred in the first place. Shooting someone and then putting the bullet back in the gun is not the same as never having fired it in the first place.[4]

A Final Study: Postproject

In October 2017, John and another Psyleron colleague, Nick Haw, wrote software to combine any amount of data that had been produced in our final standard data format. I provided John and Nick with a large body of my personal data spanning many years. I gave it to them under duress, however, noting that over the years there were many times that I was *trying* to go backward or was testing out strategies that *let* the results trend downward. None of that was indicated in the data file. I suspected that the results of the whole were not going to be significant. And they weren't. Seeing that, however, put me into one of my signature moods of righteous indignation. I said to myself, "I'll show them." Of course, at that point, I'm also watching myself react this way but am allowing the feelings anyway, because they can be put to good use. I started another study with the goal of reaching a Z_{max} score of 5 as quickly as possible and not stopping until I got there.

Long story short, I did not reach a Z score of 5. But in that effort, I generated a months-long study of about 1.7 million trials before giving up. In fact, the righteous indignation wore off early, and the study took on its own character (or unit of meaning) that seemed to settle around a Z score of about 3. One might say that this score became the norm during the study. That is, the longer the study went on at that value, the more any fluctuations from the score became emotionally unimportant—or even irrelevant. Even a strong rubber band didn't affect the score greatly because of the vast number of trials already done.

Figure 19.3 shows the postproject study with the standard random-walk chart. As can be seen, even to the end the chart continues to climb. However, the Z score remains flat. To make that clearer, figure 19.4 shows the chart

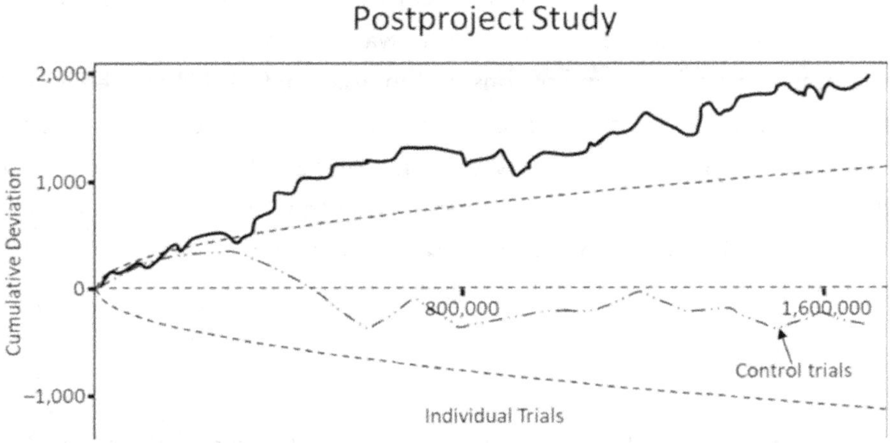

Postproject Study

FIGURE 19.3. A postproject study of 1.7 million trials with a target Z score of 5 but settling into a Z score of approximately 3. The dashed line represents the control data

from the perspective of current Z score. Once the score reached 3, it settled on that score to the end—in spite of a dip in the middle.

I did not reach my lofty goal of a Z score of 5, but the actual results should not be dismissed. The probability of ending with such a score has odds against chance of about 750 to 1.[5]

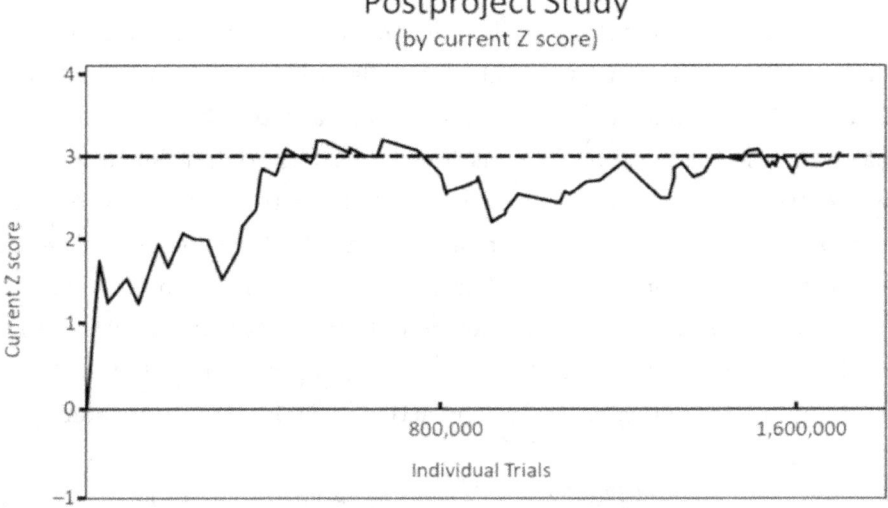

FIGURE 19.4. This chart of the same postproject study, this time shown by Z score, indicates that early in the study, a Z score of 3 is established and becomes the psychological norm for the study.

The settling of the Z score on 3 is curious, but it does have an explanation. Because the original target Z score was 5, it meant that a Z score of 3 was easier to reach—a kind of consolation prize. In fact, I chose the original target because it was clearly over my head. The score the study settled on may represent how I *actually* feel about my current abilities. I have perhaps developed a deep sense that I am a person who through training has become a Z-score-of-3-type person. We can draw an analogy to a level 3 black belt in karate: I've become a level 3 black belt in REG.

※ ※ ※

Shortly after producing that result, I discussed my idea of self-identifying as a level 3 with a colleague, who for reasons of anonymity we'll call Steve. Steve sent me his own, similar experience that had just occurred. Steve is much better than I am at the REG, and he can routinely get higher scores. In this study, he set a target of reaching a Z_{max} of 6.2 to 6.4 (don't ask me why the range). As he approached 5, his results moderated and ultimately flattened completely at that value. And though he had not completely given up on going higher, a family move forced him to end the study. His cumulative Z-score chart is shown in figure 19.5. It can be compared with my own chart: figure 19.4.

I queried Steve about his stalling at a Z score of 5, and he admitted that perhaps at some deeper level, that score reflects his own sense of ability. He is a REG level 5 black belt. So, just as my initial target has been above my pay grade, so was his. His subconscious had settled on a value at which he was most comfortable.* It's also curious that the trend values were round numbers. Round numbers help make the case that they were imposed by the mental regulator rather than being random values like, say, 2.65 or 5.35.

Steve's study was not conducted remotely, as contrasted with the rest of the data reported in this chapter. Once again, that suggests that there's nothing to recommend distance as an active variable—except insofar as one

---

* Steve's study spanned 39,413 trials. However, he tracked his progress in terms of where each session ended (sessions could be of different lengths). So, the graph of figure 19.5 (with session as the horizontal axis) represents how he experienced his progress and the psychology of significance involved.

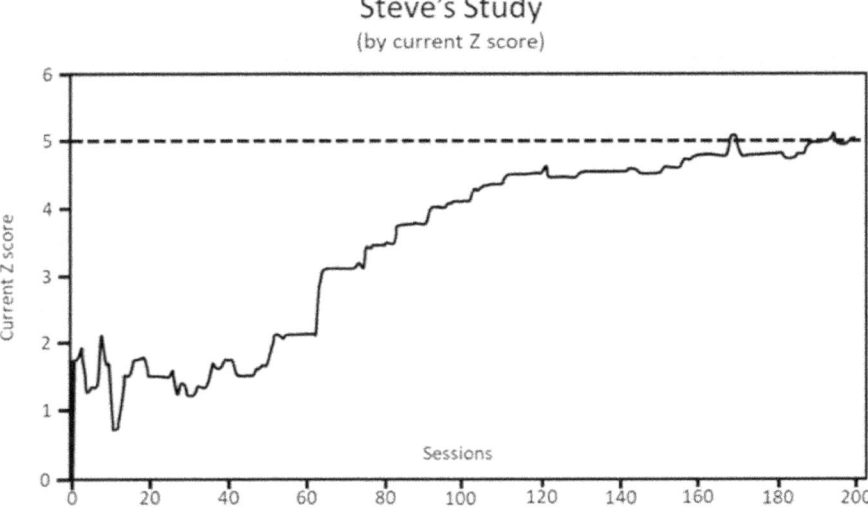

FIGURE 19.5. Steve's chart by Z score, showing a steep climb that moderates to the point of reaching a limiting value of about 5, which becomes the psychological norm for the study.

might think it *is* a variable and so react differently. In fact, during this REG postproject study I physically moved between cities, including a long stint in Maryland, where I was about 170 miles from the REG. The results during that period look very much the same as when the REG was one and a half miles away.[6]

Very much the same is of course not a rigorous statement. However, I learned that providing too much detail loses the overall intent. I found years ago that no matter what data are presented, those disinclined to believe the material on theoretical grounds will never find that it is enough. Rather, what's needed are curious minds that want to find out what this process might mean for human experience, including what value it might provide. In that regard, practical applications may take the lead even before we fully understand the theory driving them. And to that end, the next chapter tells the story of a similar field of study that took a practical path toward societal acceptance and integration. Today it contributes greatly to many people's well-being. In examining the similarities and differences between the two stories, we may get a glimpse of how the REG will find its own way forward in society.

CHAPTER 20:
PSYCHOFEEDBACK

In the late 1960s, a group of Indian yogis arrived at Council Grove, Kansas, for a conference on altered states of consciousness. The yogis had spent their lifetimes meditating, and through the discipline, had developed abilities not previously seen in the West. They could make one of their hands hot and at the same time the other one cold. They could lower their heart rates, blood pressures, and metabolisms to levels considered virtually unsustainable for life. They could shift their brain-wave patterns to approximate sleep yet be awake. Some could even push a nail clear through a hand without bleeding or showing evidence of pain. From the perspective of science, these yogis were creatures from another planet.[1]

Conventional wisdom at that time held that the conscious mind simply could not exert control over autonomic functions such as blood pressure, heart rate, body temperature, pain response, and brain-wave activity. But because those yogis clearly could, an explanation had to be developed that was consistent with current scientific thinking. The scientific establishment decided that the yogis were not actively controlling those unconscious body processes, because, well, that just couldn't be done.[2] The official line became that the yogis had found ways to classically condition their bodies—specifically, the muscular–vascular system. In that model, the yogis had taught their bodies to respond to stimuli—just as Pavlov conditioned his dogs to salivate upon hearing a bell. According to that theory, the yogis were embedding stimulus–response links in their subconsciouses so that their bodies would respond on cue. But while a debate raged throughout the halls of the scientific community, on the street it was a very different story. The new field of biofeedback came under clinical study for treatment of a variety of medical conditions, was producing good results, and was on its way to becoming a multibillion-dollar health therapy.

Today everyone accepts the idea that the autonomic nervous system can be engaged and controlled to various degrees through conscious intention and biofeedback. And today most people assume biofeedback was always accepted and that there was never a controversy surrounding it. However, many of today's' biofeedback clinicians in practice can attest to their struggles for respect in the early years.

One such practitioner is Les Fehmi, who as a young postdoctoral student in the 1960s became captivated by the possibility of controlling his own brain. Because biofeedback didn't yet exist as a field of study, Fehmi had to build his own electroencephalograph (EEG) brain-wave device. He decided to pursue the research even though others repeatedly warned him it was fringe science and would stigmatize him for the rest of his career. But when the group of yogis arrived at Council Grove, Fehmi saw the future. He witnessed the yogis perform their mind-boggling feats of control and realized the tremendous untapped human potential.[3] And Fehmi stuck with the area of study. From chairing the first US national meeting of biofeedback researchers in 1968,[4] he remains today, half a century later, an active biofeedback researcher and clinician.

He has never forgotten his early attempts to train himself. When first hooked up to a brain-wave monitor, he failed to produce the alpha waves he had targeted. He tried with increasing concentration for weeks to alter his brain's output, but it seemed, if anything, to be getting worse. Finally, after giving up and resigning himself to failure, he began to produce an abundance of alpha waves. When he stopped trying so hard and simply opened himself to whatever would be, he succeeded.

That sequence of events mirrors my own reported experience with the REG. In both Fehmi's case and my own, the wistful resignation, "Well, I tried," resulted in a breakthrough. For Fehmi, that profound moment showed him that it is *not* narrow-focused conscious intent that succeeds but an open attitude and focus that are more encompassing, more free-flowing, more giving, and wider in scope. Since that moment, Fehmi has worked with thousands of patients, helping them achieve healthier and more-adaptive mental attitudes of openness. He developed an audio program as a teaching tool called Open Focus, which has sold tens of thousands of copies as a book and as CD-guided training.[5]

Fehmi's wife, Susan, also a psychologist and biofeedback clinician, describes another issue that often arises with patients new to biofeedback. New patients tend to watch the feedback monitor closely for signs that they're entering the right mental zone. They don't want to miss it, and so, when they get into the zone as indicated by an audible tone and flashing lights, they try to freeze what they're doing. According to Susan, "They instantly build a model of a proposed brain state and try to become the model."[6] That, too, is parallel to my own experience with the REG game in what I called *posing*. It's very tempting to jump from a live *moment* into a *model* of that moment. But the two are not the same.

There are other basic parallels between biofeedback and REG-based feedback. In both cases, one must attend to inner states of mind to get the process to work. Both involve feedback about those inner states. But biofeedback is based on physical measures of the body's response, such as brain waves and skin conductance. The REG process involves no physical monitoring of the brain or body and is not a physical process as we know it. For those reasons, PEAR lab manager Brenda Dunne termed the experience *psychofeedback*.

The proposition here is that psychofeedback will find its way into society just as biofeedback did. It will have its own unique areas of inquiry and activity. So, although today it remains too strange to admit into academic study, like biofeedback it can take a more-clinical route to social acceptance. Basic research can take place in this more-practical setting as we tinker with process to find out what methods and procedures work most effectively. In other words, we'll let neuroscience and the principles of physics catch up with the reality on the street.

Clinical and Related Psychofeedback Research

The Baycrest hospital group in Toronto is testing REGs with patients who have brain damage.[7] The first studies were to see whether such patients might perform better by having diminished self-awareness caused by specific types of brain lesions. In particular, given that the two brain hemispheres interact primarily by inhibiting each other, it is possible that patients with one damaged hemisphere might show diminished inhibitory response. What I've called the *mental regulator*, which tries to dampen significance—and therefore REG results—might be less operative in such patients. The sample size was too small for meaningful conclusions, but the study showed that in at least one case of brain lesion, the patient's scores were repeatedly significant.

It's possible that a REG approach to certain forms of brain rehabilitation may succeed. That is, because one steps out of current neural activity to focus on REG results, the brain may find alternate pathways to previously damaged areas. Damage to several specific brain regions, including the amygdala and anterior cingulate cortex, can cause loss of emotional response and loss of the ability to make decisions.[8] But the REG experience itself is full of affect—from fears of success and fears of failure to fears of gain and loss—often involving a response to the rising and falling of patterns of significance. It may be, then, that when one focuses on REG output, without the normal reliance on those brain circuits, new pathways get forced in the brain so as to recover some of that experience.

Another Canadian group, at Laurentian University in Sudbury, Ontario, has worked with normal subjects in clinical settings. Dr. Michael Persinger, who organized the behavioral neuroscience program at Laurentian, developed a helmet that produces continually varying magnetic fields. Subjects under its influence show positive REG results.[9] The research group's hypothesis is that the extra energy applied to the brain somehow boosts the mind signal. I suggest a different view—again based on the idea of reduced self-regulation or inhibition. I suspect that the somewhat chaotic global field disrupts some of the mental regulator processes that normally inhibit more-effective purposeful alignment. Thus, we may have the counterintuitive result that a normally too-busy brain might benefit from being made even busier in certain ways so as to tie up the normal inhibiting response and allow a person to be more purposeful in other ways.

The current stage in the development of psychofeedback shows a clear need for the correlation of neurological activity with both self-reports and ongoing REG output. Though an obvious thing to try, there has yet to be any well-funded research in this area. However, attempts are emerging—again in a more-clinical setting due to the presence of such instruments for other purposes. The Baycrest group has done some early work with subjects trying to affect the REG while inside a functional MRI device. The group images the subjects' brain activity during the sessions. Other measures such as skin response and heart-rate variability can also be taken. So, even though psychofeedback may be directly related to the mind, it doesn't mean that the brain and body can be ignored.

Correlations between mental and physical responses are expected to be present. For example, figure 19.2 in the previous chapter shows three instances of experience when I was doing poorly, stopped to regroup, and then did well. Each chart represents a period lasting anywhere from 5 minutes to 45 minutes. That length of time is certainly long enough to analyze brain states by using today's tools, such as brain-scanning devices. And as tools get better, faster, and of higher resolution in the future, findings should be easier to come by. However, according to the discussion in chapter 18 on how neuroscience hopes to "read minds," increasing the resolution of tools may work only to a point. My (limited) experience is that the mind recoils from becoming too exposed. Therefore, the mind may use the redundant pathways available in the brain to play cat and mouse with the measures being taken to examine it.[10] In contrast, here the goal is not to achieve highly granular looks at individual thoughts but, rather, to gain some general understanding of the parts of the brain that are activated and correlated with REG success.

Another issue to be considered in future studies is that some people are simply better at the REG than others. In that regard, we can enhance the value of physiological monitoring by engaging subjects who are more naturally gifted. Given that we're now finding genes that support certain attitudinal proclivities (optimism/pessimism[11]) and specialized openness (spirituality[12]), there's no reason to dismiss the idea that some people have enhanced biological/psychological support for better REG effects. Someday this research may have the benefit of accomplished "REG yogis," who can be wired up and studied just like in the early days of biofeedback.

Mental Enhancement Using the REG

The medical and health industries focus on restoring people to normal health. That process basically involves the elimination of physical and mental disease states. But today a growing number of people want to be more than normal. We're moving toward aspirations of technology-augmented experience. So, we can explore how psychofeedback might play a role in such a future. Psychofeedback may help us achieve more-advanced states of mental well-being and maybe enhance our cerebral abilities.

As before, we look to parallels with the development of biofeedback. Biofeedback's traditional strength has been relief from such physical ailments as headaches, cold hands, anxiety, pain, and high blood pressure. But recently, advances in EEG hardware and analysis software have resulted in a new subfield, called *neurofeedback*. Neurofeedback enables the training of high levels of synchrony in the brain-wave patterns of various parts of the brain. We don't know all of the benefits that may accrue from such synchrony, but they're certainly worth exploring.

Psychofeedback embraces aspirations similar to those of neurofeedback, but from a different angle. That is, rather than alter brain states to change the mind, psychofeedback focuses on mind states to change the brain. For example, one might ask, "Why can't I seem to be able to...?" Using the model that says that various inhibitory processes in the brain support normalcy over achievement, the brain dampens many of the more interesting possibilities. With psychofeedback, we may be able to unleash new associations by stretching our minds. Stretching may enhance emotional intelligence and responsiveness, self-awareness, and even some of the elements of basic intelligence.

The US military has been testing the use of transcranial magnetic stimulation to generate magnetic pulses to a specific part of the brain in order to speed up training people in the ability to recognize patterns. The military found that by stimulating an area of the brain associated with pattern recognition, (1) trainees became able to more quickly learn to read drone video footage that had been taken in search of hidden enemy sites and installations and (2) the ability persisted after trainees ceased using the stimulation.[13]

With the REG, we might find that targeted transcranial magnetic stimulation can knock out mental regulators and give the mind greater freedom (similar to what I proposed with the Laurentian University studies mentioned above). Any such exploration would be trial and error at this point—but with REG results serving as the guide.[14]

The REG is just one tool for such exploration. Every year in Palo Alto, the Transformative Technology (TransTech) Conference convenes to discuss the growing number of tools for self-exploration and self-enhancement. Many of the devices center on good health, such as heart-rate monitors for body regulation and electroencephalograms for stress reduction. But others try to push the envelope of human experience beyond the bounds of normalcy.

The psychofeedback process suggests new ways of thinking about what we're doing with the REG. It isn't about the gadgetry. It's about how that gadgetry bootstraps our ability to think in new ways. Psychofeedback helps us by way of a growing toolbox of mental resources. I call that toolbox *knowware*. The term is nicely evocative on two fronts. First, it involves technologies to assist in knowing. Through knowware, we come to encounter new web-based associations that help our personal wide webs become more sophisticated. And second, the term is a homophone of the word *nowhere*, which conveys an important characteristic. Knowware is not external gadgetry—like a biofeedback device or even a REG. Knowware is nowhere in the physical world; it is how the personal wide web learns to handle its own activities and processes more effectively.

In this schema, we also need a term for the physical devices that provide inputs for the mind in this effort—for example, a transcranial-magnetic-stimulation device used with the REG as mentioned previously. I propose a new term for these support devices and processes: *somaware*. Somaware has *soma* as its root, meaning *related to the body, especially as distinct from the mind*.[15] Somaware generates and feeds information to knowware, and together they form the basis of a training regimen. The term *somaware* is also put forth somewhat tongue-in-cheek as a homophone of *somewhere* (when pronounced as expressively Italian), because in contrast to knowware, somaware tends to involve gadgets that are physically somewhere. Somaware also includes the feedback or information given to the mind about the state of the body. The divide between knowware and somaware sits at the point at which information enters the mind, whereupon knowware takes over. Knowware is represented by many of the concepts presented in this book, including webs of association, moments and models, disrupter bits, posing, the mental regulator, mental occlusion, the society of mind, units of meaning, units of action, meaning-action pairs, external viewpoints and CBT, layers of abstraction, alternative futures, alternative reality, and the selection effect itself.

One final example of knowware and somaware that I've mused on is the possibility of what I call IANs, for *inhabitable artificial neurons*. IANs would be REG-based neural network units that can be inserted into the brain and that would enable people to fuse with them or personally inhabit with them over time. The units would become new meaning-action pairs for the brain–mind, with their neural nets conditioned over time to target some new mental process. The IANs might also interface with external devices so as to extend bodily capabilities and link with outside AI processes.[16]

Psychofeedback Training Effects

I can offer a few personal anecdotes about changes I've noticed in myself after extensive use of the REG in a psychofeedback mode. Such anecdotes involve the aforementioned areas of basic intelligence (maybe), self-awareness, and emotional intelligence and responsiveness. If you want to skip over these stories, please go ahead.

In college, I lagged in advanced physics courses and wished I had more native ability. My brain seemed to have limitations. Recently, I dusted off an old textbook to see how I'd do with it. In particular, I was interested in what happens when I get stuck on a math problem. I found that unlike before, when I would get bogged down working through an equation, I can separate myself from the stuck part. I can almost walk around the area of my brain that is blanking on the solution, thereby giving me more ability to work on my limitations. I try to teach that area of the brain how to engage the problem or, alternatively, map around it.[17]

Self-awareness is largely the subject of this book, and following is a related example of a change I've noticed in myself. In my early twenties, I learned transcendental meditation and practiced it for years. But that early diligence trailed off, and now I tend to engage the process only occasionally—such as when stressed or anxious. Recently, just for fun, I tried a session for the first time in years and was shocked at the experience. In the past, I would repeat a mantra to myself until I entered a meditative state. This time, however, as I shut my eyes and started the mantra, my inner sense of space felt vast, cavernous. When I tried to say the mantra as I had always done, it had no effect on me. It was small, tinny, kind of perfunctory. It did not engage the bulk of the aware self I now inhabit. So rather than let that voice be lost in the cavern, I let the cavern walls *be* the mantra and resonate at the widest level of my conscious mind. Immediately, the process began to work as before—only this time as a deeper, more-awe-inspiring experience.

With regard to emotional changes I've noticed in myself, here's a quirky example. I grew up listening to pop music like most people, but there was one group I couldn't stand: Simon and Garfunkel. It wasn't that I thought they were bad. Quite the contrary. I regarded some of their songs as just too deep and too rich and evocative of a pathos I was unable to face emotionally. Their songs made me sad and uneasy to a level I could neither own nor understand, so I avoided them. That feeling is gone now, and when I hear one of those songs, I embrace its lyrical poetry, letting it fill me. Similarly, in the past, I had trouble appreciating the full majesty of a beautiful spring day. With an awareness of this emotional shortcoming, I felt a sense of loss; I was just not up to it. Today that feeling is replaced with an often soaring joy, the joy I knew I was missing.

Of course, over the years, I've lived through many other experiences such that pinpointing and isolating the cause of a specific change is problematic. The foregoing anecdotes may have had multiple causes, of which my REG work is only one. For example, writing this book has involved an intensity that has no doubt stretched me in many ways. The same is true for many of my career experiences. And naturally, simply living brings changes. However, I can't resist telling one more anecdote, because I'm virtually certain that this change was brought about by the REG experience.

When standing on a bridge or looking down from a high balcony, I've always felt the strange urge to jump. It isn't a death wish; I don't want to feel that way. It's always seemed the oddest thing to me, and plenty of others I know have the same experience. My wife has it worse than I do: she says her feet begin to tingle and she has to hold on to something as if to resist the urge. Recently, I was at the edge of a high overlook with no railing, but the feeling wasn't there. I noticed it right away. And because I'd never known the feeling to be absent in such a situation, I was intrigued. I set out to learn why.

I Googled "the feeling of wanting to jump from high places," and among the results was a 2012 research study by a graduate student group at Florida State University.[18] The group wanted to find out what causes such an urge. In the study's polling of 431 undergraduates, about a third admitted to the experience. Through the interviews, the researchers came to a tentative conclusion that when one is looking over a dangerous precipice, there is an instinctual feeling of wanting to draw back, to physically pull away from danger. But to have such a feeling suggests that at some level, the pulling back is necessary to counter some other part of you that might otherwise want to jump.[19]

When I noticed the urge was gone, I suspected that the change had to do with the REG work. Though a self-analysis, I came to a conclusion that gives perhaps a deeper level of detail to the foregoing study's hypothesis. To explain why and how requires using some of the language that has been developed here. The feeling comes from the mental regulator below the surface of consciousness that mocks up the idea of lurching over the precipice to one's certain death. It mocks up that image because that's the only way to grasp the danger. You are forced to imagine such a future if you want to know how much you want to avoid it. But because the image of jumping comes from the mental regulator buried in the subconscious, it emerges from the blackness of the deeper mind—full of emotion and feeling and looking like a suggestion for an action you might decide to take. One asks, "Why am I obsessing about seeing myself jump? Do I have a death wish?" What the REG work has done for me is to enable me to inhabit some of those deeper subconscious layers of mental processing and make them part of my consciousness. Being now in consciousness, I mock up the possibility of falling—but not with a feeling that arises from a fearful blackness generated from below. I am conscious at the level in which that mocking-up process is taking place, and so the mental regulator has nothing to do; it doesn't generate a fear-based alert.

Use of Psychofeedback for Controlling Physical Devices

Finally, I'm often asked about the use of the selection effect or mind-over-matter processes for controlling mechanical devices like robotic arms or flight simulators or even for flying real airplanes. And here we're not talking about bioconnection wires or waves of any sort but a direct mental link. The idea is that such a direct link would shorten reaction times; allow for remote, signalless operation; and give more-precise, more-nuanced device control.

In my estimation, such expectations are not realistic. They represent a fundamental misunderstanding of the selection effect. The selection effect occurs *only* when an outcome involves inherent uncertainty and when one influences the probability distribution of the outcome. With uncertainty as the starting point, this situation is the antithesis of physical control processes—and hardly the basis on which one wants to, say, fly an airplane or even open a garage door.[20] Garage door openers from the hardware store are cheaper and more reliable. There's an old story about the Buddha's arriving at the ferry with his entourage of followers. Suddenly from across the river and coming toward them over the water is a man shouting, "Master, master, I have meditated my whole life, and now I can walk across the river." The Buddha replied: "I'm sorry to hear that. The ferry costs me only a nickel."

❋ ❋ ❋

Even though clinical usage may lead the way for the REG to find acceptance in society, we still must lay theoretical groundwork to the best of our ability. The concepts of webs, models, moments, mental regulators, and units of meaning build a framework for that new realm of understanding. Interestingly, the field of psychology has evolved new thinking that closely parallels a number of the concepts put forth here—but of course in a different context. The next chapter reviews those parallels and even shows how REG theory can provide advancement for this emerging body of theory in psychology.

CHAPTER 21:
FAST, SLOW, SELF-AWARE

The field of economics has long presumed that people are rational actors. That is, when making decisions, we humans seek to maximize our positions. However, as the theory goes, we also treat others fairly—in part so that others will treat us fairly in return. Acts of sheer altruism can be seen rational insofar as they help support one's positive self-image. On the other hand, emotions sometimes cloud good judgment, taking away from our otherwise levelheaded and logical decisions.

The problem with such a theory of human behavior is that it turns out to be wrong. Israeli psychologists Daniel Kahneman and Amos Tversky ran 15 years of studies and found that at our cores, we humans are *not* rational actors. People can easily be shown to make decisions that are blatantly inconsistent with even the simplest of logic. It isn't that we're stupid; nor does the problem lie in runaway emotions. It is something completely different. We have not understood the deeper structures of the mind and how they work. Therefore, when researchers look under the hood, we simply aren't what we thought.[1]

Perhaps the biggest shock to our self-image of rationality occurred during the mid 1990s, when neuroscientists led by Antonio Damasio began to systematically study emotions and the brain. The neuroscientists found that contrary to previous thinking about emotions, emotions are at the core of good decision making. People who've lost the parts of their brains that facilitate emotional response cannot make decisions *at all*. They may sit for an hour trying to decide whether to do the simplest of things, such as whether to tie the left shoe or the right shoe first. The problem is lack of a value system that allows for choosing one alternative over another. Without being able to viscerally feel the value or meaningfulness of proposed actions, we have no basis for action. We need the brain's emotional hardware below the surface of consciousness to inform our basic evaluations. Thus, rather than that emotions *disrupt* otherwise logical action, emotions are *essential* to almost all decisions.[2]

Kahneman and Tversky conducted studies with normal subjects—whose brains were fully intact—to see how the subjects would respond when confronted with choices. The subjects were presented with hypothetical situations and were asked to make decisions. Through many experiments, the researchers developed a model of mind that comprises two separate mental-decision-making systems. One of the two is what we would call *rational,* but it is not the primary system. The primary system is the one that is used throughout our daily lives and bears little relationship to the concept of rational. Together the two systems of decision making have come to be called *system 1 fast thinking* and *system 2 slow thinking.* In 2002, Kahneman won the Nobel Prize in Economic Sciences for this work.[3]

The reason this framework of decision making is relevant here is its closeness of fit to the understanding of mind as put forth in this book. The parallels become a level of corroborating evidence. Of course, the field of psychology doesn't need my validation with regard to its findings. But I do believe the work here has something to offer the field. The REG project argues for a major *third system* of thought in human decision making. That third system is only now emerging within the human condition but promises to change the course of human experience in radical ways. To examine that proposition, we look briefly at both systems 1 and 2 and then at how and why a system 3 finds a valuable place in the schema.

System 1 Fast Thinking

Kahneman writes in his book *Thinking, Fast and Slow* that most of our daily decision making involves the concept of a web of prior knowledge. That web represents our storehouse of experience of useful connections in life. When confronted with a new situation, we draw on that web of past experiences to decide what to do next. What psychologists now call *system 1 fast thinking* is based on the use of that web.[4]

One aspect of the system 1 web is the way it provides a sense of familiarity through repetition. We favor what we encounter often, and a growing familiarity affects our decision making. People vote for a candidate whose name sounds familiar even if they cannot remember where they know the name from or why they know it. Similarly, confronted with a store shelf filled with too many choices, we tend to buy products with brand names. Essentially, if your web of mind has no data at all on an issue, seeing a name you recognize makes you feel as if you have a leg up on complete uncertainty. A familiar name is better than nothing.

Your system 1 mental web is involved in almost all of your daily activities. You grasp the meanings of windows, doors, books, lights, tables, shoes, coats, and so on because of past experience embedded in the web. Your subconscious mind naturally matches those associations to prior imagery and experience—usually with no conscious effort on your part. Even simple calculations can exist prepackaged in your personal web, such as in response to the question, How much is 6 + 4? You don't have to think about it; you just know the answer based on past training and general life usage. That system is termed *fast thinking* because of the way it is served up in an instant—perhaps multiple times per second.

Kahneman and Tversky found many interesting aspects of the associative mental web, which can be targeted for distortion in a variety of ways—with the effect of altering one's decision making. One such method is called *anchoring*. If, for example, you hear a certain number in conjunction with some decision you're about to make, that number will influence your decision; it will anchor you to that number.[5] I recently had such an experience. A newspaper ad read, "Lease this car for $64 per month." Now, I did look at the fine print, and I knew the price would climb to $95 per month if I eliminated the payment made at closing. Therefore, I was prepared to pay that amount based on my calculations. At the dealership, the salesperson's first statement after "Hello" was, "I bet you want to pay less than $199 for your lease, right?" I said "Yes—" and with that the damage was done. The salesperson anchored the new number in my head (even getting me to affirm it) and so shifted my expectation from being "something more than $64" to being "something less than $199." My lease ended up at $175 per month. Time and again, the psychologists found that people's decision making can be altered radically by such prior anchoring. And there's clearly nothing about it that is either rational or emotional in a traditional sense. It's just the way webs of mind work.

In my REG project, I too used the term *web* to describe how my mind appeared to work. My web model is in some ways even more richly described, and, in fact, looking at the web structurally helps explain the process of anchoring as well as other functions of the web. In my schema, when the salesperson put forth a number and got me to accept its position, it placed that number at the center of the active part of the web. The center is the position of normalcy, the set point from which all deviations are measured. At that point, any deviation from the set point becomes *significant*. The further the number deviates from the norm—even in a way that would be good for me—the more significant or alarming it gets. I could no longer argue for lower numbers, because they work against the mental comfort and ease provided by anything close to the current norm or set point.

Kahneman and Tversky found many other ways the web functions with its own set of principles and ways it can be played. We are totally unaware of those influences. And though for the most part, the web helps us navigate life successfully, psychology's uncovering of the mind's weaknesses means our minds can be and indeed do get richly exploited.

System 1 has its limits. Fast thinking cannot develop science and technology, because it is not very process oriented. It's more of a matching action for immediate, snap decisions. To reach beyond fast thinking, up to many of our highest achievements, we had to evolve a different system.

System 2 Slow Thinking

Our mental webs can readily serve up the result of 5 + 2 because the answer already sits in the webs we've fully formed from childhood. But those same webs will not do as well at calculating 134 X 497. That is, you probably don't have that answer prepackaged and ready to be called up. When challenged with such a problem, you can feel a different mode of thought kicking in. This is system 2, or slow thinking, which breaks a problem apart, laying it out on the mental stage as a series of steps. System 2 has given us most of science and its findings and enables us to understand the world at a deeper, more analytical level.[6] That deeper level involves abstractions of things not currently in front of us. We create and manipulate the abstractions in our minds and/or on paper. In math class, we were told, "Show your work," as evidence of using the system 2 step-by-step process rather than applying a series of system 1 overlays by trial and error until happening upon the right answer.

In the late 1980s, New Zealand political theorist and intelligence researcher James Flynn proposed that each new generation is smarter than the last. Using IQ scores taken from the course of a century, Flynn was able to study elements of the IQ tests to confirm that theory. He found that IQ has increased steadily worldwide in what is now called the *Flynn effect*.[7]

What's relevant here is the *way* we've become smarter. We're *not* better at vocabulary or the parsing of sentences or basic math. Those abilities were presumably well developed in an earlier era. Rather, the boost comes in our ability to do abstract reasoning and form hypotheticals. For example, if you asked someone born in the late nineteenth century the question—as Flynn reports having asked his grandfather—How would your feelings about race change if you woke up one morning and you were black?—the person might respond, "This is the silliest thing I've ever heard." The person would be unable to grasp or follow the purpose of such a hypothetical; it just wouldn't make any sense.[8] But today we routinely use hypotheticals and other abstractions to test out future scenarios. Hypotheticals give us more flexibility in problem solving and decision making.

System 2 uses the system 1 web of associations as a storehouse of knowledge while overlaying a new process on top of it. In that sense, system 2 is a secondary process. Associations form in the web, and if a deeper analysis is needed for decision making, then system 2 kicks in. Almost everything we see around us today—from SUVs to indoor plumbing, to the electrical grid, to the computers on our desks—are made possible through system 2 thinking.

As the scope and impact of the two systems become clearer, however, another layer of experience emerges as relevant. It's through that third layer that the decision maker can take different approaches to resolving an issue—and different approaches can lead to different decisions and outcomes. This process is easy to overlook—in part because it comes from a relatively new human experience. As we shall see, managing decision making is facilitated by a distinct mental system that emerges from the shadows. I call it *system-3-self-aware thinking*.

System 3 Self-Aware Thinking

A century ago, a new understanding of the mind emerged with the work of Freud, James, Jung, Piaget, and other early psychologists. Before their insights, we took the mind at face value, which meant that it extended only as far as we could consciously experience it. But as we learned about the subconscious and unconscious minds, we came to realize that our conscious awareness represents just the tip of a much greater whole. We know now that many things are going on inside us that we seemingly have no awareness of or that we seemingly have no control over.

The ability of psychologists and others to manipulate our decision making arises from those deeper structures of mind and brain. Our personal webs respond in ways that pass through our conscious minds to affect us at deeper levels. However, given that our deeper minds are influenced in targeted ways, it means we might be able to exert the same influences *on ourselves*. That is, we can apply back on ourselves some of the same processes to reshape our own attitudes and decisions. For example, one might say, "I talked myself into it"—a notion that may seem casual but is profound. It shows how we can separate from ourselves enough to have two active viewpoints of self. Once separated, the self can be poked, prodded, and engaged in various ways.

The famous gestalt exercise from the 1950s exemplifies such a process. In this exercise, an empty chair is placed in the center of the room, and the clinical subject or patient is implored to place his or her child self in the chair. The subject talks to that younger self, showing compassion for its fears, aloneness, and the horrible events that occurred to that vulnerable and defenseless child self. The experience is intended to heal and integrate the child self into the adult self. It also helps a more-integrated self to open up heart and mind to others because subjects become aware of how other people around them may also harbor deeply hurt children buried within.

It is here that we develop a more-modern concept of self-awareness. In the normal sense of the concept, self-awareness means to be aware of yourself, what you're doing and thinking. But the term suggests such awareness of *any* self. Through empathy, you might become aware of another's personal experience or selfness. That, too, is being self-aware: aware of another's self. The gestalt exercise of putting *your self* in a chair and separating from it is to be self-aware in that same external sense. The key is to hold two distinct viewpoints at the same time. In fact, sometimes the term *split personality* suggests that someone can display different or inconsistent selves. *Split personality* may sound like an undesirable condition, but in fact any one of us might display such splits—even over the course of only a day. Psychologists have seen how people can take on vastly different personalities at work, at home, on vacation, or with their spouses, their children, their friends, their colleagues, or strangers.[9]

Kahneman and Tversky and others who extend this research become themselves models of self-awareness. That is, they uncover general characteristics that *selves* display, characteristics that were previously undiscovered. What is now called the field of behavioral economics is itself a body of system 3 thinking by providing an outside-in viewpoint over ourselves. Such thinking leads to, for example, media literacy. One learns how oneself can be manipulated and thus learn to stand outside one's own native or reflex responses. The point of media literacy is to evaluate one's own feelings and by doing so become able to make better decisions.

That self-awareness process can extend from momentary decisions to clusters of decisions. As we come to know ourselves in multiple roles, we see how the roles interact with the world and make different decisions. For example, in choosing a beverage to drink, one might say to oneself, "I would go for the soda, but when I put my health coach hat on, I know to choose the kombucha." The statement is riddled with the use of the pronoun *I* because it shows self-awareness of multiple webs or roles or selves that can be brought to bear on a decision. That same person at some other time might reference the self as, say, a parent or educator as the role taken on for making a decision.

This expanded notion of self-awareness is based on many of system 2's features, such as modeling and the ability to mock up hypotheticals. In seeing ourselves from the outside, we can shift who we are and how we behave—at least to some degree. Social media give us the opportunity to invent aspects of ourselves and place them in the public domain to see how others will react. But there's a key difference between normal system 2 modeling and the modeling of self. When we *model the outside world,* our models are fixed and stable. When we *model ourselves,* the act of creating the model changes who we are through a dynamic feedback process. So, what may begin as a system 2 process begins to diverge from all other acts of modeling.[10]

Another aspect of decision making that is passed over in the concepts of system 1 and system 2 thinking is that people are conflicted in what they want to achieve. In neither of the other systems is there a conscious reckoning with the subconscious and unconscious aspects of mind that create explicit feelings of conflict. Through self-awareness, however, one can begin to see one's own internal reactions and then use them as tools to inform and/or change decisions. For example, you might say to a friend: "I don't want to feel this way. Let me sleep on it before I decide."

One of the criticisms of today's life orientation is that we are increasingly "self"-absorbed. However, in light of this discussion, we see how that condition represents more of a cultural shift. As the human condition encounters the self, humans become increasingly self-absorbed. Put in a larger context, Americans used to see themselves as rugged individualists, spreading across the wide-open land and taming the land's natural resources. But in learning about the subconscious and unconscious aspects of mind—while also shifting from a simpler, rural lifestyle to a complex, social urban environment—our sense of self changes. Rather than taming the outside, we become locked into an internal process of figuring out our own complexity. And we have an updated version of the gestalt chair exercise to find out about ourselves. We project aspects of our selves on social media. But in this case, it isn't done privately in a quiet room; it's out there for others to comment on as well. The self is put on public display, and the exposure creates a highly precarious situation for the more-vulnerable parts of the self. The self gets buffeted in certain ways—and at a level to which we're not yet accustomed. As a result, we're changing from *rugged* individualists to *fragile* individualists.

I do not mean this critique to be negative with respect to these changes. They are what they are. And it appears that we are evolving through a transitional phase in relation to the self. The transition represents a shift from experiencing the world as *primarily physical* in nature and instead toward seeing it as *primarily social and mental*. From a previous focus on physical-resource challenges and physical-health issues, we now find the world filled with social connectivity challenges and mental health issues. It is a process brought on by that social evolution itself, leading to a state we could call *hyperindividualism*. Hyperindividualism positions the emotional needs of a self-absorbed self as the primary focus in life. But that condition cannot stand beyond the transitional period because it makes little long-term sense. It's like trying to be happy by focusing on trying to be happy.[11]

The Three Systems Working Together

The three systems can be viewed in relation to one another by stacking them as in figure 21.1. The layering is natural because the expectation here is that the systems grew out of one another. System 1 fast thinking is the bottom

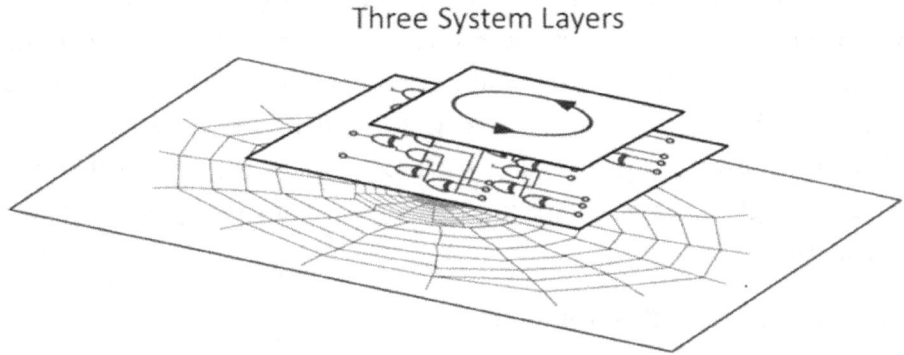

FIGURE 21.1. The three decision-making processes as layers in the mind. The bottom layer is web-based system 1, the second layer is analysis-based system 2, and the top layer is the self-aware, reflexive, loop-based system 3.

layer, the ground state of our thought processes. It involves recognition and relationships and has a spatial quality to it, as represented by a web. The objects in the web are spread out in a mental space by qualities so they can be compared—one with another. Dogs are not on top of ants or elephants but are set apart by salient characteristics like size, shape, and color. System 1 is largely state oriented, being a mental snapshot of relations as they exist at any given moment in time.[12] Its internal value system is its ability to make rapid decisions that aid in survival and well-being.

System 2 sits above system 1 and acts on the mental web with linear, step-by-step logic. It is depicted in the figure as a network of logic gates. Because it's a more structured analytic process, it allows for more-complex relations to be developed within the web's current network of associations. It builds new layers on the web, including the construction of models and the mocking up of proposed futures. System 2 is largely process oriented by stepping through time with logic rather than being spatial in nature. System 2's internal value system regards the correctness of its own logic and the relational consistency of its findings. And given that value system, it often checks its own work because the prospect of miscalculations (like calculating the wrong tensile strength of bridge trusses) can be disastrous.

Finally, system 3 rises above system 2 as a self-modeling process. It involves an iterative feedback as the self encounters the self. With each loop of self-reference, the self experiences change such that it views the world from a new perspective. It uses that self-awareness to take some measure of control of the challenges it confronts, including the way it processes its own reactions and the way it frames its own self in relation to decisions that have to be made. System 3 is the most time dependent and least spatial of the three systems. System 3's internal value system regards flexibility of choice through increased complexity and regards self-development through personal evolution.[13]

System 3 and the Selection Effect

From the position of mainstream psychology, nothing in the theory of a System 3 requires or demands the presence of the selection effect. The notion of mental webs already exists in the literature and can continue to be viewed as simply a functional description of the mind, with the brain as the physical basis. The thesis here, however, is largely the reverse. Matter becomes a functional description that any viewpoint uses to define what is not part of itself.

This inverted model of mind and matter *still* doesn't affect whether the trains run on time, but that may be only because we have not reached the tipping point in society with regard to its awareness. The selection effect becomes a more active variable as we become aware of it. In other words, its impact increases as we change our worldview to accept its impact. It sounds circular but is no different from any other previously mentioned psychological variable with positive feedback. Optimistic people tend to create for themselves an easier time in life and so have more reason for optimism; we become positive coaches for our own influences. The mind of the future determines its own fate more than it did in the past as we come to learn what states of mind affect the outcomes of events in ways that are most beneficial.

Today the selection effect sits inside a larger framework of personal web activity wherein we affect each other mostly through physically-mediated actions. The key to this direct web-to-web effect is in the ability to correlate our deep expectations in life with events that would otherwise have been unlikely to occur. We can enhance this ability by learning to purposefully impose our goals and objectives on the world in ways that (hopefully) increase harmony overall. That is, given that System 3 thinking has the value system of increased choice, one hopes that it is used to enhance the ability of others to make free choices as well. We are all in this together.

※ ※ ※

In conclusion, our growing self-awareness may be leading us to a watershed moment in human experience. The instability and uncertainty that intense self-awareness brings has shifted us from a more rugged past identification to a more fragile present identity. And while that may sound dire, it may simply be a transitional state toward an as yet undefined future human condition. Transitions sometimes have intermediary steps, and that would seem to be where we are now.

New York Times columnist David Brooks makes the point that the stage of high individualism in society leads to high levels of diversity. And though diversity is to be celebrated, such a state forms only a midpoint in a larger schema. At some point, the diversity must come together into a more cohesive whole that becomes a set of higher commonalities that in turn coalesce and build a stronger society.[14] Therefore, in closing, we look at emerging conditions that augur the possibility of greater social integration and wholeness.

CHAPTER 22:
THE AGE OF MEANING

Years ago, my sister-in-law and her family were driving to the Grand Canyon. Her daughter Samantha was about four years old and of course had no reference for the magnitude of what she was about to experience. But the family wanted to get her excited, so they told her she was going to see "a really big hole." Finally, they arrived and walked toward the edge of the canyon. As they gazed out across the vastness and majesty of the canyon, my niece asked, "Where is the hole?"

The little girl was looking for something she could get her arms around, so to speak. The canyon was simply too big, too different from her expectation. This problem is not unlike what we face with the selection effect. It is a process reflected in the very nature of space and time such that it is outside our framework of expectations. We don't know it is there, because when the course of events is altered, we tend to alter our expectations along with it. We don't have tables of significance in our pockets that we can consult, and in the end we can always chalk up unusual events to the unpredictable fluctuations of life and the complexity of nature.

However, if the selection effect exists—and I am now fully convinced it does—it's important that we know about it. At least those of us who want to begin processing the world differently. In today's fast-paced social society, web-based inflection points are everywhere; and the endless branching of possible futures gives enormous uncertainty to life and events. When one imagines oneself as a web that engages other webs in intersubjective space, a new dynamic emerges. One sees below the surface of sensory interaction and operates at a different level of engagement. One's web can influence another's and cause shifts in outcomes. That's the real process at work, and it's simply identified as the selection effect when we can catch it in action.

We can place the selection effect in a broader historical context. The past is typically characterized in terms of ages, beginning with the Stone Age followed by the Bronze Age and the Iron Age, each of them identified by the physical resource that was the primary currency of the time. The next ages were the Middle Age, the Gilded Age, and the Industrial Age, each of them identified by social organization and production methods. We live today in the Information Age, when information has become the primary currency of society. During this age, the production and transmission costs of information have dropped so precipitously that what once was scarce now flows at almost no cost. But as we've learned, there can be too much of a good thing. We are now awash in information and can't turn the spigot off. In the period following the Boston bombing, for example, the problem was not lack of data points about what had happened on the street that day. Investigators received so much data and so many images from cell phones and other recording devices that it was hard to know what comprised valuable information and what was noise.[1]

Our new human challenge, then, is not volume of information, but becoming more selective with regard to what information we attend to. Increasingly, we must sort through mountains of it to find the relatively few jewels of meaningful data. In this way, the Information Age would seem to crest, and we're headed toward a new stage of human experience. We're shifting from a focus on *raw* information to a focus on *meaningful* information. To that end, we can characterize the coming age as the Age of Meaning.

The Age of Meaning involves sorting through information to find what is meaningful. But it is far more than that. It is a deep examination of the nature of meaning itself. What brought about the Information Age was the ability to understand the very nature of information and how it gets produced, transmitted, and quantified through what was known as *information theory*. Similarly, the Age of Meaning must advance a new *theory of meaning*. For example, a while ago, I was discussing the concept of units of meaning with colleague Adam Curry, but we were having trouble understanding each other. I realized we were using the term in different ways. I was using the term to mean generic states of mind as singular units, but Adam was using the term in a sense of quantization, a unit of meaning like a unit of energy or a unit of weight. One might say, "This concept requires three units of meaning"—and indeed, such usage is already starting to occur. The *Washington Post*, for example, has established the Pinocchio measure, which quantifies on a scale of 1 to 4 the falsehoods told by public officials and which is, in effect, a unit of dishonesty.[2]

The Age of Meaning represents a profound shift in human history and experience. It becomes the first major departure from what has been the human project since the origin of our species—or any species for that matter. The past has been a struggle to overcome disease, famine, and other physical challenges. Today we've conquered those elements to a level that only two centuries ago would have been unimaginable. Certainly, we could always live longer and find better ways to distribute food across the globe. But the basic issues are no longer fundamental—only tactical. They have peaked in terms of emotional hold over us, and as we now turn our sights to new directions, the primary direction for the first time is inward rather than outward.

The turn inward gets pinpointed when we each have enough freedom from physical struggles to ask, "What is it all about?" This new journey is informed and propelled by new theories of the psyche as noted in the previous chapter and earlier. The unconscious and subconscious minds come to represent the hidden fullness of who we are. Young people today seem caught in the middle between external economic issues and their growing desire to focus inward to find out what will fulfill them. They often state that more than anything else they want to do meaningful work and lead a meaningful life. When I was growing up, few raised such issues. Meaning and meaningfulness were not explicit commodities but, rather, what might naturally occur in the course of living.

As we move toward the Age of Meaning, our growing self-awareness leads to even further analysis of our deeper psyches. As noted in the introduction, it is clear that our brains are structurally hardwired for primitive behavioral responses.[3] And because we spent most of our prehistory "in the jungle," our brains reflect what life was like in that environment. Daily experience was full of physical anxieties we no longer face today. In the jungle's web of life, everyone gets eaten—either alive or dead and sooner or later—by someone or something else. The best one can do is to protect oneself with a fortified shelter, stores of food, and other resources. So, it should be no surprise that today we continue to pursue such things as if our lives depend on it. The difference today is that there are essentially unlimited quantities of such resources relative to need. If you object to that characterization, go to a supermarket and look down the aisles. The scene is unimaginable in the vast expanse of human history and experience. Any knee-jerk response against the notion of plenty is part and parcel to our unremitting fears and anxieties under which we remain locked. What we call *greed* is really a built-in response produced by our brains. It is the never-ending promise that with more and more resources, we can move further away from the specter of hunger and death.

And lest we forget, that brain legacy is not just defensive but makes each of us aggressors as well. We did our share of eating others in the jungle. Today's quip would be to boast how we "ate the next guy's lunch." In the end, our wiring compels us onward to what amounts to a socially-agreed-upon version of obsessive-compulsive behavior. We accept it because we all have the same circuits.

The discussion of those basic inclinations and behaviors is by no means morally driven here. Rather, it is when we see through the layers of hard-wiring that we become able to develop personal and collective choice with respect to our own feelings. Do we want to continue being run by these circuits when they bring neither fulfillment nor happiness? Indeed, it's been shown that once one achieves a certain level of physical wealth and comfort, adding more does not add appreciably to well-being.[4] But that's not to say that being rich in resources is bad. Our economic framework often requires it, and wealth itself is not the point. Rather, here we address the inner experience of *how we want to feel*.

In addition to struggles with the demons of our past, a struggle is forming with possible demons of our future. The need to understand the nature of meaning is pressed on us by a variety of impending events. As noted in the introduction, within some reasonable time frame artificial intelligence will come to match—and will then exceed—our own intelligence. Many social issues will arise then: from AI's takeover of jobs to its possible unruly behavior, to AI's maniacally turning the universe into paper clips.[5] But underlying all such uncertainties is the question, "What are these AI creatures?" And by proxy, that begs the question, "What are we?" If AI becomes as conscious as it is intelligent, then there will be little doubt that it will replace us over time. Our task will be to create an orderly transition. And honestly, if that's the case, then what does it really matter? AI creatures will laugh and cry and have feelings like anyone else. And even further to that point, recent developments in machine learning suggest that human-capable AI may have to learn and grow through experience—just like children do.[6]

But AI may have no consciousness at all. Recent concepts in cognitive psychology and information theory allow for a decoupling of intelligence from consciousness. One side no longer requires the other side, as was tacitly assumed when we had only our human selves as reference points. Now, as we emerge from the Information Age, *intelligence is defined only as the ability to process information*. And it has become clear that the processing of information does not require consciousness. Weather stations do it, routers do it, desktop computers, locomotives, and anything else we call systems do it. And if we decouple intelligence from consciousness, then we are led to search elsewhere for the basis of consciousness.

Imagine that we asked a highly intelligent AI robot to sit in front of a REG and affect its output. Because the REG findings suggest that the subjective experience of a mind is necessary for the selection effect, the question is whether a robot might also succeed. The robot may respond that it fully understands the task: to make the line on the screen go up just by thinking about it. And indeed, if the robot (and other robots) were to succeed, then one would have to assume the robot had generated the required meaning field around it from its own web of associations. But if it and other robots repeatedly failed at the task, we would have a data point of evidence suggesting that inner experience is not present in them.[7]

Thus, for the first time, we have a tool in the REG that can help distinguish between consciousness and intelligence, between meaning and action, between brain and mind. By showing that the mind can do something the physical matter of the brain cannot do, we can begin working with the model of meaning and action pairs. We can see how brain and mind interact at cascading layers all the way down to the smallest level.

I had lunch one day with physicist Freeman Dyson at the Institute for Advanced Study in Princeton. Both my son Ian and his classmate Noah were doctoral students in theoretical computer science and were spending a semester at the institute with their adviser. I thought it would be nice for the two of them to meet a luminary such as Dyson, so I introduced them and at one point in our discussion about the nature of consciousness, made a play to describe the human brain/mind as intertwined meaning–action pairs consistent with this book. Dyson blocked it out, with little hesitation. He said no: the brain is hardware, and the mind is software; that is clearly the correct model of brain and mind. I could see Ian and Noah smirk at seeing me smacked down by the great man. But with all due respect, this may be a generational issue: We have been so taken by the beauty of this hardware–software model of the brain–mind for the past half century that we cling to it.[8] It gives the best of both worlds for an older worldview: it is mechanical at its base (hardware) but allows for a layer of intelligence and information processing on top (software). But as noted, intelligence per se is not consciousness. And though we acknowledge the many advances the hardware–software model of brain–mind has given us—such as much of the basis of cognitive psychology, for example—it is time to move on.[9]

The alternative model of the brain and mind is that of webs of association and meaning that I believe should be classified as fundamental structures in nature. Webs are everywhere today—from the Internet backbone to social networks, to hypertext documents, to the coming grid of interacting, self-driving cars. Of course, it was the development of hardware and software that largely brought about this proliferation of webs in society, and so, webs might be considered a derivative. However, we should reverse the order. Mental webs were and are necessary to develop hardware and software. So, the latter concepts are projections of the mind and not as fundamental as that which projects them. Any new theory of brain and mind must look another level deeper, and the notion of webs with their highly complex and entangled linkages tracks closer to the source.

The New Generation

I recently asked a Princeton neuroscience graduate student at a community dinner whether she thought the brain and mind are one and the same. She said, "During the day, we treat the brain as purely physical, of course, but at night, we sometimes have discussions about what the mind might really be." Students have always been freer to exercise their imaginations beyond what they've been told. They have to do so because the world is in constant change. Today's young people grow up with social networks and other mind-based connections that loom far more relevant than the physical objects around them. Young scientists are forced to become observationally bilingual by living in the prevailing matter-based scientific worldview of their elders while beginning to encounter a meaning-based world that is in fact very different.

Young scientists hoping to make big-picture discoveries in the field of consciousness and the relationship between brain and mind will need broader backgrounds than current training offers. Without a doubt, they will need familiarity with the principles of neuroscience, psychology, physics, and evolutionary biology. To make real breakthroughs, we need polymaths who can think through both theory and experiment at a deep level.

Principles of philosophy are also important to help overcome some of the most-difficult conceptual roadblocks. Philosophy is the original *knowware* and can help us untangle and sort through the many uses of the term *consciousness*—uses that are often different within different disciplines. For example, psychology uses the term consciousness with a lowercase c to mean the waking state. Physics uses the term *Consciousness* with an uppercase C to mean the reference point for the collapse of the quantum wave function. And biology uses it to indicate higher-order functioning in the evolution of animals.

German philosopher Thomas Metzinger, who believes mind and brain are one and the same, notes nevertheless that there may be a value in consciousness researchers' examination of their own mental states and processes. He writes, "I actually do believe that scientific research programs on consciousness and its neuro-functional correlates *could* be greatly optimized if researchers were well-traveled in phenomenal state space, if they were cultivated in terms of the richness of their own inner experience as well." He then qualifies this statement by saying, "but not because this would give them a mysterious kind of first-person 'data'—more likely, because it would thoroughly shatter their folk-phenomenological intuitions and endow them with completely new *theoretical* intuitions." Finally, he splits the middle ground with, "what is right is that first-person approaches possess an enormous *heuristic* potential, and we are currently far from realizing it." [All emphasis in the original.][10]

Materialist philosopher Michael Lockwood of Oxford echoed and extended that position through his own line of reasoning: "In short, I am suggesting that introspective psychology might have a contribution to make to fundamental physics. If mental states are brain states, then introspection is already, it seems to me, telling us that there is more to the matter of the brain than there is currently room for in the physicist's philosophy."[11]

Based on REG project findings here, I could not agree more with the usefulness of introspective psychology cultivated through individuals "well-traveled in phenomenal state space." Even if subject and researcher remain separate and distinct—that is, before newer, self-referential experimenter–subject methods become adopted—researchers will make better progress if they have a strong empathetic reach. They are tasked with grasping the experience of their subjects as closely as possible.[12]

※ ※ ※

Finally, the REG project speaks to the issue of values in nature. Values is a subject that science tends to avoid—in large measure because the scientific method for establishing facts is presumed to be value neutral: "Just the facts, ma'am." And because of that value-neutral approach, science tends to foster a worldview in which the world is itself value neutral. In a universe that is nothing more than matter in motion, there is no deeper meaning or basis for values. Thus, although humans have developed a system of values that helps us get along with each other, the values are seen as simply structured activities carried out among particles in motion. The REG experience, however, suggests a different view of values: if mind and meaning are primary in nature, then we can view aspects of our minds as representations of what the universe appears to value.

The previous chapter examined three systems of the mind that form the basis of our decision processes, and it pointed out that each of the three systems has a value system. Therefore, we might postulate these values as nature's values as well. System 1 fast thinking involves the mind as a web of associations and as a value system focused on the web's own survival, expansion, and sense of internal harmony. That's obvious at one level but quite profound at another. Life is about survival, clearly, but there's never been an underlying basis for the reasons why survival is sought. It is perhaps too fundamental or self-evident to ask how and why evolution and survival of the fittest got started in the first place. Why indeed did amino acids happen to clump together and form cells with the complexity of DNA and so forth. If, on the other hand, we suggest that associative webs are the basis of everything, then their drive to flourish through self-organization, self-integration, and growth is a favored direction in nature. Therefore, they seem to qualify as values.

System 2 slow thinking is a process that creates even more-complex and more-detailed web-based relationships. It synthesizes layers of abstraction beyond the direct perceptions and matching processes of system 1, accelerating web-based growth along many dimensions. System 2's value system is a kind of multi-dimensional explosion in layers of knowledge, including system self-correction. Once again, as favored activities along with growth and expansion, they would seem to represent values in nature. Furthermore, these activities are undertaken against the specter of disorder that occurs in nature otherwise.[13]

Finally, system 3 self-aware thinking involves self-modeling, whereby the self takes over the management of its own web structure. By taking a position outside the bounds of the current web, system 3 helps the existing web keep from becoming trapped in dead-end or slow-growth modes. It creates choice that increases alternatives for the direction of thought. In that regard, system 3's internal value system that celebrates flexibility of choice would seem to embody a value in nature. Further, collateral aspects of this direction involve purposefulness, self-awareness, self-alignment, self-integration, and both diversity and convergence. Those qualities would seem to be part of nature's value system as well.

These values may form the basis for the evolution of the universe—or at least a direction in which the universe *wants* to evolve.[14] Naturalist Pierre Teilhard de Chardin proposed that the universe is headed to an Omega Point, where fundamental values of nature reach a maximum. The values described here may be good candidates for Omega Point values. Albert Einstein weighed in on this issue but by means of a lighter touch, musing that if he could ask God one question, it would be: Is the universe friendly? He may have been asking that question in the abstract; that is, did we get lucky with the construction of this universe such that by and large we can all be safe, fed, sheltered, and otherwise content? But he may have been addressing a different issue: whether the universe could *itself* be friendly in the way that you or I might be friendly. Maybe the universe itself has a mind with choice as to how it evolves and how it treats its inhabitants. If the values we see in nature are reflections of that larger collective or universe mind,[15] then maybe the answer to this second interpretation is yes. In the Age of Meaning, those propositions are no longer idle reflections. By adopting a worldview centered on nested and evolving meaning structures of nature—including our own minds and, say, Karl Popper's World 3 abstractions—we can indeed contemplate larger units of meaning that reach beyond the grasp of our current awareness.

The discussion of values might therefore become a legitimate part of a new frontier for scientific discovery. And if we can begin to understand our own mental structure and workings as a representation of nature's fundamental values, then we have a better chance of aligning ourselves and our activities with those values. In turn, that would give us a better chance of successfully navigating the many choices we face in which there are many treacherous alternative futures. By contrast, if we do not learn who we are and how we are constructed or if we fail to do so fast enough, then our choices for the future we would aspire to may narrow.

To that end, the REG stands out as a strategic tool in an otherwise confusing social, scientific, and philosophical landscape on the relation of brain and mind. The REGs importance is more than a small adjustment factor to the causal nature of events. It points us to an organizing principle that changes everything. Indeed, the world is not what we thought. It appears to be more miraculous than we might have dared hope and literally teems with meaning. The REG has a lot to tell us about this new reality and about ourselves—certainly more than I have managed here—and provides an exciting new entry into the world of consciousness and its research. Let's use it.

SUPPLEMENTAL MATERIAL

UNITS OF MEANING

This chapter was not included in the text because it is more detailed in a way that may not interest all readers.

Imagine the following story.

> You are preparing to take an eight-hour road trip. As you get into the car, you think about the eight hours ahead of you. You envision the destination with a few points of interest along the way—maybe stopping at your favorite restaurant. During the trip, you think about how you're getting ever closer to the finish line, closing in on completion. As the last half hour approaches, you begin to get tired, but you're in the homestretch. At last, you pull into the driveway, a bit bleary-eyed—but you made it to the end!

Now play the same scene over, but this time imagine that the trip is ten hours.

> As you prepare to take a ten-hour trip, you envision the whole trip ahead of you with some of your favorite stops. You get on the road. As the last half hour approaches, you begin to get tired. You're in the homestretch. At last, you pull into your destination, a bit bleary-eyed—but you made it to the end!

The trips are clearly very similar. But why is it that on the ten-hour trip you passed the eight-hour mark and did not pay any attention to it? During the second trip, you didn't limp toward the eight-hour mark with fatigue as you did in the first trip. Indeed, it appears that one mentally paces oneself specifically so as not to get tired at an inopportune time. Getting tired at the eight-hour mark on the longer trip would have made the rest of the trip highly unpleasant and maybe even insufferable. It appears that we have the ability to frame experiences and manage them as whole units. Here we call such units *units of meaning*, and they appear to have their own properties.

The concept of units of meaning is embedded in the web model of mind. The whole mind is seen as a web of mental connections or associations, which represents the largest unit of meaning of the individual organism or self. At any given time, a set of active threads of association in the web are forming the conscious state of mind, which is itself a (sub)unit of meaning. In neuroscientist Giulio Tononi's integrated information theory, a conscious state of mind is one in which active bits of information (in my term *threads of association*) are integrated such that they cannot be pulled apart without changing the state of mind. The primary difference between the unit-of-meaning concept and that of integrated information theory is that the former includes layers of subconscious or unconscious threads of association that may be active. In fact, there can be entire units of meaning active within the mind or self at any given time that are completely nonconscious to the top-level mind.

This chapter takes a more formal look at units of meaning by using two types of diagrams as aids. It also examines units of meaning with respect to some of the unusual qualities and implications found in the REG experience. The discussion of units of meaning even touches on highly existential issues. The discussion begins with the idea of conceptual spaces.

Conceptual Spaces

Cognitive psychology has developed a framework called *conceptual spaces*, which provides a model for the way related concepts form integrated clusters in the mind.[1] The value of examining conceptual spaces is that it illuminates basic properties of units of meaning. A mocked-up conceptual space is shown in figure UM.1 and could be titled Cup Space. Cup space is the repository for the experience of cups. This space includes the placement of the many cup experiences one has had. Almost all cups are different from one another, but when we encounter a new cup, we somehow know what it is.

The study of someone's internal cup space or any such internal space involves a method for extracting it from a subject's mind. In that method, a study participant is shown a series of pairs of pictures of cuplike objects and is asked: "Which of the two is more like a cup?" Or even more specifically, "On a scale of one to 10, how different are these two cups?" After many such pairs have been presented, the responses are mapped into a best-fit graph. Objects that have been judged more dissimilar are positioned farthest away from one another on the grid, and those that are more similar to one another are closer to one another. The data may require a number of dimensions to map the space adequately because objects deemed similar in one way (such as size) might be dissimilar in other ways (such as shape). Multiple dimensions allow for the jostling of all of the objects into reasonable positions relative to one another with respect to the various dimensions that are being (tacitly) used in an evaluation. For example, in one of the early research papers on conceptual spaces, the researchers developed an animal space by using this method. They found that three dimensions allowed for a very good fit of the data, meaning that people largely considered three independent characteristics of animals when making their determinations. In this case, the three characteristics were size, ferocity, and humanness.[2]

The mocked-up cup space of figure UM.1 is shown as two-dimensional for descriptive ease. The cup in the very middle of the cup space represents the most quintessential of cups, or the average cup, as determined by a subject through the subject's experience. The cups farthest from the center are the outliers, with marginal cuplike features. When new possible cups are encountered, they are weighed against a set of relevant characteristics that have previously ordered the cups. The average cup provides a shorthand for these characteristics, presumably embodying them to the highest degree.[3] Of course, each new experience may result in an incremental adjustment of the center point itself. That would be especially true when one is learning about some new type of object or as among young children, when most objects and other experiences are new. In the figure, the lines between objects represent the threads of relationship connecting them. The relative

Cup Space

FIGURE UM.1. A two-dimensional space of cups (cup space) as a unit of meaning. The cups are positioned based on the mind's sense of their dissimilarity one from another.

lengths of threads correspond to the mental distance, or dissimilarity, between the objects involved.

An initially counterintuitive aspect of units of meaning (as developed here) is that the farther a piece of information is from the center, the more significant it is. That is, although we may be conditioned to think that items in the center are most important or most significant, with units of meaning the reverse is true. When one encounters a new cup, if it is very cuplike then it takes almost no attention or evaluation to place it in the space. One doesn't have to expend any energy examining it. In contrast, if the newly seen cup is only marginally or possibly a cup, it must be scrutinized more closely. Further from the norm means more significant attentionally. This was, of course, the central lesson of the REG. For REG space, the set point or average in the center of the space is the 50–50 red–green (or one–zero) expectation of output. When one starts to achieve a high REG score, one moves outward toward the edges of the space, where significance develops. When one reaches far enough, a mental alert will indicate that something is out of kilter.

The firing of alerts is an action previously mentioned with respect to the mental regulator (see chapter 6). A unit of meaning holds together in part by the regulation of significance through alerts by the mental regulator. The goal is always to reference the center of the unit of meaning to any other content that might be involved. An alert-level emotional response indicates that the normal sense of the space is being tested by new data. It momentarily creates uncertainty and in this sense a thread that the unit of meaning will be distorted more than is comfortable. Figure 8.3 on page 95 shows the threads of a web being stretched.

A natural question arises as to how long those mental threads can get before they're no longer meaningful—or relevant at all. That is, conceptually, they can extend an unlimited distance, such as when considering the position of a pencil in cup space. Or even beyond that example, we might ask where abstract concepts such as revenge or freedom fit into cup space. Clearly, it would be very inefficient for the mind to evaluate a pencil or the concept of revenge for cup space. If that were the case, then any object or idea one encounters would be sifted through millions of possible spaces. For more visually-based spaces (or ones otherwise sensorial), the recognition process begins with sensory neural pathways and how their matching patterns in our brains get activated. But here we'll continue addressing higher-level functions wherein significance is evaluated.

To see how spaces might limit their own scope—that is, self-limit—we look again to REG space. In REG space, the rise of significance that one experiences in moving away from the center set point of normalcy is nonlinear, or exponential. The large middle area of the space where there are low Z scores is insignificant. But at some distance from the center, the exponential of significance turns sharply upward. And although each space might have its own curve, the expectation here is that all of them are some variant of that nonlinear shape.

Regardless of the mathematical terms of the exponential, if one moves far enough away from the center the significance climbs toward infinity. That occurrence provides the basis for the boundary of the space—what has been referred to earlier as a *mental membrane* (see chapter 11). The membrane is the effective limit to a unit of meaning (or space), which is the point where high significance overwhelms any possible additional analysis. An alert takes over to end further analysis in what is essentially a blanking of the mind or a point of noncomprehension. Conditions are literally too significant in terms of the attention and emotions required to translate the current point back to the center point. That phenomenon was discussed in chapter 10 under the concept of occlusion. To draw on a physics comparison, the membrane is very much like a singularity, which is the outer boundary of a system with an internal set of laws. Inside the boundary of a space there are laws (relationships) that define the norm and other positions, and outside the membrane, those laws do not apply. The boundary cannot be crossed, because the two sides are incompatible. If one is inside the membrane, one does not leave the space by going through the boundary. To leave the space, one must shift to another framework or unit of meaning that is outside the space. So, most of the time, one is outside cup space and doesn't enter it. It is only when some of the characteristics of the target entity or object match the qualities of cup space enough (again, often beginning with neurologically encoded processing) that one finds oneself inside the space. (Obviously, this analysis is highly qualitative and needs further research and refinement.)

Figure UM.2 represents a stylized image of a unit of meaning based on the concept of significance. At the center bottom of the bowl is the set point of normalcy, for example; it is where the average cup resides in the cup-space unit of meaning. For the REG, it is the position of a 50-50 red–green result. The bowl is quite flat in the center and then turns outward and upward as the significance of these locations rises. The outer rim defines the membrane, with nothing beyond it, indicating that the significance has risen to infinity—or beyond the ability to process in this space.

The diagram includes an action ball, which represents the attention of consciousness within the unit of meaning at any given time. The action ball

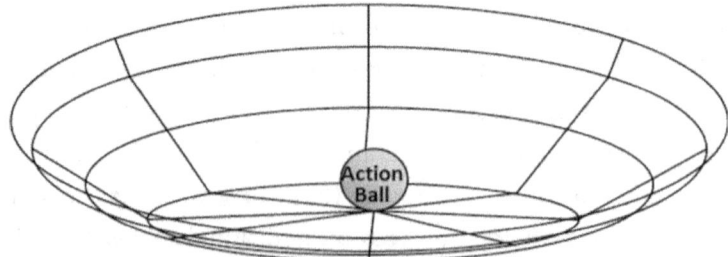

FIGURE UM.2. The unit of meaning as a bowl of significance, with (a) the bowl norm as the bottom center, (b) rising significance up the sides, and (c) the action ball representing the current position and focus of consciousness.

wants to be near the center as the comfort zone and will trend there as the lowest point in the bowl. If it moves outward, it means consciousness is being tasked—or forced—to relate to whatever entities are at that location. With cup space, it would be the evaluation of a new cup; with the REG, it would be the current score or level of significance of that score.

Bowls of Significance and Time

The process of active perception involves the mind's overlay of expectations onto reality based on past experience, with the hope that reality will conform to the image (see chapter 7). If it does, then all is well. If it doesn't, then the internal model of expectation must be revised. The selection effect was discussed as part of that process, wherein the mental pressure of the overlay can shift the probability distribution of nature's response to the overlay itself. In that sense, the selection effect must deal with the time involved in the sequence of events. That is, whereas much of the discussion about units of meaning referenced static spaces and states—even such as cup space—in reality, most units of meaning have time components. That same point was raised in the discussion of stories as potent units of meaning. A story involves a sequence of events with decision points, or forks in the road, that lead to different outcomes. We mentally create stories to manage how we want future events to play out. Once they do play out—however they do—the story or unit of meaning ends. For example, you may find that you're out of milk, and need some right away. You envision a trip to the convenience store, carry out your plan, and return home, thus ending this unit of meaning.

The psychology of these time-bounded stories is rich. But for the present purpose, we'll use the REG experience to describe some of their key characteristics. When one plans a REG session, one generally sets a target. In that sense, the event becomes a story or unit of meaning. For example, say that one proposes to achieve an ending Z score of 2.3, giving odds of 100:1 against chance. The bowl of significance begins with the action ball at the center of the bowl, which is of course the point of 50-50 expeccted red–green outcomes. That place in the bowl continues to be the most likely, or expectation, value during the event. Figure UM.3 shows a session wherein

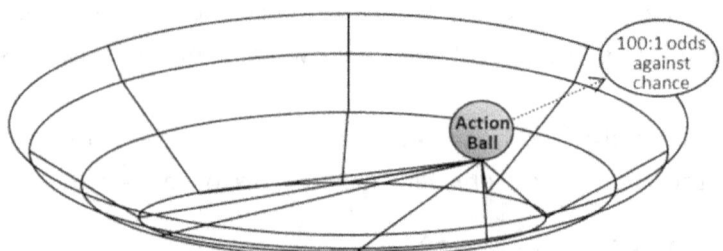

FIGURE UM.3. A bowl of significance depicting a REG session with a target score of 100:1 odds against chance. The current score is represented in the action ball of consciousness as higher scores move it up the sides of significance. Consciousness produces greater tension in the associative threads as it pulls away from the norm.

the action ball is moving away from the center as some level of significance is being reached toward the target. The top of the bowl is the point at which the target would be reached in terms of both time and (the) space. There is no implication of anything beyond that point, as the whole event would end.

The figure indicates that as the significance rises, the threads of the action ball's relation to the center set point go with it. They are increasingly stretched. Also, as visually represented, the ball is pushing against gravity in the sense of heading up the sides of the bowl. Thus, the diagram demonstrates a rubber band in the making. The action ball seems to want to snap back to the center, tumbling downhill back to the area of normalcy and expectation. The storyline or unit of meaning ends when one either reaches the target or gives up trying.

One must remember that this diagram represents states of mind rather than physical events. It is all about the awareness of what is occurring, which is highly interpretive. The action ball is the state of consciousness, not the event itself. As such, multiple similar physical events can be depicted by different bowls of significance depending on how the mind is considering them. An old adage is relevant here: that one-man's meat is another man's poison—or, each has a different bowl of significance for dinner.

Figure UM.4 shows two different psychologies for the same sequence of events. In figure UM.4 Profile A are three sessions of 1,000 trials each and each targeted to end successfully, with odds of 100:1 against chance. The three are considered separate and independent events or units of meaning. If one is indeed successful in the first session, then there is a sense of completion and accomplishment, and this unit of meaning is over. If that does occur, then one starts the second session with the knowledge of the first one having been successful. This can create a sense of confidence. Further, the first session provides something of a psychological anchoring to a new norm—a norm that one might feel more comfortable now replicating. If one succeeds in the second session, then the third session begins with even further reinforcement toward this new norm. In this scenario, then, one is successful in the third session as well.

Now we look at figure UM.4 Profile B. Here there is only one session or unit of meaning, involving 3,000 trials, which is the same total number as in the figure UM.4A scenario. Here the goal is reaching a result with odds of 1 million:1 against chance. In this case, the psychological profile of the scenario is quite different and is depicted by figure UM.4B. As shown, this single unit of meaning may be daunting, with a bowl of significance involving very steep and high sides. The effort here feels enormous compared with that in figure UM.4A, yet the overall outcome is the same in both cases. That is, to succeed three times with the odds of 100:1 with sessions of the same length as in figure UM.4A results in the same odds of 1 million:1 as in figure UM.4B.

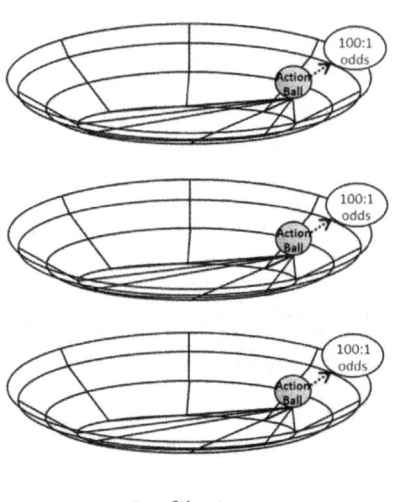 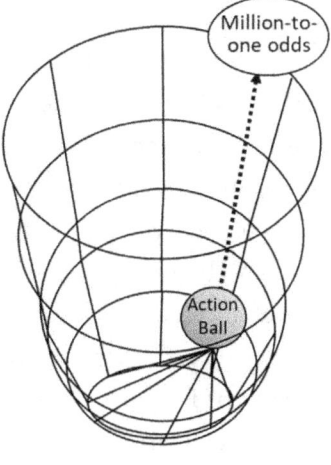

Profile A   Profile B

FIGURE UM.4. Two units of meaning—Profile A and Profile B—involving the same physical events and same overall significance but with different psychological framings.

Of course, this situation was brought up in the text, where I had an almost identical situation. I generated three studies, in which the success of the first helped me with the success of the second, and then with the third, as in figure UM.4A. But when I thought to combine the three studies into a whole and do one more to achieve odds of 1 million to one against chance, I shifted my unit of meaning to figure UM.4B. And that's when the high anxiety set in.

That experience is also very much part of managing day-to-day tasks or larger life projects. When faced with a difficult challenge, we're often encouraged not to think about the whole but to think about the individual parts and how to achieve each part in sequence. In other words, a series of baby steps gets you to the finish line. Professional athletes, such as golfers who've just won a tournament are often asked by reporters how they managed the pressure. They generally respond that they took it one hole a time.

The Trouble with Targets

Of all of the unusual facets of the REG experience, the one that stands out as the strangest and most unexpected is what I call *target aversion*. Target aversion occurs when one sets a REG target score and then works toward achieving it—as described earlier. Reaching the target would seem the logical successful conclusion of the session—at least in terms of how we think about targets and goals. But oddly, during a session one may approach the target until *almost* achieving it. But then one stops short and cannot take it over the threshold. It's an experience so self-defeating that it requires deep self-examination to grasp exactly why.

First, we'll review the two common fears in any goal-driven unit of meaning as highlighted by the REG process. One is fear of failure and the other is fear of success. Those fears are not what I call *target aversion*, but they need to be laid out to demonstrate how truly odd target aversion is.

Fear of failure occurs when a level of significance achieved in a session causes the mental regulator to fire an alert that the situation is getting tenuous. One realizes that now one has something to lose and so begins to "walk on eggshells." More generally, the mind steps out of a forward mode of thinking and adopts a sense of protecting what has already been accomplished.

With the REG game in particular, one can always undo any good state that has been achieved. Everything is always on the line, as opposed to many goals in life wherein incremental steps once achieved are done and cannot be removed—like, say, moving bricks one by one from the driveway to the house. In the case of the REG, one begins to look back "down" the significance bowl to face the potential loss, which can create a rubber band.

The fear of success, on the other hand, can relate to a potential loss of identity. That is, if one succeeds at a difficult task, one might have to reevaluate one's own sense of self. Thus, though we generally think that succeeding is a good thing, some cases can cause a real fear of going into personal uncharted territory. Using the model of the mind as a web or as a bowl of significance with the comfortable self sitting in the middle, one can feel leery about too much stretching of current threads. The comfort of the current norms can be lost, forcing many other relationships to potentially change. And once again, one must always remember that significance is in the mind. For example, if one has reached a difficult target many times before, then achieving it yet again is not necessarily emotionally significant. In this case more success of the same type or a familiar type would not be threatening.

With the structure of those fears examined, we can now take up target avoidance. I will put the conclusion straight out and then discuss it. Simply put, units of meaning do not want to end themselves. If they end, they die. And if a unit of meaning has been created specifically to reach a target, then reaching that target ends, or kills, the unit of meaning.

To explain that assertion, first note that the mind as a web is really a complex system of webs within webs. As mentioned earlier, our lives are nested in many layers of experience—from, say, walking the dog each morning to winning a life achievement award in one's profession. Many units of meaning can be active at one time. But it's also possible to focus down on a single unit of meaning that causes others to, for the most part and for some period of time, drop away. One of the thrills of movies or gambling or reading a novel is that one's consciousness becomes thoroughly soaked in a unit of meaning—to the exclusion of almost all else.

The REG experience highlights that situation because, for whatever reasons, it is all-consuming. There have been many times when I've come very close to reaching a target, only to pull away from it. I can say with confidence that as I get very close to the target, such as one or two hits away from success and completion, the significance shoots up dramatically. As I reach to press the space bar for the next trial, I almost blank out at the prospect of succeeding. *I can't imagine where I will be or what will become of me once it happens.* I am so thoroughly involved in that unit of meaning that when it ends, I am simply gone. I can't do it. (See examples in chapter 16 under the heading Courage and Vulnerability.)

Before analyzing this more fully, we can return to the idea of reading a novel—one that is lengthy and epic. As you reach the last page, you may feel pangs of sadness that the characters with whom you have grown so intimate will be done, over—and you don't want them to go. I remember watching parts of the longest Wimbledon tennis match in history, which spanned more than 11 hours. In the last set, a player must win by two games. In this match, the advantage in games swung back and forth within the narrow band for five or more hours. As time went on, it became literally incomprehensible that at some moment someone would actually win and it would all end. I almost found myself pulling for it to continue because after all, *it couldn't just end.* Furthermore, I would think that the feeling was magnified manyfold for the players themselves. Indeed, no possible scenario of random fluctuations would have produced this narrow band of ongoing results. I firmly believe that the players were locked in target avoidance at some deep level—out of the disorientation of the moment of ending. (Years later, one of those same players was involved in the second-longest match, with the last set lasting 50 games. Such a statistical improbability defies the imagination and supports the notion of the event's being psychologically regulated. It may be that the one player literally imposed a continued unit of meaning on each of the matches.)

It can be hard to see target avoidance at work in a REG session, only because targets are generally not visible in the charts. A target Z score of 2 or 3 becomes a nondescript point on the data line of a normal random-walk chart. However, there is a target that is easy to see on the charts. That is the target of zero. There have been many times when I dropped well below zero early in a session for whatever reason. Then I might stop and set my sights on reaching back to zero as the target—just to feel as if I didn't "lose." It is here that target aversion can be seen. I can show legions of sessions when I get one hit away from the target of zero and I bounce off it like a glass ceiling. Sometimes I come back and bounce off again and again—any number of times. In moments of being one or two hits away from the target, I can feel the fear overtake me. My mind literally blocks my ability to keep thinking. A

Log Entries: Target Avoidance

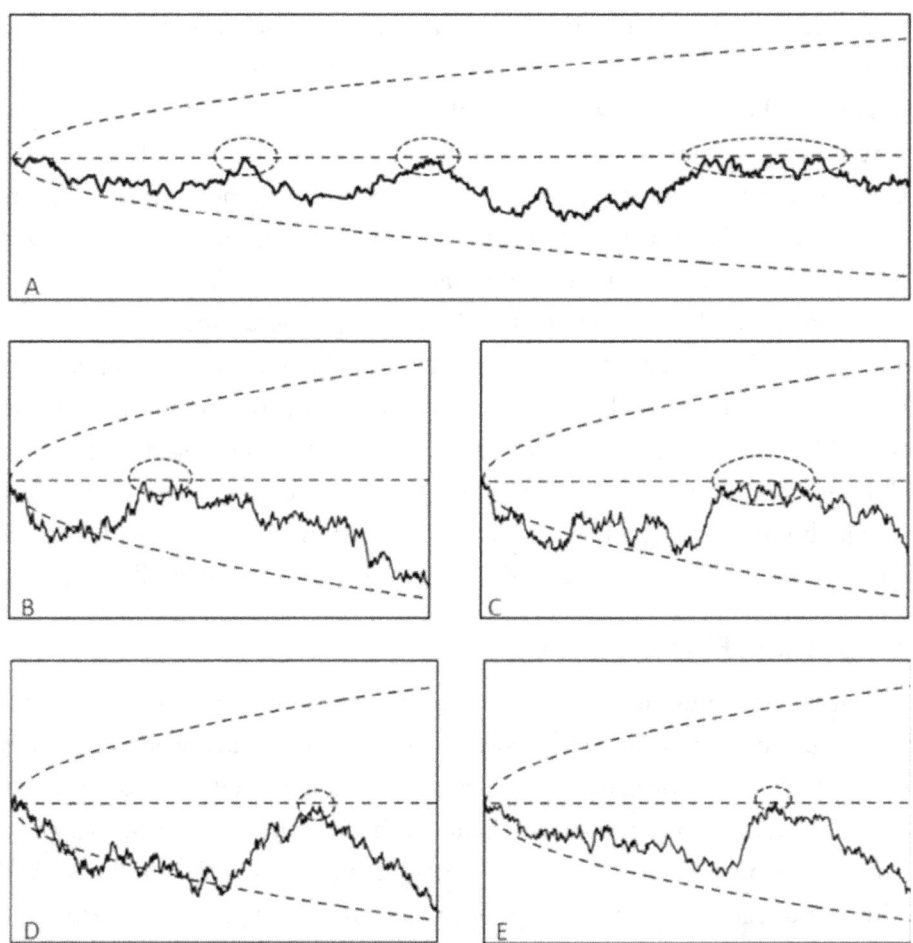

FIGURE UM.5. Five random-walk charts showing target avoidance. In each case, the target was set as zero after initially falling well below zero. But when the target is approached, it is avoided.

rubber band takes over just to get away from the target. Figure UM.5 shows five such charts (among many). The four smaller charts (B through E) are scaled similarly for easy comparison. That is, the parabolas of the two charts directly overlay.

Part of the theory of target aversion can be developed by how one finds a way around the issue. To beat it is to begin to understand it. I have found two ways to beat target aversion. The first is to stop playing when near the target. That itself can be hard because the unit of meaning is, as stated, all-consuming. But to stop is to break the spell—especially when setting the mind briefly on something else, like reading the paper. Then, when one comes back to the game, one is external to the unit of meaning that was so dominant moments ago. From that outside vantage or viewpoint, the idea of getting the last hit or two is trivial, because it doesn't mean what it did before. There is no emotional involvement—though it doesn't take much to reassume the unit of meaning if one wants to or is not careful. So, one easily reaches the target, and the unit of meaning ends. But in this case, one doesn't die with it, because one is already mostly outside it.

A second method for succeeding is to change the target from a Z score of zero (in these cases) to some greater number. With a new, higher target, reaching zero is no longer significant. It is passed by without a second thought. This process is very much as described at the beginning of this chapter, wherein one rethinks an eight-hour road trip into a ten-hour one. Given this reframing, when one reaches the eight-hour mark—the actual end of the drive—one is pleasantly surprised and not tired at all.

Targets and Physical Death

If units of meaning do not want to end themselves, then we can see how a most basic element of the physical survival instinct has been encoded in our biology. For an organism, physical death is the ultimate unit of meaning that ends. Thus, to approach physical death is to approach infinite significance or incomprehensibility. It is the organism's point of singularity. And I further suggest that the concept of units of meaning precedes concepts of biology, evolution, and the organismic drive to survive. That is, biological theory assumes that organisms want to survive, but as noted earlier, the basis of that desire is not inherent in the theory. Through the concept of units of meaning, however, the source of that drive can be hypothesized.

I have come to believe that an organism, as a unit of meaning, cannot fully, mentally grasp the experience of its own death. It is a life-level target avoidance. If circumstances force one close to the point of death, a recoil shuts down further processing. In Tolstoy's *War and Peace* there is a moment when Prince Andrei is contemplating the next day's battle, and he is certain that he will die. He tries to grasp the fullness of the implications and the significance of blinking out of the world. Tolstoy writes, "He looked at the row of birches shining in the sunshine, with their motionless green and yellow foliage and white bark. 'To die... to be killed tomorrow... That I should not exist... That all this should still be, but no me...'"[4]

Neuroscientist Christof Koch tells the story of a dream he had in which he comes face-to-face with the fact of his own death. He experienced the imminence of his end of consciousness rising to the point of utter incredulity. He reports being deeply shaken by the experience and becoming "perhaps wiser, but no happier." And since that time, that certainty of death has remained with him.[5] As another example, it is often reported that for people facing a moment of death during, say, a fall or a car accident, time is experienced in slow motion.[6] Such individuals may even have the sense of externalizing their viewpoint from their body.[7] In effect, they must get away from the implications or the significance of the moment, which may even cause them to black out to avoid it. In that regard, fainting from shock is perhaps another example, wherein one's current unit of meaning is taken so close to its outer boundary that the mind cannot process it.

Professional or public atheists (a self-given term) sometimes note that from an atheistic position, physical death isn't so bad when taken in a broader context of the web and the circle of life. There is plenty of meaning to be had in the wonder and beauty of nature. All of that may be true, but it further suggests that to deal with the ending of the life-level unit of meaning, one cannot face it from the inside and attempt to cross it. One has to circumvent it by creating a framework in which one's own life is nestled inside a larger framework or unit of meaning. Like the REG, one can face reaching a target point (in this case, death) only by being outside it through a larger context. This model also explains why nonatheists so vehemently react to atheistic statements. It's one thing for an atheist to talk about his own ending of a unit of meaning, but when that model is overlaid on another, there can be a visceral recoil for all the reasons described here.

The idea of an afterlife is often considered to be a coping mechanism for reluctance to face the fact of one's own physical death. As seen here, this is clearly true. But alternate assertions about the implications of death, as in the atheistic naturalist statement given earlier, are coping mechanisms as well. Both attempt to negate the power of the life-level event on the biological unit of meaning as experienced from the inside. The point is that none of us can face death from the inside unless it is couched in some larger framework. That's just how units of meaning work.[8]

What it does is to make one ponder why the universe is built this way. And without treading on sacred territory, so to speak, I will further some thoughts on the issue. As discussed in chapter 12 and elsewhere, there would appear to be units of meaning that are larger than single organisms. These units of meaning can be momentary—such as a sports team's gelling—or more-permanent groupings as a collective unconscious or even a Gaia-level mind. As such units of meaning reach "upward" in scope, there are reasons to believe (as discussed earlier) that they can decouple from anything physical through the layering of abstraction. The meaning side of a meaning-action pair references another meaning as its action side. In that process, a stable system is created that has no physical base at all. At least—that seems to be the case experientially—and it suggests that there is much we do not yet know about the structure of the universe.

Science and Bowls of Significance

Last, we use the concept of units of meaning to circle back to the discussion of the decline effect in scientific research (chapter 18). There we proposed that high levels of expectation may help drive initial study results to be significant and that later studies on the same subject may show a decline in significance relative to the first study. We'll use bowls of significance to model this course of events.

Figure UM.6 represents the psychological profile of a scientific study about to take place. The key to this model is that two connected bowls of significance are involved rather than one, as might be expected. The bottom bowl of the figure represents what we classically regard as active, which is why it is shown in solid lines. In this bowl, the center represents the set point of the null hypothesis, which is the idea that there will be no positive result for the variable being tested in the study. Up the sides of the bowl represents what would be supportive findings. Higher up the side of the bowl comes the point of significance, indicating a bona fide significant positive result. So, during the study, the action ball must go up the side of the bowl some reasonable distance for the study to show confirmed scientific significance.

But there is another bowl, which is "floating" in the mental space of the study. If there were to be a positive finding in the study, then this null hypothesis bowl would have been incorrect from the very beginning. The positive result would indicate—after the fact—that a positive finding is not "significant" in the larger sense. Rather, a positive finding indicates that the target condition is in fact natural or the norm all along, and we simply discovered that fact through the study. The dashed bowl shows this future condition, wherein a positive result emerges. In this case, the bottom of the top bowl (the center point of normalcy) is the top point of the bottom bowl

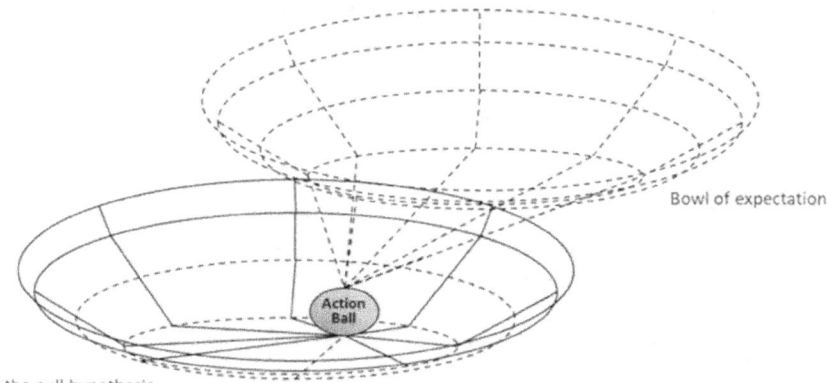

FIGURE UM.6. Linked significance bowls representing the classic image of a scientific study. The lower bowl places the null result at the center bottom, with significance running up the sides. The upper bowl represents the expected or implicit bowl should a positive result emerge as a new fact of nature. That is, a point of significance on the lower bowl becomes the new-found norm of the upper bowl.

(the point of positive significance). Said another way, if a positive result emerges—and holds up—the null hypothesis bowl fades, and ever after, the top bowl is what we call *reality*.

Now, it's possible that in the history of science (just for the sake of argument), scientists did not actively consider the dotted upper bowl much at all. "Objective" science perhaps demanded full focus on the bottom bowl. But I suspect that increasingly, there is a tendency to adopt the upper bowl from the very beginning of a study. As described in chapter 18, there is the pressure to have a positive result for all kinds of reasons such as career, reputation, jobs, and financial reward. As society shifts from being slower paced and more observational to being more decision based and more actively involved, it seems to be the case that scientists, like all others, begin to pressure the environment to show what they want it to show. And given our prodigious ability to mock up futures, we mock up the future we want to see, which in this case is the upper bowl in a study. Figure UM.7 shows how the scientists may be inverting primary and secondary bowls from the start so as to make the upper bowl the primary.

There is nothing disingenuous about this process. As noted, if a positive finding occurs, then indeed the upper bowl was right all along. That approach also comes under the heading of active perception, as described in chapter 8, wherein one overlays onto reality a given norm of expectation. Once imposed, reality either confirms the pattern expected by conforming

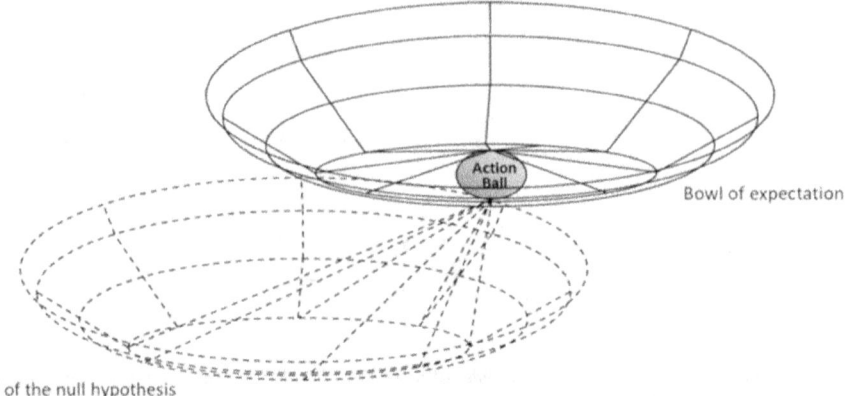

FIGURE UM.7. An alternate version of linked significance bowls of a scientific study, this time where the proposed variable is seen to be already "real," as would be the case with a subsequent positive finding. Adopting this bowl from the start pressures reality to conform to it.

to it—or it doesn't. But the stronger the overlay, the more it may force reality to conform.

At this point in the scientific sequence, attitude can shift, as described in the course of the Colorado experiment. It may be that once the upper bowl is confirmed, the scientists feel free to readopt the lower bowl. And in doing so, they have nothing to lose, because they have verified the reality of the proposed study variable. In shifting to the lower bowl, they become objective scientists again—relative to what the world currently knows—as they seek to quantify just how significant their findings are relative to existing norms. The proposition here is that in doing so, they no longer prop up the early findings, and so they tend to disappear. And even more dramatic, it's possible that their adoption of the lower bowl as a way to stress-test future results might actually pull the future results lower than they might have been otherwise. Given the bowl imagery, this is literally a case of the bottom dropping out of the results.

※ ※ ※

Much remains to be learned about units of meaning. The REG process is a valuable tool because for whatever reason, it causes people to become narrowly locked into specific units of meaning. That lets us isolate experience relative to the normal condition of life, with its many layers of units of meaning that are active at any given time. Bowls of significance then become a method of visualizing the psychology of individual or interacting units of meaning and how they are bounded and described.

This discussion covers only one person's findings—though in part confirmed by other colleagues who report similar experience. And I have tried to steer the findings away from a level of detail that might regard individual differences. That is, because this domain of research is potentially vast and almost completely unexplored, the findings reported here are more basic and universal. I feel confident that there are many more general principles to be found well before we arrive at the nuances of individual difference.

RUNNING YOUR OWN REG PROJECT

Personal experience leads to increased awareness, and that's certainly true with the selection effect. You can try the REG yourself by running your own project at whatever length and magnitude interests you. To that end, I will describe a framework for developing your own project and will include guidelines and tips. I know that even this small amount of direction would have saved me a lot of time (years!) and made my experience more productive.

REGs can be purchased on the market for as little as $50. They're units typically used for other applications (and marketed as RNGs), but with appropriate software (check availability), they will work in this context. So, interest in running a project should not be blocked by a purchasing issue. Along with the device, you will of course need a computer or laptop to connect it to. As an alternative, there are phone apps emerging, but they're of limited use for any data-driven project. They typically do not store data and so are not well suited for tracking changes in your experience.

Based on the original PEAR lab program, we have identified two basic applications for REG use. The first, which formed the basis of my long-term project, involves the attempt to affect the REG output directly and in real time. One sits facing the computer screen and receives visual and/or auditory feedback on the one/zero bits being produced. This format enables you to monitor and correlate your mental states with the physical events in front of you. It also incorporates a concept of purpose training. As indicated earlier, I use the term *purpose training* rather than the more common one—*intention training*—because I consider purpose to be deeper than intention (see chapters 9 and 16). That is, because it's critical to success, purpose involves meaningfulness and caring, and intention is usually more dispassionate and utilitarian. It may be just a matter of one's definitions, but the distinction here helps clarify the focus of the training. The selection effect is about your own web of mind and how it connects meaningfully to entities and events around you, including your deeper purposes in life. When you focus in this way, it lets the REG output tell you when your frame of mind is strong enough to affect the world and possibly change the course of events.

The second type of experience available for the REG is the setup exemplified by the PEAR-style FieldREG program (see chapter 4). With FieldREG, you track the course of an event to receive insights about it. The REG output patterns can tell you the meaningfulness quotient during parts of the event. That is, the REG output seems to respond to richer levels of meaningfulness and so display different patterns. For example, you might engage in an activity as simple as reading the newspaper and let the REG tell you what parts of what stories seem to touch you most deeply. FieldREG is appropriate for people who have already accepted the idea that there may be value here rather than for people seeking to confirm whether it works at all. That's because the results are highly interpretive—and less suited for research scoring and levels of statistical significance. You decide what the output charts are telling you. I address FieldREG here (even though it was not the basis of my project) because in the REG workshops I've run, upwards of 80% of people affirm that their primary interest is in this application. Following are a few FieldREG tips before I turn to a Reflector-style personal-development-oriented project.

Tips for FieldREG

A FieldREG-style program is easy to set up and operate (depending on the software involved). It runs in the background of some event, and the results are reviewed and interpreted after the fact. The setup doesn't have to be located near the event—as indicated by the distance discussion of chapter 19.

Typically, FieldREG is run to monitor a single event or a series of isolated single events. And though this format does not generally make for a long-term project, it is possible to create a more comprehensive study or program. One of our users undertook a yearlong project in which he kept FieldREG running almost every day. In effect, he was chronicling his waking hours in a REG version of a GoPro camera. But, that said, the rest of these tips have to do with the monitoring of a single event.

When you first start using FieldREG for the tracking of events, you'll probably be tempted to keep the computer nearby and look at the screen periodically to see what's happening. Or, during the event, you may think about the fact that it is running—in part to try to goose it to show something interesting. Pretty quickly, however, you'll learn to let that go, trusting that it will tell you what you need to know. And as you do, it will.

Interpretation of the results is the key to FieldREG. First, it's always exciting when the REG chart goes far outside the parabola lines of significance, such as seen in the FieldREG examples in figures 4.1 and 4.2. However, such behavior is not necessary to receive information of value. Consider it a gift when a dramatic chart happens; but it is not essential. The main things to look for are abrupt and sustained changes in direction and other patternings of the chart line. The example in figure 4.1 demonstrates an abrupt and striking "turn of events." In this experience, Justin felt his experience and attitude shift, and the chart reflected it. With such changes in chart direction, there is no universal meaning or interpretive code. You have to reflect on the experience and see what kind of insight the chart gives you about it. The point is that the experience of the event is natively remembered by the physical actions that occurred. FieldREG shifts your attention to the course of the inner experience of the event. It gives you a parallel tracking of the event from that inner perspective.

Figure SM.1 is an example of another FieldREG experience—in this case, one of my own. The event was a cordial breakfast that I had with my former boss and business mentor, Martin Tuchman. It occurred shortly after I left that business and started working full-time on Psyleron and this research. For the first 40 minutes or so of the breakfast, we discussed my former company, its current dealings, and bits of news about some of the staff. At that point, the conversation shifted to my new endeavor, Psyleron, and my REG work. The resulting chart shows clearly the two different periods. So, in

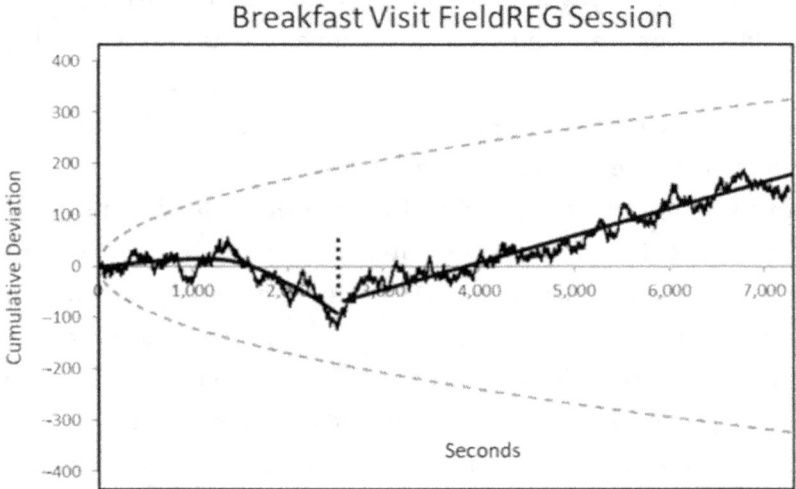

FIGURE SM.1 Breakfast event lasting about two hours, with two approximate trend lines and dotted vertical line showing the approximate point at which the discussion shifted topics.

spite of the fact that the data line never reached outside the parabola, it still gave valuable information.

We can examine the two periods of the chart for more insight into the interpretation process. The first topic—how things are going at the office—put me back into that work frame of mind. And because I'd been an executive at the company, I began feeling the weight of the job again. The chart arced down and continued in that direction. But the moment we shifted to the second topic—my new venture and work—the chart changed direction. In that second period, there is an initial burst upward. But then the chart displays a measured, steady rise. That is, the slope of the line does not seem to reflect wild or unbridled excitement. As I examined the chart later that day, I realized that I indeed hold just the attitude that seems to be shown. I am measured in my attitude, am in it for the long haul, am committed to this research as my life plan rather than something that's exciting just for the moment. The awareness of my own steady resolve was very meaningful to me at the time—and something that years later I still remember. The chart itself has long since been filed away, but I still retain the feelings I took away from it.

There are times when a chart is striking for an opposite reason—that is, for its sheer lack of anything's appearing at all. Such a chart may mean that nothing of deeper significance was going on, that nothing touched you enough for you to so indicate in the REG output. If it's even more exaggerated in its lack of pattern, that may indicate what's referred to earlier as *baseline bind* (also referred to as a *brain-dead chart*). The chart acts constricted—is not able to do anything. Such a result can indicate either too much tightness and control—with no flowing energy in it—or misplaced and begrudged effort. One may need to revisit the basic purposes that led to or drove the event. But again, you'd have to consult with your inner feelings to find out.

In summary, the real value of FieldREG is that it gives a way to connect with and articulate your own deeper feelings about selected events in your life. And overall, it's best to have fun with it. Projecting too much weight or skepticism on the results can, as noted, tend to tighten the output. On the other hand, with a relaxed, mildly expectant attitude, FieldREG will probably work for you and give you insights in interesting and unexpected ways.

REG Training Projects

This section covers the basics for projects involving direct engagement with the REG output. It will touch on elements of attitude, preparation, settings, scoring, and goals. It will also mention tools that can help in future research efforts. You can put together a program for yourself that involves personal training or that extends to include basic research to help move the field forward.

We start with attitude. It's a simple discussion but not optional. You just need to be open to possibilities. Attitude is more relevant to success than it is in the traditional, dispassionate scientific-study model. As noted earlier, a coach will get much better results from athletes if that coach truly believes the athletes can win and instills in them that very feeling: that they can in fact win. But you can be open and *also* skeptical. The point of personal experience here is that it creates a feedback process wherein you change over time. As you become more and more attuned to your own mental activity, you should experience new and interesting states of mind. That itself leads to a growing sense of exploration, which in turn can lead to better REG results.

Along the way, you'll probably devise innumerable REG strategies. In a *moment,* you'll find some thought or frame of mind that seems to drive the results positively, perhaps repeatedly. You will declare that you have found the final answer to the whole mystery and can't wait to publish it—only to have it stop working when overused. (If you detect an autobiographical element here, you are of course correct.) Those *moments* and their aftermaths are all part of the process.

Moments of meaningfulness often drive the results. Similarly, frustration and dashed hopes go with the territory. But each time you get frustrated, the next time you come back you'll see that frustration encapsulated as your last frame of mind. In doing so, you have moved past it. You now see it from the outside and can use it as a stepping-stone toward more-successful states of mind.

Preparation

Regardless of the kind of REG work you plan to undertake—either personal or as part of institutional research—you will have to develop two perspectives. First and foremost, you are engaged and hoping to achieve good results, and that engagement may be all-absorbing. But we are analytical creatures, and soon you'll find yourself watching what you're doing and what's going on, so that you can know what seems to work and what doesn't. In my case, this was an extreme separation into a subject's viewpoint engaged and an experimenter's viewpoint looking on. Just be aware of this split in attention so that you can make sure you don't become too analytical. Or, if you do plan to be more research oriented, be aware that the analytical mind tends to work against good results.

If I were to do my project over again, I would consider a simultaneous program of meditation. As noted earlier, meditators have shown a propensity to do better on the REG, and it makes sense based on my limited personal experience as well. Results come from one's own self-engagement, self-awareness, and self-alignment. Meditation can take a number of different forms, of course. But the basic idea is to turn inward in a mindfulness process. Even if it doesn't help a great deal with the REG results, if you're going to focus inward anyway, I think mindfulness gives many added personal benefits. There is a real need for formal studies involving meditators, with formal measures of meditative expertise. We need to know how many hours of quality meditative training (demonstrated by the effect on brainwave patterns or mental signatures) help correlate with REG success.

Another element of preparation involves keeping a journal, as described in chapter 3. It is hard to keep a journal, I fully admit. It is not easy to describe your REG experience with the evolving nuances of your mental states. But that's precisely why it is valuable. You will not integrate or solidify these experiences—or even remember them—if you do not either write them down or talk about them with others. Consider journaling to be half the effort of the REG experience.

Finally, I believe that running the REG from a remote location is a good practice, if you can set it up. (As of this writing, commercially available remote access program TeamViewer is free of charge for personal use, and it works extremely well.) Remote operation helps you grasp the enormity of what you're doing, and it can have a profound effect on your psyche. This isn't what you were taught in science class.

Running a Session

When sitting down to a session, make sure you won't be rushed. Be in a quiet place. If you're conducting a study with other study participants, they should be allowed to continue working with the REG as long as they want. Feeling hurried constricts the mind as one tries to push with too much intention. That's almost always counterproductive because it shuts down the more ranging quality of the deeper mind and its ability to latch onto meaningfulness. On the flip side, if one is *too* unhurried, there is a danger of stretching the process out. It can be like having very little work to do at the office and simply putting in time as the main goal. Productivity—and the REG score—tend to go nowhere. You will always learn something in the process (even if it's only to confirm that without purpose, very little happens), but the cost in time is high. Running sessions for too long (I am fully guilty) causes the decline effect to almost always set in for at least three reasons:

(a) it all becomes routine, with no differentiation of one bit from the other, so there is no driver for the results; (b) the mind gets bored and begins to feel as if the only way to get you to stop is to do badly; and (c) as the deeper mind begins to feel as if you're inexplicably forcing more and more openness on it, it now has time (since nothing is going on of interest) to object and try to shut the process down.

The software you use should include visual feedback and auditory feedback. Which of them you use (or both or neither) is a matter of preference. If you're attempting to meditate with eyes closed, then you will probably want to use just the audio feedback. You're also free to change it up. However, the nature of the feedback is such a significant variable (I believe) that if you're being formal in your work, you may want to run separate studies for separate feedback modes.

When you start, you may have formulated a strategy for how you will use your mind. However, you'll find that such strategies can shift within minutes or even seconds of starting. For example, many times I've told myself I will work slowly and deliberately on each new trial, carefully preparing my mind to press the space bar for each one. Very shortly, however, I find myself holding down the space bar and firing trials rapid-fire. For some reason, a sense of urgency takes over. Again, the point is to watch yourself and learn your own thoughts and behaviors.

Finally, knowing when to quit or stop is an acquired skill. As I described earlier, when you're under water—meaning, your score is below zero—or you're in a bad rubber band, you might feel an urgency to keep going until you can turn things around. Just be aware of your inability to stop, and with time, you'll get a handle on it. So don't beat yourself up over it.

Scoring and Significance

The classic measure of significance is the Z score—the measure that tells you the odds of the result's being produced by chance once the session is over. And the session length had to be fixed ahead of time. So, you say you'll do 50 trials, and at the end, you have a Z score that can be converted to odds. The two tables in appendix C cover some basic ending Z scores. For example, getting 34 hits out of 50 gives a Z score of 2.55 with a probability of 186:1

against chance. You can also use this procedure to create a longer study, such as running 30 segments of 50 trials each. You work on each segment on its own but then also combine them together, stringing them end to end. That multisegment or multiple-session framework can be helpful in that it lets you lose track of the current significance level of the combined score. I found that to be a good thing, because not knowing the score (particularly if it's becoming highly significant) can moderate the emotional reaction. It keeps the mental regulator from kicking in with an alert to pull the score back down.

One of the most helpful scoring measures in practice is the Z_{max} score. With that measure, you also start a new session (or with the Reflector software a new segment within a session), which zeros the score, and then you try to get as positive (or negative) a cumulative Z score (Z_{max} score) as possible before stopping. You don't have a fixed end. The Reflector program keeps track of and displays the Z_{max} score during each ongoing segment—that is, the high score reached at any time since the beginning. With the Z_{max} score, you can go for broke at any instant and not worry about being at a good score at the end of a fixed-length session. In other words, it lets your energy be more spontaneous, *moment*-like, blowing it all right now. It isn't like a track runner who must reserve some energy for the end. Furthermore, positive results can feed positive feelings to create a positive feedback loop that can last for some period. At some point, however, the score will start to fall back due to a loss of the *moment* or due to the onset of a rubber band or due to a deeper fear of success or even due to just chance fluctuations that you are not controlling. After such a crest and dropping in score, you can sometimes push through these periods and recoup to drive an even higher Z_{max}. But at some point, you realize you aren't going to get back to the last high, and so it's time to stop. You can then restart and try again. Also note that you can string segments together—and even sessions together—to form a single Z_{max} score. But in looking across sessions (with the Reflector software, at least), you will have to calculate the Z_{max} yourself. And you can never calculate having started from the middle of a segment—say, after a particularly good run. You have to start at the beginning.

Finally, some colleagues and I are rethinking the whole focus on Z scores. Z score is a measure of significance. As it turns out, focusing on significance—when states of mind react to significance—creates a feedback loop that then creates chaos. Another measure is a focus on the percentage of hits you produce. So, for example, if you make 52% hits on many segments or sessions in a row, it can begin to reinforce the sense that you can keep doing it. And that result chains together to produce a higher Z score or Z_{max} score than you might otherwise feel comfortable achieving when focused directly. We are trending toward that approach. However, be aware that the fact that you will later convert this percentage to a Z score means you will still get wrapped into feelings of significance.

Regardless of which statistical measure you use, you must also remember that probabilities are sensitive to how many attempts you make. For example, reaching a Z_{max} of 2.75 is significant at the 20:1 level as shown by the Monte Carlo simulation in appendix B—*but only if that was your first try*. If you try 20 times or even 10 and get this result, it is not significant. That is, on average, every 20 tries should produce one such result. And in 10 tries, you would expect, roughly speaking, to get such a result about half the time. However, if you get a Z_{max} score of 4, then according to the Monte Carlo simulation, such a result should occur only one time in 1,443 tries. In this case, you can try many times and still feel good about the significance when it occurs.

Other Types of Data Collection

The data collected during REG sessions are the individual REG bits drawn from individual trials.* In the future, however, we will need to collect physiological data on the subjects involved because, for instance, changes in skin conductivity can signal tension. Brain waves can be monitored, too, as can heart-rate variability, in order to help with the systemic states of the mind-body. To date, almost nothing has been done regarding those measures.

---

* Some systems fire multiple bits for each trial and then take the majority result to be the final binary hit or miss. You can keep all such bits if you want to—under the possibility that the sum of all bits will give meaningful results. But generally speaking, a goal-driven process doesn't seem to care how it gets to where it's going.

Such studies would immediately add to the body of research data and help move the field forward.

We also need a running commentary by subjects themselves. Real-time commentary could be highly illuminating if a scoring method were developed for relating the output bits to standardized classes of psychological states. If you're working just by yourself, then keeping a journal and making notes during and after (and before) sessions can serve the purpose in a preliminary way. You might even try talking into a recording device as you work and having it electronically linked to the results. But it may be that having to talk interferes with the mind such that it cannot produce good results. Or, recording may instead become natural, fade into the background, and not affect results. We simply need to do the research.

Finally, as noted in chapter 20 on psychofeedback, it is worth exploring a process of temporary alteration of brain function through transcranial magnetic stimulation or other new technologies. Because the brain seems deeply involved in the subroutines of the subconscious that create alerts and attempt to draw the scoring back down to expectation values, it may be useful to disrupt those mental regulators. Through the years, I have distinct awareness of the locations in my brain of certain feelings that seem to emanate from them. Whether those feelings are real or not is something that needs to be tested. Transcranial-magnetic-stimulation devices and/or EEG monitoring might help resolve the issue. Work is waiting to be done in many new areas of this research, and each new effort will add another piece to the puzzle of our human nature and its capabilities.

The Fingertip Exercise

The following is a somewhat random exercise you might try—just to get a feel for how the REG process can change you. I offer it as one very small guidepost related to self-integration. It is something I stumbled onto because it is a yoga exercise I have occasionally done.

Sit in a chair or on the floor. Extend your arms out sideways, parallel to the floor, palms down, and make fists. Now extend the middle finger of each hand and start making small circles with your arms, perhaps several inches in diameter at the fingertips. You can do this with your eyes open or closed.

Now, try to feel the tips of each of the two extended fingers simultaneously. You'll probably find that your mind wants to shift back and forth between attending to one fingertip or another. When I had my wife try this, she said she could feel both of them at the same time—but then she exclaimed that, no, that's not right. She found herself shifting her attention very quickly back and forth between each hand.

I believe that through the REG process, I have developed a level of brain integration that may or may not have value but is at least a marker of change. Part of the trick to my success at this task is that I pull back from *being* my brain to *feeling* my brain—both hemispheres of it—in action. I experience the hemispheres as each feeling a fingertip (each hemisphere controls the opposite hand) simultaneously. My attention is on the hemispheres' experiencing the fingertips, which I myself experience as an integrated whole. More on this process in seeing and working with the brain from the outside in is described in chapter 12 in the bioREG section. Anyway, give it a go.

Goals Recap and Final Words

If you've read this far, then presumably you don't need me to tell you why you might want to undertake your own project or study. But I will recap the major ones I see. Feel free to add to it. Following are four basic reasons for trying the REG experience yourself.

- You want to see for yourself whether the selection effect really exists—that is, to see whether it truly is possible for the mind to directly alter REG output.
- You want to have your own deeper feelings displayed back to you in a totally new and novel way, giving insight into this level of experience.
- You want to become more purposeful and effective in life by using the REG as a purpose-driven training device.
- You want to push the boundaries of our current human understanding of this phenomenon and thereby add to the growing body of research.

Jack Nicklaus, arguably the greatest golfer of all time (or at least one of the two greatest), was asked recently why he thinks interest in golf is waning.

He replied that golf has three basic problems: First, it is too expensive. Second, it is too slow. And third, it is just too hard. The REG process avoids two out of three. It isn't expensive—the devices can be inexpensive. It isn't slow—that is, even though it can involve hours of engagement, the time flies by in the same sense as one gets absorbed into any computer activity or video game and loses track of time. But last, I do think it is too hard. At least it's too hard relative to the levels of success we have come to expect given a certain amount of time put into a training process. We're not used to failing almost 50% of the time we try something. However, because the long-term goals are really about changing one's own self in fundamental ways and/or adding to the body of research findings, there's no metric for how long it should take. The fact that it's possible at all to achieve some level of success is pretty remarkable. Those are the aspects I personally focus on.

In the end, I suspect that I may not be the best judge of the difficulty or ease that others will have with the process. Due to my scientific upbringing and early inculcation into a mechanical worldview, I am clearly not the best candidate for success overall. Others may be better suited, having less analytically convoluted and self-sabotaging tendencies. Or not. We don't yet know all the workings of the mind or how individual differences may vary outcomes. But it seems that anyone can experience enough to confirm that the effect is real. And if you become an accomplished REG yogi, I would certainly love to hear about it.

Last, we theorize—rightly or wrongly—that with more people working at this task and becoming more self-reflective in the process, the more everyone will succeed in the future. As a groove of acceptance and normalcy reshapes the collective mind web or larger meaning field, it will become more natural for everyone. Someday it will even be taken for granted.

But right now, we have to take the hill, so each new individual's efforts are valuable. Whatever drives you to become engaged, or whatever your goals might be with it, I wish you good luck. And most important, be sure to share your experience with others.

MIND LAMP GAMES

These games are drawn from the Mind Lamp user manual to show how one might engage the Mind Lamp. The section is titled "Seven Ways to have a Great Experience with your Mind Lamp."

Experience #1: The Pet Lamp

Set the Mind Lamp on a table or desk where you will see it often. Now think of it as being a pet, like a dog or cat. As a pet, it reacts based on your relationship with it. Giving the Mind Lamp a personality and engaging it in this way often seem to work for getting the best results. It gets you imagining how it might feel from the "inside." So when it turns a color, consider why it may have turned that particular color when it did. How were you thinking about it? or, What was going through your mind at that moment? Over time, see if you can pick out patterns of what it does in relation to what you're thinking or how you or others around you seem to make it react. You can do this in both white-to-color mode and rainbow mode. If this seems to be working for you, take it one step further and let the Mind Lamp become an extension of yourself. In this case its reactions are actually your own thoughts at a deeper level, and so it can give you a window into your subconscious.

Experience #2: Intention Training with a Score

You can try your hand—that is, your mind—at helping the lamp become a color by intending that color. This is the classic mind-over-matter test and can be used for training intention. If you want to score your results, use white-to-color mode. To begin, first write down what color you want (it helps in remembering later). Then try to bring that color into being. Write the result next to your color. After each try, you can pick a new color, or you can keep going with the same color and try multiple times. The odds of getting one trial correct are one in eight, because there are eight colors, all of which are equally likely to occur. For more than one trial, you can calculate the odds by using notes on page 19.

Experience #3: Pulling against the Odds

In rainbow mode, the lamp meanders from color to color and sometimes sits on one color for a while. But you'll notice that it tends to drift in one direction of the color wheel more than the other. In fact, it is quite significant to get the lamp to make a full circuit around the color wheel in the backward direction of red-orange-yellow-green-cyan-blue-purple-magenta-red. See how good you can get at moving it in that direction.

Experience #4: The Oracle

The lamp can function as a window into your subconscious for decision making. Deep inside yourself, you may know more than you think you do about a situation, and you may even have some access to the future and scenarios about how things may best play out. To use the oracle, you create an answer set that pairs each answer with a lamp color, such as the set below. Feel free to create your own set—particularly when you associate some personal meaning with individual colors. Then, in a somewhat meditative state, you clear your mind and ask a question. When a color comes up, see what it says! Be sure to write down your answer set ahead of time. Also write down your questions and results. That way you can look at what actually happens in relation to the answers given. This is best done in white-to-color mode because the odds for each color's coming up are the same.

Experience #5: Synchronicity

In white-to-color mode, sit and read a book or magazine or do something so that you're not focused directly on the Mind Lamp. But write down each time the lamp turns a full color (be sure not to miss any!). See whether a pattern forms over the course of an extended period of time, like an hour. For example, see if one color seems to come up far more than would be expected. Or see which of the color types—warm colors (magenta, red, orange, yellow) or cool colors (green, cyan, blue, purple)—tend to dominate. If you see a pattern developing, write down how you feel about it—in particular, whether it seems totally natural, as if the Mind Lamp has been designed with such a bias in mind (it hasn't), or not.

This works on the same principle as synchronicity. For example, have you ever learned a new word that you think you've never seen before, and then suddenly you start seeing it everywhere? Having the Mind Lamp show a consistent (rather than random) behavior is the subconscious's locking into a pattern and then starting to predict it. That prediction is something of a mental overlay on reality that tends to shift how events actually play out.

Experience #6: Group Efforts in Harmony

Most of these games can also be experienced with another individual or with a group of people working together. For example, in white-to-color mode, a group can focus on getting the lamp to become a particular color. The group intention , if truly aligned, does become stronger than an individual could effect alone. If the Mind Lamp gives the group's color, then you can use that excitement and energy to focus on a goal, such as world peace, group harmony, success in a project, prosperity, or healing for another individual.

Experience #7: Group Competition

Mind-over-matter success is easiest when everyone is pulling in the same direction. But sometimes it's fun to compete. Engaging in mind duels or mental arm wrestling can sometimes raise everyone's energy level and drive up the results. In white-to-color mode, have two people or two groups pick a target color and see which can get their color first. This way, even if a stray color (neither individual's or neither group's target color) comes up, the group can keep going until one or the other group succeeds.

Finally, if you happen to have more than one Mind Lamp —

Put the Mind Lamps next to each other. Try (alone or in a group) to get the colors of two or more lamps to sync up into the same color. This can be in white-to-color mode or rainbow mode. Alignment of colors (more than two lamps is very unusual) can give an especially strong sense of working together and locking into a goal.

APPENDICES

APPENDIX A:
RANDOM OUTPUT AND THE XOR MASK

The REG is engineered to avoid the influence of normal physical factors such as temperature fluctuations, vibrations, and electromagnetic waves. To that end, the device has been shielded and made as tolerant as possible of variable environmental conditions. However, it does use a comparator with a threshold to determine what is ultimately a one and what is a zero. The comparator can result in slight deviations from the perfect mean of 50-50 output. Therefore, an additional software step is used, which is called an XOR (exclusive or) mask, or, more generically, bit scrambling. Bit scrambling makes sure that regardless of these fluctuations, the results will be 50-50 and will always pass tests for randomness of the mean regardless of external physical influences and conditions.

As shown in table A.1, each next output bit from the REG (as read left to right) is put through the next bit of the XOR mask. The mask simply alternates between ones and zeros, as shown. Each input bit is compared with the mask bit, and there is a rule for what becomes the output bit.

- If the input bit and the XOR bit are the same, the resulting output bit will be a zero.
- If the input bit and the XOR bit are different, the resulting output bit will be a one.

By this process, the output bits no longer correspond to any physical meaning that might have been in the input stream. For example, if there were many more ones in the input stream corresponding to some environmental or force influence, the output stream would no longer reflect this. In the example of table below, the input stream has 10 ones and 2 zeros. But the output stream has 6 ones and 6 zeros. And although that balanced output ratio will not always be the case for any short segment of data (or it would not be random), it will be the case overall.

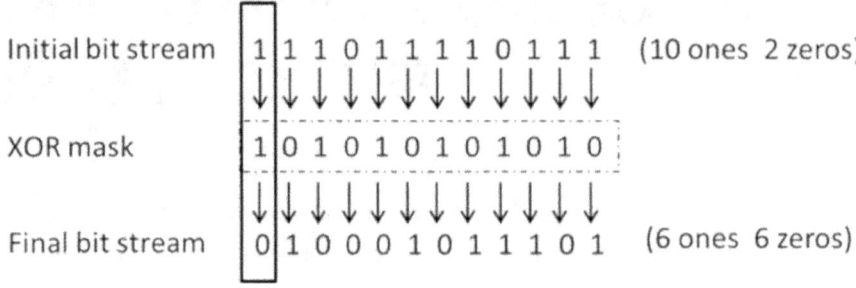

It can be noted that the Psyleron REG-1 used in these studies involves an even more-complex XOR process. First, the unit has two internal REGs that are XORed against each other. That result is then XORed with a pseudo-random algorithm (rather than the alternating one and zero mask). This process helps ensure not only that the mean value is 50-50 overall, but also that there are no other regular patterns in the data stream. True randomness involves not only a stable 50-50 mean but no other patterns in the data as well.

APPENDIX B: Z_{MAX} SCORE MONTE CARLO SIMULATION

The following table represents data from the simulation of 1.5 million sessions, each session consisting of 12,000 trials. It shows how often the threshold Z_{max} value (or "Number of sessions reaching Z_{max}" as labeled in the table) was reached between a lower bound of 100 trials and an upper bound of 12,000 trials. The upper bound was chosen for practical reasons; none of my data reported for Z_{max} purposes involved more than this number of trials. The lower bound was chosen to avoid early readings from small samples. The simulation was run by generating 20 GB of data with the same REG used to produce the actual data and then segmenting the data into individual sessions or "starts."

Z_{max}	2.5	2.75	3.0	3.25	3.5	3.75	4.0	4.25	4.5	4.75	5.0
Number of sessions reaching Z_{max}	146,422	83,289	44,437	21,767	9,959	4,322	1,796	695	239	75	28
<p value for sessions reaching Z_{max}	.1	.056	.03	.015	.0067	.0029	.0012	.00047	.00016	.00005	.00002
Probability of Z_{max} occurring by chance	One in 10	One in 18	One in 34	One in 69	One in 151	One in 347	One in 835	One in 2,158	One in 6,276	One in 20,000	One in 53,571

Z_{max} Score Monte Carlo Simulation Table

APPENDIX C:
TERMINAL Z SCORE TABLE

50 Trial Segments

Total Trials	Total Correct	Terminal Z Score	Probability p<	Chance Odds: 1 out of:
50	25	0.00	0.5	2
50	26	0.28	0.4	3
50	27	0.57	0.3	4
50	28	0.85	0.2	5
50	29	1.13	0.13	8
50	30	1.41	0.08	13
50	31	1.70	0.04	22
50	32	1.98	0.02	42
50	33	2.26	0.01	84
50	34	2.55	0.005	186
50	35	2.83	0.002	429
50	36	3.11	0.001	1,070
50	37	3.39	0.00035	2,865
50	38	3.68	0.00012	8,547
50	39	3.96	0.00004	27,027
50	40	4.24	0.00001	90,909
50	41	4.53	2.9E-06	344,828
50	42	4.81	7.5E-07	1,333,333
50	43	5.09	1.8E-07	5,555,556

Note: p values < .05 (odds against chance of greater than 20:1) are considered significant.

100 Trial Segments

Total Trials	Total Correct	Terminal Z Score	Probability p<	Chance Odds: 1 out of:
100	50	0.00	0.5	2
100	51	0.20	0.42	2
100	52	0.40	0.34	3
100	53	0.60	0.27	4
100	54	0.80	0.21	5
100	55	1.00	0.16	6
100	56	1.20	0.12	8
100	57	1.40	0.08	13
100	58	1.60	0.055	18
100	59	1.80	0.036	28
100	60	2.00	0.023	43
100	61	2.20	0.014	71
100	62	2.40	0.008	125
100	63	2.60	0.005	200
100	64	2.80	0.0026	385
100	65	3.00	0.0013	769
100	66	3.20	0.00069	1,449
100	67	3.40	0.00034	2,941
100	68	3.60	0.00016	6,250
100	69	3.80	0.00007	14,286
100	70	4.00	0.00003	33,333
100	71	4.20	0.00001	100,000
100	72	4.40	5.4E-06	185,185
100	73	4.60	2.1E-06	476,190
100	74	4.80	7.9E-07	1,265,823
100	75	5.00	2.9E-07	3,448,276

GLOSSARY OF TERMS

action *See* units of action.

action ball An image used to represent the current point of awareness within the generalized "significance bowl" diagram of a unit of meaning.

alternative reality The proposed realm in which possible future states exist in the present in something akin to a waveform and can be partially guided into being by using the selection effect.

anomalies research The study of events that do not conform to our understanding of normal causal process within the mechanical model of the universe, thus considered anomalous.

baseline The zero Z-score line in a random-walk chart.

baseline bind The tendency for a random-walk chart to adhere more closely to the zero Z-score line than would be expected by chance. The subject appears to cause this effect for various psychological reasons.

Bayesian reasoning A form of analysis whereby an original expectation or model is updated through a comparison between the expectation and the subsequent actual events leading to an adjusted model that will be applied to future events in an ongoing iterative process.

biofeedback The use of physiological-monitoring devices to inform the host of relevant states of brain or body. The process trains for achieving specific desired body conditions, such as warmer hands or reduced muscle tension.

bowl of significance A visual construct or model for a unit of meaning that is shaped like a bowl with a set point or norm at the bottom middle as the point of least significance in the bowl and the sides of the bowl representing related mental states that are increasingly more significant.

conceptual space   A cluster of associated experience that is organized around a central set of characteristics in which the elements of the set in the space are visually spread out and in relationship in accordance with the characteristics.

control run   A data set produced with the REG, wherein no subject is attempting to influence the results. It is used for confirming that the REG device is functioning properly on its own.

disrupter bits   The concept that the mind inserts interrupts into its own mental flows to make sure it does not lose track of current environmental circumstances.

goal-driven process   Action intended to achieve a predesignated future state.

hit   The output of a single trial in the REG game when the result is in the direction of prestated intention. In the project described in the text, a hit is generally represented by a green result. Related: *See* miss.

intention   A condition of consciousness in which consciousness proposes a future desired state and then seeks to bring that state into being. Here intention is considered subservient to the concept of purpose , which is the underlying driver of the desire to bring about the future state.

intersubjective field   *See* intersubjective space.

intersubjective space   The concept that individual minds exist in a shared mental domain or space or set of common mental dimensions and that minds can engage each other through that common platform. Also called *intersubjective field*.

law of attraction   The popularized principle that one attracts things, occurrences, and events into one's life based on the direction of one's own thoughts and expectations and that the expectation of success or failure draws a result that becomes a self-fulfilling prophecy.

Glossary of Terms

layers   The concept that the mind forms units of meaning with larger ones nested around smaller ones and whose layers nominally include seven levels as shown by the REG experience, which become representative of life activity as well. A simple model for these layers is a book, with its words, sentences, paragraphs, sections, and chapters.

MAP   *See* meaning-action pair.

meaning   The basic structure of the mind, whereby all information links that make up the web of mind are meaning experiences when viewed from the inside. So, while typically, the word *meaning* is about something—as in "the storm means trouble"—here meaning is itself the foundation of mental experience. We are built out of meaning.

meaning-action pair, or MAP   The proposition that the universe builds complexity through the interaction of first-person meaning and third-person action, which build on each other, with meaning striving to both perceive and shape the action counterpart, which in turn feeds back onto enhanced meaning. Mind and brain form a basic meaning-action pair.

meaning field   The characterization given to the experience of nested, somewhat discrete layers of self cognitively or physically felt around the body. So, while the concept of self is generally described here in terms of webs of association, the actual experience of a layer of self can be characterized as a meaning field.

mental membrane   The idea that a mental web, unit of meaning, or conceptual space does not trail off to infinity but is bounded by a barrier that defines inside the conceptual space from outside it.

mental pen   A REG game strategy whereby a desired future state is visually impressed on reality. The term comes from the sense of "perception in reverse" whereby green or any desired visual result is imagined coming out from the eyes to paint itself on the actual landscape of future events.

mental regulator   An agent of the brain–mind composed of the interaction between the emotional and prediction subsystems, which together develop a set of norms based on past experience and which fire alerts up to the conscious mind when those norms are sufficiently violated.

miss The output of a single trial whose result is not in the direction of intention. In the REG project described in the text, misses are usually represented by a red result. Related: *See* hit.

null hypothesis A procedure used in science whereby a condition is defined as a counter to or rejection of a proposed phenomenon, so that if subsequent study results do show the phenomenon (and violate the null hypothesis), it is an indication that the phenomenon under study does in fact exist (is significant).

occlusion The way the brain–mind causes certain mental processing to be unavailable because conditions have risen to a level of significance that is too challenging for the self to contemplate at the moment.

parapsychology The academic field studying extrasensory perception, first developed by J. B. Rhine at Duke University in the 1930s. *See* anomalies research.

PEAR laboratory *See* Princeton Engineering Anomalies Research laboratory.

posing The act of watching one's own states of mind—particularly during the biofeedback or psychofeedback process—and then trying to capture and reapply a state of mind to reproduce a desired effect.

prediction system or predictive system The portion of the brain–mind and its neural circuits that gather information from the environment, make a model, and predict future events and that tends to overlay its findings on current events to *see* how closely the events match the expectation , thus allowing for an ongoing update of the model in a Bayesian-like process; forms part of the mental regulator. *See* Bayesian reasoning.

Princeton Engineering Anomalies Research laboratory, or PEAR laboratory A research laboratory at Princeton University that operated from 1979 to 2007 studying (1) anomalous effects produced by the mind's interaction with sensitive physical systems and (2) the process of remote viewing. *See* anomalies research *and* remote viewing.

psychofeedback Feedback given to a user attempting to influence a physical device directly with the mind. In contrast with biofeedback, psychofeedback involves no physical-sensory brain–body intermediates such as electromagnetic waves or other physical forces. The REG software applications Reflector and FieldREG are psychofeedback games.

Psyleron   The company founded by Herb Mertz and John Valentino in 2005 to produce and sell REG and REG-related devices for research as well as to encourage general public exploration of consciousness.

random   Events with no predictable outcomes; more specifically here, a situation involving a set of possible outcomes that have equal probabilities of occurring such that no alternative is more likely to occur than another.

random-event generator (REG)   An electronic device that generates random output. True random output is generally based on quantum physical fluctuations or other natural processes, with outcomes that cannot be predicted. Typical sources for fluctuations include thermal noise and reverse-bias diode tunneling. Also called a random-number generator (RNG)—specifically when the output is a binary 1 or 0. *RNG* is the favored term for mainstream applications (as opposed to more-specialized consciousness research) that require randomness, such as cryptography.

random-walk   The pattern made by a sequence of binary random results, as displayed in a chart format. The chart generally builds from left to right, with hit results shown as short line segments headed to the right and up, and with miss results shown as short line segments headed to the right and down in a pattern sometimes also referred to as a *drunken walk* because the randomness causes the line to meander as if unsteady.

REG   *See* random-event generator.

REG output   One or more results of individual REG trials in the form of a sequence of binary results, represented by ones and zeros, green squares and red squares or any other such binary representation.

remote viewing   A process whereby a person attempts to view a scene at a distant physical location (the target site) through the mind's-eye and with no other physical or sensory information. Sometimes the person attempts to gain the information about the target site through the viewpoint of another person who is at the target site.

RNG *See* random-event generator.

run The sequence of REG output trials whose result is all the same, such that the run ends with the first instance of an opposite result. The sequence green, green, green, green, red would be a run of four greens.

selection effect The propensity of the mind to select one desired outcome from a set of possible outcomes and then apply itself so as to shift the probability structure of events to favor the desired outcome.

set point A central or most likely expectation value within a web of associations, unit of meaning, or bowl of significance often formed in the subconscious.

shoulds The auxiliary verb *should* made into a noun to represent the feeling of what one expects should happen, in which the mind experiences a *should* as an impulse toward the unfolding of events in a certain direction (usually a set point of normalcy). There are two types of shoulds : shoulds of expectation (or prediction), as in "He should come home soon," and shoulds of rightness (or value), as in "She should treat her mother better."

significance The quality of being worthy of attention and which statistically represents the extent to which the null hypothesis is being violated or, conversely, the extent to which an alternative proposed hypothesis is being confirmed.

Society of Mind The proposal put forth by computer scientist Marvin Minsky of MIT's artificial intelligence lab stating that the most effective artificially created minds consist of competing and cooperating agent/resources that together enhance the decision-making process in robot perception and action and that this concept appears to correlate with the human mind involving agents and resources that operate in the subconscious.

subconscious mind Mental processes that occur below the surface of conscious awareness and a term generally used in this book rather than *unconscious mind* based on the idea that some parts of this domain can be brought to the surface of conscious awareness through mental training.

threads of association The connections of meaning in the mind, displayed as lines connecting or associating mental objects one to the other.

trial A single output result from the REG, such as a red state or a green state.

UM *See* unit of meaning.

unconscious mind Mental processes that are deeply embedded in the psyche and not directly accessible to the conscious mind and that cannot be made to be so (in the context used here).

unit of action The half of a meaning-action pair that represents behaviors of outside events as seen, defined, or characterized by a unit of meaning. *See* unit of meaning *and* meaning-action pair.

unit of meaning, or UM The half of the meaning-action pair that represents sentience or awareness and that characterizes or defines observed units of action. Units of meaning are singular integrated states, however limited or extended. *See* unit of action and meaning-action pair.

web of association The concept of the mind as an integrated set of associations or hyperlinked set of data and whose representation of the connections appears as a set of interconnected threads. (*See also* threads of association.) Webs of association can be nested, with the largest such web being considered a *web of mind* and in an individual instance of a web of association also being called a *unit of meaning*. *See* unit of meaning.

web of meaning Another term for a web of associations *See* web of association.

web of mind A term for a web of association when involving the largest or whole of a mind (the full mind) *See* web of association.

Z score A standard statistical measure of significance that takes sample size into account. In the REG context, it is approximated by the mathematical formula $((Hits*2)-trials)/sqrt(trials)$ or—given n as the total number of trials and h as the total number of successes—$(h*2-n)/sqrt(n)$. *See* chapter 2 for a description of the types of Z score that appear in the text.

NOTES

Introduction

1. Daryl Bem (2011). "Feeling the Future: Experimental Evidence for Anomalous Retroactive Influences on Cognition and Affect." *Journal of Personality and Social Psychology* 100, 407-425. Also Bem, D. J., Tressoldi, P., Rabeyron, T., and Duggan, M. (2014). "Feeling the Future: A Meta-analysis of 90 Experiments on the Anomalous Anticipation of Random Future Events," which reports on high significance of combined results from a number of labs replicating the original work.
2. Dean Radin, *Journal of Scientific Exploration* 2004, 18(2): 253-273.
3. Garret Moddel, Zixu (James) Zhu, Adam Curry (November 2011). Laboratory demonstration of retroactive influence in a digital system. In *AIP Conference Proceedings* 1408(1): 218-231). See p. 224.
4. Meta-analysis of mind-matter interaction experiments: 1959 to 2000," Dean Radin Boundary Institute) and Roger Nelson (PEAR Laboratory). Can be accessed through http://boundary.org/bi/articles/rngma.pdf. Meta-analysis of 515 experiments shows results that are 16 standard deviations from expected standard error. (Also see Bosch H., Steinkamp F., and Boller E., *Psychological Bulletin*, American Psychological Association 2006, 132(4): 497-523. This meta-analysis shows significant results, but much smaller effect, having removed several hundred studies based on selection criteria. The selection criteria are criticized in Radin D., Nelson R., Dobyns Y., and Houtkooper J., "Reexamining psychokinesis: Commentary on Bosch, Steinkamp and Boller meta-analysis." *Psychological Bulletin* 2006: 529-532. Radin also reports on another meta-analysis in his book *Entangled Minds*, attempting to remove all possible criticism—still highly significant. See Dean Radin, *Entangled Minds*. New York: Paraview Pocket Books, 2006, pp. 275-276.
5. The tendency for the effect size to decline over the course of a series of studies or even within a study is ubiquitous in REG and other research into anomalies. It is so prevalent that it has been given its own name as a variable: the decline effect. It was first articulated by J. B. Rhine in in his original ESP studies conducted at Duke University beginning in the 1930s. Over time, the variable has come to take on a more clinical term: the series position effect. That is, the effect size is (in part) a function of how early or late a given data segment is relative to the whole body of work for a given subject or experiment. See note under Chapter 2 #1 (below) regarding PEAR laboratory findings. Also see note under Chapter 18, #3 (below) regarding the decline effect in other areas of science.

6. *Heretics of Science: Robert Jahn,* Episode S01E5, BBC documentary, August 2, 1994. Interview with Steven Weinberg, minute 16 (accessed December 9, 2016), http://www.tvshowtime.com/en/show/257843/episode/4303632.
7. See Marc Wittmann, *Altered States of Consciousness.* Cambridge MA: MIT Press, 2018, p. 116.
8. Here we are speaking about research freely undertaken rather than industry or career workers who may or may not embrace the work given to them.
9. To my knowledge, there has been no systematic study of the attitudes of researchers relative to the subject matter, because such a study would be very difficult to undertake for a variety of reasons. The general concept was brought to my attention by both Brenda Dunne and Robert Jahn in private conversations, when they noted that that seemed to be the case. However, there have been extensive studies regarding subjects' orientations regarding the possibility of psychic effects and subsequent performance. Parapsychologist Gertrude Schmeidler coined the term *sheep-goat effect* and conducted extensive such studies. *Goats* are those who do not believe in paranormal effects; *sheep* believe paranormal effects are possible. Studies have repeatedly shown that sheep perform better than goats. See Lance Storm, The Sheep-Goat Effect. *Psi Encyclopedia*, July 2017. Found at https://psi-encyclopedia.spr.ac.uk/articles/sheep-goat-effect (accessed October 23, 2018). Finally, there is a famous counter-case, which is that of psychologist Susan Blackmore. Blackmore began her career as an enthusiastic parapsychologist. However, early on she became disillusioned by lack of positive findings, and moved into more mainstream psychology, becoming a critic of parapsychology. Thus, when the argument about the need to be a "believer" is brought up, she takes exception. While it is perhaps unfair to introduce a new variable to explain the (dare we say) anomaly of Blackmore, I regard the concept of believers to be an overly simplistic representation of relevant states of mind involved. The real action with the REG appears to be with the subconscious, and a conscious stated belief in something only tends to be correlated with what the subconscious believes. Blackmore has shown herself to be a highly analytical, first-rate cognitive scientist. Thus, it may be that in her case a native predisposition to hold a certain orientation in psychology trumped her excitement inherent in finding the unexplainable phenomena of parapsychology. Later in this book there is extensive discussion about subconscious expectation and mental regulators.
10. I have had numerous conversations with two of the researchers—Garret Moddel and Adam Curry—concurring with much of this narrative.
11. The decline effect (see note 5 above) is thought of here as being driven by a psychological state that shifts from engagement and meaningfulness to detachment and habituation (or boredom).
12. The experimenter effect concept is so prevalent in anomalies research that there is a chapter dedicated to it in the recent industry reference, *Parapsychology, A Handbook for the 21st Century,* editors Etzel Cardeña, John Palmer, and David Marcusson-Clavertz. Jefferson, NC: McFarland, 2015. See chapter 22: pp. 293-300.
13. Sam Harris. *The Moral Landscape.* New York, Free Press, 2010, p. 180.
14. Princeton Engineering Anomalies Research (PEAR) Laboratory manager Brenda Dunne, in a personal communication, summer 2006. Context was a scientist arguing

about the validity of reported mind influence-related data. It is worth noting that Galileo had a similar experience, complaining in a letter to Kepler that some philosophers who opposed his discoveries had refused even to look through a telescope. Also, in 2017 Harvard psychologist Stephen Pinker was asked in an interview by neuroscientist Sam Harris, "What are you most certain of such that if the data contradicted it you would have to say that the data were in error?" He responded, "That the mind is completely determined by the physiological activity of the brain." But to his credit, as an open-minded scientist he continued, "So, if there were apparent demonstrations of precognition, telepathy, mind over matter, of the soul's surviving the death of the brain, I would look at those data twice." Waking Up Podcast 2017, minute 1:21; https://www.youtube.com/watch?v=8-Jbiuu_t_0&t=4056s (accessed April 23, 2018).

15. Originally called *"Yes!* Organic Market and Bookstore." The market has since been relocated, and, sadly, the bookstore eliminated.

Chapter 1

1. Lynne McTaggart, *The Field*. New York, Harper, 2008, pp. 109-110.
2. Robert Jahn, personal communication, June 2014.
3. The PEAR lab's second major area of study was the direct interaction of two minds through the concept of remote viewing. In this process, one person (the receiver) tries to receive information about another person's (the sender's) visual and other experience at an unnamed remote site.
4. John Bisaha and Brenda Dunne, "Precognitive Remote Viewing in the Chicago Area: A Replication of the Stanford Experiment," (1979). *Journal of Parapsychology*, 43: 17-30. See also John Bisaha and Brenda Dunne, "Multiple Subject and Long-Distance Pre-Cognitive Remote Viewing of Geographical Locations," chapter in Charles Tart, Hal Puthoff, and Russel Targ, eds., *Mind at Large: IEEE Symposia on the Nature of Extrasensory Perception*. New York: 1979, Praeger Special Studies, pp. 107-124.
5. Andy Schneider, *Daily Princetonian*, February 15, 1984. See http://theprince.princeton.edu/princetonperiodicals/cgi-bin/princetonperiodicals?a=d&d=Princetonian19840215-01.2.5&e=-------en-20--1--txt-txIN------- pp. 1, 3 (accessed June 4, 2017). For recollections of the event, see also Robert G. Jahn and Brenda J. Dunne, *Molecular Memories*. Princeton, NJ: ICRL Press, 2015, pp. 76-77.
6. Research carried out at SRI International, The Princeton Engineering Anomalies Research Laboratory, Psycho-physical research Laboratories, Mind Science Foundation, Rhine Center, Science Unlimited Research Foundation, and others. A summary of major laboratories involved in this research is found in George P. Hansen, *The Trickster and the Paranormal*. Bloomington, IN: Xlibris, 2001, pp. 205-209.
7. See the metastudies referenced in note 4 of the introduction.
8. Robert G. Jahn and Brenda J. Dunne, *Margins of Reality*. New York: Harcourt Brace Jovanovich, 1987, pp. 91-119.
9. Robert G. Jahn and Brenda J. Dunne. "Science of the Subjective." *Journal of Scientific Exploration* 11(2): 209-210.
10. Some differences in male/female data sets are reported in Brenda J. Dunne, "Gender Differences." *Journal of Scientific Exploration* 12(1): 15-16.
11. Personal communication with PEAR lab founder Robert Jahn, fall 2005.

12. Personal communications with PEAR lab manager Brenda Dunne, February, 2009.
13. Dan Brown, *The Lost Symbol*. New York: Anchor, 2010, p. 67.
14. Ibid., p. 82.
15. *Dateline NBC*, October 15, 2009. Transcript: http://www.nbcnews.com/id/33280724/ns/dateline_nbc-newsmakers/t/secrets-lost-symbol/#.WU7UT-kpDLg (accessed January 8, 2017).
16. *New York Times*, February 10, 2007, Science section. See www.nytimes.com/2007/02/10/science/10princeton.html?pagewanted=all&_r=0 (accessed October 19, 2016).

Chapter 2

1. Brenda J Dunne, York H. Dobyns, Robert G. Jahn, Roger D. Nelson, "Series Position Effects in Random Event Generator Experiments." *Journal of Scientific Exploration* 1994, 8(2): 197-215. Also see the appendix to this paper with literature review in this subject throughout the history of parapsychology research.
2. We use the standard level of significance —the $p<.05$ level—corresponding to odds of less than one in 20 of occurring by chance. That is, if one engages in 20 sessions, there is a high probability of getting at least one that shows this level of significance by chance alone—and without a real effect.
3. The full PEAR chart includes a third data line, which is the baseline data set. In this condition, subjects were tasked with keeping the data line as close to the center line (Z score of zero) as possible. Indeed, the line does stay within the expected nonsignificant zone and between the two other lines. It is not included in the text chart because it has difficulty fitting on the same scale due to the statistical difference between the other data lines. The High and Low conditions are evaluated on a one-tailed basis, and the baseline data line is evaluated on a two-tailed basis. As such, the baseline appears to go outside the parabola of significance in the chart (because the y-axis is cumulative deviation) but is correctly noted as not significant at $p<.0867$. For the full chart, see Robert Jahn and Brenda Dunne, Consciousness and the Source of Reality. Princeton, NJ: ICRL Press, 2011, p. 63.

Chapter 3

1. This journal entry was modified (i) to remove some of the original jargon, or shorthand, that I tend to use and (ii) to add more clarity where needed. Such modifications for clarity are also made on journal entries that appear later in the text.

Chapter 4

1. John cannot remember exactly how many messages were in this message set, but it was enough (at least five) such that one would not expect this message to occur even once a day.
2. Through phone calls to Psyleron, we hear many stories of customers' using FieldREG for a variety of applications.
3. This may or may not have been the most-recent data I had produced, but it was extracted blind to the results and represents a large body of data.

Chapter 5

1. In the formal sense, beginning a project after starting with a good result is itself not statistically legitimate. Had the results been bad, then I would never have thought of this project. But it captured my imagination, and that is what mattered for me to set a goal. This issue is taken up again in chapter 17.

Chapter 6

1. Ironically, grandmothers with funny hats do appear to be historically significant. I discovered that the field of neuroscience uses the concept of so-called grandmother cells. *Grandmother cells* was an original, tongue-in-cheek reference to the idea that certain neurons in the brain will fire when you think of or see your well-loved grandmother. That is, before such neurons were actually found, they might be characterized through a sarcastic statement such as, "You can't really believe that your brain reserves a network of cells for thoughts of your grandmother!" (See Leonard Mlodinow, *Elastic*. New York, Pantheon, 2018, p. 78.) Indeed, we know now that certain cells do in fact respond and fire repeatedly upon encountering the same meaningful stimuli, including images of well-known individuals.
2. See Wikipedia entry on loss aversion: https://en.wikipedia.org/wiki/Loss_aversion (accessed September 18, 2018). Also see Daniel Kahneman, *Thinking, Fast and Slow*. New York: Farrar, Straus and Giroux, 2016, p. 301, regarding the brain's giving priority to bad news over good.
3. Jonah Lehrer, *How We Decide*. New York, Houghton Mifflin Harcourt, 2009, pp. 105-106.
4. Richard Restak, *The New Brain*. New York: Rodale Press, 2003, p. 109.
5. Richard Herrnstein, *The Matching Law*, edited by Howard Rachlin and David Laibson. New York: Russell Sage Foundation and Harvard University Press, 1997, pp. 15-22.
6. William Newsome, lecture, Princeton University, April 21, 2009.
7. Jonah Lehrer. *How We Decide*. New York: Houghton Mifflin Harcourt, 2009, pp. 28-34. Also see Science Channel, *Through the Wormhole*, season 3 Episode 8 minute 26, "The Subconscious Mind."
8. Psychologist and Nobel laureate Daniel Kahneman has popularized the notion of this normalizing process as "system 1" for "fast thinking" of the mind. It is the associative, fast-acting decision-making part of the mind that references one's past experience. See Daniel Kahneman, *Thinking, Fast and Slow*. New York: Farrar Straus and Giroux, 2011, pp. 71-73.
9. There are many known regulator processes in the brain–mind, but I have not come across a description of this kind of regulator. I use the general term *mental regulator* because it seems to be inherent to the way the mind regulates against change.
10. Daniel Kahneman, *Thinking, Fast and Slow*. New York: Farrar, Straus and Giroux, 2011, p. 72 (see also Chapter 21).
11. Krissy Brady, "This is Why You Get More Anxious After Something Good Happens." *Huffpost,* April 9, 2019; https://www.huffpost.com/entry/anxiety-good-things_l_5ca78fc1e4b047edf959e2fe. (Accessed September 10, 2019)
12. Alice Park, "The two faces of anxiety." *Time*, December 5, 2011.

13. It is possible that our basic relationship with the experience of change may be shifting generation after generation. Certain kinds of change are becoming so present that change itself may become a new norm. In such a case, if conditions stop changing at some point in the future, that, too, could create an alert. By way of analogy, a study that was conducted in which mice were reared in the presence of loud atonal music found that the mice became distraught to the point of derangement when the music stopped. Norms are expectations for future conditions based on past conditions.

Chapter 7

1. I once again note that I adapted this entry from my log so it would be more readable.
2. This result may sound impossible because the vending machine would be using a pseudorandom algorithm immune to any selection effects. However, such algorithms often use seeds drawn from environmental conditions such as current clock time to the hundredth or thousandth of a second, which themselves can be subject to selection effects. The PEAR lab conducted some pseudorandom experiments with highly provocative results, in part depending on the nature of the psudorandom design. The experiments had one design—for example, that generated a pseudorandom bit stream running in the background, with a cycle of about 60 hours before the sequence started over. Here the bit that was returned to the subject depended on the exact instant that the keyboard was pressed, which itself introduces a possible nonpseudorandom component subject to selection effects. Thus, true pseudorandomness may itself be more the exception than the rule. See Robert G. Jahn and Brenda J. Dunne, *Consciousness and the Source of Reality*. Princeton NJ: ICRL Press, 2011, pp. 117-120.
3. Ciro Conversano, Alessandro Rotondo, Elena Lensi, Olivia Della Vista, Francesca Arpone, and Mario Antonio Reda, *Clinical Practice and Epidemiology in Mental Health* 2010 6: 25-29. Published online May 10, 2010. Accessible at https://www.ncbi.nlm.nih.gov/pmc/articles/PMC2894461/ (accessed September 18, 2018).
4. See Anil Seth lecture The Neuroscience of Consciousness, Royal Institution, January 2017, accessible at https://www.youtube.com/watch?v=xRel1JKOEbI, minute 27-28.
5. See Wikipedia entry "Active Perception," https://en.wikipedia.org/wiki/Active_perception (accessed September 18, 2018). The development of AI robotics is now driving the development and use of this theory.
6. There is ongoing debate in cognitive psychology as to how this update process works with the brain–mind. One of the contenders is called *Bayesian reasoning* (see Anil Seth lecture The Neuroscience of Consciousness, Royal Institution, January 2017, accessible at https://www.youtube.com/watch?v=xRel1JKOEbI minute 26-30), distinguished because it involves a compact mathematical model for how expectations are calculated given prior knowledge and experience of similar events. After a new instance of an event unfolds, the outcome—whether supporting or refuting the expectation—is fed back into the prior probability to form a revised expected probability for the next instance.
7. This phenomenon points out that the decline effect in general should not be thought of as just a decline in impact. Rather, here is a change in *direction* of the impact. Where before the results moved away from the norm, now they move back toward the norm just as dramatically. So, it may be the case in general that once one is capable of a

positive-going effect, then a decline in scoring may not be due to a lack of effect but, rather, to a negative directional effect.

Chapter 8

1. Jordan Lewis, "Why Does Time Fly as We Get Older?" *Scientific American*, online guest blog, December 13, 2013. Found at http://blogs.scientificamerican.com/mind-guest-blog/2013/12/18/why-does-time-fly-as-we-get-older/ (accessed October 19, 2016). See also Marc Wittman, *Felt Time* (Cambridge, MA: MIT Press, 2017), pp. 83-91.
2. Marian Sigman, "Why does Infant Attention Predict Adolescent Intelligence?" University of California. *Infant Behavior and Development* 20 (2), 1997: 133-140.
3. Alan Slater and Michael Lewis editors, *Introduction to Infant Development*. Oxford, England: Oxford University Press, 2011, in chapter 6, Scott Johnson and Alan Slater "The Development of Intelligence in Infancy," pp. 115-116, found at http://www.psy.miami.edu/faculty/dmessinger/c_c/rsrcs/rdgs/cognitive/Intelligence_in_Infancy.pdf (accessed October 19, 2016). I was involved in such research studies at Educational Testing Service 1979–81. See ETS research database for other related studies by Michael Lewis at http://search.ets.org/researcher/query.html?col=rsrchr&op0=&fl0=AU%3A&ty0=p&tx0=Lewis,+Michael&qt=+&st=41.
4. An early branch of psychology called *associativism* (before formalization of the current field of psychology) postulated that the mind functions primarily based on a sequence of associations. Associativism's roots go back to Plato and Aristotle but the conception was supported by Enlightenment philosophers John Locke, David Hume, Thomas Hobbs, David Hartley, and others. Locke coined the term *association of ideas*, which embodied what would become the basic thesis. The discussion focused on the nature of memory as a stream of consciousness fed by associations rather than a theory about the mind's structure in general. Today the presence of hypertext linkages enables us to think more broadly about how the mind forms a complex network of associations. See Howard C. Warren, *A Brief History of Association Psychology*. New York: Charles Scribner's Sons, 1921.
5. For physical systems, we might say that some item has been "stretched beyond the moment of elasticity," at which point it has deformed and will not return to its original shape.
6. Leonard Mlodinow notes in his book *Elastic*, New York: Pantheon Books, 2018, pp. 18-19, that humans embrace change more than all other animals do. Change involves growth and evolution, and so, humans are primed to self-evolve much more readily than other animals are. The concept of the mental regulator is seen here as the counterbalance to that tendency. Most of our lives are involved in norms, and only what I call *moments* are the perhaps dopamine-fueled instants when we let go of norms as we reach toward an insight.

Chapter 9

1. Although I was not present at this event myself, I wrote notes based on staff reports shortly afterward. According to one who was present, one student in group seven (my designation) claimed that the lamp peeked red 23 times in a row without turning red or any other color. Such an occurrence strains credibility, and I redescribed it as "more times than they could keep track of."

2. Marvin Minsky, *The Society of Mind*. New York: Touchstone Books, 1986, p. 8.
3. Ibid., p. 20.
4. This concept of a cacophony of chaotic activity existing below the surface of consciousness in the mind has origins in a theory by Oliver Selfridge, an early AI scientist in the late 1950s. Selfridge developed "pandemonium theory" to represent how the mind is constructed, with independent subconscious routines or demons working to solve initially independent sections of tasks such as pattern recognition in a stimulus. However, the concept had to be broadened later as its fully bottom-up nature was indeed pandemonium in that it lacked some of the needed ability to hierarchically organize. Thus, the society of mind became a more effective concept in AI practice and a better model of activities in the human mind. See Wikipedia entry "Pandemonium architecture" found at https://en.wikipedia.org/wiki/Pandemonium_architecture (accessed December 4, 2018). Also see Stanislas Dehaene, *Consciousness and the Brain*. New York: Penguin Books, 2014, pp. 175-177.
5. The terms meaning *field* and *field of meaning* were first used (to my knowledge) in a conversation between David Bohm and Renee Weber as transcribed in, Renee Weber, "Meaning as Being in the Implicate Order Philosophy of David Bohm: a Conversation," pp. 444-445.
6. Marvin Minsky, *The Emotion Machine*. New York: Simon & Schuster, 2006, p. 8. Here Minsky explains why he uses the term *resources* in this book as the elements of the society of mind concept, in effect replacing or superseding the term *agent*.
7. Dean Radin, *Supernormal*. New York: Deepak Chopra Books, 2013, p. 276.
8. Ibid., pp. 276-277.

Chapter 10

1. Deborah Racey, Michael Young, Dennis Garlick, Jennifer Pham, and Aaron Blaisdell. "Pigeon and human performance in a multi-armed bandit task in response to changes in variable interval schedules." *Learning & Behavior* 2011, 39, 245-258. Also see Richard Herrnstein, *Matching Law*, p. 13.
2. Marc Wittmann, *Altered States of Consciousness*. Cambridge, MA: MIT Press, 2018, p. 58.
3. Of course, from a research standpoint it was intriguing.

Chapter 11

1. Ruth Rosenbaum, "Exploring the Other Dark Continent: Parallels between Psi Phenomena and the Psychotherapeutic Process." *Psychoanalytic Review* February 2011, 98(1): 73. Also personal communications.
2. Ibid., p. 60.
3. Ruth Rosenbaum, personal communication, November 2018.
4. Ruth Rosenbaum, "Exploring the Other Dark Continent: Parallels between Psi Phenomena and the Psychotherapeutic Process," p. 66.
5. Ibid., p. 59-60. It is interesting that just two years after Freud's first mention of telepathy, a neuropsychiatrist named Hans Berger invented the electroencephalograph (EEG) and that the impetus for his work on the EEG had come from a personal experience as a young man that had fostered a belief in telepathy. See Leonard Mlodinow,

Elastic, New York, Pantheon Books, 2018, pp. 111-112. Also see Wikipedia entry for Hans Berger regarding first use of EEG.
6. Ibid., p. 60.
7. Poll conducted by Poll Position, as reported nationally January 12, 2012, in the *New York Post*, the *New York Times*, the *Christian Science Monitor*, and others. See, for example, http://denver.cbslocal.com/2012/01/12/poll-finds-43-percent-of-people-believe-god-helps-tebow-win/ (accessed October 26, 2016).
8. Andrew Newberg, Eugene d'Aquili, and Vince Rause, *Why God Won't Go Away*, New York: Ballantine Books, 2002, pp. 123-125. Also pp. 108-109 regarding psychological advantages of belief to overall health.
9. Daniel Goleman, "Probing the Enigma of Multiple Personality." *New York Times*, June 28, 1988. See http://www.nytimes.com/1988/06/28/science/probing-the-enigma-of-multiple-personality.html?pagewanted=all (accessed June 12, 2016).
10. To some degree, the presence of multiple top-level minds is seen in the left and right hemispheres of the brain when the corpus callosum connecting them is severed. The two hemispheres function somewhat independently and can be addressed sometimes separately. For example, one might raise a right arm (controlled by the left hemisphere), and the right hemisphere, having now caused the action, must create a story about why it happened.
11. F. Diane Barth, "Our Many Selves," *Psychology Today* (online) April 1, 2011. See https://www.psychologytoday.com/us/blog/the-couch/201104/our-many-selves (accessed September 13, 2018).
12. Alan Hugenot, "The Nature of Consciousness," video. See https://www.youtube.com/watch?v=yByEQfaD314 minute 11:50 (accessed March 25, 2016).

Chapter 12

1. Antonio Damasio, *Descartes' Error*. New York: Penguin Books, 2005 (first published 1994), pp. 3-5.
2. See *Psychology Today*, January 16, 2012, excerpt from Jenni Ogden, "Trouble in Mind." Oxford, England: Oxford University Press, 2012. See https://www.psychologytoday.com/blog/trouble-in-mind/201201/hm-the-man-no-memory (accessed October 26, 2016).
3. Christof Koch, *Consciousness : Confessions of a Romantic Reductionist*. Cambridge, MA: MIT Press, 2012, pp. 65-66.
4. Ibid., p. 43. Also see Antonio Damasio, *Descartes' Error*. London: Penguin Books, 1994, p. 252, wherein the spirit and soul are ascribed to be completely organism material states but acknowledging how those states come about through a complex interaction with all parts of the body and environment and that the environment itself is generally structured based on previous influences of the individual itself—a somewhat tangled feedback loop.
5. Jenni Ogden, *Psychology Today*, January 16, 2012, excerpt from "Trouble in Mind." Oxford, England: Oxford University Press, 2012. Found at https://www.psychologytoday.com/blog/trouble-in-mind/201201/hm-the-man-no-memory (accessed October 26, 2016)

6. Karl Popper and John C. Eccles, *The Self and Its Brain;* Wilder Penfield : *Mystery of the Mind;* Sir Charles Sherrington, *Man on His Nature;* R. W. Sperry, "Mind-brain interaction: Mentalism, yes; dualism, no." *Neuroscience* 5, 196.
7. Wilder Penfield, *Mystery of the Mind.* Princeton, NJ: Princeton University Press, 1975, pp. 75-82.
8. C. G. Jung, *Memories, Dreams, Reflections.* New York: Vintage reissue, 1989, p. 136, stating: "The relationship between doctor and patient, especially when a transference on the part of the patient occurs, or a more or less unconscious identification of doctor and patient, can lead to parapsychological phenomena. I have frequently run into this." In this passage, Jung indicates that parapsychological phenomena, or what I call *direct shared meaning,* come with an empathetic connection of doctor to patient and the openness and transference from patient to doctor and back.
9. Larry Jameson and Beth Jameson, *Brain Injury Survivor's Guide.* Denver: Outskirts Press, 2007. Excerpt of book from "Beth's Brain Injury Blog" entry of January 11, 2011; http://blog.brain-injury-online.com/2011/01/understanding-brain-injury-whats-next.html (accessed June 5, 2014).
10. See Wikipedia "Cognitive Behavioral Therapy," including extensive references; http://en.wikipedia.org/wiki/Cognitive_behavioral_therapy (accessed August 4, 2017).
11. See Christof Koch, *Consciousness,* p. 103, referencing work of Karl Popper and John C. Eccles. See also http://www.informationphilosopher.com/solutions/scientists/sperry/ for views of Nobel laureate Roger Sperry regarding the interaction of brain and mind (accessed July 12, 2017).
12. Stuart Hameroff, "Quantum computation in brain microtubules? The Penrose–Hameroff 'Orch OR' model of consciousness." The Royal ?Society, 1998. See http://www.quantumconsciousness.org/sites/default/files/1998%20Hameroff%20Quantum%20Computation%20in%20Brain%20Microtubules%20The%20Penrose%20Hameroff%20Orch%20OR%20model%20of%20consciousness%20-%20Royal%20Society_0.pdf.
13. Max Tegmark, "The importance of quantum decoherence in brain processes." Physics Review E, July 2, 1999. Pdf file accessible through https://arxiv.org/abs/quant-ph/9907009 (accessed August 7, 2017). For a simpler description of his own paper and its implications for arguing against the brain as a quantum computer, see Max Tegmark, *Our Mathematical Universe.* New York: Knopf, 2014, pp. 205-208.
14. Neuroscientist Christof Koch notes that the probability function associated with a presynaptic action potential causing a postsynaptic action potential to be fired could be a mechanism (the only mechanism) for a nonmaterial mind to influence the brain by determining the firing sequence or a given individual instance. So, though the probability distribution of action potential firing would remain constant, individual instances would be targeted over others (see Christof Koch, *Consciousness,* p. 104). Although he largely dismisses this proposed mechanism based on the lack of any possible causal force to be present, I propose the selection effect as the causal force, though as noted before, force is not the appropriate characterization. For further discussion regarding the probabilities of neurotransmitter release (synapse firing) and how local conditions and feedback processes can change them, see http://www.nature.com/nrn/journal/v10/n5/full/nrn2634.html (accessed June 26, 2017). Also see Khan Academy

article "The Synapse", https://www.khanacademy.org/science/biology/human-biology/neuron-nervous-system/a/the-synapse (accessed June 26, 2017), in part reading: "[A] sending neuron can 'dial up' or 'dial down' the amount of neurotransmitter it releases in response to the arrival of an action potential. Similarly, a receiving cell can alter the number of receptors it puts on its membrane and how readily it responds to activation of those receptors. These changes can strengthen or weaken communication at a particular synapse."

15. Ilya Prigogine, *The End of Certainty*. New York: Free Press, 1996, pp. 44, 68-69.
16. This can be in two ways. First, as noted, synapse firing can simulate a thermodynamic system, wherein the patterns of various neural clusters in effect represent different temperatures. Second, the brain is an actual thermodynamic system with constantly fluctuating local temperatures as seen by fMRI machines as blood concentrations change. The random component of neuron firing may be affected by such fluctuations, as may be the speed at which neurotransmitters and other chemicals traverse the synaptic cleft. That in turn affects the sequence of subsequent neuron firings.
17. The concept of consciousness altering the timing of a given neuron's firing through quantum mechanical processes has been proposed by Nobel Laureate Sir John Eccles with supporting work by German physicist Friedrich Beck. A downloadable summary is available at *www-physics.lbl.gov/~stapp/eccles.pd*f, (accessed December 4, 2018).
18. See Khan Academy article "The Synapse"; https://www.khanacademy.org/science/biology/human-biology/neuron-nervous-system/a/the-synapse (accessed June 26, 2017).
19. Each new point in time can be considered an initial condition, with all synapses fixed in a phase space associated with their time to fire, such that the time evolution of the ensemble would very quickly show instability. This models a thermodynamic system wherein work is constantly being done such that conditions are not moving toward a final rest state of equilibrium. Rather, the brain is always moving away from any notion of equilibrium with respect to its previous state.
20. Most recently (2015), three mathematical physicists provided proof that there is a broken link between microscopic properties of matter at the quantum level and their coalescing into macroscopic properties. There is no causal force linkage that bridges the gap and allows all macroscopic properties to be known with certainty from the underlying quantum states. See Toby S. Cubitt, David Pérez-García, and Michael Wolf, "The Un(solv)able Problem." *Scientific American* October 2018, 319(28): 37.

    One additional issue can be addressed regarding the proposed mind–matter model. It involves the issue of energy balance. The argument exists that if mind were to affect the brain from some external position, it would have to affect the energy balance in the brain. That is, to apply a force or pressure on the brain such that it is redirected in any way would mean that the system would gain (probably heat) energy. The gain in energy in this situation would appear to come from nowhere. And this situation is not seen (although it is dubious with regard to whether tools exist today to measure it in situ). In any event, with the bioREG concept as a selection effect, it may not work with energy at all, or if there is, it may remain so small as to be undetectable in the complex brain system. Synapses will fire anyway, idling at many times per second. So, to affect the timing of that firing based on inherent uncertainty would not necessarily involve a model based on energy application.

21. Two theories postulate possible changes in the speed of light. One suggests that the early universe had different properties, leading to a much faster speed: See Daniel Oberhaus, "Scientists Think the Speed of Light Has Slowed, and They're Trying to Prove It." *Motherboard*, December 6, 2016, at https://motherboard.vice.com/en_us/article/8q87gk/light-speed-slowed (accessed September 13, 2018). A second theory suggests that the speed of light is based on its interactions with virtual charged particles in the quantum vacuum of space, and if the density and mix of those particles change based on their interactions with radiation, the speed of light may change. See Jesse Emspak, "Speed of Light May Not Be Constant, Physicists Say." *Live Science* April 27, 2013. Found at https://www.livescience.com/29111-speed-of-light-not-constant.html (accessed September 13, 2018). Although these theories would be characterized as simply physical properties at work, at least the first theory could be thought of as the universe's interacting with itself.

22. Amanda Gefter, "The Evolutionary Argument Against Reality." Theatlantic.com. Reprinted from *Quanta* magazine, April 21, 2016; https://www.theatlantic.com/science/archive/2016/04/the-illusion-of-reality/479559/ (accessed September 13, 2018).

23. In mid 2018, a meme made the rounds wherein a word was repeated, and people described what they heard. In general, people heard either *laurel* or *yanny*, and those who heard one or the other were absolutely adamant that to hear the other must indicate a hearing problem. I myself heard *laurel* and was shocked to find out almost half of people heard *yanny*. The takeaway is that reality depends on the specific hearing system of the individuals involved.

24. See Ken Wilber, editor, *Quantum Questions*. Boulder: Shambhala, 1984. This book consists of excerpts of "mystical writings" from mostly early quantum physicists, including Werner Heisenberg, Erwin Schrödinger, Albert Einstein, Louis de Broglie, James Jeans, Max Planck, Wolfgang Pauli, and Arthur Eddington. We can add to the list (as per Robert G. Jahn and Brenda J. Dunne, *Quirks of the Quantum Mind*. Princeton, NJ: ICRL Press, 2012, pp. 157-239) Niels Bohr, Eugene Wigner, John von Neumann, Carl von Weizsäcker, and Percy Bridgman, all of whom addressed the concept of consciousness as having nonphysical implications. Finally, there is David Bohm, who discusses physics and consciousness in his book *Wholeness and the Implicate Order*. New York: Routledge, 1980.

25. John A. Wheeler, "How Come the Quantum," in *New Techniques and Ideas in Quantum Measurement Theory*, Annals of the New York Academy of Sciences, vol. 480. New York: New York Academy of Sciences, 1986, p. 305.

26. Ibid., p. 313.

27. Renee Weber, ""Meaning as Being in the Implicate Order Philosophy of David Bohm: a Conversation," in *Quantum Implications: Essays in Honour of David Bohm*, Editors B. J. Hiley and F. David Peat, London, Routledge & Kegan Paul, 1987, p. 443.

28. Amanda Gefter, *Trespassing on Einstein's Lawn*. New York: Bantam, 2014, p. 289.

29. Renee Weber, "Meaning as Being in the Implicate Order Philosophy of David Bohm: a Conversation," p. 439.

30. In fact, there is a third meaning-action pair, which is we who are looking on. But for purposes here, we ignore our own presence.
31. For example, a rock, as an aggregation of smaller observers, will not be looking back at a human observer. But there can be interactions among particles and photons bouncing back and forth as part of the observational process.
32. Hilbert Spaces were developed in the early 20th century, named after the German mathematician David Hilbert.
33. Case Western Reserve University, "Einstein's 'spooky action' common in large quantum systems, mathematicians find," May 28, 2013. See https://newatlas.com/quantum-entanglement-ubiquitous/27836/ (accessed December 5, 2018).
34. By *individual level* is meant an individual parent that might help select a genetic mutation for its offspring. By *species level* is meant the possibility of a group mind's helping statistically influence the members of the species to produce a desirable mutation somewhere among the members. This basic concept is perhaps supported by the fact that evolution is exponential over time, gaining speed as more complex organisms and species have more complex webs capable of overlaying needs, desires, and expectations on the mutation process itself.
35. Karl Popper and John C. Eccles. *The Self and Its Brain*. Berlin: Springer International, 1981, pp. 56-60.
36. Karl Popper, *Knowledge and the Body-Mind Problem*. London: Routledge, 1994, pp. 31-33.
37. Sir James Jeans, *The Mysterious Universe*. London: Pelican Books, 1938, reprint of 1931 2nd edition, p. 137. See https://archive.org/details/TheMysteriousUniverseSirJamesJeans for download (accessed May 12, 2017).

Chapter 13

1. On a somewhat humorous side note, in 2010 at an event marking the closing of an almost century-old Princeton restaurant, I met a woman who had been living on Mercer Street in the early 1950s. She described how, at age four, she would see Einstein on his morning walk and would run up to him saying, "Good morning, Dr. Iodine."

Chapter 14

1. I did continue with the session. I had two misses and then five more hits, giving 10 for 12 overall.

Chapter 16

1. This proposition does not preclude other, nonpurposeful states of mind from having effects. In fact, sometimes daydreaming connects with the output of the REG and creates large effects. However, even here, one can suppose that the connection and impact represent the mind's finding an outlet to purposefully mirror the feelings in the daydream.
2. Amy Wrzesniewski and Barry Schwartz, "The Secret of Effective Motivation." *New York Times*, July 6, 2014. Op-Ed. See https://www.nytimes.com/2014/07/06/opinion/sunday/the-secret-of-effective-motivation.html (accessed October 26, 2016).

3. Of course, here again, one could say that what lies behind the intent is the deeper purpose of examining one's own mind. This is patently true, but regardless of the characterization, the act of applying intention on the self can bootstrap the very strength of one's purpose that drives it. It becomes a feedback loop.
4. Curtis Marean, "The Most Invasive Species of All." *Scientific American* August 2015: 33-39.
5. I almost always avoid using the term *machine* to characterize humans or their behavior, but the expression is too good to pass up here.
6. Christopher Clarey, "Djokovic Loses Battle of Trajectories (His Is Fading)." *New York Times* sports, June 7, 2017.
7. Ben Rothenberg, "Halep, Resigned to Defeat, Finds Out It's Not Over Till It's Over." *New York Times* sports, June 7, 2017.
8. This is also not to say that changing one's mind immediately and completely at any given time suddenly changes one's circumstances. Just as you may have units of meaning about yourself, others have units of meaning about you as well. Those outside units create outer boundaries that impress on you and in which you fit. In order to change your circumstances, you have to use the change in your own attitude and orientation to effect change in that outer boundary. That is, you have to change others' minds about yourself, and you have to shift the prevailing attitude as well as circumstances to support your new model.
9. For Gates, Musk, and Jobs, see Michael Simmons, "Studies Show That People Who Have High 'Integrative Complexity' Are More Likely to Be Successful," May 15, 2018. Found at https://medium.com/the-mission/studies-show-that-people-who-have-high-integrative-complexity-are-more-likely-to-be-successful-443480e8930c. For Bezos, see article by Steven Levy, "Jeff Bezos Wants Us All to Leave Earth—for Good." *Wired*, October 15, 2018. As Bezos colleague George Dyson said, "It was almost incomprehensible how technically engaged Jeff was in every part of the discussion." Found at https://www.wired.com/story/jeff-bezos-blue-origin/ (accessed October 16, 2018).

Chapter 17

1. See Wikipedia entry on episodic memory found at https://en.wikipedia.org/wiki/Episodic_memory (accessed October 12, 2018).
2. See Wikipedia entry "Reality Distortion Field"; http://en.wikipedia.org/wiki/Reality_distortion_field (accessed December 26, 2017).
3. See documentary *The Joy of Sox*, by Joel Leskowitz, about the Boston Red Sox 2004 World Series champions. Discussion of monitoring for heart entrainment and other physiological syncing as well as crowd effect, minutes 13:00-17:30.
4. Lynne McTaggart, *The Power of Eight*. New York, Atria Books, 2017, pp. 32-36.
5. Dr. Bernard Grad of McGill University and its affiliated Allen Institute ran studies from the 1960s to the 1980s examining the effect that healers had on rates of seedling growth or on water that was then used to help grow the seedlings. See Bernard Grad, "A Telekinetic Effect on Plant Growth." *International Journal of Parapsychology* 5 (1963): 117-33, and Bernard Grad, "A Telekinetic Effect on Plant Growth II." *International Journal of Parapsychology* 6 (1964): 473-98. I personally spent the summer of 1984 working with Dr. Grad, studying the effect of magnets placed around

water that was then used to grow the seedlings to see whether this process would duplicate the effect of healers. In fact, such was partially found to be the case, though there was no evidence that healers themselves involved a similar physical magnetic process (unpublished). See also S. M. Roney-Dougal and J. Solfvin, "Field Study of Enhancement Effect on Lettuce Seeds: Their Germination Rate, Growth and Health." *Journal of the Society of Psychical Research* 66 (2002): 129-143.

6. Lynne McTaggart, *Power of Eight*, pp. 49-50.
7. An extensive list of simultaneous inventions can be found at https://en.wikipedia.org/wiki/List_of_multiple_discoveries (accessed August 27, 2018).
8. Nicholas A. Christakis and James H. Fowler, *Connected*. New York: Little, Brown and Company, 2009, pp. 41-43.
9. Ibid., p. 44.
10. Ibid.
11. Dean Radin, *Supernormal*, pp. 39-40.
12. Reza Aslan, *Zealot*. New York: Random House, 2013, pp. 30-31.
13. French philosopher Jacques Derrida, for example, critiqued our insistence that narratives follow a linear storyline, which is the case with so much of (reductionist) science. Derrida considered that truth was found in stories that embody the complexity of connection and interactions and that real narratives are neither linear nor as simple as science tries to make them. See article "Material Storytelling—Learning as Intra-active Becoming," Kenneth Mølbjerg Jørgensen and Anete M. Camille Strand, in *Critical Narrative Inquiry*, editors Kenneth Molbjerg Jorgensen and Carlos Largacha-martinez. Nova Science Publishers, 2014, pp. 62-63.
14. Nicholas A. Christakis and James H. Fowler, *Connected*, p. 26.
15. The Gaia hypothesis was developed by James Lovelock and Lynn Margulis, who spent many years trying to defend the concept as good science, describing interrelations in the biosphere as systemic and highly complex. Over time, the public sense of it has expanded to personify the biosphere as something of a living entity. Various interpretations of the theory mirror the various possibilities of a collective agent described here—from a complex mechanical feedback system to a self-regulating organism, to a more-self-aware information-processing agent.
16. Kurt Gödel's incompleteness theory is relevant here. Gödel proved mathematically that any logical system considered to be complete (like the entire universe), includes propositions that cannot be supported within the system itself. That is, certain propositions can be supported only by having the complete system evolve (in effect stepping out of itself) to a higher-level position from which to assert the truth of the propositions. At that point, the whole has been augmented by the arrival of this new position—which must now be included as part of the whole and which once again results in propositions that cannot all be confirmed within this larger system.
17. ESPN broadcast of US Open tennis tournament semifinals, September 6, 2018.
18. The site election.princeton.edu (accessed November 6, 2016).
19. My own project attests to this fact. Figure 15.2 shows how closely I tracked the minimum of what I needed to succeed in this unlikely outcome.

Chapter 18

1. Jonah Lehrer, "The Truth Wears Off." *The New Yorker*. December 13, 2010. Available online at http://www.newyorker.com/magazine/2010/12/13/the-truth-wears-off (accessed October 4, 2016).
2. Ibid.
3. WNYC Studios podcast with Jonathan Schooler. "The 'Decline Effect' and Scientific Truth" aired June 29, 2012. See transcript at https://www.wnycstudios.org/story/219360-decline-effect-and-scientific-truth (accessed October 16, 2012). Also, paper presented by Jonathan Schooler at the Society for Scientific Exploration conference, June 11, 2011. "The Decline Effect: Exploring Why Effect Sizes So Often Decline following Repeated Replications." Boulder, CO.
4. Brian Nosek, "Estimating the Reproducibility of Psychological Science." *Science* August 28, 2015. See description in Ed Yong, "How Reliable Are Psychological Studies?" *The Atlantic*, August 27, 2015, accessible at https://www.theatlantic.com/science/archive/2015/08/psychology-studies-reliability-reproducability-nosek/402466/ (accessed December 26, 2017).
5. See Rachel E. Gross, "Psychologists Call Out the Study That Called Out the Field of Psychology." *Slate* March 3, 2016. http://www.slate.com/blogs/the_slatest/2016/03/03/psychology_study_that_induced_the_reproducibility_crisis_was_wrong.html (accessed July 2, 2017).
6. See Benedict Carey, "Psychology Itself Is Under Scrutiny," July 18, 2018; https://www.nytimes.com/2018/07/16/health/psychology-studies-stanford-prison.html (accessed July 23, 2018).
7. Matthew Hutson, Artificial Intelligence Faces a Reproducibility Crisis. *Science* February 16, 2018; http://science.sciencemag.org/content/359/6377/725 (accessed August 27, 2018).
8. B. J. Dunne, Y. H. Dobyns, R. G. Jahn, and A. Thompson. "Series Position Effects in Random Event Generator Experiments." *Journal of Scientific Exploration* 8(2), 1994: 197-211.
9. Markus Maier and Moritz Dechamps, "Observer Effects on Quantum Randomness: Testing Micro-Psychokinetic Effects of Smokers on Addiction Related Stimuli," *Journal of Scientific Exploration,* Vol. 32, No. 2, June 2018, p. 281.
10. WNYC Studios podcast with Jonathan Schooler (see note 3 above).
11. Joshua Kirsch, "European Effort to Computer-Simulated Brain Draws Fire." *New York Times*, July 8, 2014. https://www.nytimes.com/2014/07/09/science/european-effort-for-computer-simulated-brain-draws-fire.html (accessed August 9, 2017).
12. Stefan Theil, "Why the Human Brain Project Went Wrong—and How to Fix It." *Scientific American* October 1, 2015. See https://www.scientificamerican.com/article/why-the-human-brain-project-went-wrong-and-how-to-fix-it/ (accessed May 3, 2017).
13. Catherine Clifford, "Japanese scientists just used A.I. to read minds and it's amazing," January 8, 2018; https://www.cnbc.com/2018/01/08/japanese-scientists-use-artificial-intelligence-to-decode-thoughts.html (accessed September 12, 2018).
14. See Giulio Tononi, Olaf Sporns, and Gerald Edelman, "Measures of degeneracy and redundancy in biological networks." *Proceedings of the National Academy of Sciences*

(USA) 96(6): 3257-3260, March 16, 1999. Found at http://www.pnas.org/content/96/6/3257.full (accessed June 12, 2017). Note that the concept of redundancy in the context of brain science is more technically called *degeneracy*. The term *degeneracy* is not used in the text because of general associations with the word. However, the formal concept of degeneracy describes conditions in which there are no one-to-one correspondences between input and output states of the brain. In those cases, processing routes cannot be uniquely identified, and the term *degenerate* is used to indicate the presence of possible alternative pathways. By contrast, in engineering systems, redundancy involves the implementation of multiple identical systems to achieve the same goal, such as a backup unit. The brain generally does not use identical backup systems but ones that function equivalently.
15. Philip Ball, "Quantum Physics May Be Even Spookier Than You Think," *Scientific American*, May 21, 2018. Found at https://www.scientificamerican.com/article/quantum-physics-may-be-even-spookier-than-you-think/ (accessed September 12, 2018).
16. An exception has been noted wherein the strong nuclear interaction has a more unusual binding curve with distance, but this is true in general.

Chapter 19

1. Pam Belluck, "Holly the Cat." *New York Times*, January 19, 2013. See https://well.blogs.nytimes.com/2013/01/19/one-cats-incredible-journey/ (accessed July 3, 2016).
2. Robert G. Jahn and Brenda J. Dunne, *Consciousness and the Source of Reality* (Princeton, NJ : ICRL Press, 2011) pp. 161-166. See table on page 163 labeled "Off-Time Remote."
3. An alternative measure of success that also does not require a fixed length session uses a statistic called the Bayes Factor (BF). The Bayes Factor continually updates the likelihood that the ongoing results are produced by a true effect as set against chance (the null hypothesis). One can stop the session or study when the result reaches a desired level of significance.
4. Recall that this is one of the very first perplexing experiences I had with the REG, as described in Chapter 3. I likened it to the action of tides moving in and out.
5. Here I use the ending Z score rather than the Z_{max} score to calculate the odds, even though the end point had not been preset. I do so because I had locked into a Z score for hundreds of thousands of trials and so consider it fixed at whatever reasonable end point might have been chosen. Also note that as the study goes on, to maintain a constant Z score the cumulative deviation chart line (see figure 19.3) must continue to rise. If it becomes flat for any length of time—which indicates randomness—then the Z score would begin to decline.
6. I ran a calculation on the results of the Maryland period alone. If scaled up to the size of the full study, it would have produced an overall Z score of 2.50. And although that's not as high as the 3.0 of the overall study, it would still have been highly significant and is simply part of the general fluctuation of results on a moment-to-moment basis. Looked at in another way, the cumulative or current Z score was 2.25 at the start of this period, and when the period ended, the score had risen to 2.55. In other words, the data set continued to move in a positive direction through this period, significantly helping the overall data set achieve its final score.

Chapter 20

1. Les Fehmi, personal communication, Princeton, NJ, Spring 2013.
2. Mark S. Schwartz and Frank Andrasik editors. *Biofeedback: A Practitioner's Guide*. New York: Guilford Press, 2003, p. 4.
3. Les Fehmi, personal communication, Princeton, NJ, Spring 2013.
4. See Les Fehmi biography at http://www.amazon.com/Les-Fehmi/e/B001JP2GPM (accessed July 2, 2017).
5. Les Fehmi and Jim Robbins, *The Open-Focus Brain*. Boston: Trumpeter Books, 2007, pp. 30-31.
6. Susan Fehmi, personal communication, Princeton, NJ, Spring 2013.
7. Morris Freedman, "Mind-Matter Interactions and the Frontal Lobes of the Brain," University of Toronto and Baycrest Health Sciences. Presentation at Society for Scientific Exploration conference, June 22, 2016. For abstract, see http://www.fmbr.org/SSE-abstracts/2016/SSE-PA-2016Abstracts.pdf (accessed October 26, 2016).
8. Antonio Damasio, *Descartes' Error*, 2005, pp. 133-134.
9. Joey Caswell, Mark Collins, Lyndon Juden-Kelly, and Michael Persinger, "Gravitational and Experimental Electromagnetic Contributions to Cerebral Effects upon Deviations of Random Number Variables Generated by Electron Tunneling," Laurentian University. *International Letters of Chemistry, Physics and Astronomy* 11, 2013: 72-85.
10. Giulio Tononi, Olaf Sporns, and Gerald Edelman, "Measures of degeneracy and redundancy in biological networks."
11. Optimism and pessimism may in fact be partially influenced by separate genes. For optimism, see Denise Mann, "Optimism May Be Partly in Your Genes," September 16, 2011, at http://www.webmd.com/balance/news/20110916/optimism-partly-in-your-genes#1 (accessed March 12, 2017). For pessimism, see John Ericson, "Is Pessimism Genetic? Research Shows Your Outlook Might Be Cloudy by Genetic Design," October 10, 2013, at http://www.medicaldaily.com/pessimism-genetic-research-shows-your-outlook-might-be-cloudy-genetic-design-259573 (accessed March 13, 2016).
12. Dean Hamer, *The God Gene*. New York: Anchor Books, 2004, pp. 70-76. Subjects with this genetic variation appear to be more naturally open, which is a trait that may directly affect the ability to succeed in the REG process.
13. R. Douglas Fields, "Amping Up Brain Function: Transcranial Stimulation Shows Promise in Speeding Up Learning." *Scientific American* November 25, 2011. See https://www.scientificamerican.com/article/amping-up-brain-function/ (accessed August 10, 2017).
14. However, it might also be the case that the ability would decline over time as the brain–mind finds other neural pathways to compensate for the significance it is experiencing.
15. See https://www.vocabulary.com/dictionary/somatic (accessed August 20, 2018).
16. It may be that even with today's devices, a person could learn to inhabit a simple calculator's circuitry to some degree—or at least feel that way. The person would have to develop a new meaning structure surrounding the input and output neurons and a kind of empathy related to the calculator. However, this would seem to be more of a mental representation of experience than the experience itself, given the rigid, gated, deterministic nature of calculators. In any event, empirical studies may lead to unexpected findings, as is so often the case in science.

17. Because there is no controlled before and after or possible ABA experimental design that can be run with respect to this proposition, it remains anecdotal. So, it is unclear how much better or faster I may be at solving problems relative to the earlier time. However, it feels faster, and without a doubt the mental process or exercise I describe makes working through stuck situations much less frustrating.
18. J. L. Hames, J. D. Ribeiro, A. R. Smith, and T. E. Joiner, "An urge to jump affirms the urge to live: An empirical examination of the high place phenomenon." *Journal of Affective Disorders* February 2012: 1112-1120.
19. See http://www.nbcnews.com/health/body-odd/weird-urge-jump-bridge-explained-f424037 (accessed February 25, 2017).
20. In contrast, bioiofeedback or neurofeedback is being tested and in some cases is already used for the control of physical devices because the brain side of the signal is far more reproducible and reliable.

Chapter 21

1. It calls to mind the story of quantum physicist Wolfgang Pauli, who once shouted out during a lecture, "That's not even wrong."
2. Antonio Damasio, *Descartes' Error*, 1994, pp. 193-194. Also see pp. 70 and 83-84 for a basic description of this thesis in relation to brain function and regions.
3. Kahneman received the Nobel Prize without Tversky because Tversky had earlier died of cancer and so was not eligible to share the prize. Also, the designation *behavioral economics* was not proposed by Kahneman and Tversky but was based on their work—in part (perhaps) because there is no Nobel Prize in psychology.
4. The system 1 and system 2 designations were first used by psychologists Keith Stanovich and Richard West. See Kahneman, p. 48.
5. Daniel Kahneman, *Thinking, Fast and Slow*. New York: Farrar, Straus and Giroux, 2011, pp. 119-122.
6. Our reverence for logic is perhaps why artificial intelligence first developed in an image of a system 2 creature. Like the crew member character Data in *Star Trek: The Next Generation*, a commonly proposed new life-form we might create is one of pure logic. Of course, these stories—including the story of the character Mr. Spock in the original *Star Trek*—have intuited that without emotions, there is no creative passion. Further, we now find that artificial intelligence is more effective when created in the image of system 1 rather than system 2. When a system is allowed to develop as an associative web, it can learn more effectively. However, such machine-learning processes begin to function like black boxes in the same way that each of our human minds are black boxes when viewed from the outside. An AI robot mind is trained by setting up a hardware/software "brain" and then feeding it lots of experience. How it internally organizes the data becomes a mystery, in effect—even to the programmers. They can see the associative connections of its web, but the connections don't mean anything from the outside—only its behavior in response to new stimulus. In this framework, system 2 reverts once again to a support process.
7. The Flynn effect was so named by Richard J. Herrnstein and Charles Murray in their book, *The Bell Curve*. Free Press, 1994, p. 307. For a summary discussion, see Flynn Effect Wikipedia entry (accessed December 20, 2017). It is perhaps also worth noting

that since the beginning of the current century IQs have begun to decline, maybe related (speculatively speaking) to some aspects of social media as well as the impact of our increasingly poor diets on learning.

8. James Flynn, TED talk, 2013. See https://www.ted.com/talks/james_flynn_why_our_iq_levels_are_higher_than_our_grandparents#t-1310241 Minute 12:20 (accessed October 25, 2017).

9. The extreme version of this condition—multiple personality disorder or dissociative identity disorder—as discussed in chapter 11.

10. In this sense, many aspects of psychology and neuroscience, such as the work described here, become more than normal scientific modeling. Their very activity has the quality of self-awareness. What they uncover, then, are not static truths. The uncovering of such truths means they will now enter a feedback process that will change them. We saw this process at work in chapter 18, with the problems of replicating psychological studies.

11. The dynamic of fragility is of course highly complex, and I only propose that growing self-awareness is a major factor. Noah Berlatsky notes in his October 10, 2018, article "Are millennials really to blame for the decline in the liberal arts?" that some of the fragility of younger generations is created by parents who withhold money for education based on their desire for "marketable" courses of study. This leads to a decline in a general well-rounded education that emphasizes personal development, thus adding to stressful conditions. See https://www.nbcnews.com/think/opinion/are-millennials-really-blame-decline-liberal-arts-ncna911941https://www.nbcnews.com/think/opinion/are-millennials-really-blame-decline-liberal-arts-ncna911941 (accessed October 17, 2018).

12. However, as discussed earlier, a web can hold episodic memories that include a time element in a sequence of events. But even an episodic memory has a snapshot quality in the sense of "remember that *Star Trek* episode called "The Trouble with Tribbles"?

13. In his book *Elastic*, Leonard Mlodinow develops another high-level schema regarding human modes of thought. This schema sees two distinct modes: conscious, analytical problem solving on one hand and unconscious, more-intuitive problem solving on the other. The former is what he calls *centralized top-down and linear thinking by the conscious mind*; the latter is a decentralized elastic thinking formed by the interaction of lower-level neural clusters. Those clusters create novel associations that the conscious mind would not think of. We will call Mlodinow's description of mental structures the *problem-solving schema*.

I will attempt to subsume this two-level problem-solving schema into the three-level schema currently under discussion that is based around decision making (fast, slow, and self-aware thinking). We call this schema the *decision-making schema*. So, whereas problem solving and decision making are somewhat different activities, they are highly related. Problem solving is often a precursor to decision making and can be folded into the latter.

First, both schemata acknowledge and revolve around the personal wide web of knowledge—the basic fabric of the mind. In the problem-solving schema, one uses that web along with an analytical process to consciously arrive at solutions. In the decision-making schema, the same problem-solving activity is more granularly divided into simple problems and more-complex ones. If a problem is simple, then the web finds a model and simply applies it in what is called *system 1 fast thinking*. This mode of problem solving is not addressed in Mlodinow's discussions, perhaps because the problems to be solved in his analysis are never that simple or straightforward. They are *problems*. More-complex problems in the decision-making schema require invoking system 2 slow, or linear analytic, thinking, which is more along the lines of Mlodinow's conscious thinking. Thus, what is called *conscious thinking* in the problem-solving schema maps closely into what the decision-making schema calls *system 2 slow thinking*. So, though Mlodiow speaks of one problem-solving mode, with the decision-making schema we have two. Already then, we have reconciled the two-process schema into the three-process one.

This issue of unconscious problem solving, however, does require an extension within decision-making schemata to fully reconcile the two schemata. Nowhere in the decision-making schema is this aspect of mind explicitly addressed. Kahneman does discuss the many ways our own web can be made to affect our decisions at an unconscious level, such as with priming and anchoring described in the text. But there is no explicit use of one's unconscious mind to form novel associations—as opposed to prepackaged models from past experience—so as to help one's conscious mind with beneficial decision making.

The problem-solving schema proposes that the unconscious mind can give creative insights to the conscious mind that would never have been achieved otherwise. Therefore, to begin reconciling the two schemata with regard to unconscious thinking, we will include the notion of subagents or subwebs into the description of the associative web—the web being the basis of either schema. Subagents or subwebs form an alternate description of Mlodinow's multiple neural clusters as structured concepts of the mind. For Mlodinow, these lower-level resources operating outside consciousness—given the freedom to engage each other—can produce novel associations. Here we simply reimagine them as volitional subagents of a complex web in the decision-making schema. Subagents engage in intermediate decisions at the unconscious level that become insights and hunches that are made available to the top-level decision-making conscious mind.

We can do more in the reconciliation process. The book *Elastic*—ostensibly about problem solving—is implicitly about decision making as well. Mlodinow encourages us to use our unconscious minds as resources, so in effect he is proposing that *we make decisions about how to treat our own minds*. That is, in order to use elastic (creative) thinking as a personal tool, we have to decide to do so. To use elastic thinking becomes a decision, which then requires careful application back onto oneself. Thus, the entire discussion becomes an aspect of system 3: self-aware thinking.

14. David Brooks, "The Strange Failure of the Educated Elite," *New York Times*, May 29, 2018, p. A23.

Chapter 22

1. See April 20, 2013, *Washington Post* article at https://www.washingtonpost.com/world/national-security/inside-the-investigation-of-the-boston-marathon-bombing/2013/04/20/19d8c322-a8ff-11e2-b029-8fb7e977ef71_story.html?utm_term=.27d796f4a107 (accessed July 19, 2018).
2. Roger Cohen, "Trump's Nemesis in the Age of Pinocchio," *New York Times* Op-Ed, August 11, 2018.
3. See Lynn Margolies (former Harvard Medical School faculty member), "Are Your Decisions from Your Evolved or Primitive Brain?" *Psych Central*, 2016 (accessed September 11, 2018, from https://psychcentral.com/lib/how-to-tell-if-your-decisions-are-from-your-evolved-or-primitive-brain-2/).
4. Andrew T. Jebb, Louis Tay, Ed Diener, and Shigehiro Oishi, "Happiness, income satiation and turning points around the world." *Nature Human Behaviour* January 2018, 2: 33-38.
5. Nick Bostrom, *Superintelligence*. Oxford, England: Oxford University Press, 2014, p. 150.
6. See Matthew Hutson, "How researchers are teaching AI to learn like a child." *Science* May 24, 2018; http://www.sciencemag.org/news/2018/05/how-researchers-are-teaching-ai-learn-child (accessed September 11, 2018).
7. Dean Radin, chief scientist at the IONS Institute, provided the first look into this domain by using a Linux computer as a control during an experiment. "[A] computer running Ubuntu Linux was programmed in Java to simulate a human participant. This 'robot' participant automatically initiated a test session with the experimental setup every hour on the hour, around the clock. Neither the web server nor the double-slit apparatus could tell if a human or a robot was on the receiving end of a given session, thus providing a rigorous way to test if human observation made a difference." See p. 19.
8. Edward Ashford Lee notes in his book *Plato and the Nerd* that humans have used a series of models to describe the brain–mind dating as far back as the ancient Greeks. Thinkers have tended to use metaphors based on the technological experience of the times. For example, Lee references computer scientist John Daugman's statement that Freud proposed a "hydraulic construction" as the basis of the unconscious. Before that, Descartes, Hobbes, and others used models of the mind based on clockwork metaphors. See *Plato and the Nerd*. Cambridge MA: MIT Press, 2017, p. 181.
9. This is not to mean that we will do less hardware and software in the future. We produce more iron today than in the Iron Age, and more industry than in the Industrial Age. It isn't the volume of activity involved, but whether the concept forms the leading edge of our thinking and activity.
10. Thomas Metzinger, "Reply to Hobson: Can there be a First-Person Science of Consciousness ?" PSYCHE, August 2006, 12(4): 1-5. Found at http://journalpsyche.org/files/0xaafd.pdf (accessed January 5, 2017). With regard to the reference to "mysterious kind of first person 'data,'" the ability to affect an outside physical system is not mysterious in the sense of being cloaked in anecdotal subjective reporting. Rather, self-reports can be correlated with REG output data.

11. Michael Lockwood, *Mind, Brain and the Quantum*. Oxford, England: Basil Blackwood, 1989, p. 176.
12. Today there are an estimated 50,000 neuroscientists doing research and publishing yearly worldwide as of 2012 and 2014: see Christof Koch, *Consciousness,* p. 41, and Elaine Biech, *Training and Development for Dummies* (Hoboken, NJ: John Wiley & Sons, 2015, p. 31). Most of them are engaged in research intended to grow our knowledge about the brain in support of better physical and mental health. However, it does provide the opportunity to explore the interface between brain function and mental states by listening to subjects and trying to feel what they feel—and as reflected in brain activity.
13. The tendency for nature to move toward disorder largely in the absence of webs of mind could suggest that disorder is also a value in nature. I believe this is true in some respects. Were it not for disorder's dampening of the ongoing impact of any event over time through a dissipation of its energy, our universe would have "gone critical" with each slightest of events and would not have remained stable. However, the term *value* here would still be contestable because the tendency toward disorder is a result of statistical mechanics rather than being subjectively driven, as is the case with ordering principles. That is, values are perhaps only values when futures are driven by the mind through choice to produce favored outcomes over other possible outcomes.
14. One can of course argue that the universe is headed toward a heat death such that these would-be values will come to naught. However, given the trajectory of increased consciousness and intelligence that these values appear to follow and the abilities that attend them, we might do well to suspend judgment on the ultimate disposition of matter and energy in the far future.
15. As Martin Luther King Jr. intoned, "Let us realize that the arc of the moral universe is long, but it tends toward justice."

Units of Meaning

1. Peter Gärdenfors, *Conceptual Spaces*. Cambridge, MA: MIT Press, 2000, pp. 4-8.
2. A conceptual space such as cup space is a relatively static model, but other spaces can be highly dynamic. They can depend on the particular unit of meaning that is operating and, specifically, the point from which it views the data in the space. For example, the psychological distance between 6 times 7 as associated with the number 42 is different from the distance between 42 as associated with 6 times 7. See Michael Lewis, *The Undoing Project*. New York: W. W. Norton, 2017, pp. 112-114. This reference also discusses a more nonparametric evaluation of distance as resulting from the number of features that are found to be in common. For example, in cup space, the measure of distance might be less visually nuanced but based on yes/no specific features like, does it have handles? And if so, the same number? And are its sides straight or curved?
3. Note that there may be no average cup, in that the absolute center point of the space has no cup positioned there. Similarly, there may be no average animal in animal space. The space might be empty, or, even if it contains an animal we would not typically think of that animal as best typifying all animals. Still, however, that position holds a unique reference spot.
4. Leo Tolstoy, *War and Peace*, pp. 1813-1814, downloaded from planetpdf.com.

5. Christof Koch, *Consciousness*, pp. 75-76.
6. Marc Wittmann, *Altered States of Consciousness*. Cambridge, MA: MIT Press, 2018, pp. 6-8.
7. Marc Wittmann, *Altered States*, p. 117.
8. Also, the fact that many people die peacefully from old age or from a chronic illness can be explained by the idea that over time, as physical energy wanes, the membrane of self becomes less defined and rigid. People may begin to psychically merge with their surroundings and in that sense become part of a larger and more-time-expanded unit of meaning. The process of death then becomes more of a flow than an abrupt discontinuity.

INDEX

All figures are designated with "f" as in: Dunne 24f1.1 Glossary terms are in bold as in: biofeedback **315**

NUMBERS

2001: A Space Odyssey, 107
2016 presidential election example, 206–207

A

action ball, 276–277, 276fUM.2, 277–278, 278fUM.3, 279fUM.4, **315**
active overlay, 82–83, 277, 288–289
Age of Meaning
    artificial intelligence (AI), 260–261
    defined, 258
    goal shift, 259–260
    greed, 260
    information theory, 258
    intelligence, 261
    new generation, 263
    units of meaning, 258–259
    values, 266
    Washington Post's Pinocchio rating example, 259
agents/resources, 103–105
AI (artificial intelligence), 15, 103–104, 260–261, 341n6
Alcoholics Anonymous (AA), 132–133
alternative reality
    actuality and, 167–168
    defined, **315**
    Einstein déjà-vu, 159
    Mertz trials, 159–161, 162, 163–166, 167–168
    uncle & niece encounter, 161
Amazing Randi, 27–28
amygdalae, 69–70, 74

analytic director, 138
anchoring, 247–248
animal space, 273
anomalies research, **315**
anoxia, 144
Antifragile: Things That Gain from Disorder, 205
ants, 122
artificial intelligence (AI), 15, 103–104, 260–261, 341n6
associative space, 153–154, 155f12.2
associativism, 329n4
attitude, 81, 295–296, 336n8

B

baseline, **315**
baseline bind, 87–88, 87f7.4, 295, **315**
Baycrest hospital studies, 235–236, 237
Bayes Factor, 339n3
Bayesian reasoning, **315**, 328n6
behavioral economics, 251
believers vs. debunkers, 9–10, 324n9
biofeedback, 233–235, 238, **315**
bioREG, 145–146, 146–147
Blackmore, Susan, 324n9
Bohm, David, 151, 152, 330n5
bowl of significance, **315–316**. *see also* significance
Brain Injury Survivor's Guide, 144
brain vs. mind, 11–13, 15, 71, 145–147, 151, 261–264, 332–333n14, 333–334n20
brain-dead charts. *see* baseline bind
brains & human experience
    active overlay, 82–83, 277, 288–289
    amygdalae, 69–70, 74

brains & human experience *(cont'd)*
   anoxia, 144
   biofeedback, 233–235, 238
   bioREG, 145–146, 146–147
   brain awareness, 143–145
   Brain Injury Survivor's Guide, 144
   brain mapping, 141–143, 216
   brain rehabilitation via REGs, 236
   brain vs. mind, 11–13, 15, 71, 145–147, 151, 261–264, 332–333n14, 333–334n20
   change, 328n13, 329n6
   cognitive behavioral therapy (CBT), 144–145
   consciousness. *see* consciousness—humans
   death, 11–12, 284–286, 346n8
   dualism, 147
   Elastic, 329n6
   energy balance, 333–334n20
   EU brain mapping project, 216
   evolution. *see* evolution
   exploratory response, 121–124, 123f10.3, 124–126, 125f10.4
   feelings. *see* feelings
   Fehmi, Les, 234–235
   Fehmi, Susan, 235
   Flynn, James, 249
   free will, 146
   habituation, 92
   Herrnstein, Richard, 72, 121–122
   inhabitable artificial neurons (IANs), 240, 340n16
   intersubjective space/field. *see* intersubjective space/field
   intuition, 4
   IQ scores, 249, 341–342n7
   Jameson, Beth, 144
   Jeans, James, 157
   knowware, 239, 240
   layers of the mind, 109–112, 119–121
   Lockwood, Michael, 264
   loss aversion, 69–72, 74
   meaning fields, 110
   meaning machines, 83
   meaning-action pairs (MAPs), 153–157, 153f12.1, 214–215
   medial frontal cortex, 70
   memory, episodic, 197
   mental membrane, 131–132, 275–276
   mental regulator, 74–78, 85–87, 86f7.3, 91, 96, 106f9.1, 107, 108–109, 120–121, 236, 274–275, 328n13
   Metzinger, Thomas, 263–264
   microtubules, 146
   Mlodinow, Leonard, 329n6
   Mysteries of the Mind: A Critical Study of Consciousness and the Human Brain, 142
   Necker cube, 123, 123f10.3
   negative feedback cycle, 74–75
   neurofeedback, 238
   neuroscience. *see* neuroscience
   observer-dependent reality, 148–152
   occlusion process, 120–121, 275–276
   Open Focus, 234–235
   parapsychology (psi), 7–8, 130–131, 213, 324n9
   Penfield, Wilder, 142–143
   perception, 81–82, 123, 150
   personal-wide web, 94–96, 94f8.2, 95f8.3
   Phi: A Voyage from the Brain to the Soul, 176
   Popper, Karl, 157
   posing, 124–126, 125f10.4, 235
   prediction process, 73–74
   psychology. *see* psychology
   quantum uncertainty, 146, 147
   redundancy/degeneracy, 218, 338–339n14
   rubber-band effect, 42–44, 43f3.2, 67–68, 75–76, 117, 183
   selection effect & brain modeling, 217
   somaware, 239–240
   spirituality, 132–135
   subconscious. *see* subconscious—humans
   synaptic cleft, 147
   thermodynamic uncertainty, 146–147, 333n16, 333n19
   Tononi, Giulio, 176, 272
   transcranial magnetic stimulation, 238–239
   Transformative Technology (TransTech) Conference, 239
   trials & studies. *see* trials & studies—human
   units of action, 153, 155–156
   units of meaning. *see* units of meaning
   US brain project, 216
   Why God Won't Go Away, 134–135
   World 3, 157
Brooks, David, 256
Brown, Dan, 30

C

caring, 184–185
CBT (cognitive behavioral therapy), 144–145
change, 328n13, 329n6

Index   349

chaos control, 205
cognitive behavioral therapy (CBT), 144–145
cold fusion, 209, 214
computers
  agents/resources, 103–105
  artificial intelligence (AI), 15, 103–104, 260–261, 341n6
  consciousness, 3–4, 4–6, 8–11, 15, 261
  feelings, 10
  intuition, 5
  Minsky, Marvin, 103–104
  random-event generator (REG). see random-event generator (REG)
  Star Trek/Star Trek: The Next Generation, 341n6
  subconscious, 103–105
  trials—prisoner-warden, 3–4, 4–6, 8–11
conceptual spaces, 272–277, 274fUM.1, 276fUM.2, **316**
conflict, 252
Connected, 200, 201, 203
connected self, 137–139
conscious intention, 102–109, 181–182, 305–306, **316**
consciousness—computers, 3–4, 4–6, 8–11, 15, 261
consciousness—humans. *see also* brains & human experience; feelings; psychology; subconscious-humans
  action ball, 276–277, 276fUM.2, 277–278, 278fUM.3, 279fUM.4
  after death, 11–12
  bioREG, 145–146, 146–147
  brain awareness, 143–145
  brain vs. mind, 11–13, 15, 71, 145–147, 151, 332–333n14, 333–334n20
  conscious intention—connect, 105–107
  conscious intention—direct, 107–109
  conscious intention—Mind Lamp game, 305–306
  conscious intention—reflect, 102–105
  conscious intention—vs. purpose, 181–182, 183
  decision-making. *see* decision-making
  definitions by discipline, 263
  dualism, 147
  energy balance, 333–334n20
  exploratory response, 121–124, 123f10.3, 124–126, 125f10.4
  free will, 146

Global Consciousness Project, 50
Herrnstein, Richard, 72, 121–122
integrated information theory, 272
integrative complexity, 190
  vs. intelligence, 15
International Consciousness Research Laboratories (ICRL), 50
layers of the mind, 109–112, 119–121
Lockwood, Michael, 264
Margins of Reality: The Role of Consciousness in the Physical World, 27–29
meaning fields, 110
meaning-action pairs (MAPs), 155, 214–215
Metzinger, Thomas, 263–264
microtubules, 146
models, 101–102, 124, 187–189, 190. *see also* shoulds of prediction
Necker cube, 123, 123f10.3
neuroscience. *see* neuroscience
observer-dependent reality, 148–152
occlusion process, 120–121, 275–276
PEAR (Princeton Engineering Anomalies Research) laboratory. *see* PEAR (Princeton Engineering Anomalies Research) laboratory
personal-wide web, 94–96, 94f8.2, 95f8.3
philosophy, 263–264
psychology. *see* psychology
quantum uncertainty, 146, 147
shoulds of prediction, 79–81, 80f7.1, 85–88, 86f7.3, 106–107, 106f9.1
shoulds of rightness, 83–88, 84f7.2, 86f7.3, 106–107, 106f9.1
synaptic cleft, 147
thermodynamic uncertainty, 146–147, 333n16, 333n19
Tononi, Giulio, 176, 272
webs of associations/meaning. *see* webs of associations/meaning
contagion, 200–201
control run, 59, 59f5.1, 169–170, 170f14.1, 316, 344n7
Cook, Ian, 50, 56
Corcoran, Barbara, 49, 50
courage, 182–183
crash house, 50
creation myths, 201–202
cup space, 272–274, 274fUM.1, 275, 276
Curry, Adam, 3, 4–6, 50, 115–116, 258–259

D

Damasio, Antonio, 245–246, 331n4
daydreaming, 335n1
de Chardin, Pierre Teilhard, 266
death, 11–12, 284–286, 346n8
debunkers vs. believers, 9–10, 324n9
decision-making. *see also* consciousness—humans; subconscious—humans
   anchoring, 247–248
   conflict, 252
   disorder, 345n13
   Elastic, 342–343n13
   feelings and, 245–246
   fragility vs. ruggedness, 252–253, 342n11
   gambling, 69–70, 70–71
   gestalt exercises, 250–251
   hyperindividualism, 253
   hypotheticals, 249
   Kahneman, Daniel, 245, 246, 247, 251
   loss aversion, 69–72, 74
   medial frontal cortex, 70
   Mlodinow, Leonard, 342–343n13
   neuroscience of, 142–143, 245–246
   problem-solving, 342–343n13
   rationality of, 245
   self-awareness, 251–253
   studies of, 245, 246
   System 1 fast thinking, 246–248, 253–254, 253f21.1, 265
   System 2 slow thinking, 248–249, 252, 253f21.1, 254, 265, 341n6
   System 3 self-aware thinking, 250–255, 253f21.1, 265–266
   Thinking Fast and Slow, 246
   transitional period, 253, 255
   Tversky, Amos, 245, 246, 247, 251
   values, 265–267, 345n13
decline effect, 212–216, 286, 289, 323n5, 328–329n7
degeneracy/redundancy, 218, 338–339n14
Derrida, Jacques, 337n13
DID (dissociative identity disorder), 135–139
disorder, 345n13
disrupter bits, 123, 124–125, 125f10.4, **316**
dissociative identity disorder (DID), 135–137
diversity in society, 256
Don't Think of an Elephant! 70
drunken-walk charts. *see* random-walk/drunken-walk charts

dualism, 147
Dunne, Brenda, 23, 24f1.1, 27–29, 235
Dyson, Freeman, 262

E

Eccles, John, 142
Educational Testing Service, 25
ego self, 137–139, 156, 165, 185
Einstein, Albert, 148, 149, 159, 266
Elastic, 329n6, 342–343n13
emerging agency, 202–204
empathy, 184–185
energy balance, 333–334n20
ESP (extra sensory perception), 50, 213
evolution
   de Chardin, Pierre Teilhard, 266
   future selves, 15–16
   individual vs. species levels, 335n33
   loss aversion, 69
   Omega Point, 266
   units of meaning, 154, 156
   values, 266
experiments. *see* trials & studies
exploratory response, 121–124, 123f10.3, 124–126, 125f10.4
"Exploring the Other Dark Continent," 130

F

fears, 185–187, 280–281
feelings. *see also* consciousness—humans; psychology
   amygdalae, 69–70, 74
   attitude, 81, 295–296, 336n8
   believers vs. debunkers, 9–10, 324n9
   caring, 184–185
   in computers, 10
   courage, 182–183
   decision-making, 245–246
   empathy, 184–185
   fears, 185–187, 280–281
   gambling, 69–70, 70–71
   intuition, 4, 5
   James, William, 90
   jinxing, 43–44
   jumping impulse, 242
   layers of the mind, 111
   loss aversion, 69–72, 74
   Mertz, Herb. *see* Mertz, Herb
   micropsychology, 44
   models, 101–102, 124, 187–189, 190

feelings *(cont'd)*
  moments, 89–93, 91f8.1, 95, 108–109, 188–189, 190, 296
  personal-wide web, 94–96, 94f8.2, 95f8.3
  in researchers, 9–11
  rubber-band effect, 42–44, 43f3.2, 67–68, 75–76, 117, 183
  sheep-goat effect, 324n9
  shoulds of prediction, 79–81, 80f7.1, 85–88, 86f7.3, 106–107, 106f9.1
  shoulds of rightness, 83–88, 84f7.2, 86f7.3, 106–107, 106f9.1
  surge patterns, 42
  during trials, 8
  vulnerability, 182–183
Fehmi, Les, 234–235
Fehmi, Susan, 235
FieldREG, 53–55, 54f4.1, 55f4.2, 56f4.3, 196–197, 292–295, 294fSM.1
file-drawer effect, 212
fingertip exercise, 301–302
Fleischman, Martin, 209
flocking/schooling/swarming behavior, 203
Flynn, James, 249
foundational physics, 218
fragility vs. ruggedness, 252–253, 342n11
free will, 146
Freud, Sigmund, 105, 131

G

Gage, Phineas, 141
Gaia hypothesis, 203–204, 337n15
Galileo, 324–325n14
gambling, 69–70, 70–71
gestalt exercises, 250–251
Ghostbusters, 70
Global Consciousness Project, 50
go high vs. go low, 36
goal-driven process, **316**
Gödel, Kurt, 337n16
Grad, Bernard, 336–337n5
grandmother cells, 327n1
group mind/web, 197–204, 199f17.2

H

habituation, 92
Harris, Sam, 11, 324–325n14
Haw, Nick, 50, 228
healer studies, 336–337n5
Herrnstein, Richard, 72, 121–122

Higgins, Bill, 49–50
hitting, 35, **316**
H.M., 141, 142
Hoffman, Donald, 150
Holly (cat), 221–222
Hugenot, Alan, 136–137
hyperindividualism, 253
hypotheticals, 249
hysteria, 200–201

I

IANs (inhabitable artificial neurons), 240, 340n16
ICRL (International Consciousness Research Laboratories), 50
incompleteness theory, 337n16
information theory, 258
inhabitable artificial neurons (IANs), 240, 340n16
integrated information theory, 272
integrative complexity, 190
intelligence, 15, 261
intention. *see* conscious intention
International Consciousness Research Laboratories (ICRL), 50
intersubjective space/field. *see also* webs of associations/meaning
  associative space, 154, 155f12.2
  Connected, 200, 201, 203
  contagion, 200–201
  creation myths, 201–202
  defined, **316**
  emerging agency, 202–204
  flocking/schooling/swarming behavior, 203
  Gaia hypothesis, 203–204, 337n15
  GAS SCARE, HIGH SCHOOL, 200–201
  Gödel, Kurt, 337n16
  group mind/web, 197–204, 199f17.2
  Holly (cat), 221–222
  hysteria, 200–201
  incompleteness theory, 337n16
  Jung, Carl, 201, 332n8
  Lovelock, James, 203–204, 337n15
  madman scare, 201
  Margulis, Lynn, 203–204, 337n15
  McTaggart, Lynne, 199
  memes, 199–201, 334n23
  Memories, Dreams, Reflections, 332n8
  neuroscience, 143
  PEAR (Princeton Engineering Anomalies Research) laboratory, 130–131
  psychotherapy, 130

intersubjective space/field *(cont'd)*
    received truths, 202
    rituals, 201
    Rosenbaum, Ruth, 130–131
    seedling studies, 199
    shared-meaning space, 143
    sports teams, 133–134, 198, 199f17.2
    stories, 197–204
    telepathy, 131
intuition
    computers, 5
    humans, 4
IQ scores, 249, 341–342n7

J

Jahn, Robert G., 21, 22, 27–29, 30
James, William, 90
Jameson, Beth, 144
Jeans, James, 157
jinxing, 43–44
Jobs, Steve, 197
journaling, 46–47, 79, 84–85, 91–92, 297
jumping impulse, 241–243
Jung, Carl, 201, 332n8

K

Kahneman, Daniel, 245, 246, 247, 251
knowware, 239, 240
Koch, Christof, 285, 332–333n14

L

Lakoff, George, 70
law of attraction, **316**
layers of the mind, 109–112, 119–121, **317**
Lehrer, Jonah, 210
life lessons—courage & vulnerability, 182–183
life lessons—empathy & caring, 184–185
life lessons—intention & purpose, 181–182
life lessons—many small deaths, 185–187
life lessons—no limits, 187–190
Locke, John, 329n4
Lockwood, Michael, 264
loss aversion, 69–72, 74
Lovelock, James, 203–204, 337n15

M

magician, 54–55, 55f4.2
mapping of brain, 141–143

MAPs (meaning-action pairs), 153–157, 153f12.1, 214–215, **317**
Margins of Reality: The Role of Consciousness in the Physical World, 27–29
Margulis, Lynn, 203–204, 337n15
matter, 147–148
McTaggart, Lynne, 199
meaning, **317**
meaning, units of. *see* units of meaning
meaning fields, 110, **317**, 330n5
meaning machines, 83
meaning side, 151
meaning-action pairs (MAPs), 153–157, 153f12.1, 214–215, **317**
media literacy, 251
medial frontal cortex, 70
meditation, 105–106, 233, 240–241, 296–297
memes, 199–201, 334n23
Memories, Dreams, Reflections, 332n8
memory, episodic, 197
mental membrane, 131–132, 275–276, **317**
mental pen, 120, **317**
mental regulator
    and brain lesions, 236
    cat & mouse game, 108–109
    change, 328n13
    defined, **317**
    emotion & prediction agents, 86f7.3, 106f9.1, 107
    examples of operation, 76
    jumping impulse, 242–243
    magnetic fields study, 236
    mental pen, 120–121
    moments, 91
    negative feedback cycle, 74–75
    occlusion process, 120–121
    rubber-band effect, 75–76
    set points, 75–76, 77, 92
    shoulds and, 85–87, 86f7.3
    success and, 76–78
    units of meaning, 274–275
    webs of associations/meaning, 96
Mertz, Herb
    agents/resources, 104–105
    analytic director, 138
    anchoring, 247–248
    changes in after trials, 240–243
    childhood, 13–15
    connected self, 137–138
    conscious intention, 102–103, 105, 106–109

Mertz, Herb *(cont'd)*
   Dyson meeting, 262
   Educational Testing Service, 25
   ego self, 137–138, 156, 165, 185
   Einstein déjà-vu, 159
   exploratory response, 121, 124–126, 125f10.4
   feelings—alarm, 107–108
   feelings—alternative reality, 159–161, 164
   feelings—anxiety, 171–172
   feelings—courage, 182–183
   feelings—déjà-vu, 159
   feelings—empathy, 185
   feelings—exhilaration, 45
   feelings—fears, 186–187
   feelings—giving up, 126–127
   feelings—indignation, 176–177, 228
   feelings—moments experienced, 89–90, 91–92, 91f8.1, 108–109
   feelings—new feelings, 39
   feelings—"red pill" frustrations, 96–97
   feelings—resignation, 67–68, 80f7.1, 132, 134
   feelings—rubber-band effect, 42, 67–68
   feelings—self-identity, 135, 137–138
   feelings—shoulds of righteousness, 84–85, 84f7.2
   feelings—vulnerability, 182–183
   fingertip exercise, 301–302
   focused awareness, 145
   journaling, 46–47, 79, 84–85, 91–92
   jumping impulse, 241–243
   layer building, 157–158
   layers of the mind, 119–121
   life lessons—courage & vulnerability, 182–183
   life lessons—empathy & caring, 184–185
   life lessons—intention & purpose, 181–182
   life lessons—many small deaths, 185–187
   life lessons—no limits, 187–190
   loss aversion, 71
   The Matrix, 96–97
   meditation, 240–241
   mental pen, 120
   mental regulator, 77–78, 107–109
   Mind Lamp, 194–196
   moments, 89–90, 91–92, 91f8.1, 108–109
   Monty Python and the Holy Grail, 87
   niece at Grand Canyon, 257
   the other, 135, 137
   PEAR (Princeton Engineering Anomalies Research) laboratory, 25
   Princeton University, 15, 24–25
   Psyleron Company, 32–33, 50, 115–116
   random-event generator (REG) training, 33, 56, 119–121, 175–176
   Reflector, 37–38
   remote viewing conference, 33–34
   rubber-band effect, 42–44, 43f3.2, 67–68, 117, 183
   self-alignment, 62–63
   Simon & Garfunkel, 241
   spirituality, 134
   story of virus, 194–196
   target aversion/avoidance, 283–284
   therapy, 131
   trial chances for success, 162–163
   trial goals, 12–13, 302–303
   trials—alternative reality, 159–161, 162, 163–166, 167–168
   trials—brain dead, 87–88, 87f7.4
   trials—distance, 223–228, 226f19.1, 227f19.2
   trials—feelings, 40–42, 41f3.1
   trials—FieldREG, 292–295, 294fSM.1
   trials—grandmother images, 67
   trials—initial success, 39–40
   trials—moments, 91–92, 91f8.1
   trials—posing, 124–126, 125f10.4
   trials—rigged scoring, 44–46
   trials—seedlings, 336–337n5
   trials—shoulds of prediction, 79–80, 80f7.1
   trials—shoulds of rightness, 84–85, 84f7.2
   trials—Studies 1-4, 178f15.2
   trials—Study 1, 56–57, 56f4.3, 60–61, 62f5.3
   trials—Study 2, 59, 59f5.1, 60–61, 62f5.3
   trials—Study 3, 60–61, 60f5.2, 62f5.3
   trials—Study 4, 116–121, 118f10.1, 119f10.2, 168–169, 171–173, 175, 177–179, 177f15.1
   trials—subsequent successes, 40–46, 41f3.1
   trials—warm-ups, 167
   trials—Z max, 228–230, 229f19.3, 229f19.4
   Tuchman, Martin, 293
   tulip moment, 89
   Valentino introduction, 31–32
   Valentino reunion, 170, 173
   Wimbledon match, 282
Mertz, Ian, 262
Metzinger, Thomas, 263–264

micropsychology, 44
microtubules, 146
Mind Lamp, 51, 99–101, 193–196, 193f17.1, 305–307
mind reading, 217–218, 237
mind vs. brain. *see* brain vs. mind
mind-over-matter. *see* selection effect/mind-over-matter
Mindsong, 50
Minsky, Marvin, 103–104, 135
missing, 35, **318**
Mlodinow, Leonard, 329n6, 342–343n13
Moddel, Garret, 3, 4–6
models, 101–102, 124, 187–189, 190. *see also* shoulds of prediction
moments, 89–93, 91f8.1, 95, 108–109, 188–189, 190, 296
monkeys, 73
Monte Carlo simulation, 223, 300, 313–314
Monty Python and the Holy Grail, 87
motives, instrumental vs. intrinsic/inner, 182
multiple personality disorder (MPD). *see* dissociative identity disorder (DID)
Murphy, 24f1.1, 25–26
Mysteries of the Mind: A Critical Study of Consciousness and the Human Brain, 142

N

Necker cube, 123, 123f10.3
negative feedback cycle, 74–75
Nelson, Roger, 50
neurofeedback, 238
neuroscience. *see also* brains & human experience
    anoxia, 144
    Brain Injury Survivor's Guide, 144
    Damasio, Antonio, 245–246, 331n4
    decision-making, 142–143, 245–246
    Eccles, John, 142
    feelings, 245–246
    Gage, Phineas, 141
    grandmother cells, 327n1
    Harris, Sam, 11, 324–325n14
    H.M., 141, 142
    intersubjective space/field, 143
    Jameson, Beth, 144
    Koch, Christof, 285, 332–333n14
    mapping of brain, 141–143
    mind reading, 217–218, 237
    Mysteries of the Mind: A Critical Study of Consciousness and the Human Brain, 142

neurofeedback, 238
Penfield, Wilder, 142–143
Persinger, Michael, 236
Phi: A Voyage from the Brain to the Soul, 176
selection effect, 217
Sherrington, Charles, 142
Sperry, John, 142
Tononi, Giulio, 176, 272
The New Brain: How the Modern Age Is Rewiring Your Mind, 70
Nicklaus, Jack, 302–303
null hypothesis, 169, 287–288, 287fUM.6, **318**

O

observer-dependent reality, 148–152
occlusion process, 120–121, 275–276, **318**
odds. *see* Z scores
Omega Point, 266
Open Focus, 234–235

P

pandemonium theory, 330n4
panpsychism, 151–152
parapsychology (psi), 7–8, 130–131, 213, **318**, 324n9
PEAR (Princeton Engineering Anomalies Research) laboratory. *see also* Psyleron Company
    academies, 31
    Amazing Randi, 27–28
    baseline bind, 87–88, 87f7.4, 295
    Brown, Dan, 30
    data, 27–29, 36, 36f2.2, 326n3
    decline & closing, 29–30
    defined, **318**
    Dunne, Brenda, 23, 24f1.1, 27–29, 235
    established, 22–23
    FieldREG, 53–55, 54f4.1, 55f4.2, 56f4.3, 196–197, 292–295, 294fSM.1
    goals of, 23–24
    Higgins, Bill, 50
    intersubjective space/field, 130–131
    Jahn, Robert G., 23, 27–29, 30
    The Lost Symbol, 30
    Margins of Reality: The Role of Consciousness in the Physical World, 27–29
    Mertz, Herb, 25
    Mindsong, 50
    Murphy, 24f1.1, 25–26

PEAR *(cont'd)*
   random-event generator (REG) devices, 26–27, 27f1.2, 36, 36f2.2
   remote viewing, 325n3
   "Science of the Subjective," 28–29
   series position effect, 213
   testing devices, 24f1.1, 25–27, 27f1.2, 36, 36f2.2
   trial—pseudorandomness, 328n2
   Valentino, John, 31
Penfield, Wilder, 142–143
perception, 81–82, 123, 150
Persinger, Michael, 236
personal-wide web, 94–96, 94f8.2, 95f8.3. *see also* webs of associations/meaning
Phi: A Voyage from the Brain to the Soul, 176
philosophy, 263–264
physics
   associative space, 153–154, 155f12.2
   Bohm, David, 151, 152
   cold fusion, 209, 214
   Dyson, Freeman, 262
   Einstein, Albert, 148, 149, 159, 266
   Fleischman, Martin, 209
   foundational physics, 218
   Galileo, 324–325n14
   intersubjective space/field, 154, 155f12.2
   Jeans, James, 157
   matter, 147–148
   meaning side, 151
   meaning-action pairs (MAPs), 153–157, 153f12.1, 214–215
   observer-dependent reality, 148–152
   panpsychism, 151–152
   Pons, Stanley, 209
   postselection, 218–219
   quantum entanglement, 154, 219
   speed of light, 334n21
   webs of associations/meaning, 151–152
   Wheeler, John, 148, 150–151
pigeons, 72, 122
placebo effect, 214–215
Pons, Stanley, 209
Popper, Karl, 157
posing, 124–126, 125f10.4, 235, **318**
postselection, 218–219
prediction process, 72–74, **318**
Princeton Engineering Anomalies Research (PEAR) laboratory. *see* PEAR (Princeton Engineering Anomalies Research) laboratory

Princeton University, 7, 15, 21, 24–25, 33. *see also* PEAR (Princeton Engineering Anomalies Research) laboratory
prisoner-warden trials (computers), 3–4, 4–6, 8–11
problem-solving, 342–343n13
pseudorandomness, 328n2
psychofeedback. *see also* FieldREG
   Baycrest hospital studies, 235–236, 237
   defined, **318–319**
   Dunne, Brenda, 235
   goals of, 238
   knowware, 239, 240
psychology. *see also* consciousness—humans
   analytic director, 138
   anchoring, 247–248
   antipsychotic drugs, 210
   ants, 122
   associativism, 329n4
   Bayesian reasoning, 328n6
   behavioral economics, 251
   Blackmore, Susan, 324n9
   Brooks, David, 256
   cognitive behavioral therapy (CBT), 144–145
   conceptual spaces, 272–277, 274fUM.1, 276fUM.2
   connected self, 137–139
   daydreaming, 335n1
   decision-making. *see* decision-making
   decline effect, 212–216, 323n5
   dissociative identity disorder (DID), 135–137
   diversity in society, 256
   Don't Think of an Elephant! 70
   ego self, 137–139, 156, 165, 185
   ESP (extra sensory perception), 50, 213
   "Exploring the Other Dark Continent," 130
   feelings. *see* feelings
   Freud, Sigmund, 105, 131
   gambling, 69–70, 70–71
   gestalt exercises, 250–251
   Ghostbusters, 70
   habituation, 92
   Herrnstein, Richard, 72, 121–122
   Hoffman, Donald, 150
   Hugenot, Alan, 136–137
   hyperindividualism, 253
   intersubjective space/field. *see* intersubjective space/field
   Jung, Carl, 201, 328n8
   Kahneman, Daniel, 245, 246, 247, 251

psychology *(cont'd)*
   Lakoff, George, 70
   Locke, John, 329n4
   media literacy, 251
   medial frontal cortex, 70
   micropsychology, 44
   mind-over-matter research, 8
   monkeys, 73
   The New Brain: How the Modern Age Is Rewiring Your Mind, 70
   parapsychology (psi), 7–8, 130–131, 213, 324n9
   perception, 150
   Phi: A Voyage from the Brain to the Soul, 176
   pigeons, 72, 122
   prediction process, 72–74
   psychofeedback. *see* psychofeedback
   psychosis, 210, 215
   psychotherapy, 130
   replicability studies, 211–212
   Restak, Richard, 70
   Rhine, J. B., 50, 213, 323n5
   Rosenbaum, Ruth, 129–131
   Schmeidler, Gertrude, 324n9
   Schooler, Jonathan, 211, 216
   selection effect and, 254–255
   self-awareness, 251–253
   split personalities, 251
   talk therapy, 105
   Thinking Fast and Slow, 246
   Tononi, Giulio, 176, 272
   Tversky, Amos, 245, 246, 247, 251
   verbal overshadowing, 211, 215–216
psychosis, 210, 215
psychotherapy, 130
Psyleron Company. *see also* PEAR (Princeton Engineering Anomalies Research) laboratory
   Cook, Ian, 50, 56
   Corcoran, Barbara, 50
   crash house, 50
   Curry, Adam, 3, 4–6, 50, 115–116, 258–259
   defined, **319**
   downsizing, 115–116
   FieldREG, 53–55, 54f4.1, 55f4.2, 56f4.3, 196–197, 292–295, 294fSM.1
   goals of, 32
   Haw, Nick, 50, 228
   Higgins, Bill, 49–50
   Mertz, Herb. *see* Mertz, Herb
   Mind Lamp, 51, 99–101, 193–196, 193f17.1, 305–307
   Nelson, Roger, 50
   Princeton University move, 33, 50
   Reflector, 34–35, 35f2.1, 37–38, 37f2.3
   REG-1, 312
   start-up, 32–33
   SyncTXT, 51–52
   trial—freshmen (High School NJ), 99–101
   trial—magician, 54–55, 55f4.2
   trial—meditator, 106
   Valentino, John, 32–33, 51–52, 115–116, 228
   Wilson, Justin, 50, 53–54, 54f4.1
purpose training, 291–292
purposefulness, 181–182, 183

Q

quantum entanglement, 154, 219
quantum uncertainty, 146, 147

R

Radin, Dean, 344n7
random, **319**
random-event generator (REG)
   active overlay, 82–83
   applications for, 291–292
   bioREG, 145–146, 146–147
   brain rehabilitation, 237
   brain vs. mind, 12–13, 71
   connected self, 138
   defined, **319**
   disrupter bits, 123, 124–125, 125f10.4
   feelings influence on, 8
   FieldREG, 53–55, 54f4.1, 55f4.2, 56f4.3, 196–197, 292–295, 294fSM.1
   goal of games, 35
   journaling, 46–47, 79, 84–85, 91–92, 297
   layers of the mind, 109–112, 119–121
   life lessons—courage & vulnerability, 182–183
   life lessons—empathy & caring, 184–185
   life lessons—intention & purpose, 181–182
   life lessons—many small deaths, 185–187
   life lessons—no limits, 187–190
   loss aversion, 70–72, 74
   meaning fields, 110
   mental pen, 120
   mental regulator, 75, 77–78, 120
   micropsychology, 44

random-event generator *(cont'd)*
  Mind Lamp, 51, 99–101, 193–196, 193f17.1, 305–307
  moments, 89, 90, 108, 296
  Murphy, 24f1.1, 25–26
  output, **319**
  PEAR (Princeton Engineering Anomalies Research) laboratory device, 26–27, 27f1.2, 36, 36f2.2
  posing, 124
  Psyleron Company. *see* Psyleron Company
  purchasing, 291
  random-walk/drunken-walk charts. *see* random-walk/drunken-walk charts
  Reflector, 34–35, 35f2.1, 37–38, 37f2.3
  REG space, 275
  REG-1, 32–33, 312
  remote REGs, 222, 297
  Schmidt, Helmut, 21–22
  set points. *see* set points
  shoulds of prediction, 80, 80f7.1, 85
  as a social change tool, 266–267
  squares, red vs. green, 35f2.1, 37, 37f2.3
  statistics. *see* statistics
  surge patterns, 40–42, 41f3.1
  SyncTXT, 51–52
  training on, 28, 33, 56, 67–68, 119–121, 175–176
  trials—human. *see* trials & studies—human
  unit of meaning (UM), 109
  XOR (exclusive or) mask/bit scrambling, 311–312
random-number generator (RNG). *see* random-event generator (REG)
random-walk/drunken-walk charts. *see also* trials & studies—human
  control run, 170f14.1
  defined, 34–36, 35f2.1, 36f2.1, **319**
  Mertz trials. *see* trials & studies—human: Mertz
  PEAR (Princeton Engineering Anomalies Research) laboratory data, 36, 36f2.2, 326n3
  Psyleron trials—magician, 54, 55f4.2
  Psyleron trials—Wilson, 53–54, 54f4.1
  significance, 35
  surge patterns, 40–42, 41f3.1
  target aversion/avoidance, 283fUM.5
received truths, 202

redundancy/degeneracy, 34–35, 37–38, 218, 338–339n14
Reflector, 34–35, 35f2.1, 37–38, 37f2.3
REG (random-event generator). *see* random-event generator (REG)
REG space, 275
remote viewing, 33–34, 49–50, **319**, 325n3
replicability studies, 211–212
resources/agents, 103–105
Restak, Richard, 70
Rhine, J. B., 50, 213, 323n5
Rhine Research Center, 50
rituals, 201
RNG (random-number generator). *see* random-event generator (REG)
Rosenbaum, Ruth, 129–131
rubber-band effect, 42–44, 43f3.2, 67–68, 75, 117, 183
run, **320**

S

Schmeidler, Gertrude, 324n9
Schmidt, Helmut, 21–22
Schooler, Jonathan, 211, 216
"Science of the Subjective," 28–29
selection effect/mind-over-matter
  2016 presidential election, 206–207
  active overlay, 82–83
  artificial intelligence (AI), 15, 261
  attitude, 81, 295–296
  baseline bind, 87–88, 87f7.4, 295
  bioREG, 145–146, 146–147
  brain modeling, 217
  brain vs. mind, 11–13, 15, 71, 145–147, 151, 261–264, 332–333n14, 333–334n20
  decline effect, 212–216, 323n5
  defined, 17, **320**
  Dunne, Brenda, 23, 24f1.1, 27–29, 235
  feelings. *see* feelings
  historical context, 258
  Jahn, Robert G., 21, 22, 27–29, 30
  Mind Lamp, 51, 99–101, 193–196, 193f17.1, 305–307
  mind reading, 217–218, 237
  motives, instrumental vs. intrinsic/inner, 182
  neuroscience, 217
  PEAR (Princeton Engineering Anomalies Research) laboratory. *see* PEAR (Princeton Engineering Anomalies Research) laboratory

selection effect/mind-over-matter *(cont'd)*
    physical device control, 243
    placebo effect, 214–215
    postselection, 218–219
    psychofeedback. *see* psychofeedback
    psychology and, 254–255
    Psyleron Company. *see* Psyleron Company
    random-event generator (REG). *see* random-event generator (REG)
    Reflector, 34–35, 35f2.1, 37–38, 37f2.3
    scientific community, 7–8
    stories, 196, 205–207
    SyncTXT, 51–52
    tennis game example, 205–206
    trials—human. *see* trials & studies—human
    uncertainty, 243
    Weinberg, Steven, 7–8
self-alignment, 62–63
self-awareness, 251–253
Selfridge, Oliver, 330n4
series position effect, 213
set points
    defined, **320**
    examples of, 74–75
    mental regulator, 75–76, 77, 92
    models, 187–188, 248
    moments, 91
    in REG games, 75, 274, 275, 276, 278, 287
shared-meaning space, 143
sheep-goat effect, 324n9
Sherrington, Charles, 142
shoulds of prediction, 79–81, 80f7.1, 85–88, 86f7.3, 106–107, 106f9.1
shoulds of rightness, 83–88, 84f7.2, 86f7.3, 106–107, 106f9.1
significance
    defined, **320**
    random-walk/drunken-walk charts, 35, 326n2
    units of meaning, 274–280, 276fUM.2, 278fUM.3, 279fUM.4, 287–289, 287fUM.6, 288fUM.7
    Z scores, 37, 86–87, 300
Simon & Garfunkel, 241
Society of Mind, 104, 135, 240, **320**
somaware, 239–240
spacetime, 149
Sperry, John, 142
spirituality, 132–135
split personalities, 251

squares, red vs. green, 35f2.1, 37, 37f2.3
SRI International (formerly Stanford Research Institute), 7
Star Trek/Star Trek: The Next Generation, 341n6
statistics
    Bayes Factor, 339n3
    control run, 59, 59f5.1, 169–170, 170f14.1, 316, 344n7
    data collection, 300–301
    file-drawer effect, 212
    go high vs. go low, 36
    hitting vs. missing, 35
    Monte Carlo simulation, 223, 300, 313–314
    null hypothesis, 169, 287–288, 287fUM.6
    prediction process, 72–74
    Radin, Dean, 344n7
    random-event generator (REG) game goal, 35
    random-walk/drunken-walk charts. *see* random-walk/drunken-walk charts
    rubber-band patterns, 42–44, 43f3.2
    scoring trials, 298–300
    significance. *see* significance
    surge patterns, 41–42, 41f3.1
    threshold effect, 213–214
    XOR (exclusive or) mask/bit scrambling, 311–312
    Z scores. *see* Z scores
stories
    aliveness, 207–208
    Antifragile: Things That Gain from Disorder, 205
    chaos control, 205
    Derrida, Jacques, 337n13
    FieldREG, 196–197
    group mind/web, 202–204
    intersubjective space/field, 197–198
    Jobs, Steve, 197
    memory, episodic, 197
    Mertz & the Mind Lamp, 194–196
    selection effect, 196, 205–207
    shared, 198–202
    Taleb, Nassim Nicholas, 205
    units of meaning, 205–207, 277
studies. *see* trials & studies
subconscious—computers
    agents/resources, 103–105
    artificial intelligence (AI), 103–104
    Minsky, Marvin, 103–104
subconscious—humans. *see also* consciousness—humans
    2001: A Space Odyssey, 107

biofeedback, 233–235, 238
conscious intention—connect, 105–107
conscious intention—direct, 107–109
conscious intention—reflect, 102–105
conscious intention—vs. purpose, 181–182, 183
defined, **320**
Fehmi, Les, 234–235
Fehmi, Susan, 235
Freud, Sigmund, 105, 131
intersubjective space/field. *see* intersubjective space/field
Jung, Carl, 201, 332n8
meditation, 105–106, 233, 240–241, 296–297
mental regulator. *see* mental regulator
Mind Lamp games, 306
Minsky, Marvin, 103–104
models, 101–102
neurofeedback, 238
Open Focus, 234–235
pandemonium theory, 330n4
problem-solving, 342–343n13
Selfridge, Oliver, 330n4
shoulds of prediction, 106–107, 106f9.1
shoulds of rightness, 106–107, 106f9.1
Society of Mind, 104
structure of, 103
talk therapy, 105
webs of associations/meaning. *see* webs of associations/meaning
yogis, 233, 234
synaptic cleft, 147
SyncTXT, 51–52

T

Taleb, Nassim Nicholas, 205
talk therapy, 105
target aversion/avoidance, 280, 281–284, 283fUM.5
TeamViewer, 297
telepathy, 131
The Lost Symbol, 30
The Matrix, 96–97
"The Truth Wears Off," 210
thermodynamic uncertainty, 146–147, 333n16, 333n19
Thinking Fast and Slow, 246
threads of association, 94, 95f8.3, 188, 272, 275, **320**. *see also* webs of associations/meaning

threshold effect, 213–214
time, 277
Tononi, Giulio, 176, 272
transcranial magnetic stimulation, 238–239
Transformative Technology (TransTech) Conference, 239
trials & studies—computers, 3–4, 4–6, 8–11
trials & studies—human, 141–143
   attitude factor, 8, 295–296
   baseline bind factor, 87–88, 87f7.4, 295
   Baycrest hospital studies—psychofeedback, 235–236, 237
   believers vs. debunkers factor, 9–10, 324n9
   clinical drugs trials, 210, 214–215
   cooperative effect factor, 28, 130–131
   data. *see* statistics
   daydreaming factor, 335n1
   decision-making studies, 245, 246
   decline effect factor, 212–216, 286, 289, 323n5, 328–329n7
   defined, 34, **321**
   distance factor, 29, 222, 230–231
   feelings. *see* feelings
   FieldREG, 53–55, 54f4.1, 55f4.2, 56f4.3, 196–197, 292–295, 294fSM.1
   fingertip exercise, 301–302
   Florida State University study—jumping impulse, 242
   gender factor, 28
   gestalt exercises, 250–251
   Grad studies—seedlings, 336–337n5
   healer studies, 336–337n5
   inhabitable artificial neurons (IANs), 240, 340n16
   intersubjective space/field, 130–131
   Jahn studies—mind-over-matter, 22
   journaling, 297
   knowware, 239, 240
   Lehrer, Jonah, 210
   magnets factor, 336–337n5
   Margins of Reality: The Role of Consciousness in the Physical World, 27–29
   McTaggart study—seedlings, 199
   meditation factor, 105–106, 296–297
   Mertz trial goals, 12–13, 302–303
   Mertz trials—alternative reality, 159–161, 162, 163–166, 167–168
   Mertz trials—brain dead, 87–88, 87f7.4
   Mertz trials—distance, 223–228, 226f19.1, 227f19.2

trials & studies—human *(cont'd)*
    Mertz trials—feelings, 40–42, 41f3.1
    Mertz trials—FieldREG, 292–295, 294fSM.1
    Mertz trials—grandmother images, 67
    Mertz trials—initial success, 39–40
    Mertz trials—moments, 91–92, 91f8.1
    Mertz trials—posing, 124–126, 125f10.4
    Mertz trials—rigged scoring, 44–46
    Mertz trials—seedlings, 336–337n5
    Mertz trials—shoulds of prediction, 79–80, 80f7.1
    Mertz trials—shoulds of rightness, 84–85, 84f7.2
    Mertz trials—Studies 1-4, 178f15.2
    Mertz trials—Study 1, 56–57, 56f4.3, 60–61, 62f5.3
    Mertz trials—Study 2, 59, 59f5.1, 60–61, 62f5.3
    Mertz trials—Study 3, 60–61, 60f5.2, 62f5.3
    Mertz trials—Study 4, 116–121, 118f10.1, 119f10.2, 168–169, 171–173, 175, 177–179, 177f15.1
    Mertz trials—subsequent successes, 40–46, 41f3.1
    Mertz trials—warm-ups, 167
    Mertz trials—Z max, 228–230, 229f19.3, 229f19.4
    military studies—transcranial magnetic stimulation, 238–239
    Mind Lamp games, 305–307
    mind reading studies, 217–218
    mind-over-matter historical studies, 7
    moments factor, 296
    PEAR (Princeton Engineering Anomalies Research) laboratory trials—pseudorandomness, 328n2
    Persinger studies—magnetic fields, 236
    projects, running of, 291–303
    psychofeedback. *see* psychofeedback
    Psyleron trials—HS freshmen (NJ), 99–101
    Psyleron trials—magician, 54, 55f4.2
    Psyleron trials—meditator, 106
    Psyleron trials—Wilson, 53–54, 54f4.1
    purpose training factor, 291–292
    random-event generator (REG). *see* random-event generator (REG)
    random-walk/drunken-walk charts. *see* random-walk/drunken-walk charts
    remote operations, 297
    remote REGs, 222, 297
    replicability studies, 211–212
    result visibility factor, 28
    rubber-band effect factor, 42–44, 43f3.2, 67–68, 75, 117, 183
    Schmeidler, Gertrude, 324n9
    "Science of the Subjective," 28–29
    sessions, preparations for, 296–297
    sessions, running of, 297–298
    sheep-goat effect factor, 324n9
    somaware, 239–240
    squares, red vs. green, 35f2.1, 37, 37f2.3
    statistics. *see* statistics
    "Steve" trials—Z max, 230–231, 231f19.5
    target aversion/avoidance factor, 280, 281–282, 283fUM.5
    TeamViewer, 297
    time factor, 29
    training factor, 28, 33, 67–68, 119–121, 175–176
    "The Truth Wears Off," 210
    Z scores. *see* Z scores
    Zeno's paradox, 171, 177
Tuchman, Martin, 293
tulip moment, 89
Tversky, Amos, 245, 246, 247, 251

U

UM (units of meaning). *see* units of meaning
unconscious mind. *see* subconscious—humans, **321**
units of action, 153, 155–156, **321**
units of meaning (UM)
    2016 presidential election example, 206–207
    Age of Meaning, 258–259
    animal space, 273
    conceptual spaces, 272–277, 274fUM.1, 276fUM.2
    cup space, 272–274, 274fUM.1, 275, 276
    death, 284–286, 346n8
    decline effect, 286, 289
    defined, **109**, 153, **321**
    evolution, 154, 156
    mental membrane, 275–276
    REG space, 275
    road trip example, 271
    significance, 274–280, 276fUM.2, 278fUM.3, 279fUM.4, 287–289, 287fUM.6, 288fUM.7
    skyscraper analogy, 155–156
    stories, 205–207, 277

units of meaning *(cont'd)*
　target aversion/avoidance, 280, 281–284, 283fUM.5
　tennis game example, 205–206
　time factor, 277
　War and Peace, 285
　Washington Post's Pinocchio rating example, 258–259

V

Valentino, John
　data compilation program, 228
　Mertz introduction, 31–32
　Mertz reunion, 170, 173
　PEAR (Princeton Engineering Anomalies Research) laboratory, 31
　Psyleron Company downsizing, 115–116
　Psyleron Company start-up, 32–33
　SyncTXT, 51–52
values, 264–267, 345n13
verbal overshadowing, 211, 215–216
vulnerability, 182–183

W

War and Peace, 285
Washington Post, 258–259
web of mind, **321**
webs of associations/meaning. *see also* consciousness—humans; intersubjective space/field
　attitude, 336n8
　Bohm, David, 152
　defined, **321**
　panpsychism, 151–152
　personal-wide web, 94–96, 94f8.2, 95f8.3
　set points. *see* set points

threads of association, 94, 95f8.3, 188, 272, 275
ubiquitous nature of, 262
units of meaning. *see* units of meaning
Weinberg, Steven, 7–8
Wheeler, John, 148, 150–151
Why God Won't Go Away, 134–135
Wilson, Justin, 50, 53–54, 54f4.1
World 3, 157

X

XOR (exclusive or) mask/bit scrambling, 311–312

Y

yogis, 233, 234

Z

Z scores
　conscious thought, 86–87
　defined, 37, **321**
　Mertz trials—distance, 224–225, 226f19.1
　Mertz trials—posing, 124–125
　Mertz trials—rigged scoring, 45
　Mertz trials—Study 4, 116, 117–118, 118f10.1
　Mertz trials—Z max, 228–231, 229f19.3, 229f19.4
　Monte Carlo simulation, 223, 300, 313–315
　scoring trials, 298–300
　shoulds, predictive vs. rightness, 85
　Z max scores, 223, 224–225, 226f19.1, 230, 299–300, 313–314
Zener cards, 50
Zeno's paradox, 171, 177
Zhu, Zixu (James), 3, 4–6

www.ingramcontent.com/pod-product-compliance
Lightning Source LLC
Chambersburg PA
CBHW070121110526
44587CB00017BA/2798